Theories of the Soundtrack

The Oxford Music/Media Series
Daniel Goldmark, Series Editor

oxford
music/media series

OMM

Theories of the Soundtrack

James Buhler

OXFORD
UNIVERSITY PRESS

OXFORD
UNIVERSITY PRESS

Oxford University Press is a department of the University of Oxford. It furthers
the University's objective of excellence in research, scholarship, and education
by publishing worldwide. Oxford is a registered trade mark of Oxford University
Press in the UK and certain other countries.

Published in the United States of America by Oxford University Press
198 Madison Avenue, New York, NY 10016, United States of America.

© Oxford University Press 2019

Library of Congress Cataloging-in-Publication Data
Names: Buhler, James, 1964– author.
Title: Theories of the soundtrack / James Buhler.
Description: New York : Oxford University Press, 2019. |
Series: The Oxford music / media series | Includes bibliographical references and index.
Identifiers: LCCN 2018006090 (print) | LCCN 2018007713 (ebook) |
ISBN 9780199371099 (updf) | ISBN 9780199371075 (cloth : alk. paper) |
ISBN 9780199371082 (pbk. : alk. paper)
Subjects: LCSH: Motion picture music—History and criticism. | Film
soundtracks—History and criticism. | Motion picture music—Philosophy and
aesthetics.
Classification: LCC ML2075 (ebook) | LCC ML2075 .B844 2018 (print) |
DDC 781.5/4201—dc23
LC record available at https://lccn.loc.gov/2018006090

This volume is published with the generous support of the Gustave Reese Endowment of the
American Musicological Society, funded in part by the National Endowment for the Humanities and
the Andrew W. Mellon Foundation.

To Leslie and Judi

CONTENTS

ACKNOWLEDGMENTS

This book grew out of an essay on critical theory and the soundtrack that David Neumeyer commissioned for *The Oxford Handbook of Film Music Studies*. When I was done, that essay had become three, and they are included in this volume in revised form as the basis for portions of chapters 5, 7, and 8. Even as I drafted that essay, I recognized the value of expanding the material into something more comprehensive. I was inspired especially by Dudley Andrew's *The Major Film Theories* (1976) and *Concepts in Film Theory* (1984) and Francisco Casetti's *Theories of Cinema, 1945–1995* (1999); both authors offer excellent surveys of major trends in film theory, but, in keeping with so much film scholarship, which even today insists that film is a visual medium, none of these texts discusses theories of the soundtrack in any detail. In fact, they rarely mention the soundtrack at all, which puts them at a disadvantage in the present, when film music studies and sound studies are rapidly becoming prominent fields of inquiry.

My initial draft sought to be comprehensive, tracing speculative thinking about film music and sound from the silent era up to the present day, but it proved unwieldy, yielding a manuscript more than twice the length of the current one. With the guidance of my tireless and extremely patient editor at Oxford University Press, Norm Hirschy, who quickly found a sympathetic (anonymous) reader to look over the manuscript, and David Neumeyer, I was able to cut and reorganize that manuscript into this final form, now refocused on major theories of the soundtrack. I want to take this opportunity to thank all three—Norm, David, and the anonymous reader—for their work in helping me deliver a slimmer and much improved book.

I have been working on this project for almost a decade now, and many people have offered feedback over the years when I have presented research from this book at conferences, in lectures, and in the classroom. The "Music and the Moving Image" conference held annually at New York University has been especially important to shaping this project, and many portions of this manuscript had their first presentation there. I want to thank Ron Sadoff and Gillian Anderson for their tireless work in ensuring that this continues to be an annual event. I have benefited not only from the responses to my paper presentations but also and even more so from the strong community of scholars that the conference attracts, and the field would be much less cohesive without it. I have also presented material from this book at many other academic conferences. I delivered a selection from the final chapter on the soundtrack in the age of digital media on a panel organized by Joan Titus for the American Musicological Society. The passage on *Hugo* (2010) from that chapter was first presented on a panel organized by James Deaville and Mary Simonson for the Society of American Music. I first presented ideas about scoring practices in action films on a panel at the Society for Music Theory organized by Mark Richards, and ideas about postclassical cinema were first tried out on a panel organized by Carol Vernallis for the Society of Cinema and Media Studies. Another panel at the Society of Cinema and Media Studies organized by Lea Jacobs and Jeff Smith offered me an opportunity to present ideas on the transition to sound, as did an invitation from Carlo Cenciarelli to talk about cinematic listening in the early years of the sound film at a conference on "Listening Cinematically" and an invitation from Jeremy Barham to talk about transition-era cinema at a conference on "Hollywood's Musical Contemporaries and Competitors in the Early Sound Film Era." Daniel Goldmark asked me to participate in a conference honoring Claudia Gorbman's *Unheard Melodies*, which allowed me to present my ideas about focalization that found their way into chapter 7. I thank all of these organizers for inviting me to contribute to their conferences and panels.

I have benefited greatly over the years from many conversations with friends and colleagues, who have offered me insights, comments, and feedback and have posed useful challenges that have spurred me to think better about the issues at hand. My thanks go to Gillian Anderson, Jeremy Barham, Kyle Barnett, Michael Baumgartner, Sally Bick, Julie Brown, Carlo Cabellero, Kutter Callaway, Justin Capps, Charles Carson, Carlo Cenciarelli, Jee-Weon Cha, Juan Chattah, Kevin Clifton, Annette Davison, James Deaville, Kevin Donnelly, Rebecca Eaton, Phil Ford, Rebecca Fülöp, Will Gibbons, Daniel Goldmark, Kariann Goldschmitt, Claudia Gorbman, Helen Hanson, Erik Heine, Berthold Hoeckner, John Howland, Julie Hubbert, Brian Hyer, Jennifer Iverson, Lea Jacobs, Michael Klein, Charlie Kronengold, Frank Lehman, Neil Lerner, Justin London, Jean Ma, Marty Marks, Brooke McCorkle, Matt McDonald, Cari McDonnell, Miguel Mera, Stephen Meyer, Tahirih Motazedian, Scott Murphy, Michael Pisani, Nathan Platte, Katherine Quanz, Sarah Reichardt, Mark Richards, David Roche, Ron Rodman, Colin Roust, Ron Sadoff, Jeff Smith, Robynn Stilwell, Joan Titus, James Wierzbicki, Anna Windisch, and Ben Winters. Carol Vernallis has been especially generous in support of the project, always willing to Skype and brainstorm on short notice whenever I ran into difficulty. Eric Dienstfrey has rescued me on more than one occasion with a quick read of a section dealing with the history of sound technology. Alex Newton helped me develop ideas about the contemporary soundtrack that first appeared in our coauthored article on the original Bourne trilogy, a brief portion of which is reprinted in chapter 9. Mark Durrand has proved a good friend and an exceptional foil as I honed my ideas on music in action film.

At the University of Texas, I am fortunate to be surrounded by excellent friends and colleagues on the music theory faculty: Byron Almén, Eric Drott, Robert Hatten, the late Ed Pearsall, John Turci-Escobar, and Marianne Wheeldon. Their support has made my work much easier. Sonia Seeman ran a reading group during the early stages of my work on this book and portions of chapters 2 and 3 were first read by that group. An informal faculty film studies interest group whose nucleus consisted of Kirsten Cather, Sabine Hake, Hannah Lewis, David Neumeyer, David Prindle, Tom Schatz, and Janet Staiger met two or three times a semester for much of the time I worked on the manuscript, and the group read and offered incisive feedback on many excerpts of book, which is much stronger for it. Janet also kindly shared her draft translations of parts 5 and 6 of Jean-Louis Comolli's "Technique et idéologie" that greatly sped up work on chapter 8. Eric Drott helped me devise translations to some particularly obscure passages of Comolli's essay. I most heartily thank the stalwarts of the faculty happy hour crew—Charles, Eric, Hannah, and Marianne—for the weekly good cheer and sanity. May our weekly meetings long continue!

I am grateful to have been blessed with excellent graduate students during my work on this project. Matt Young, Emily Kausalik, Alex Newton, Ally Wente, Colleen Montgomery, Stefan Greenfield-Casas, Catrin Watts, and Steven Rahn have all passed through our program during this time, and they have been a source of wisdom and common sense.

Ever since I arrived at the University of Texas at Austin in August 1999, the institution has assisted me with timely leaves, research and conference funding, and the opportunity to develop courses around the soundtrack. I received two research leaves from the university to work on this project: a Faculty Research Assignment early in the process that gave me time to research the theory of silent film accompaniment (most of which did not make it into the current volume), and a Dean's Fellowship at a key point that allowed me to write a large portion of the manuscript. I have also received a number of smaller equipment grants from the Butler Faculty Fund in the Butler School of Music, from the College of Fine Arts Creative Research Grant, and from the Office of the Vice President for Research to explore digital sound production techniques. These grants have been crucial to my understanding of the contemporary soundtrack, and chapter 9 would look very different had I not been able to explore these digital production techniques on my own using the same software and much of the same equipment as professional composers and sound engineers use. I am most thankful for the steadfast support from the deans of the College of Fine Arts, Robert Freeman and Douglas Dempster, and from the directors of the Butler School of Music, B. Glenn Chandler, Glenn Richter, and Mary Ellen Poole, all of whom have enthusiastically encouraged me to focus my work in the area of soundtrack studies.

I want to offer special thanks to two colleagues. Hannah Lewis has been a model colleague, always willing to read material and offer helpful advice on short notice. My frequent collaborator, David Neumeyer, went far beyond the call of duty, read and edited the entire manuscript twice, and asked the right questions to allow me to reshape the contents of the book into an intelligible whole as I cut it down. The book is much better for the interventions of Hannah and David, and I am incredibly grateful for their help.

I give a personal note of thanks to my family. My parents both loved the movies, and some of my fondest childhood memories are going regularly as a family to a small storefront cinema in Glencoe, Minnesota, in the 1970s and seeing whatever was showing that night. My mom favored musicals and my dad westerns, both declining genres at the time (and which they sought out whenever older films played on television), but mostly they just enjoyed going to the cinema. I am grateful that they passed this love along to me.

Finally, I owe a very large debt of gratitude to Leslie Bush, my partner now for more than thirty years and the person who has done more to make sure this project got done than anyone, and my daughter, Judi, who has just embarked on her own intellectual journey of college. They have been my constant companions in watching films, both at home and in the cinema, and have showed patience, humor, and love whenever the demands of the project spilled over into family time, which was unfortunately all too often. This volume is dedicated to them.

Portions of chapter 5 and 7 were first published as "Ontological, Formal, and Critical Theories of Film Music and Sound," in David Neumeyer, ed., *The Oxford Handbook of Film Music Studies* (New York: Oxford University Press, 2014), 188–225. ©Oxford University Press.

Portions of chapter 7 were first published as "Gender, Sexuality, and the Soundtrack," in David Neumeyer, ed., *The Oxford Handbook of Film Music Studies* (New York: Oxford University Press, 2014), 366–82. ©Oxford University Press.

Portions of chapter 8 were first published as "Psychoanalysis, Apparatus Theory, and Subjectivity," in David Neumeyer, ed., *The Oxford Handbook of Film Music Studies* (New York: Oxford University Press, 2014), 383–417. ©Oxford University Press.

Portions of chapter 9 were first published as James Buhler and Alex Newton, "Outside the Law of Action: Music and Sound in the Bourne Trilogy," in Carol Vernallis, John Richardson, and Amy Herzog, eds., *Oxford Handbook of Sound and Image in Digital Media* (New York: Oxford University Press, 2013), 325–49. ©Oxford University Press.

1

Introduction

From its beginnings in the later nineteenth century, film—"moving pictures"—posed problems for critics, philosophers, and others concerned with the nature of art. At one level it was an abstract question: could film, a product of mechanical reproduction, be an aesthetic object at all? At another level, it was a matter of mechanics and effects: what did film do, and how did it do it? At still another level, it was a matter of cultural hierarchy: how did film as a popular art form relate to the very well-established categories of the theater, painting, opera, and so forth? The first systematic attempts to make sense of film as an emerging art form began to appear in the 1910s (Lindsay 1916; Münsterberg 1916), and by the 1920s, theories of film based in the art of editing began to proliferate.

When recorded sound and filmed image were combined into the sound film, the task of theorizing the moving pictures only became more difficult. Sound films had been an experimental form almost since the beginning of the cinema itself, but relatively few theorists had much to say about them. A variety of questions were nevertheless raised whose consideration became urgent after sound film became common, first in newsreels and short musical films in the early to mid-1920s, then in feature films after the success of *The Jazz Singer* (1927) and *The Singing Fool* (1928). The commercial success of talking and singing film completely changed the industry, but theorists did not really begin to tackle the sound film in a systematic way until around 1930, when the techniques of the sound film first began to codify and the European film industry converted to sound film production. To demonstrate what it was that early theorists were confronted with in the soundtrack, I begin with five examples, all essentially one-shot shorts. These films trace the prehistory of commercial sound film and demonstrate how, from the invention of cinema, a range of approaches to the mechanical synchronization of sound existed that would come to preoccupy film theorists.

Five Vignettes of Early Sound Film

The year c. 1895: "Dickson Experimental Sound Film." A man, evidently William Dickson (Edison's primary collaborator on the motion picture camera), plays a violin, as two other men dance in time to the music, a number from the very popular operetta, *Les Cloches de Corneville*, by Robert Planquette. The backdrop is draped in black, setting off the figures; a large recording horn looms in the foreground. Because the recording reproduces only the sound of the violin and Dickson's fingers are hard to see, it is difficult to evaluate the quality of the synchronization. This short film in its modern reconstruction by Walter Murch is, moreover, precisely that, a reconstruction, with significant doubts about its accuracy due to uncertainty about frame rate among other things. Nevertheless, the large movements of the violin bow and the dancing figures produce a convincing impression of synchronization in the reconstruction.

This is an image of origin before origin: an experimental film made before any moving pictures had yet to be shown in public, it was not intended to leave the laboratory. As it was not viewed publicly until its modern reconstruction, it also had no direct influence on other early sound films. Yet it exhibits many of the traits of early sound films including a static camera, a single shot that makes the film seem like a recording of a slice of reality, a dark backdrop that produces a sharp contrast between foreground and background, and a recording technique that focuses on capturing the foreground sound (the violin) rather than the general sound of the scene (which might have included the footfalls of the dancers). Even before it arrived, the sound film was already a construction.

The year 1905: "Dranem Performs 'Five O'Clock Tea.'" Armand Dranem, a French music hall artist, walks out on stage and begins to sing and move about. He performs a comic music hall act, a gentle parody of British manners. The camera remains stationary throughout the number, and Dranem plays to the camera as though it was his audience. Though Dranem shuffles about the stage during the instrumental interludes between verses, no footsteps sound. The focus of the sound recording is on capturing the voice and accompanying orchestra, not his whole performance.

The result is a film that is obviously postsynced, shot to playback, and the effect is more akin to an illustrated phonograph recording than the recording of a slice of reality.

The year 1913: "Nursery Favorites." Three men appear onscreen singing. They are evidently on a small stage, with a fireplace located prominently in the background, and they direct their song to the camera, which serves as a stand-in for the audience. As they complete their short song, they turn and throw some objects to the rear of the stage, which land in perfect synchronization with a prominent thump. A giant strolls onstage singing, and then the Queen of the Fairies appears in the fireplace, saying she will cast a spell. Soon the stage is filled with a whole set of fantastic characters, many singing brief songs using familiar lyrics from nursery rhymes. Between songs, the characters speak with the patter of stage repartee.

Like "Dickson Experimental Sound Film" and "Dranem Performs 'Five O'Clock Tea,'" "Nursery Favorites" utilizes a single shot, but the perspective of the sound recording is quite different. The Edison apparatus used for "Nursery Favorites" featured an improved recording mechanism that allowed sound to be recorded at a greater distance than the standard recording horn of the time. The sound recording here thus mimics the film image in providing a reproduction of the overall scene. Unlike Dickson's film or "Five O'Clock Tea," the sound recording has not been optimized to capture the musical performance (or the dialogue, much of which is just barely intelligible); instead, the recording aims for reproducing the sound of the general setting. The result is the impression of canned theater, as though a stage performance has been recorded and then (poorly) reproduced.

The year 1923: "A Few Moments with Eddie Cantor, Star of 'Kid Boots.'" After a brief fanfare, Cantor walks onstage in front of a black backdrop. The recording of the voice is clear and distinct, a marked improvement over the first three films we have considered. It seems closely miked, and the film gives little sense of the theatrical space except that Cantor treats the camera like it is a theatrical audience. The sound design resembles the minimalist staging, which produces the effect of a spotlight performance. The dark backdrop and Cantor's static body emphasize the movement of his lips, which display perfect synchronization with the impressively clear sound recording. After a series of disconnected jokes, Cantor shifts to a song, explicitly cueing the unseen conductor to begin the music. As he sings, Cantor also grows more animated, though he is careful not to stray too far from his original mark, and his footfalls are never audible. The song ends with applause, presumably from an offscreen audience; Cantor exits the frame; and the image fades. An inconspicuous cut, masked somewhat by the applause, brings Cantor back for the second part of the film, which replicates the first formally: Cantor telling jokes and then a song performance.

Overall, then, the film presents a recorded performance, but not the canned theater of "Nursery Favorites." The recording process now uses a microphone rather than a recording horn, and the microphone allows the abstraction of the voice from the context of its performance even while sound and image are recorded simultaneously. The audience applause for the song is notable for how it emphasizes the silence—especially the lack of laughter—elsewhere. Is this audience real or was the sound of applause added later? As with "Five O'Clock Tea," "A Few Moments with Eddie Cantor" is more a representation of a performance than a reproduction of one.

The year 1926: "Introductory Speech by Will H. Hays." Hays approaches the camera, winding his way between a table with some sort of box or machine on it in the background along the left edge of the frame, a small table sitting in the foreground in the lower left of the frame with a pile of three books, and a chair, only the arm of which is visible along the right side. The background is otherwise black, with a "VC" ornament (Vitaphone Corporation) hovering in the upper right. The identity of this curious set is uncertain, but it seems to suggest a small study. With the extremely precise diction and careful large gestures of an experienced public speaker, Hays envisions Vitaphone as part of the ongoing story of the development of cinema: "Tonight we write another chapter in that story. Far indeed have we advanced from that few seconds of shadow of a serpentine dancer thirty years ago when the motion picture was born to this public demonstration of the Vitaphone synchronizing the reproduction of sound with the reproduction of action."

Hays's meticulous articulation demonstrates well the precision of the synchronization, even as his broad gestures point to a difficulty in representing public speech. Aside from the moving lips, action in the image here seems indeed to distract, as the gestures, rather than reinforcing the words as they would in a public setting, take on an autonomous, almost monstrous quality.

Although each of these films captures a recording of a performance, they display a surprisingly wide variety of approaches as to how recorded sound should construct that performance. With the exception of the Cantor film, they all consist of a single shot, and they each present a continuous recorded performance. Nevertheless, they vary in the extent to which they regard the recording as a reproduction or a representation. Each of them approaches the camera as a stand-in for the audience, playing to the camera if not always explicitly addressing it. Each of them, moreover, is dominated by the soundtrack. If synchronization means image and sound are redundant—that the soundtrack sounds precisely what the film already shows or vice versa (and this is a line of argument that director Sergei Eisenstein especially would develop in his writings, a line of argument that would be echoed by theorists all the way to the 1960s)—in the case of these short sound films, it is the image far more than the sound that seems superfluous. In the case of "Five O'Clock Tea," this is literally the case as the phonograph recording was made first, and the film was shot to playback to that recording, a procedure that would remain common in musicals through the era of the classical sound film. The others all involve recording a fixed perspective as sound and image were made at the same time. But sound and image do not necessarily or even generally record the same perspective. In fact, only "Nursery Favorites" attempts to match image and sound perspective; the others all adopt strategies that focus on capturing clear singing and dialogue. That is, the shorts emphasize the quality of the sound reproduction and the fact of synchronization; the quality of the image, by contrast, is more utilitarian. The "redundancy" of synchronization proves, even in these relatively rudimentary one-shot sound films, to be a less-than-stable concept.

Of course, many classical film theorists would scarcely acknowledge these films as "real" cinema, since they contain virtually no editing, and the movement in the image consists largely of moving lips, which emphasizes the illusion of speech (or singing). These films are not "filmic" or "cinematic" in a way that Rudolf Arnheim (1933), Siegfried Kracauer (1997), or Jean Mitry (1997), for instance, would recognize. The hostility to sound from those invested in the silent film came from the inversion of filmic values that the talking and singing film seemed to impose. In the early sound film, as the name implies, sound came first. If, initially, sound film also seemed to insist on being the recording of reality, the variety of approaches in these sound shorts suggests that "reality" was itself a construction from the beginning, and usually less than it appeared. The art of recording worked to mold the sound before the horn or the microphone so that it recorded only certain sounds. Phonography may have espoused the value of fidelity, but it usually simply managed the recording situation through abstraction so that only the sounds wanted were captured (Lastra 2000). In any event, with respect to sound film, the far greater impression of reality comes from the audiovisual figure of synchronization than from the fidelity of the sound, and for dialogue and music usually a clear or well-balanced sound seems more realistic even when it is a fabrication.

The Hybridity of Sound Film

The theoretical claim that these early sound films are not cinema belongs to ontological concerns about the nature and essence of cinema best framed by André Bazin's collection of essays, *What Is Cinema?* (2005). Bazin wrote hardly at all about the soundtrack, and so he does not figure largely in this book, but he did articulate a very influential realist theory that argued for a guiding idea of film as total cinema, "as a total and complete representation of reality," a recording of the world. In a famous essay, "The Myth of Total Cinema," Bazin argued that the idea of a complete automatic recording predated the existence of the cinema. "Every new development added to the cinema must, paradoxically, take it nearer and nearer to its origins. In short the cinema has not yet been invented!" (21). As Tom Gunning (2001) notes, Bazin's myth of total cinema was a response to the mechanical separation of the senses that had been inaugurated with the phonograph (14–16). Cinema both required that separation and answered "a desire to heal the breach. In other words, Bazin's total cinema is a response to a previous sense of desperation and division" (16).

Film, then, was born incomplete, half an invention that was designed to complement and complete the phonograph. In a caveat explaining the motion picture camera for the patent office, Thomas Edison (1888) wrote: "I am experimenting upon an instrument which does for the Eye what the phonograph does for the Ear, which is the recording and reproduction of things in motion" (1). The idea of cinema followed from the success of the phonograph, which had precedence in both conception and execution. He went on to consider their combination:

> By gearing or connecting the Kinetograph by a positive mechanical movement, a continuous record of all motion as taken down by the Kinetograph and continuous record of all sound as taken down by the phonograph and by substituting the photograph recording devices on the Kinetograph for a microscope stand and objective, it becomes a Kinetoscope and by insertion of the listening tubes to the phonograph into the ear the illusion is complete and we may see and hear a whole opera as perfectly as if actually present although the actual performance may have taken place years before. (2–3)

Thus, the Kinetoscope is a kind of monstrous scientific device for replicating opera. A microscope is attached to a large cabinet containing a long strip of celluloid with a sequence of images attached. A light source illuminates a frame of the celluloid from behind and the frames move past the gate in succession. This allows anyone looking into the microscope to have the impression of images in motion. Mechanical gearing connects a phonograph to the mechanism that moves the celluloid strip through the Kinetoscope, allowing the two to work in synchronization. Just as the user peers into the cabinet through the microscope, so too the user places rubber tubing attached to the diaphragm of the phonograph in the ears. The impression delivered by the cabinet, presuming it functioned properly, would be the synchronization of image and sound, a reproduction of reality. This device is obviously complex, and the monstrous quality of the Kinetoscope (which with ear tubes was known as a Kinetophone) is evident in Figure 1.1. But its basic principles are not really much different from taking in a video on an iPhone with headphones.

The promised synchronization of Edison's original apparatus proved elusive, and, as it developed, cinema's status as incomplete came to mark it as mute. When fictional films became the dominant commercial form, they became known as "silent photoplays." This original status of the moving picture as mute pushed cinema in two directions that will be familiar to those who have studied the topic of disability: on the one hand, a reformist valorization of muteness as the distinctive property of the moving picture; on the other hand, an ableist drive toward completeness and unity, toward Bazin's (2005) "myth of the total cinema" that would restore to film what it was missing and so make it a complete reproduction of the world. In both cases, the binary dynamic constructs cinema around lack and its muteness as a loss. The former leads to the construction of muteness as a magical state, a miracle of sense, the

FIGURE 1.1 Early Edison Kinetophone, combining Kinetoscope and phonograph.
Credit: Thomas Edison National Historical Park.

exception that reinscribes the compulsory character of the normative complete state. The latter leads to the sound film. With respect to the former, the nonnormative body is one that is exceptional, out of control, or at least not subject to the full force of the norm. That is where its magical properties derive from and also what makes muteness productive for art, where lack can be transformed into pathos as a celebration of resilience overcoming adversity. This construction affirms the power of the norm even as it appears to transcend it, because it marks muteness as other, as a state beyond. It is the tale of redemptive overcoming, as when Beethoven, for instance, is presented as wrestling with his deafness and is able to surmount it. So in terms of aesthetic theory as it evolved into the 1920s, the silent film became a distinctive art form by virtue of its lack, which it displayed in pure form: the muteness of film bestowed on it its visual dominance and gave gesture and movement the mark of eloquence. If silent film seemed to promise even to present a distinct ontology—*moveo ergo sum*—it did so by virtue of its original lack.

The deafness and muteness of the silent film apparatus had been long recognized by the 1920s, and its prostheses of music and pantomime were incorporated into the form to produce an affinity, often the appearance of an integral whole. Yet because the music in particular did not belong directly to the apparatus, it could bestow a meaning that was not strictly in the film or could clarify what might otherwise be inscrutable. The relation was in essence allegorical. As I have written elsewhere:

> Music did not substitute for the missing voice, as one common theory has it, so much as it underscored the absence of the voice, the muteness of the apparatus, the failure of translation. The face could not say what it would express. The silence of the cinema was in this sense a sign of its absolute rootedness within a speech the audience did not—could not—hear. The muteness of the film then marked the limit of universal expression as silence. As the sound of the voice's absence, music played the face's displaced presence to plumb the depths of diegetic interiority. (Buhler 2010, 39)

Entwining music and muteness into an allegorical complex, the silent film also created a representation that worked with an interiority that was hidden but still in play. Although the pantomimic code allowed actors to exteriorize some of this hidden content, and the play of emotions across the face in close-up especially pointed to interior emotions and motivations at work, music could seize on these visual signs and transform them into something more definite without thereby also collapsing the depth of character or negating the occult status of interiority. The music sounded like feelings feel, perhaps, but music did not thereby become the feeling. For one thing, the music emanated from theater musicians, most often in a special arrangement made by the theater's music director from music in its library or improvised by its organist, not from the screen. Yet since the relation was allegorical, the fact that music did not belong to the film did not diminish its impact. It was common for film theorists of the silent era to point out how film was conducive to fantasy, and this related not just to the overt content of exotic settings and the fiction articulated by the edited images but also to the way music seemed to give access to a fantasy-filled allegory of interiority.

The introduction of sound film dissolved the affinities of mute cinema, declared them unnatural, and forced film to speak through another body. Talkies "enforced normalcy" (R. Johnson 2017, 2);[1] that is, the new sound film invented and imposed a system of "compulsory synchronization" that mimicked the unity of sound and image in "normal" perception. Initially, it took the form of a rigid mimetic synchronization. That talkies untied the tongue of

---

[1] Russell Johnson (2017) notes that the 1920s were a period when oral instruction to the deaf was heavily promoted, but it was a movement that had been strong since the late nineteenth century—essentially the whole period of the silent film—so the shift to sound film was unlikely to have been unduly influenced by the cultural attitudes toward deafness except insofar as they encouraged the myth of total cinema.

film (Green 1929), restored sound to the image, unified what had been divided, and yielded a more perfect reproduction of the world (Bazin 2005; Gunning 2001)—all of these attributes gave a representation that conformed to the normal, the typical, the ordinary, the conventional arrangement of the senses. The heightened realism of the union made a reality of the normal, typical, ordinary, conventional representation that it returned. Moreover, the early talking film yielded a representation without depth and interiority: characters were simply as they presented themselves; the soundtrack defined them much as the image did, and mimetic synchronization insisted that the sound belonged to the image.

Yet the established conventions of the silent film also challenged talking film so that the addition of recorded sound initially appeared itself not so much as a return to unity but as a new prosthesis. Therefore, to contemporaneous theorists like Arnheim (1997) and other critics like Hilda Doolittle (H. D.) (1927), the talkies initially seemed a kind of natural monster, where the voice was uncanny, neither belonging properly to the image nor yet separable from it (Spadoni 2007). The hybrid quality of sound film, its heterogeneity, had to be purified, turned into a complex but still singular medium.

Sound Film, an Audiovisual Medium

In the age of the silent film, when the music that normally accompanied the images was not considered a fixed part of the film, the claim that film was a visual medium made a certain amount of analytical sense, even if the story (rather than the images) in fact dominated the conception of commercial film even then. With the coming of the sound film, which mechanically linked image and sound, the visual dominance of film could only be maintained through habit and repeated declaration, ritualistically chanted, as Sarah Kozloff (1988) puts it, "like a charm to ward off evil" (9). "Story" continued to dominate the sound film, and the soundtrack, like the images, was generally subordinated to the task of storytelling. But the medium of the storytelling was not primarily the images with the sounds as an added special effect. Dialogue was from the beginning of the sound era considered a key element (dialogue had in fact been a key element of the silent film as well, as the abundance of dialogue cards attests), and for most of the transition and even into the classical era, the priority in production fell on the vocal portion of the soundtrack. There is a reason after all that they are called *sound* films, *talkies*, and *musicals*. Indeed, as the complaints of directors and other film workers during the transition era make clear, the early sound film was dominated by the capture and synchronization of sound. The whole routine of film production was upended and restructured to ensure that sound, especially dialogue, was captured with clarity and with a continuous flow. In the early years of the transition, dialogue frequently determined the blocking and editing, since speaking actors needed to be visible and in the proximity of a microphone, and cuts would almost invariably follow the delivery of the lines.

The hostility toward dialogue among many directors and theorists stems in large part from the imposition of sound and especially dialogue. Director William C. de Mille complained to one reporter how sound had upended the old studio hierarchy: "while once he had been a director of pictures, now he was nothing but [sound engineer] Roy Pomeroy's very earnest assistant, with promise that if he displayed due diligence he might again be promoted to be a director" ("Too Much Vocal Attention" 1928, 7). Edwin Hopkins (1928) was even more explicit that dialogue was the central stratum of the new sound film. "A great revolution is taking place in motion pictures. Voices are presumably being added to films. In reality what is taking place is that films are being added to voices" (845). As filmmakers adjusted to the new situation and recovered elements of the earlier visual style, this was not really done at the expense of the soundtrack. The much-vaunted "Painted Doll" sequence from *The Broadway Melody* (1929), for instance, was guided by its soundtrack. In histories of film, this scene is often held up as an example of early sound film overcoming the restrictions of sound technology to restore something of the camera movement and editing patterns of the silent film. Yet such claims are misleading. If the camera was "freed" in this sequence and allowed to regain much of its mobility from the silent era, this was because the music was prerecorded and the whole thing shot to playback. The sequence has many more edits than the other musical performances of the film, but the visuals, though "spectacular," do not determine the sequence; the music does. Similarly, the ostentatious visuals of the Busby Berkeley musicals from the mid-1930s are closely tied to, even motivated by, their music.

If film production during the transition era moved quickly away from the ideal of recording and mimetic synchronization, of filming a fiction staged for the camera in order to reproduce it, and returned to the notion of film as a fiction constructed in the filmmaking process, especially editing, this does not mean that film returned to being the visual medium it was in the silent era. The camera regained its former mobility, and scenes were again shot in a manner resembling the practice of the silent film; but dialogue and song were hardly diminished in significance, and dialogue in particular continued to be of primary importance, governing blocking, shot selection, and editing patterns, because dialogue was fundamental to the story. Indeed, synchronized dialogue became the zero point of sound film practice, even though film theorists, critics, and directors like Arnheim, Eisenstein, and René Clair continually marginalized the audiovisual figure of synchronization when it was not simply condemned for redundancy.

Given the status of the talking film as the dominant commodity after 1930, theorists found it impossible to ignore these films, and they needed to speak to the actuality of sound to domesticate it to the image if for no other reason. Consequently, a body of theory on the soundtrack did emerge, but it was a largely antagonistic theory, and its terms were often implicitly stated. Music as a more compliant sound received somewhat more favorable attention from theorists, but generally film theory through the 1970s treated the soundtrack as supplemental, a superfluous addition. Because music was only needed strictly speaking when it was a realistic (i.e., diegetic) element of the depicted scene, music was also an excellent model for this supplemental status, which may in part account for its positive treatment from such writers as Eisenstein, Pudovkin, Kracauer, and Mitry.

Film Sound and "Occult Aesthetics"

If the soundtrack, especially music, has never been the neglected theoretical object that it is sometimes presented as (Prendergast 1977), the continued visual bias of film theory means that its treatment has remained somewhat concealed. Kevin Donnelly (2014) astutely notes the soundtrack's "occult" status, which nicely captures both its hidden character as a theoretical object and the magical properties often attributed to it, from sound vivifying the pictures to music saving the film (2). Here, I want to distinguish "hidden" from "neglected" and suggest that its occult quality lies, as Donnelly suggests, in the fact that synchronization especially is not a simple figure but a difficult one. "Retaining a sense of the occult means realizing that hidden aspects might be the most important ones, and that by their obscured nature, the most important to pin down" (72). Christian Metz once quipped that "the movies are difficult to write about because they are easy to explain" (quoted in Neumeyer 2015, 29), and there is something to this about synchronization as well. Synchronization appears simple enough, especially if we presume redundancy, but it is actually a rather difficult figure to explain because it is not really the uniform state we pretend. Often the synchronization is clear enough, but frequently the lips are hidden, the face is turned or obscured by shadow or by a veil or mask, the voice comes over a telephone or over a loudspeaker, and so on. There is an indefinite variety of such semisynchronized cases, many of which may be at any moment ambiguous but rarely threaten our belief in synchronization. Indeed, often they strengthen it. As Mark Kerins (2011) notes, contemporary digital surround sound with its capacity to move the sound around the theater complicates this situation even further but again without threatening our basic belief in synchronization however it might affect the actual practice (262–63). The occult status—whether in classical or in contemporary film theory—is acknowledged in a term like "synchronization" and its work hidden and assigned to the image in a term like "redundancy," which eliminates the play of synchronization in a single concept.

The sound film is itself at base analytic: it separates image and sound and records and reproduces them with separate technologies. Playback of a synchronized sound film is a kind of synthesis where our senses of vision and hearing fuse the stimuli of the two technological streams into a unity so that the voice we hear from the speakers seems to come from the body we see on the screen. This trick makes it seem as though reproducing is simply the inverse of recording that returns an identity in the ideal case (Altman 1980b): where recording analyzes into component parts, reproduction synthesizes the unified experience. But this unity, though appearing natural, is incomplete and only a limit case. Indeed, the relation between the streams is more or less arbitrary, and in fact neither depends on the other: in principle, any recordable sound or set of sounds can be placed against any filmable image (Altman 1980a, 6). As Britta Sjogren (2006) notes, "all sounds . . . are equally separate from the image track in that they are only 'married' in the final instance, brought together in the composite film print: prior to this, they are separable elements which can be 'placed' anywhere one wishes relative to the picture" (6). Of course, few films exploit such radical autonomy of image and sound, just as few films have been satisfied to simply record image and sound in tandem as a seeming mechanical identity. And as the five vignettes I started this chapter with suggest, synchronization yields a particular construction of difference more than an identity.

Both classical and contemporary theorists have generally started from this implicit scenario, which is structured by poles of mimetic synchronization on the one hand and autonomy of sound and image on the other. From Eisenstein and Pudovkin through Hanns Eisler and Theodor W. Adorno to Kracauer, classical film theory formulated a basic opposition between synchronization (or parallel) and counterpoint around this scenario, and Donnelly (2014) merely continues a long tradition when he writes, "matching or not matching sound and image (so-called parallel and counterpoint) might be construed as different ways of thinking" (1). Where synchronization is troubled by the figure of redundancy, counterpoint is haunted by indifference.

What is concealed by this formulation are other concerns, often exposed at the poles, such as that what appears "real" under the press of mimetic synchronization is often fabricated; sounds of violence—punches, kicks, gunshots—especially are rarely the actual sounds they represent. In the early days of sound film, this was because loud sounds often overmodulated the soundtrack; today it is often because they sound too puny for the power they are meant to represent. Michel Chion (1994) notes that synchronization is a powerful audiovisual figure because it can weld sound and image together over a much wider range of variability than we might initially think (224). He calls this process "synchresis" (63), and even in cases where we become aware of a disjunction—a small child, say, speaking with an adult voice—we still are willing to attribute that voice to that body for the purposes of the fiction.

Synchronization also has other important effects that are easily lost when the theoretical emphasis falls on redundancy. "A focus on synchronization," Donnelly (2014) writes, can help us "radically [rethink] . . . the 'space' between sound and image" (1). First, mimetic synchronization establishes an indexical bond between sound and image. Synchresis reminds us that this bond may not be real, but it is virtual, and it can be actualized in the diegesis. In this way, sound comes to have its source in the image. The reverse case of the image indexically calling forth a sound, director Robert Bresson claims, never occurs (cited in Burch 1981, 90). Ironically, synchronization secures a certain precedence for the image that it enforces through terminology that understands sound with respect to the image, notably the distinction between onscreen and offscreen (Percheron 1980; Kalinak 1992).

Second, mimetic synchronization is less a mark of realism than a mark of pertinence. Synchronized bodies are important bodies, bodies that the film cues us to pay attention to. The audiovisual figure of synchronization, in other words, divides an image into foreground bodies and background bodies, those that have synchronized sounds associated with them and those that do not, and then it imports "narrative sense" to naturalize the hierarchical formation of an ordered fictional world. Such hierarchical work of synchronization is evident in the preview screening of "The Duelling Cavalier" in *Singin' in the Rain* (1952). In the scene, Lina plays with her necklace, which makes a loud rumbling sound; she turns away from the microphone, which audibly changes the volume and timbre of her voice; Don throws his staff, which lands with a loud thud; and so forth. The humor of the scene comes from the misbehavior of sound, which is not unrealistic but instead simply a faithful recording. The scene is disorienting because the sound seems narratively impertinent. R. F. Simpson, the studio head, wonders about the sound of the pearls because they are incidental to the scene, simply part of the costume, but their thunderous sound suggests an inexplicably ominous tone. The thud of Don's staff makes it seem like the throwing of the staff rather than his entrance is the important matter. The changing perspective of the microphone emphasizes Lina's turning head rather than her words. Synchronization does not reinforce the narrative hierarchy in this scene but rather runs against it. The sound traces out a line of sound effects without narrative cause, and the humor indicts it as improper, not because it lacks sufficient fidelity with the promicrophonic sound but because it reproduces disordered reality rather than the fiction of hierarchy.

In contrast to mimetic synchronization, counterpoint has been the critically favored term by some theorists precisely because counterpointed sound is not redundant with the image. Counterpoint reveals a novel potential to the sound film, aspects of the audiovisual relationship that cannot be achieved (or at least are difficult to achieve) in other ways. But it also creates inherently ambiguous asynchronous figures and juxtapositions where image and soundtrack grow remote. At one extreme, anempathetic music or sound can nevertheless remain expressive: a death occurs, say, and the sound of the motor keeps going, happy children resound in the background, joyful music plays on the radio, and so forth. Composer Max Steiner (1937) recognized the dramatic power of this device: imagine, he says, a nightclub with a jazz orchestra playing and a daughter notified of her father's death: "it would be absolutely wrong to change from the hot tune in progress to music appropriate to her mood. . . . [N]o greater counterpoint has ever been found than gay music underlying a tragic scene" (224–25). The juxtaposition registers the indifference of the world (Chion 1994). At the other extreme, music or sound simply goes its own way with a kind of absolute indifference, an indifference that ceases even to be expressive. At this extreme, the figure of counterpoint is conceived in such a way that it does not impinge on the image and so does not call into question visual dominance, even if the indifference might make us wonder about its relevance.

Early theorists of the sound film such as Eisenstein and Arnheim were especially hostile to dialogue, but even later writers such as Eisler and Adorno, Kracauer, and Mitry continued to harbor serious misgivings over it, probably because dialogue offered the greatest threat to the claim that film is a visual medium. The better argument against dialogue, which was voiced early, has always been that it makes sound film irreducibly anthropocentric. Béla Balázs (2010b) had suggested already in 1924 that the silent cinema treated things and people equitably by refusing speech to both. "Since [a mute object] does not speak less than human beings, it says just as much" (23). In 1938, Arnheim inverted the formulation. Sound film, Arnheim said, "endows the actor with speech, and since only he can have it, all other things are pushed into the background" (Arnheim 1957, 227). By favoring some figures with dialogue, sound film marks those who speak as special objects.

Other arguments against dialogue worked to separate film from theater. Writing in 1930, director René Clair (1988), for instance, thought that the talking film would "survive only if the formula suitable to it is found, only if it can break loose from the influence of the theater and fiction, only if people make of it something other than an *art of imitation*" (58, emphasis in original). The viewpoint was common, even in the earliest days of the transition. Director William C. de Mille, for instance, was quoted by *Variety*: "The new form is going to be dominated more thoroughly by the technique of the picture than by the technique of the stage. . . . The talking picture will not be a stage play photographed. It will be a motion picture that talks" ("Too Much Vocal Attention" 1928, 7). And this line of argument would continue throughout the classical era, parodically summarized by Alberto Cavalcanti (1939): "A play is all speech. Words, words, words" (31). Theater and film are similar, then, but theater is dominated by dialogue, whereas film is dominated by the image. This distinction would be picked up by many subsequent theorists, including Kracauer and Mitry, although neither opposes the sound film per se. Dialogue in film, like sound in general, therefore becomes a property or extension of the image, and this idea, which remains dominant, was revoiced by Metz, Gilles Deleuze, and even in modified form by Chion and David Neumeyer.

The conception makes for a neat distinction between film and the-ater, but it also conceals the importance of dialogue to film, which is often governed by the rhythms and needs of dialogue. That observation does not mean that such films are "really" species of recorded theater. Even in films governed by dialogue, the dialogue is usually structured differently, pithier and without theatrical cadences. And the dialogue occurs with images, which emphasizes different things depending on whether the image speaks (as in synchronized dialogue), listens (as in a reaction shot), or shows something else (as in a voiceover, in a shot showing the subject of conversation, or in a shot of something else suggesting a distracted camera) (Kozloff 2000, 100). The more important factor to film dialogue, however, and one that is not often scrutinized, is that it is designed to be recorded, edited, and mixed. Among other things, this means that the pace and delivery of film dialogue can be far more nuanced, with much more emphasis in the writing to finding ways to allow the actors to draw out the "grain" of the voice to suggest layers of char-acterization. Even in the case of direct sound and improvised dialogue, the di-alogue is still designed to be recorded, with emphasis falling on capturing the "reality" rather than scripting of speech. Like the image, recorded dialogue is a material to be worked on in editing and mixing the film, not the thing itself.

Music, not dialogue, has been the preferred theoretical object, in part be-cause it is a more compliant partner to the image; in part because it is unreal, a special occult object; and in part because its work is not well understood by audiences. This is true of both classical and contemporary theory. If Claudia Gorbman (1987) describes film music as largely "unheard," this does not mean that audiences do not hear it in the way that they do not hear the inaudible sound edits, only that it is unobtrusive much like the editing of a film is in-conspicuous. Music remains accessible but out of sight, like the reverse side of the image. On the other hand, music associates with the image in a different way than effects and dialogue do. When it is nondiegetic and unreal, music can express what the image in itself cannot, especially characters' moods and feelings. And this expression in turn posits a psychological world hidden be-neath the surface of the images. Music divides the image into exterior and interior, into visible and hidden regions. With unreal music, the psychology of the characters can be more evident, can appear more real. This mimetic im-pulse of film music has been often criticized, presumably because it suggests the inadequacy of the image, but nevertheless the idea that music underscores feeling remains generally accepted, even basic to the theory of film music, and we will encounter the idea repeatedly in the pages that follow, for instance, in the discussions of Aaron Copland, Gorbman, Kathryn Kalinak, and Annabel Cohen. Indeed, even theories that object to music expressing feeling will generally accept that music often needs to take flight from the image in a lyrical extension if it is going to productively engage the film (Jaubert 1937; Eisler and Adorno 1947).

This Volume

A theory of the soundtrack is concerned with what belongs to it, how it is effectively organized, and how its status in a multimedia object affects the nature of the object, the tools available for its analysis, and the interpretive regime that the theory mandates for determining the meaning, sense, and structure that sound and music bring to film and other audiovisual media. Beyond that, a theory may also delineate the range of possible uses of sound (and music), classify the types of relations that films have used for image and sound, identify the central problems, and reflect on and describe effective uses of sound in film. My goal in this volume is not to provide an exhaustive historical documentation but rather to sketch out the range of theoretical approaches that have been applied to the soundtrack over time, and to do that within the broad conceptual frame already outlined in this introduction. For each approach, I present the basic theoretical framework, consider explicit and implicit claims about the soundtrack, and then work to open the theories to new questions about film sound, often by putting the theories into dialogue with one another. The organization is both chronological and topical: the former in that the chapters move steadily from early film theory through models of the classical system to more recent critical theories; the latter in that the chapters move equally steadily through—and highlight—central issues for each generation: the problem of film itself, then of image and sound, of adequate analytical-descriptive models, and finally of critical-interpretative models.

Chapters 2 and 3 provide an overview of how sound and music were addressed in classical theories of film. Chapter 2 examines several major theories that emerged during the transition to sound film, when even the definition of the sound film was contested. I begin by discussing the specificity of sound film and its seeming inherent hybridity, since it combined two disparate technologies: camera and projector for the image, microphone and loudspeakers for the sound. Here, the idea that sound film would specialize in mimetic synchronization, in making a recording of the world, came into conflict with ideas that an artwork needed to be specific to its medium on the one hand and with the edited nature of the silent film on the other. The theories of sound film that arose during the transitional decade from 1926 to 1935 focused on the closely related forms of recorded theater and silent film and worked to articulate how sound film differed from them. They also gave considerable attention to asynchronous sound in part because it was a figure specific to sound film (or in any event more difficult to produce in other art forms) and in part because asynchronous sound had affinities with montage. The chapter focuses on five important theorists who wrote prolifically during the transition years: Sergei Eisenstein, Vsevolod Pudovkin, Béla Balázs, Rudolf Arnheim, and Harry Potamkin. The first four are well known: Eisenstein and Pudovkin as directors, Balázs and Arnheim as cultural critics (Balázs also worked as a screenwriter, and Arnheim would go on to an important academic career). Potamkin, also a critic, is not as well known since he died young and his essays were not collected into a book until the 1970s. But he offers a distinct approach—the "compound cinema"—that manages to escape the theoretical quandaries faced by other writers during the transitional era.

Chapter 3 examines theories after the sound film had been codified. The theories produced during this period are less concerned with whether sound film is a viable artistic form than in mapping the terrain. As such, the characteristic forms of theory became the grammar and typology: the goal was to map the potential formal relations between image and sound. Despite the commercial dominance of talking films, theorists during this period continued to insist that film was primarily a visual medium. This manifested itself especially in a theoretical suspicion of dialogue and the "redundant" audiovisual figure of mimetic synchronization; indeed, considering the importance of dialogue to talking films, theorists actually had little to say about it other than to recommend that filmmakers keep dialogue pithy, vernacular, and subordinated to the images at the level of construction. Music in many respects served as the preferred theoretical soundtrack object because it was much less likely to call into question the visual dominance of the medium. Moreover, because background music often only had a nebulous relation to the narrative (theorists at the time called it "unreal") that did not accord with the terms of realistic representation, music also required theoretical explanation.

To show the range of ideas that this line of thinking inspired, I look at six theoretical models focusing on the treatment of music. I open with a discussion of Eisenstein's concept of vertical montage and consider the modes of synchronization that he developed from the concept. I then turn to Aaron Copland's typology of functions for film music. Copland worked as a composer in Hollywood and produced several variants of this list of functions, as well as a list of reservations. I next consider Hanns Eisler and Theodor W. Adorno's *Composing for the Films*, one of the most important theoretical treatments of film music. Eisler also worked as a composer, first in Europe and then in Hollywood during World War II. Adorno was also a trained composer, who is best known for his writings on critical theory. I focus on their response to Eisenstein, their critique of Hollywood practice, and their list of "bad habits," which is similar to Copland's reservations. The chapter concludes with discussions of three formal typologies offered by Raymond Spottiswoode, Siegfried Kracauer, and Roger Manvell and John Huntley. Spottiswoode was a British theorist and documentary filmmaker. Kracauer was an important cultural critic in Frankfurt during the Weimar Republic and became an academic when he immigrated to the United States. Manvell and Huntley were both prolific authors who worked for the British Film Institute. The typologies of Spottiswoode, Kracauer, and Manvell and Huntley all seek to map the conceptual space of the image–sound relationship in film. Spottiswoode and Kracauer develop their typologies within the context of general theories of film, whereas Manvell and Huntley are concerned specifically with understanding the place of music in film.

Each subsequent chapter takes up a topic and charts its development over a portion of the historical range from the 1960s to the present. Chapter 4 starts with the issue of the "film language" and examines how the concept served to ground film semiotics. Both film and music have been called universal languages, and this language-like quality meant that both areas were inviting objects to the emerging academic field of semiotics. The concept of "film language," much like "musical language," had an informal sense that related to materials and devices that could be assembled to make a sensical arrangement that resembled a syntax. In this informal sense, the concept worked as a vague analogy. Jean Mitry, a French film historian and theorist, thought the analogy with language was useful but limited. Film is a language because it communicates, but it does not have grammar and syntax like verbal language. He would make an analogous argument with respect to rhythm in assessing film's similarity to music. After looking at Mitry's contribution, I turn to film semiotics proper and consider especially the influential work of Christian Metz, who inaugurated the field. Metz attempted to understand film as a language using the tools of structural linguistics. Like Mitry, Metz ultimately rejected the idea that film is a language, but he also shifted the focus from grammar to signification. The importance of this shift can be seen in his analysis of "aural objects," where he examined sound as a characteristic of the image, which becomes a way of acknowledging that sounds signify somewhat differently than images do in film while upholding the visual dominance of film. The chapter closes with a discussion of Gilles Deleuze's concept of the movement-image. Deleuze, a philosopher, was not concerned with the film language per se, but he did presume that filmmakers think in images, and his mode of analysis drew extensively from the semiotic tradition of Charles S. Peirce. Deleuze himself offered mostly cryptic comments about the soundtrack, especially as it relates to the movement-image of classical cinema. I use the typology Deleuze developed for the movement-image and seek analogues in the treatment of the soundtrack.

In chapter 5, I consider the topic of formal theories and models, starting with the movement of so-called neoformalism in film studies and then examining four models that have affinities with it. Neoformalism emerged in film studies about the same time that Metz abandoned his search for a semiotic basis for a film language and turned instead to narratology and psychoanalysis. Neoformalism in fact shares many concerns with semiotics, structuralism, and Russian formalism, the last of which is the historical basis for neoformalism in film studies and had a decided influence on the development of structural linguistics and structuralism. Following a brief overview of neoformalism, I look at a number of scholars working within the tradition. Film analyst and historian Kristin Thompson presents a manifesto for the analytical approach of neoformalism. Film historian David Bordwell draws an analogy to musicology to formulate a different research program for film studies based around the study of the art form. Noël Carroll, a philosopher and film theorist, proposes an account of how music serves to modify the narrative situation. Thompson, Bordwell, and Carroll are closely associated through institution and coauthorship, and although they do not agree on all particulars, their work does show a broad shared vision of research.

The other authors considered in chapter 5 are not as closely aligned, but they each share a similar concern with analysis and they all work to develop models of how the music subsystem works in relation to the other subsystems of film. Kathryn Kalinak, a film historian working on film music, develops a working model for film music from an analysis of *Captain Blood* (1935), and I organize her model to reveal better its underlying theoretical structure. Nicholas Cook, a music theorist, proposes a model of pairwise multimedia interactions that is useful especially for disentangling and assessing the claims of other theories of media interaction. David Neumeyer, a music theorist and historian of the soundtrack, reworks Michel Chion's concept of vococentrism into a full model of the integrated soundtrack. Annabel Cohen, an experimental psychologist, has over the past twenty-five years developed an increasingly intricate cognitive model of how film music is perceived that confirms a number of speculations and presumptions of other theories. Although taking a very different methodological approach, Cohen produces a model that is similar in many respects to other formal theories. The similarities and above all differences of emphasis in these models illustrate the range of potential for this kind of theoretical work.

Chapter 6 focuses on narratology, like semiotics a descendant of structuralism that developed outside of film studies and was later applied to film. In some respects, these approaches resemble neoformalism (and there is more than a little overlap), with an emphasis on the film (or soundtrack) as the object (which has now become a text). The chapter opens with a discussion of narratology in film. The second section covers narratological theories of the soundtrack, especially music, which was one of the first subsystems of film to have its theory rewritten in explicitly narratological terms. Film historian Claudia Gorbman's *Unheard Melodies* (1987) made a key intervention here, as she combined narratology with aspects of the then-dominant psychoanalytic theories to produce a compelling new reformulation of music's place in the soundtrack. The remainder of this section considers contributions by Chion,

Giorgio Biancorosso, Robynn Stilwell, Jeff Smith, and Ben Winters—all scholars working on the soundtrack—and it traces how the basic conceptual distinction of diegetic and nondiegetic music that Gorbman introduced has evolved. The next section looks at the important narratological concept of focalization as it applies to music in film. To amplify the range of the concept, I engage film music historian Guido Heldt's recent book on narrative level and work.

Chapter 7 considers critical theories of the soundtrack, and chapter 8 examines how aspects of these critical theories have been combined with psychoanalysis. Critical theories are in some respects the flip side of neoformalism and structuralism: where neoformalism and structuralism seek a disinterested perspective, critical theories insist on political interest; where neoformalism and structuralism require objectivity, critical theories reveal that objectivity as subjectively constructed. When scholars today say "film theory," they usually have in mind one of the modes of critical theory (Marxism, postcolonialism, feminism, queer theory, critical race theory), or the so-called apparatus theory (considered in chapter 8) that combined semiotics, Marxism, and Lacanian psychoanalysis into a heady mix that would dominate debates in film theory for much of the 1980s. Critical theories nevertheless draw on many of the same analytical tools as neoformalism and structuralism but put them to different critical ends. Because critical theories aim to reveal, analyze, and explain a political interest that is concealed in a general ideology, the analysis often takes hermeneutical form where the political interest is read out of the structure of the film, which is at the same time understood as a concealed ideological stratum. The forms and structures of the film are assumed to be determined by the ideological forces of society. Critical theories thus often engage in ideology critique, distinguished from older forms of ideology critique in being more focused on deconstructing forms, techniques, and structures rather than identifying explicit ideological contents. Critical theories are also often concerned with the analysis of power, the traditional modalities being race, class, and gender. In current usage race is usually expanded to include issues of ethnicity and colonialism, and gender expanded to include issues of sexuality and orientation.

Specifically, chapter 7 is devoted to general issues of critical theories and the soundtrack. The first part considers its origins in Marxism, the analysis of ideology, postcolonialism, and issues of labor. The largest portion of this section examines the theory of musical topics (musical topics are conventional musical passages that signify generally like "stormy" or stereotypically like "Indian") and subjects the concept of musical topic to ideological critique. The second part of the chapter contains a lengthy discussion of how debates over gender and sexuality have influenced thinking about the soundtrack. The analysis of gender and sexuality forms one of the major branches of critical theory, and in terms of the soundtrack it has developed the deepest literature.

Chapter 8 examines the influential film theory that derived from the intersection of semiotics, Marxism, and psychoanalysis. The resulting so-called apparatus theory proved contentious but very influential, especially the concept of suture, which provided a model for film spectatorship and subjectivity. Though apparatus theory itself is rarely embraced today in full form, many of its concepts have remained useful. This chapter concludes with a section on neo-Lacanian theory and uses it to explicate the very influential soundtrack theory of Michel Chion.

Chapter 9 serves as a conclusion to the whole project, arguing that the conception of digital and "new" media in terms of "convergence" has emphasized a shift in both aural and visual dimensions toward a general purpose rendering fixed on producing distinct feelings and sensations and away from a reproduction and screening of real events. This turn away from semiotic indexicality as a grounding for film has met considerable resistance, which has revealed the extent to which film theory remains bound to a conception of film as a recording of reality and ultimately to André Bazin's "myth of total cinema," however much film theory also understands film as a representation and so recognizes whatever reality it represents as inherently and necessarily constructed. This chapter concludes by sketching out some theoretical implications of the soundtrack in the context of digital media.

2

Early Theories of the Sound Film

Introduction: The Specificity of the Sound Film

The earliest theories of sound film attempted to determine its nature and aesthetic possibilities by asking what was specific to it. They asked: What is sound film? What are its fundamental bases? How, if at all, does it differ from silent film and recorded theater? What is the role and status of recorded sound? How do image and sound relate? Is synchronization an accidental, emergent, or ontological relation? In particular, these theories responded to the basic fact that the sound film combines two sets of distinct technologies: camera, film, projector, and screen, on the one hand, and microphone, record, phonograph, and loudspeakers, on the other. Sound on film substitutes a sound strip for the phonograph record and a sound head for the needle, but the technologies remain distinct even when image and sound are printed together on the medium of film. Despite the fact that sound film was supposed to restore the unity of sight and sound denied in the reproduction technologies of (silent) film, phonograph, and radio, the distinctions in technology for reproducing image and sound prompted theories that emphasized the basic hybridity of the sound film apparatus and so also conceptual opposition of the two sets of technologies.

In several lengthy articles and a short book written in the late 1920s, American cultural critic Gilbert Seldes offered one of the first extended public attempts to theorize the new sound film. Drawing on a critical tradition that grounded the cinematic art in the specificity of the medium of film and in the technique of montage, Seldes sought to ground sound film similarly in the specificity of the medium as such, which he located in the properties of the technology, notably in the division between the camera and the microphone, between the screen and the speakers: "The essential problem of the talkie is to find the proper relation between the camera and the microphone" (Seldes 1929b, 298). Seldes, who was neither explicitly for nor against the talking film, recognized artistic possibilities in the divided apparatus, and consequently saw **23** no need to yoke them together to form a unified perspective, as many writers committed to sound film as a recording medium distinguished by its ability to unite image and sound do. Seldes, in fact, argued that attempts to enforce a unified perception was one of the major difficulties of the talking film because it so restricted the possibilities of the camera. The difficulty of the talkies, their lack of action and mobility, followed not from the nature of the medium per se, but from (1) the immobility of the microphone and (2) the demand for mimetic synchronization, the demand that camera and microphone reproduce the same perspective. Given the state of the technology in the early transition years, the result could only be an unnecessarily static camera.

To break the impasse, Seldes explicitly rejected the model of perceptual realism that dominated the thinking of those who developed the technology. As a doctrine, perceptual realism insists that the technology should mimic human perception, and the rule of mimetic synchronization grew out of this doctrine, construing the apparatus as a recording device for the senses of seeing and hearing. Other writers of the time, notably Vsevolod Pudovkin, would question whether mimetic synchronization yielded an adequate model of perceptual realism, but Seldes attacked the notion that there was a good reason for the talking film to be dominated by mimetic synchronization. Instead of accepting perceptual realism as the basis for the sound film, then, Seldes instead looked for ways of putting the technological differences between camera and phonograph, screen and loudspeaker into aesthetic play. The point, he said, was not to impose an artificial unity by synchronizing the two technologies in a way that forced the technologies to conform, but rather to find a way to allow each technology to follow the nature of its mechanism and to regulate the result so that they coordinated in an artistically convincing way even if they did not express an identity. Seldes analyzed the situation thus:

> The voice in the talkies is recorded by one mechanism, the movement by another. . . . The microphone is comparatively stationary; the camera is mobile to the highest degree. From this separation of function it should have been clear at the start that, while the voice might go on steadily, the camera could leave it behind, could show not only the listeners, but whatever else was relevant to the action at the moment. The producers immobilized the camera in favor of the microphone; the result was not a new form of entertainment—the true talkie—but a combination of movie and phonograph. (1929a, 455–56)

For Seldes, the early conception of the sound film was too bound to the recording of the voice, which had the effect of turning sound film into something resembling an illustrated phonograph recording.

Seldes's analysis perceptively recognized that the phonograph and the cinema have differing representational conventions, and the theory he developed is more interesting than most from the early transitional era in that it locates an aesthetic ground for sound film that allows the talkie to define a medium specific to it rather than understanding it either as a mere recording of an event or as a silent film plus sound recording. Seldes's theory focused on how to reconcile speech with camera mobility, by which he primarily meant editing rather than camera movement during a shot. And along with preserving the editing of the image, he sought a purposeful (rather than mechanical) place for dialogue. He argued that the talking film must show "a feeling of the necessity for speech which the talkies can use in relation to silent pictures—speech not as an accident, not as a toy, not as an additional attraction, but something demanded by the nature of the whole which they have created" (Seldes 1929c, 147). For talking film to become an art in the way silent film was an art, it had to "become thoroughly itself—to be not symphonic music, not opera, not movie—but a distinct thing, growing and changing in accordance with its own laws, as human beings grow, as all the arts grow" (154). The double technological base of the talking film made this a complex demand, and one that would not be answered until the parameters of sound film had been worked out and codified in the 1930s.

Seldes's approach emphasized the technological basis of the sound film and attempted to draw the nature of the sound film from that. Most theorists of the sound film during the transition period focused less on the technologies as ontological determinants and more on preserving the editing procedures from the silent film, even when they looked for the artistic grounds of sound film's specificity. These theorists, which include most of the authors covered in this chapter, were concerned about the emphasis on dialogue turning sound film into talking film, and like Seldes they worked to denaturalize—or at least question the necessity of—the audiovisual figure of mimetic synchronization. But in general they understood the ontology of film to lie in the representational capacities of montage (the edited moving image), and argued that an effective sound film therefore needs at least to preserve the montage of silent film or find novel ways of extending it.

In this chapter, I examine in depth the views of five important theorists who wrote during the transition to sound. Each of these authors recognizes the great technological advance of the sound film, but they are all troubled in some fashion by how dialogue fundamentally altered the cinematic values that had been established with the silent film. The unrelenting mimetic synchronization of the early talking film made for a difficult audiovisual figure, hard to work in editing and deeply hierarchical in content. On the one hand, the moving lips of the image are difficult to part from the voice. Sound frequently does not allow the same freedom of editing as does the image, as edits in the middle of a word radically alter the meaning or even render it meaningless. The sounds, especially the voice, are also "sticky"; once dialogue and image were affixed to one another, filmmakers initially found it difficult to cut away until the full line had been delivered. This considerably slowed the tempo of the editing and forced the rhythm of montage to follow the delivery of dialogue rather than the theme or action. On the other hand, talking also transformed the structure of the image, or rather forced a new hierarchical arrangement on it. Synchronized bodies are important bodies, and characters speaking dialogue command the image to a much greater degree than was the case in the silent film. The theories considered in this chapter therefore give significant attention to synchronized dialogue and asynchronous sound. Because of its important place in the silent cinema, music continued to receive substantial attention from theorists, who often invoke it not just for a set of metaphors but also to imagine an ideal relation of sound and image.

The Statement on Sound and the Concept of Counterpoint

I begin with the response to sound film from the Soviet Union. When sound film was commercially introduced, Sergei Eisenstein and Vsevolod Pudovkin were two of the most important directors of Soviet cinema. The "Statement on Sound," written by Eisenstein, Pudovkin, and Grigori Alexandrov with the passion of a manifesto, appeared in 1928 before any of the signatories had seen a sound film.[1] The authors argue that synchronized dialogue is antithetical to montage: "Sound used in this way [as synchronized dialogue]," the authors direly warn, "will destroy the culture of montage, because every mere *addition* of sound to montage fragments increases their inertia as such and their independent significance" (Eisenstein, Pudovkin, and Alexandrov 1988, 114, emphasis in original). The idea of inertia is inspired, as it recognizes a stickiness to synchronized sound that makes editing sound film much more fraught than images alone. But the problem lies not just in the way the segments of sound film are more resistant to montage. The inertia also makes the segments less pliable, and the authors feared that synchronization as a mechanical principle (rather than a theme or even a story) would come to determine the montage, partly to ensure the illusion of reproduced reality, partly because sound and image condense into a difficult audiovisual figure whose unity isn't merely an ideological illusion.[2]

---

[1] The "Statement on Sound" was first published in July 1928 and appeared in English translation in October of that same year in the journal *Close Up*. The more commonly encountered translation appears in Eisenstein (1975), which was first published in 1942.

[2] Arguably, Eisenstein would come to reorient his whole conception of montage around this recognition. Whereas his conception of montage during the silent era remained principally concerned with cutting and joining on the basis of purposefully developing a conflict on the basis of a theme, his later conception of montage was a much more general principle that suffused all of the arts. In terms of film it meant that he gave much more analytical attention to montage within the shot. This had the effect of making his later theory of montage much more diffuse.

To counteract the inertia and to restore the flexibility of montage, sound cannot be simply synchronized with the image but must rather be "treated as a new element of montage (as an independent variable combined with the visual image)" (Eisenstein, Pudovkin, and Alexandrov 1988, 114). The authors thus advocate for a "new orchestral counterpoint of visual and sound images." Famously, they argue that *"only the contrapuntal use* of sound vis-à-vis the visual fragment of montage will open up new possibilities for the development and perfection of montage" and urge that *"the first experimentations in sound must aim at a sharp discord with the visual images"* (114, emphasis in original). Counterpoint thus becomes synonymous with montage and with the asynchronous use of sound. The latter would also become the privileged theoretical mode of sound, since it is not redundant with the image.

In Soviet theory of the silent film, as in much film theory of the 1920s, montage was considered the constructive element of film and also what distinguished cinema from other arts (Eisenstein 1988, 113). As early as 1926, Eisenstein had defined his artistic principle as "the rational constructive composition of effective elements; the most important thing is that the effect must be calculated and analyzed in advance" (75). And montage was the primary method to do this in film. The authors of the "Statement on Sound" argue that sound film has the potential to solve certain "imperfections" in the methods of silent film (Eisenstein, Pudovkin, and Alexandrov 1988, 114). Sound, they say, offers "an organic escape" from "blind alleys" of silent film that include intertitles and "explanatory" sequences (long takes) (114). Silent film frequently required the use of these devices or complicated alternatives that resulted in "fantastical montage constructions" that were difficult for audiences to follow (114). Sound film, the "Statement on Sound" argues, provides fresh solutions to these intractable problems.

Sergei Eisenstein and Counterpoint

Writing in the wake of the "Statement on Sound," Eisenstein (1988) remained enamored of the idea of the sound film, so much so that he could assert that "the whole future of our cinema and an as yet unimagined range of opportunities for social influence lies with sound cinema" (129). He dubbed this new form of film, one guided by audiovisual counterpoint, "absolute sound cinema," in which sound would be "organized by means of the cinematic recording of noises and untempered sounds." These sounds would in turn be distributed across the film in a planned fashion: "neither anarchically nor by recording sounds 'as they really are' but by the strict organization of the selection of sounds and it is by no means obligatory for these sounds to correspond to the event that is taking place" (131).

Although his enthusiasm for sound film continued after Hollywood and Europe had converted to talking pictures, he remained unconvinced of dialogue's efficacy: "I think that a 100 per cent talking film is nonsense and I believe everyone agrees with me" (200). Nevertheless, Eisenstein understood that the international success of the talkie meant that sound film would have to deal with dialogue in a substantive way. He favored a freer approach to it than deployed in Hollywood, arguing, for instance, that matching of volume to image scale was often unnecessary in the cutting of dialogue. "All depends on the intention of the author of the film. In order to eliminate a particular effect or to produce an unexpected effect, you can and must emphasize the discrepancy between the sounds and the distance of the filmed object from the camera" (133). Thus, Eisenstein shifted the basis from mimetic reproduction to directorial planning: the intention of the director convincingly executed would make sense of any treatment of sound. Although the mimetic synchronization of a mechanically reproduced scene might seem natural, Eisenstein argued that it presented an acute danger because the director tacitly ceded control to the machine. Eisenstein's formulation, by contrast, demanded that any deployment of synchronized sound be meaningful. Such a meaningful deployment of synchronization occurs, for instance, when the intention or theme of the film requires such an alignment, or when the conflict between image and sound could be brought to its greatest pitch through synchronization rather than mismatch.

Eisenstein remained too suspicious of synchronized dialogue to pursue these options during the early years of the transition to sound; and when he returned to develop the concept of vertical montage, his attitude toward dialogue had changed sufficiently that he no longer required a special theory of montage to handle it. In summary, then, Eisenstein's ultimate evaluation of the audiovisual counterpoint comes down to deciding on its efficacy for articulating the theme of the film.

Vsevolod Pudovkin and Asynchronous Sound

Like Eisenstein, Pudovkin privileged counterpoint and asynchronous sound long after the "Statement on Sound" was published, but even in his theoretical writings from the transitional period, Pudovkin's underlying issue with synchronized sound was less the redundancy of image and sound per se than the fact that mimetic synchronization was a mechanical figure that often ran counter to the needs of the story and theme. Because of its proximity to the story, Pudovkin's account of counterpoint and asynchronous sound was also more easily accommodated by Hollywood than Eisenstein's more thoroughly dialectical one.

Pudovkin argues that "the first function of sound is to *augment the potential expressiveness of the film's content*" (1949a, 156, emphasis in original). Sound, Pudovkin says, allows for a deeper presentation of the content and for a more rapid delivery of information. For Pudovkin, the audiovisual figure of mimetic synchronization, though not a necessary condition for sound film and often unduly naturalized as though it was, nevertheless adheres in the idea of the sound film and can be used in an aesthetically successful manner whenever it increases expressiveness. Consequently, compared to Eisenstein, Pudovkin focuses more on the indexical qualities that arise from the asynchronous relationship than any all-encompassing meaning that emerges from their formal juxtaposition.

Analyzing the formal possibilities for treating dialogue in sound film, Pudovkin notes that an exact coincidence of image and dialogue is only one option, and often the least interesting because it tends to make film into a species of recorded theater, especially when a single shot is used to cover the scene. Pudovkin deems this approach to be extremely primitive, essentially a reversion of film to a simple medium of recording as in the earliest days of silent film. He finds the related approach of editing the scene to follow the dialogue with each change of speaker bringing a cut to the image of the new speaker to be something of an improvement, because it at least recognizes that film receives its power from selecting pertinent elements from the whole and giving them emphasis. But this approach does not resolve the basic issue. In this case, Pudovkin argues, "the director has made of montage and editing no more than a cold verbatim report, and switched the spectator's attention from one speaker to another without any emotional or intellectual justification" (1949a, 159). The procedure, in other words, leads to an empty formalism, one that simply follows the dictates of the raw material, rather than articulating that material in a way that responds to a thematic need of the film.

Nothing in the sound film, however, binds image and sound into a necessary unity, and in fact the sound strip permits cutting just as readily as the image. "The sound record on film is, in general, as pliable a material as the pictures film on which the image is recorded. This record can be cut and edited, more—on occasion it must be cut and edited" (1949b, 81–82). Even in cutting dialogue, the rhythms of editing image and sound do not need to coincide (1949a, 168). Pudovkin argues that asynchronous sound is a technical means of domesticating the technology, allowing the sound film to eliminate the dead intervals of mimetic rendering and to synchronize its rhythms instead to the theme. "Directors lose all reason to be afraid of cutting the sound strip if they accept the principle of arranging it in a distinct composition. Provided that they are linked by a clear idea of the course to be pursued, various sounds can, exactly like images, be set side by side in montage" (170). Indeed, "sound film will approach nearer to the true musical rhythm than silent film ever did, and this rhythm must derive not merely from the movement of artist and objects on the screen, but also . . . from exact cutting of the sound and arrangement of the sound pieces into a clear counterpoint with the image" (171).

The metaphor of counterpoint, which appeared prominently in the "Statement on Sound," becomes for Pudovkin a dominant concept to theorize an alternative to an all-determining mimetic synchronization, and the musical origins of the metaphor are hardly coincidental. Music in fact holds a privileged place for Pudovkin (and many writers on the sound film) in theorizing the soundtrack. "This sequence of images is but one of the rhythmical lines," Pudovkin writes, and he is adamant that in the sound film the "music is never an accompaniment but a separate element of counterpoint; but sound and image preserve their own line" (1949a, 172).

THE CASE OF *DESERTER*

Pudovkin uses the final sequence from his film *Deserter* (1933) to illustrate this idea. This sequence shows a workers' demonstration and the setbacks as the workers fight with police. It passes through a variety of moods as drivers caught in cars grow agitated and the workers clash with the police, but the music emphasizes throughout "courage and the certainty of final victory" (1949a, 164). According to Pudovkin, the music plays neither the details nor the suspense of the sequence but traces only "a gradual growth of power" (164). Pudovkin finds this music effective because it allows the film to articulate both the momentary fluctuations in fortune (through the aggressive cutting of the image to represent the violence of the fighting) and the larger arc of eventual success. The musical treatment, he says, "reminds the audience that with every defeat the fighting spirit only receives new impetus to the struggle for final victory in the future" (165). In his account of this sequence in *Film Acting*, he adds: "The music guides the line of the portrayal of the inner content representation of this historic march to certain victory, consciousness of which cannot, for us, be separated from perception of a worker marching into battle" (1949b, 94). The image traces the intricate rhythms of the "objective perception of events," whereas "music expresses the subjective appreciation of this objectivity" (1949a, 164–65), though it might equally be said that the image traces the fractured, localized subjective impressions of workers caught in the melee, whereas music expresses the objective reality (the power of collective action) that binds the moment together under the surface of appearance. Moreover, either the music was composed to the sequence or the images of the final confrontation were edited to the music, as cuts of particularly violent actions are timed to aggressive hits in the music. As a result, music and image are at this moment not so much in counterpoint as in a relation of complementation, which collapses the distinction between objectivity and subjectivity altogether to emphasize the power of collective action.

The treatment of sound in *Deserter* overall is striking in this respect. In most of the film, especially the early portions, sound is deployed specifically to individuate: characters speak, workers make sound through their labor, even individual ships and machines seem to distinguish themselves by the particularity of the noise they emit. Writing about this film, Pudovkin expresses a preference for "real sound because ... sound, like visual material, must be rich in its association, a thing impossible for reconstructed sound to be" (1949a, 173). Pudovkin points to the elaborate preparations needed to record real ship horns (173); but in *Deserter*, the horn effects in the initial scene in the port, which Pudovkin terms "a symphony of siren calls," seem as if they were synchronized from a library in postproduction; they do not settle with the image but instead seem to float above the scene like sound effects in silent film practice, and, moreover, there seems no particular thematic reason for this disassociation. We hear the sound of a horn and its aural marks of proximity lead us to expect to see *that* ship—the inertia of the association makes it sound like the recording has been imposed on the situation since it fits neither the image nor the imagined fictional space. But it also is not sharply drawn enough to make sense as a contrapuntal contrast, even if Pudovkin himself believed that it achieves the effect of contrapuntal syncopation.[3] In fact, Pudovkin's diagnosis of the issue here seems uncharacteristically confused. It is not the fact of a "real" sound that matters but the particularity of the reverb, which taps the representational potential of sound film's "inertia"—the tendency of sound to particularize and to become a component of the image—to facilitate the construction of offscreen space, a task that directors and technicians in the Hollywood studios had by and large mastered by the time Pudovkin was making his film.

Although most sounds in the film have a particularizing, individuating effect, the one notable exception is the sound of a crowd, which is collective, and as Pudovkin points out the crowd is qualitatively different than the quantity of individuals that combine to form it (1949a, 168). The crowd, Pudovkin says, takes its identity from the emotion or thought that binds it into a unity of force (168–69). But the handling of sound in the early portion of the film seems to suggest the way the technology of the sound film conspires against the representation of the collective, constantly deploying sound and image montage to dissolve it back into a set of individuals. This fits Pudovkin's conception of the crowd:

The conflicting processes at work within the groups to produce this result afford immediately obvious dramatic material, and accent upon the

---

[3] In a later scene in the port the use of reverberation did help force the horns into the aural background, and it may have been experiences like this that convinced Pudovkin that recording the sound in "real" space was a method to manage this issue.

characteristics of individuals is an integral part of the creation of a living mass. What real method can there be of creating this qualitatively altered mass of individuals save by the editing of close-ups? (1949a, 169).

Montage, then, becomes the method for representing a dialectical understanding of the crowd, the collective mass coming into being. Really, only in the concluding demonstration sequence does the crowd form into a qualitatively distinct entity. That is, in *Deserter*, the task of collectivization belongs to the music, in particular to the march that concludes the film, and that sequence is itself a kind of reversion to silent film practice. The result is that the film makes a rather ambivalent artistic statement about the inherent politics of the sound film technology.

In any event, to return to the issue of counterpoint, it is not so much the precise status of the subjective and objective as their initial opposition and then the varying paths and rhythms they take through the material—paths and rhythms determined by the representation of the theme—that is decisive for Pudovkin, since this is what allows the contrapuntal relationship to form. "The crux of the matter is, of course, that the emotion derives from far deeper elements integrated as a result of the combination of two lines—the objective representation of reality in the image and the revelation of the profound inner content of the reality in the sound" (1949b, 95). The goal is dialectical understanding, and this dialectical understanding emerges from the interplay, which allows for moments of both concordance and opposition (96).

PERCEPTUAL REALISM

Although an advocate for counterpoint and asynchronous sound, Pudovkin consistently invoked a model of perceptual realism to ground his theoretical intuitions about the relationship of image and sound. This too made his conception consistent with the emerging classical system.

> There must be borne in mind the relative importance of every character, or, from another point of view, the logical course of interest of the eager spectator, for the rhythm here found will determine the actual course of his attention, and therefore, in the end, the unity and clarity of his reaction to the film. (1949b, 89)

Audiences, he argues, frequently want to see the effects that words have on those to whom they are addressed more than the speaker who delivers them because the reaction of the listener is the element that is most dramatically pertinent. "Would a director of any imagination handle a scene in a court of justice where a sentence of death is being passed by filming the judge pronouncing the sentence in preference to recording visually the immediate reactions of the condemned?" (1949a, 161).

Pudovkin also argues that this kind of perceptual realism justifies even more elaborate deployments of asynchronous sound to increase the dynamism between image and sound. The world, he claims, does not unfold in the same way that we perceive it, for our perception selects from all that is available to fix first on this element and then that. It is this difference that marks perceptual realism as subjective (1949a, 158). The route of our attention follows pertinence; what we attend to is dependent on our interests, needs, and emotional state. "The tempo of [a viewer's] impressions varies with the rousing and calming of his emotions, while the rhythm of the objective world he perceives continues in unchanged tempo" (158). The apparatus itself—both film and sound recording—records just that objective world, not a subjective impression; that is the power of film to reveal what we do not immediately perceive but also its deficiency inasmuch as its interests do not align with our own. The machine can be brought into better alignment, however, through editing, which allows the presentation to be selective and so to better mimic the impressions of our immediate perception. Sound allows film to move even closer to rendering human perception in machine form (158).

Pudovkin imagines a scene modeled on an attempt to follow the reality of perceptual attention. He argues that because a simple reproduction of sound, however faithfully rendered, is not subjectivized, it has no point of audition to ground it in a lived reality. In one frequently cited passage, he writes:

> In actual life, you . . . may suddenly hear a cry for help; you see only the window; you then look out and at first see nothing but the moving traffic. But *you do not hear the sound natural to these cars and buses*; instead you hear still only the cry that first startled you. At last you find with your eyes the point from which the sound came; there is a crowd, and someone is lifting the injured man, *who is now quiet*. But, now watching the many, you become aware of the din of traffic passing, and in the midst of its noise there gradually grows the piercing signal of the ambulance. At this your attention is caught by the clothes of the injured man: his suit is like that of your brother, who, you now recall, was due to visit you at two o'clock. In the tremendous tension that follows, the anxiety and uncertainty whether this possibly dying man may not indeed be your brother himself, *all sound ceases* and there exists for your perception total silence. Can it be two o'clock? You look at the clock and at the same time you hear its ticking. *This is the first synchronized moment* of an image and its caused sound since first you heard the cry. (1949a, 157–59, emphasis in original)

Editing for sound film, Pudovkin argues, ought to follow a similar procedure, guided by the presumed subjectivized, psychological flow of image and sound that reveals the unity of the total experience. The point, he claims, is to "augment the potential expressiveness of the film's content" (156), and this can only be accomplished if the director anticipates the audience's reactions.

Editing should be instrumentalized to prepare the psychological place of the audience in advance: "A relationship between the director in his cutting room and his future audience can be established only if he has a psychological insight into the nature of his audience and its consequent relationship to the content of the given material" (160). Indeed, "the director in editing makes himself the first, as it were the fundamental spectator" (1949b, 90).

Although the scene that Pudovkin outlined is more elaborate and more thoroughly subjectivized than would be typically attempted in films produced under the classical system (whether in Hollywood or elsewhere), editing image and sound to direct audience attention to points of narrative pertinence rather than simply showing dialogue delivery is a functional norm of the system, as is evident in the important place that the reaction shot of a character listening played in the formation of the style. The general representational scheme of perceptual realism with an added psychological dimension would ultimately prove the dominant one in Hollywood and elsewhere. Pudovkin shows that strict mimetic synchronization often fell short of the representational goal of perceptual realism. Indeed, mixing synchronous and asynchronous treatments of sound often conforms better to perceptual realism, while also making possible more fluid editing patterns.

Béla Balázs and the Physiognomy of the Voice

Béla Balázs, a Hungarian critic, librettist, screenwriter, and director, wrote some of the most incisive theory of film from the 1920s through the 1940s. His *The Spirit of the Film* was published in 1930; an extensive revision was published in 1945 as *Theory of the Film*. He had previously written *Visible Man* (published in 1924), an important theoretical treatment of silent film, and the subsequent volume attempted to extend those insights to the sound film.

In *The Spirit of the Film*, Balázs argues for possibilities of sound film that avoid the reduction to the naïve realism presupposed by mimetic synchronization. Sound film, he says, should "approach the reality of life from a totally different angle and open up a new treasure-house of human experience" (1970, 197). Balázs advocates an asynchronous treatment of sound on similar grounds: sound and image should each work in their own way to unfold a subjective perception. At the same time, he concedes that mimetic synchronization exerts a strong influence in sound film—people are predisposed to look for sources of sounds—resulting in the tendency to favor shots where image and sound coincide, especially for dialogue.

The predisposition of sound film toward synchronization means that it is inherently more hierarchical than the silent film. Although the latter also organizes its images hierarchically, with the face serving as the privileged object, that hierarchy is both more formal and more fluid than that of the sound film: silent film establishes a basic equality between people and things. Objects in silent film, Balázs says, "share with human beings a quality of silence that makes the two almost homogeneous, and hence enhances the mute object's vitality and significance. Since it does not speak less than human beings, it says just as much" (2010a, 23). Each communicates not through speech but through physiognomy, through the gestures of an expressive face revealed in close-up, a face that he believes things possess as much as people. Sound film, "burst[ing] upon the scene, with catastrophic force" (2010b, 183), changes this relation, not just because it restores language to people and so sets them again apart from things but also because synchronization foregrounds and individuates. Synchronization marks pertinence. Balázs recounts a scene that begins "by showing us the raging tumult of a great crowd in long shot. The camera then dollies in towards a single individual. The sound camera does likewise. And what emerges from the mass is not just an individual face, but an individual voice, a personal utterance" (193). The actual words of this utterance are beside the point: it is only the fact of synchronization that matters to this individuation.

Balázs is quick to argue that dialogue is "the least edifying element of the sound film" (2010b, 208). Instead, he contends that the performance of dialogue, the manner of its delivery, not the words themselves, is what distinguishes screen dialogue (194). This focus on the "sensuous impression" of the delivery offers the potential of revealing what might be termed a vocal physiognomy, the aural face of the voice. If conventional discursive meaning recedes into the banality of the script, this vocal physiognomy, its play of expressive intonation, opens like the play of expression across the face of things to hermeneutic reading; this face becomes legible through the repetition that recording makes possible. "Sound film dialogues differ from other dramatic dialogues in that they are uttered only once, and once and for all. Every nuance of intonation is final and fixed for all time" (207). Recording is fundamental to this effect. This is a crucial insight, and one that will be frequently neglected in subsequent theory.

As the close-up reveals the human face to be one among the faces of things, so too a physiognomy of sound reveals the human voice to be one among the voices of things. This is at least the utopian promise of the talking film. For Balázs, as for many sound technicians of the time, the microphone is analogous to the microscope, which had opened up a new order of the world to visual inspection.[4] The microphone similarly transforms the sound film, whose importance lies in allowing us to hear "the intimate language of nature." Sound film, Balázs says, permits "the voices of things themselves . . . to speak" (2010b, 186). Although the sound film forces a profoundly regressive

---

[4] On the analogy between the microscope and the microphone, see Abbate (2016, 807–8).

movement on film art, Balázs nevertheless also recognizes that it "opens up a new sphere of experience," "a reality . . . that has never before been depicted" (189), and offers "new objects of representation" (184). This is especially true of the sound close-up, which in this respect resembles its image counterpart: the sound close-up "can transmit auditory impressions of which we are only in the rarest of instances aware with the unaided ear. . . . We hear, but simply do not become conscious of these soft, intimate sounds, since they are drowned out by the everyday noise as if by an avalanche of sound" (194). This voice of things, their vocal physiognomy, only becomes legible as an object of synchronization; recording alone does not suffice because the voice of things remains remote without the image to connect "voice" to object. "We are so unfamiliar with the intimate sounds of nature and the world of objects that we simply do not recognize them unless we see the images to which they belong" (186). The capability to synchronize image and sound offers sound film a distinct advantage in this sense over radio, since in the latter the sound must always be explained by another sound, usually through the intervention of a commentator's voice. And a similar advantage obtains for synchronized over asynchronous sound. With synchronized sound, the source is shown so the recognition is immediate rather than mediated.

It is with this understanding that Balázs approaches the concept of counterpoint, which he does not reduce to asynchronism. In the sound film, he argues,

> we should not hear, or only hear, what we can already see. The acoustical dimension should not just reinforce the effect of natural reality, but should use sound to emphasize something that we might otherwise have overlooked. It should awaken ideas and associations in our minds that the silent image on its own might have failed to arouse. And it will do so by juxtaposing sound montage and image montage contrapuntally, like two melodies. (2010b, 198)

Balázs agrees with many early critics of sound film that sound should not simply be redundant with the image and that synchronization needs a justification beyond being just naturally given. But he identifies and traces a kind of mutual legibility of the two domains, the way sound can emphasize and awaken what is not immediately apparent in the image. And the reverse is also the case.

> A figure on film listens to a song on a gramophone. We see the effect. The recorded voice dissolves into the original voice, and this acoustic montage signals a change of scene. We now hear that we are somewhere else, though we do not yet know where. We hear that the singer is now present. We do not yet know what she looks like, but we know already, with mounting expectation, that she is significant. (2010b, 199–200)

The point, then, is the appearance of this contrapuntal relationship of image and sound, the way the montage of image and the montage of sound are each directed toward making the physiognomy of the other apparent and legible, not whether the formal relationship happens to be synchronous or asynchronous. In the case of revealing the voice of things, the relationship is liable to be synchronous, since the sound's significance as a "voice" is tied to the recognition of its source and being represented in the world. But in the case of familiar sounds like human voices, knocks, and so forth, the relationship is at least occasionally liable to be asynchronous, and not only or even primarily because synchronizing such sounds is highly redundant. Rather, because they are so recognizable, these types of sounds are also strongly indexical, and the previous example of the gramophone audio dissolve is doubly so. In the example, the gramophone serves as an index of the voice that motivates the dissolve, and the voice itself is an index to the singer after the dissolve.

The reaction shot is prototypical of this sort of indexical use, which is indispensable for creating the expansive diegetic space of sound film. Balázs draws a subtle but important point from it. In a reaction shot, he notes, "when sound enters the image space, we do not see its source. We do not see the speaker. We see only the listener, and we too become listeners" (2010b, 198). If the effect is to make evident that "the acoustical space of the scene is larger than the space that is shown within the frame" (198), it does so by creating an indexical play of absence that knits the audience into the scene on a point of identification that appropriates the voice's address. The indexical effect is usefully (i.e., artistically) unstable if also a bit perilous, as it traces a circuit of desire propelled by the central absence.

The whole of *Romance* (1930), one of Greta Garbo's early talking pictures, turns on this circuit, which is something like the film's theme, with the voice serving as a conduit to an imagined, recollected world and the promise to return the object of desire to its place of originary plenitude. Early in the film, a dissolve from a phonograph quite similar to the one Balázs mentioned motivates the film's central flashback. The signification is more complex than the situation Balázs described, however, because the gramophone record in *Romance* is also semiotically iconic. That is, it does not point to the moment of vocal inscription on the record (index), but instead triggers a memory of a particular performance that the recording recalls through resemblance (icon) rather than being the thing itself.

For Balázs, the reaction shot operates through displacement and the semiotic power of the index, as it is productive of imagined space by virtue of its insertion into and activation of this circuit. "A face in close-up. A call. Startled, the face listens and turns. We do not yet know who has called. The camera roams slowly through the space. The voice gets louder, comes closer. Until, finally, the speaker appears in the frame" (2010b, 198). The reaction shot serves as a lure for the camera, the shot's indexical character animating the camera, which responds as though reacting to this circuit of desire opened by asynchronous sound, and sending it looking for the sound's source.

From this example of the reaction shot, as well as that of Pudovkin's scenario of subjectivized sound discussed previously, we recognize that the power of asynchronous sound lay not so much in its autonomy from the image as in the way it productively defers synchronization; like consonance in musical counterpoint, the point of synchronization retains its structuring force. This power of asynchronous sound, then, was akin to that of actual contrapuntal dissonance and derived from the destabilization rather than negation of synchronization. Asynchronous sound is, in other words, a figure of displacement and disorder, which is what made it both artistically productive and perilous. Unless carefully handled, asynchronous sound, even something as ubiquitous as a reaction shot, can create the impression of a "voice from nowhere," that is, as unanchored in the space represented by the film. In fact, Rudolf Arnheim, as we will see, objects to the reaction shot for precisely this reason. Balázs, keenly sensitive to the circuit of desire that underlies asynchronous sound, is on the contrary more measured in his assessment, recognizing that "such voices from nowhere do however acquire a certain pathos that may render them impersonal, ghostly and oracular, qualities that are not always appropriate" (2010b, 205). Balázs evaluates the efficacy of the figure not on its absolute effect of unruliness but on the basis of its representational function. This allows him to discern in the contours of this offscreen voice the outlines of what Michel Chion (1994, 1999) calls the acousmêtre, the acoustical being.

Balázs also recognizes the peculiarly specific and yet indefinite quality that sound brings to its articulation of offscreen space. Although he thinks that sound film gives a more concrete impression of space than does silent film, this impression is nevertheless essentially ambiguous and uncontainable in the absence of synchronization. Sound might seem "impossible to abstract . . . from space," since characteristic timbral shifts from the reverberant qualities of space and distance mean that sound "always possesses a particular spatial character, which derives in turn from its point of origin" (2010b, 189). Moreover, unlike theater, which possesses only the sound of the auditorium so that the drawing room on stage carries the same acoustical imprint as the cathedral or the forest glen, sound film has the capacity to record position in space and so also the markers of space (189–90). But sound itself, Balázs suggests, only gives an imprecise spatial sense. "Sound is hard to locate. The emission of a sound will thus have to be visually indicated either with a striking gesture or with a close-up of its source" (196). Sound, he famously says, "casts no shadows" (187); it has no angles, edges or sides (188); and it moves easily around corners (196). It is also amenable to combining with other sounds in a fashion that makes them impossible to separate. Consequently, sound "does not establish space" (189) or create "figures in space" (187), and "its capacity to determine perspective and direction" was actually quite limited (189).

Given the care and subtlety that Balázs brings to his theory of film, it is somewhat surprising that his account of audio recording is so lacking in nuance, so wedded to an ontology that took recording as first and foremost a reproduction rather than a representation. He understands audio recording as primarily a technical discipline, one that does not permit judgment and taste to intervene as is the case in cinematography. "The same sound from a single identical source," he claims, "cannot be recorded in three different ways by three different sound-camera operators; it cannot be 'interpreted,' as is possible in any optical image of that same object. A sound cannot be completely altered by the subjective temperament, the personal attitude of the camera operator, while still remaining the same sound" (2010b, 192). This is as much as to claim that the recording apparatus is a neutral medium that does not color the sound, as though microphone choice and placement do not ultimately matter on any plane other than fidelity to the source.

Typical of the historical moment, this statement also captures the crux of the problem for early sound film. Theorists had—and to a surprising degree continue to have—great difficulty breaking the identity of sound with its represented source: "Recorded sound is, indeed, not even representation" (2010b, 192). And being outside of representation, recorded sound seems to drag the sound film toward being a recording of the world. This conception was resisted time and again by writers from very different theoretical and ideological commitments because it threatens a "dubious relapse into the theatrical" (193). For Balázs, since reproduced sound itself has no way to distinguish itself as a representation, this danger has to be managed through the specificity of the medium of sound film.

> If the sound film is to become a new genre on a par with the other arts and with the silent film, it must use sound not just as a complementary element that merely enriches dramatic scenes, but as a dramatic event of central, decisive importance and as the basic motif of the action. (205)

The theme, the idea, must "be made specific to the sound film" (205). And it attains this specificity through a unique and characteristic articulation: "A motif belongs absolutely to the sound film only if it makes sense only in a sound film and nowhere else" (206). This is Balázs's succinct formulation of the specificity thesis for sound film. To be an art, sound film needs to find and exploit the artistic potential specific to it. And this means that it can be neither silent film nor recorded theater. When he returned to revise *The Spirit of the Film* into *Theory of the Film*, he would indeed wonder whether sound film could in fact be an art at all.

Rudolf Arnheim and the Unity of Sound

Rudolf Arnheim was a German psychologist and Berlin-based film critic who wrote extensively on film and radio in the 1920s and 1930s. After arriving in the United States in 1940, he became a professor and developed an influential theory of art based on the principles of gestalt psychology. Although *Film as Art* (1957), a revision and substantial abridgement of his *Film als Kunst* (published in 1932 and translated into English simply as *Film* in 1933), is considered a classic of film theory, he seldom wrote on the topic after his arrival in the United States, in part because he could never reconcile himself to the art of the sound film.

Arnheim agrees with Balázs on the requirement of medium specificity, but at the same time he finds it to be one of sound film's most vexing issues. Writing about the early sound film, he grants that the talking film is a suitable replacement for theater but is uncertain whether sound film is viable—sufficiently specific—as a medium in its own right. The difficulty of sound film is not its mechanical inadequacy—even for music, he says, the reproduction is excellent and he was surprisingly unsentimental about the resulting displacement of musical labor, whose standardization under mechanical reproduction he saw as one of the virtues of the technology (1997, 29). Throughout the transition to sound, Arnheim grants the technology its accomplishment: "Sounds come from the loud-speaker much as they are in real life, fundamentally unchanged" (1933, 224). He makes this concession not so much because he did not hear the difference—he acknowledges that the apparatus had difficulties reproducing sibilants and that theater acoustics had not yet been designed for reproduced sound (229)—but because he is interested in how the drive toward a realism defined by mimetic synchronization affects the art of film. If silent film is itself a mimetic art, sound film takes the mimetic impulse much further. Any proper aesthetic claims that the sound film raises, Arnheim concludes, cannot lie in inadequate fidelity of reproduction, which is merely a technical issue, but in its accomplishments of mimetic synchronization, and ultimately in that which the apparatus promises. The sound film, he says, poses its most difficult aesthetic challenges—indeed, calls its own possibility as art into question—precisely in its full adequacy, which endows the film with a reproductive fidelity that both fills out the material and hardens it, or makes it less supple to work artistically.

Even in its rudimentary commercial form of 1928, the reproduction compelled and amazed—it created, Arnheim says, a feeling of wonder that encouraged a regression to a naïve, childlike state (1997, 30). He also acknowledges the real draw of sound film, even admitting that it "gets under your skin far more than silent film" (30). Yet he also contends that this attraction of wonder ultimately undermines the foundations of its art. "In the split second that this happens, however, film art abdicates its hard-won place back to the peepshow" (30).

The peepshow metaphor points not only to a cheap entertainment organized around a somewhat illicit spectacle and display but also to a change in the conception of the representation (1933, 283). Silent film is, Arnheim said, framed; its representation is contained not so much to serve as a window on the world as to give a particular view. If this view remains partial, it is nevertheless a composed, primarily graphic space that stages a "competition between division of the picture and movement within an area" (1997, 30). The sound film, by contrast, turns the frame edge into "the demarcation of a hole," and the resulting space is less graphical than theatrical (1997, 30; see also 1933, 236–37), as sound constantly makes the audience aware of what lay beyond the frame line. This has the effect of making offscreen space in sound film far more compelling than in silent film because it appears immediately, without needing to be indicated positively by the image. But it also has the effect of increasing the impression of realism, so that the audience is placed within a "panopticon ideal," believing that they are seeing and hearing a recording of an actual event rather than a representation (1933, 283). With the sound film, the frame edge becomes a mask of a wider world, and it organizes the screen around the peephole's dynamic of concealment and revelation, which also opens a circuit of desire. When the audience hears a sound whose source is not shown, they wonder where it comes from and strain to move the opening of the "hole" to reveal the source.

The increased impression of realism, Arnheim suggests, means that synchronized sound imposes stronger obligations on the representation than does the image of silent film, and this places especially severe limits on editing. "The unity of sound demands I also keep the picture unchanged" (1997, 31). This concept of the unity of sound commits Arnheim to a fairly rigid ontology of recording—"synchronism . . . serves to unite picture and sound as they appear in reality" (1933, 260)—that sits uneasily with his notion of art as a human construction. It also confuses—or rather insists upon an identity of—the theatrical space of the recording (the set) with the diegetic space that it represents in the film. With the increased fidelity of the representation, Arnheim says, "the artistic part of the work will be more and more focused upon what is set up and enacted *before* the camera" (1933, 285, emphasis in original). The unity of sound makes sound film an excellent medium for recording theater, but the identity that this unity imposes on the representation and the way it constrains editing make it less suitable—or at any rate somewhat questionable—as a medium in its own right (1997, 32).[5]

---

[5] Arnheim actually considered silent film, sound film, radio, and presumably recorded sound and later television to be modes of the same artistic medium, all of which he classified as species of film (1933, 276–77). Film in this sense was the art that derived its laws from the "naturalistic [mechanical]

The unity of sound designates two distinct planes. First, it refers to the temporal unity of recorded sound and entails the recognition that sound in itself cannot be cut with the same freedom as the image. A moving image, even an action, can be cut up and reassembled into a new sequence in a way that is not the case for sounds, which, when edited, he claims, "always seem to be ripped in two" (1997, 35). Second, the unity of sound refers to the synchronized unity of sound with its depicted source—mimetic synchronization—that ensures the grounding of sound in the depicted space. The primary difficulty this unity poses to the art of sound film is that it seems to yoke editing to mimetic synchronization in ways that make sound film shots difficult to work with as material. Much as the "Statement of Sound" noted the "inertia" of synchronized sound, the unity of sound means that editing is fundamentally the task of joining segments of sound film where each film segment is hardened by this relation to sound into something quite different from, and much less supple than, silent film because it requires both elements.

> Sound montage always operates as an interference with the acoustical continuum—the actual continuity is interrupted and pieces that do not belong together are joined together. Thus sound montage is only possible when the scene of action changes, because this anyhow represents an interference with natural continuity . . . ; but not within a scene with a constant auditory locale, because the abrupt change in the intensity of the sound destroys a sound situation that had been planned homogeneously. (1933, 246)

Cutting within a scene, Arnheim thinks, can therefore occur only under the special conditions that obviate the need to edit the sound. "Thus either the camera must only be moved short distances, for which sound *montage* seems unnecessary; or else the change must be effected at a moment when there is complete silence" (246). Generally, the latter means planning the acoustical space of the scene such that there is no background ambience and then making the actual picture edits on the silence between lines of dialogue. This in turn requires, among other things, sufficient space between lines that actual silence prevails. To permit cutting, then, Arnheim recommends short speeches and the avoidance of complete songs, since they do not introduce the silences required for effective editing.

Arnheim notes that most sound features and shorts from the time utilize more cutting during synchronized talking and singing sequences than this,

---

reproduction of all the diverse manifestations of optics and acoustics" (277). In each of its modalities, film was essentially mimetic—it had to accept the "presentments of reality" that the recording device automatically and mechanically captured and then the artist reworked by "selection and grouping."

but he declares such editing generally ineffectual and inartistic. For instance, unlike Balázs or Pudovkin, he doubts the efficacy of the reaction shot:

> As long as we saw the singer, the song warbled meaningfully from his lips. However, as soon as the picture changed in the middle of the verse and showed, for instance, the listeners on the balcony, the song remained helplessly suspended in the acoustical space—a good example of the impossibility of transferring the technique of montage from silent film to acoustical film. (1997, 35)

The suspension of sound in acoustical space implies that sound generally requires a visual anchor, a depicted source; otherwise, sound floats disconcertedly in an unlocatable (dimensionless or infinite) space, what he terms "the dark void," akin to Balázs's "voice from nowhere." Arnheim specifically faults *The Singing Fool* (1928) on its use of the reaction shot: the filmmakers, he writes,

> have not yet realized . . . that during an acoustical [i.e., synchronized sound] sequence no change of perspective may occur: Al Jolson sings his love song in front of our eyes, and our ears hear it, too, but in the middle of the verse the picture jumps to the girl to whom the song is dedicated, and the melody is ripped from his mouth and left floating in the dark void. (Arnheim 1997, 36–37)[6]

Arnheim is also critical of the process of multiple camera shooting, common in the early years of sound film, which uses the continuity of the soundtrack as a kind of master shot for subsequent picture editing (1933, 263). He thinks the general microphone placement of the arrangement limits the variety of camera angles to those of negligible (and so mostly less useful) difference. Synchronization and the continuity of the sound do not, he thinks, in themselves suffice to hold the assemblage together when a sequence exhibits mismatch between shot scale and sound scale, leading to "a psychologically most irritating severance between pictorial and sound impressions" (244). Joining shots of different scale can also disorient, even if the unity of sound is respected individually for each shot.

---

[6] We might find Arnheim's concern for the anchoring of sound overdrawn—his examples do not always seem especially well chosen, and this is symptomatic of a larger issue with the concept of unity of sound—but early sound films could produce unsettling effects where sound did not seem to sit in the image due to the absence of clear synchronization cues, and it is likely that such situations were more noticeable during the transition period, when the whole process was novel, than today, when many of the devices have been habituated into convention. These effects were (and remain) most noticeable with postsynchronized dialogue, as in Hitchcock's *Blackmail* (1929), but they also appeared to a certain degree with unsynchronized sound effects and with typical analytical editing if the cutting moved about the space too drastically. These effects would persist until filmmakers developed a workable auditory hierarchy.

> In sound film a most curious phenomenon occurs—some entire picture is shown, say a group of people talking, at a distance of about twelve feet; then follows a close-up. The people are now seen much larger; but suddenly their voices also sound much louder; and thereby the impression is given that the camera and the audience have moved abruptly forward, have rushed right up to the group. The cut now arouses the illusion that the camera is moving through space. That is a superfluous and disturbing effect. (244–45)

Such mobility was usually considered a virtue in the silent film, where it could be assigned to the camera. What Arnheim finds disturbing about its appearance in the sound film is not so much the mobility per se but rather how synchronized sound seemingly subjectifies its impression. The mobility of the sound film, due to the impression of reality that the synchronized film brings to it, seems to conjure up the presence of some unseen character. Cutting through space in sound film, Arnheim says, "turns the camera, an invisible receptive organ, into a conscious subject playing a separate part in the picture" (245). The issue is not the subjectification of the viewpoint per se, which Arnheim recognizes as an ordinary element of film, but rather the inability to assign this subjectified position to a character within the depicted space of the film; the result is a view that is particularized rather than general but nevertheless unanchored.

Perhaps because Arnheim understands the unity of sound as not just a basic obligation of sound film but as one of its central aesthetic problems, he is open to probing its limits. He argues, for instance, that sound offers film far better potential for playing artistically with the ambiguities of offscreen space than does the silent film, where the offscreen always needs to be mediated by the onscreen (via, say, a look) (1933, 240–43). Offscreen sound, he notes, is especially effective in marking the limit of the frame, reminding the audience of that part of the scene that is not visible (and that this absence is fundamental to the sound film's analysis and depiction of space) (242). This constitutes the positive, potentially creative side of the conception of the screen as a hole. He also entertains the possibility that image and sound could be treated in a form of montage to forge novel combinations that produce magical and fantastical effects:

> Animals may be made to speak with human voices, men with animal voices, a child like an old man. When someone sits down, the upholstery may sigh in human tones; if tea is poured out of a pot it may sound like the rushing of a waterfall; if a big gun is fired, a little squeak may be heard. A crane may begin to talk with clanking jaws, and a box on the ears may howl like a siren. But the records must be so made that a feasible time-space unity results. Otherwise, the intended effect, which consists in presenting a grotesque combination as a natural unity, will be destroyed. (264)

The magical effect derives from the fact that the sounds seem to inhere in the image as a "new, natural seeming unit." Not so much an instance of image-sound montage—though Arnheim calls it that—this instance of stylized sound is akin to the use of sound in animation. Yet the formulation also recognizes, inadvertently or not, that the unity of sound does not so much belong to the material per se as a natural product, as it is itself a construction or audiovisual figure, one whose marks of stylization have been technologically effaced so as to appear natural. The potential of that formulation, left untapped by Arnheim though consistent with his broader aesthetic principles, would in fact serve to organize the practice of sound film as it was codified in the 1930s.

Arnheim concedes that the premise of asynchronism makes sense as an aesthetic principle. "Sound is always superfluous, in fact detracts from the effect," he says, "unless it conveys something that is not already conveyed by the picture. The same is of course true *vice versa* of the pictures" (1933, 251–52). Indeed, "the principle of sound film demands that picture and sound shall not do the same work simultaneously but that they shall share the work—the sound to convey one thing and the picture another, and the two jointly to give a complete impression" (251). The doctrine of counterpoint, he acknowledges, works from a convincing premise, that sound cannot serve as a mere "enhancement" of the silent picture. Sound film is not silent film with sound added. Nevertheless, he sees the inferences that advocates of asynchronous sound draw from this premise as faulty. "It is correct that we do not need to hear what we already see. But there are possibilities in having sound and picture supplement each other contrapuntally, without our having to explode the visual-acoustic unity with real dynamite" (1997, 40). By contrast, mimetic synchronization constitutes sound film's basic "presentment of reality" and the way that dialogue in particular is transmuted from a medium in its own right back into a material for sound film. "In theory, the method of asynchronism sounds more refined, more exclusive, more aesthetic. In reality, it is inadequate, since it gets bogged down in its concept, rather than searching for the embodiment of the thought in uncut, unadulterated reality itself" (41).

Sound film, Arnheim suggests, is fundamentally wed to reality in a way that silent film is not. The issue here is the confusion between art and reality. Silent film does not confront the issue in this respect, because, although mimetic in image, its muteness marks it as profoundly other than the world. But sound film differs because its representation is infinitely closer to reality, virtually a reproduction. Therefore, sound film gives the illusion of being a "closed piece of reality," and that piece of reality cannot be divided without doing violence to it. Moreover, if it is reassembled with other sounds, the status of synchronism becomes doubtful.

If I see images of the criminal investigation department at work in Fritz Lang's *M*, and if I hear the voice of the chief of police as a sort of lecture accompanying it, I will not be under the impression that the actual voice is floating invisibly above the scene of the crime. I will easily be able to keep separate things which do not belong together. In René Clair's example [of the pursuit of the coat at the opera house in *Le Million*], though, the things that do not go together are fit together so cleverly that the viewer cannot help combining them psychologically. The result? Not a metaphor, but a fake. (1997, 41)

Adherence to the principle of asynchronism leads to faulty thinking about the relationship of sound and image, to awkward and improper juxtapositions of sound and image, and to filmmakers concerning themselves too much with devising ingenuous if unworkable situations for asynchronous sound rather than with the basic selecting and grouping sequences of sound film.

For Arnheim, one of the most vexing problems of asynchronous sound is its inherent ambiguity, which makes it difficult to use in many of the extended ways that the counterpoint theorists advocate. He thinks the metaphorical use of sound not anchored in the image or even selective sound modeled on subjective perception or thought is a dicey proposition because such sounds are liable to be confused with offscreen sound:

The danger always exists that the viewer will misunderstand such a montage of image and sound and expect the sound to come from the scene; when the drunkard at the bar hears the warning voice of his far-off wife, the viewer will quite likely look around for the woman in the picture, assuming that since he can hear her, she must be nearby. (1997, 51)

The difficulty is that asynchronous sound in itself simply specifies a formal relation between image and soundtrack, that both offscreen sound and the metaphorical and subjective rendering of sound share the asynchronous formal relation, and that audiences have a very strong predilection to presume in the first place that asynchronous sound is diegetic sound whose source is not shown. Essentially, Arnheim believes that asynchronous sound is almost always taken to be indexical, with a strong expectation for later synchronization that serves to incorporate what has previously been offscreen space. Asynchronous sound, he thinks, is also inherently unnatural, as it substitutes one sound for another, running contrary to the strongly indexical property of the sound film. Sound always becomes an attribute of the image to which it is joined.

Music and voiceover offer exceptions because they are handled in such a way that it is clear that they reside in "separate realms of reality" and appear "to be joined together only via the montage" (1997, 51). With respect to voiceover, Arnheim offers the following example, which allows the image to drift away from depicting the body of the voice:

We can have the speech of a narrator continue in a feature film when he is no longer visible because the scene has changed. We hear and see, for instance, the mother praising the virtuous changes in her daughter's life, but while the motherly voice continues to speak, we see the daughter dancing in a nightclub with licentious men. (51)

If Arnheim shows intimations of recognizing what others from the period call "commentative" sound (see chapter 3) and what will come to be called "nondiegetic" sound by narratological film theory (see chapter 6), he remains cautious about it. Such asynchronism, he says, must be treated with extreme care: "with every application of asynchronism, the two spheres must be clearly divided, so that those which have only been connected by the artist are not construed as being part of the same real scene" (51).

Even though Arnheim points to background music as the best example of consistently viable asynchronous sound, the potential for confusion extends to it as well. In the silent film, the role of accompaniment and its location in theater ensure a clear separation. "The very essence of an accompaniment is that it shall not be a part of the play but that it shall supervene from a completely separate sphere. In silent film this separation was definitely assured, because there were no sounds except the music." The sound film is different because in it "the sounds are part of the scene of action on screen, and the danger is that the audience will project the accompaniment into it" (1933, 271). In contrast to the silent film, music in the sound film is not so much an accompaniment as a form of asynchronous sound, and the ambiguity of the latter therefore extends to the status of the music. Because music in sound film cannot easily mark itself as accompaniment, the audience is predisposed to connect even the music "to the scene of action, and, should [a spectator] even hear the voice of a young girl sitting alone in the forest accompanied by a large orchestra, he quite rightly wonders how such luxury comes to exist in the wilderness" (1997, 51).

Arnheim's "quite rightly" is worth pondering. Its discursive work in the passage is to naturalize an assumption about sound film, namely, that it represents a recording of the world, and that the film is therefore a reproduction of the real world, or at any rate that it represents a world that follows the same principles as our own. A spectator "quite rightly wonders" only because the spectator "knows" our world does not enjoy such luxury and believes the screened world must be similar. If the girl in the forest shows no signs of "hearing" this music, how does the music relate to the rest of the film, where is it located, and to whom is it addressed? These are basic issues of nondiegetic or extradiegetic space, and the nondiegetic would require conceptual work, some practical exemplars, and theoretical intervention before filmmakers were convinced that the audience would not in fact "wonder" in just the way Arnheim describes.

A basic issue of music as background during this period was that music needed to be marked as belonging to a separate realm from the action, so the status of its mood as a kind of commentary would be apparent. The music, Arnheim says, could not be indifferent to the action, but it also had to be sufficiently distinct that it avoided projecting

> individual elements of synchronism—as when we hear, for instance, the marching music necessary when a troop of soldiers and a military band march through the picture. The accompaniment here assumes the character of a sound that reverberates from within the scene, and it tended to do this during the silent film era as well. (1997, 50)

Arnheim is not claiming that music should not sound with marching troops, only that with the image of marching troops the status of the music would, unless handled very carefully, become ambiguous as to whether it belonged to the (diegetic) action or belonged to another (nondiegetic) realm as a music commenting on the situation or evoking a mood. Music, he thinks, can serve as mood music only to the extent that it does not allow itself to be confused with potential diegetic music from the scene. Otherwise, it is liable to appear like a "reverberation" of the action but without certainty as to its status.

Perhaps one reason Arnheim finds background music problematic is because it mimics the emotional action too closely, and so reverberates in a somewhat similarly ambiguous way. In any event, he thinks background music inflects sound film toward melodrama, that is, toward a form of recorded theater, especially when the music manages to articulate itself as accompaniment. "The musical accompaniment, be it necessary for technical reasons or not, turns sound film into a melodrama, thereby tarnishing its artistic purity unbearably. If sound film is to have any purpose at all, it will have to provide for its acoustics solely by means of the reproduction of sounds" (1997, 37). The problem of synchronizing music too closely with drama is that it breaks down musical form for the needs of drama, and the mimicking of the action creates a kind of "naturalistic illusion."

Arnheim finds a general mimetic relation that allows a certain interior rhythm of the image to be drawn out by the music according to its own logic to be a more satisfactory use of music.

> Frequently, though, [music] avoids such naturalistic illusion and touches simply on the rhythm of the on-screen action with sounds that are obviously of extraneous origin. This happens when, for instance, the accompaniment assimilates the beat of oars visible on-screen into the melody, or underlines the rhythm of the montage cut with a precisely synchronous musical rhythm. On the other hand, we find such accompaniment of the image with synchronous music, sounds, or sound effects consciously dispensing with illusion in the American animated films. In general,

though, as we said, musical accompaniment makes do entirely without such synchronism, whether of a naturalistic or stylized character; it speaks its own musical language, which fits the picture not through a similarity of external forms, but through the relationship of expression to the picture. (1997, 50)

Sound film is not a species of silent film, a silent film with sound added, and Arnheim draws a provocative and illuminating parallel to arranging a musical piece to explain how sound film in fact should relate to silent film. In adapting a piano piece for piano and violin, he argues, an arranger could simply have the violin supplement the piano. But this procedure would only color the original. The violin part would remain supplemental, since it lacked necessity. The resulting arrangement might be charming, but it would not actually be artistic in Arnheim's terms, because the violin remains superfluous to the conception. To be artistic, the arrangement would have to intervene in the original to such an extent as to make the piano alone insufficient and the violin a necessary part. A sound film similarly cannot just be a silent film with a soundtrack added. Just as the piano part must change to allow the violin to become a necessary part of the arrangement, so too the image of the silent film needs to be recast so that it can allow the soundtrack to become a necessary part of the sound film. This is an appealing, surprisingly far-reaching comparison that does much to clarify Arnheim's thinking about the relation of sound and image, even if its conclusion runs somewhat counter to his aim.

First, in keeping with his analysis of the principle of asynchronism noted previously, Arnheim suggests that in the piano and violin arrangement "piano and violin are not doing the same thing simultaneously—they would only distract one another or each make the other superfluous" (1933, 278). They would indeed if the whole arrangement followed such a procedure, but moments of doubling are in fact quite common in music of this kind, and a compositional practice that eschewed them entirely would resemble the distortions of austere asynchronism that he notes in film. "Sound film demands counterpoint; but this does not necessarily mean that the pictorial motif and the sound motif should always contrast with one another" (256). The point, however, should not have been to proscribe such simultaneity—in framing it thus and accepting the seemingly arbitrary prohibition, for instance, on the synchronized shot of a ticking clock, Arnheim inadvertently hews too closely to the canon of asynchronism—but to insist that the points of simultaneity (but also of difference) must follow from the aesthetic idea being expressed. This formulation also adheres better to his general aesthetic principles than does his acceptance of a weak form of asynchronism, which skirts rather than addresses the central aesthetic difficulty. As he states elsewhere (and directly in keeping with this reading of the metaphor), "Frequently, . . . sound and picture will play the same melody. . . . [S]ound and picture, each in its own way, unite different impressions to give a homogeneous effect" (257–58).[7]

Second, his inadvertently extended metaphor reveals a truth that he otherwise suppresses: the centrality of the soundtrack to the conception of sound film. Sound might be essential to the sound film, but Arnheim remains committed to the priority of the image: "even sound film has not changed the fact that the visuals of a film still determine its invention and design" (1997, 45). The primary role of the piano in a piece for violin and piano, however, is invariably one of (necessary) accompaniment, and in reworking the piano piece the arranger would recast the piano part accordingly. Extended to the sound film, the metaphor suggests that the image must not just leave room for, but must actually adapt itself in support of, the soundtrack.

Given his profound skepticism and even hostility toward what he calls the "faultless film," it is worth returning to the question of why Arnheim nevertheless commits himself so thoroughly to a rather extreme realist position of his own on sound film. If Arnheim initially grants sound film its technical perfection to better understand the aesthetic challenges it might pose, his continued insistence on sound film's foundational realism seems less generous and more confused. It is less generous because realism and the mimetic synchronization with which it is allied are contrary terms to the creative acts of construction that he sees as essential to art. Silent film becomes for Arnheim the superior form of film art because its peculiar limitations allow it to sit at the center of a clear and distinct artistic domain where the medium is homogeneous and the material can be readily formed into novel and meaningful figurations through framing and editing. Sound film, by contrast, presents a more complex and heterogeneous material, and it lacks a clear and distinct domain, on the one hand seeming derivative for much of its technique on the silent film, and on the other hand, its most characteristic form, the talking film, being situated very close to theater.

His continued insistence on sound film's foundational realism is also more confused because Arnheim never articulates why he feels he must commit to mimetic synchronization for sound film even as he objects to the "faultless film" at which the fidelity of recording aims. In Arnheim's account, sound film often seems condemned, not by its own lack of possibility, but by his theoretical straightjacket that requires it to be first of all a reproduction and then to be rejected either because it strays from the mimetic ideal or because it hews too closely to it as a reproduction.

---

[7] In a later passage, Arnheim elaborates thus: "A sound-film scene is only comprehensible if picture and sound are apprehended simultaneously. Nor do the two detract from each other; for they are not doing the same thing at the same time in different ways, but supplementing one another to form a whole" (1933, 243).

The clarification of this confusion lies in Arnheim's understanding of art and material. In particular, an art form in his view requires a homogeneous material, a single medium. The complex nature of the material of sound film means that it always threatens to dissolve into a heterogeneous compound of image and sound, two mediums each supplementing the other without binding necessity, and so to present itself as a hybrid art form, which in Arnheim's view would make sound film a lesser art, indeed really no art form at all. His concept of the unity of sound, then, is designed to ensure that sound film adheres to the aesthetic principle of a medium: "sound film—at any rate real sound film—is not a verbal masterpiece supplemented by pictures, but a homogenous creation of word and picture which cannot be split up into parts that have any meaning separately" (1932, 213). Yet the critique of synchronism implies that synchronized sound is mostly redundant, superfluous, and so not effectively a homogeneous medium, and this critique gains purchase because the technological separation of the recording technologies for image and sound implies an operative analytical separation in concept. Arnheim evidently had difficulty formulating an understanding of a singular medium of sound film sufficiently robust that it could encompass a relation between image and sound that was neither one of complete identity nor one of simple arbitrary hybridity. In any event, this confusing impasse ultimately leads Arnheim to reject sound film, but for quite unpersuasive reasons.

Harry Potamkin and the Compound Cinema

Harry A. Potamkin was an American Marxist critic, and he started writing about film just as Vitaphone and Movietone were beginning to establish the sound film as a viable commercial medium. Inspired by I. A. Richards and other critics whose work would be codified by the New Criticism (L. Jacobs 1977, xxxi),[8] Potamkin's writing has a strong formalist bent, and he is concerned especially with locating principles of cinematic unity. Initially, he shows a critical preference for the silent film because he finds in it a "purity" of artistic approach that makes its principles of unity readily apparent (Potamkin 1929a, 282).[9] At the same time, already in his earliest essays, he recognizes the potential for compound forms in addition to the pure simple form, an

---

[8] Lewis Jacobs actually says Potamkin was inspired by the New Critics, but that movement did not emerge until after Potamkin's death.

[9] Though not published until 1929, this essay was written in 1927, when sound film was only beginning to gain a foothold. Potamkin's thinking evolved significantly in the interval between the article's conception and its publication, and one of the most striking changes is the displacement of the "simple" silent film by the compound cinema as the dominant form.

important concession that will allow him to rework his theory of film to accommodate the emergence of sound film.

Potamkin's confrontation with the Soviet directors' "Statement on Sound" and other writings persuaded him that the pursuit of purity was in fact "an evasion" (1977, 49). He recognized that the appeal of "purism" lies in its consistency and the ease with which it can articulate and realize principles of unity. But he came to understand that "purism" posited a unity that is too easy and so something of a mirage. It attains its consistency "by exclusion and not by inclusion; by the intensity of the irreducible and not by the intensity of a complete experience" (49). He concludes that "the objection to sound [film] cannot be absolute" (1929b, 34). "To force the movie constantly into its simplest form [i.e., silent film] is to keep it forever simplistic, a lisping, spluttering idiot" (1977, 48). The simple form of cinema, silent film, remained viable after the advent of sound film, but it is a first, not a definitive, form.

Potamkin argues the cinema could only realize its full potential by becoming "compound." How does the sound film, as a compound form, achieve a unified presentation as art? That is, how does the sound film integrate sound so that it appears not as an effect but as a basic element of form? He thinks the early years of the sound film are hard to untangle because the industry obstructed the continued development of the silent film while inhibiting the emergence of any new form of cinema not bound to a mimetic mode of reproducing dramatic dialogue. This state of affairs made it difficult to know what belonged to the nature of sound film on the one hand and to the nature of commercial filmmaking on the other. He concedes that commercial talking film almost always substituted "muttering for uttering" (1930a, 11). But the confusion of that current moment when the technology and the business were in an uncertain state could offer no final indictment of cinematic speech, since the fact that silent film had continually sought ways to represent speech, even though it resulted in a profound contradiction between "the realistic lip-mimicry in a film of concentrated time and emotion" (1929e, 35), made recorded dialogue virtually inevitable. Moreover, the basic technique of montage was actually compound in implication: it involved bringing unlike elements together, even though it might be restricted to the simple medium (1977, 44).

Although arguing for the compound cinema, Potamkin agrees with the critique that sound film would "need to be *preconceived* on the basis of one sense" for it to appear unified (1929h, 175). He reconciles compounding with unity by asserting that this singular sense is itself compound rather than simple. Even the silent film, he notes, was not as singular as its advocates assume; silent film is not "a visual medium" but rather a "visual-motor" one (175). Sound film retains these visual-motor coordinates and compounds them with new ones that produce a higher, more complex unity:

Time and space are its structural elements. Upon these are imprinted the emphases of pitch (light sound), distribution (color-values, sonar tones), etc. Time and space, visual motor fundaments, determine, however, the placement of these emphases. They comprise within themselves: scale, duration, alternation, counterpoint, simultaneity, climax. . . . The film contains also elements that are visual and that are visual-tactile (textural), as well as—in the sound film—those that are sonar; but these elements must be submissive to the visual-motor. (175)

The point, then, is ultimately subordination of sound to image, but in a way that sound also appears necessary, as "irrevocable in the structure," rather than as something added, supplementary, and ultimately superfluous (1930a, 16).

Compound sound cinema is therefore inherently hierarchical, requiring submission and subordination in a way that the simple silent cinema did not. The sound film, Potamkin thought, should be "a sound-sight compound working in an interrelated sound-sight pattern" (1929a, 295), which allows a play determined by the planned structure of the particular film. Potamkin recognized such a formation in Lewis Milestone's treatment of dialogue in *The Front Page* (1931), where the director

correctly gauged the quantity of speech and its velocity (the relation of speech to visual-motor density) and thereby, for the first time, presented the principle that though the plane of correlation in the cinema is visual-motor, the vocal element in the compound may, if the subject-matter requires, set the pace for the unit. (1933, 30)

Yet this positive critical observation is very much the exception in Potamkin's writing about sound film. Despite his openness to sound on a theoretical level, Potamkin remains, like so many writers of the time, fundamentally suspicious of it, especially when it is deployed mimetically or when it evokes the theater.

Potamkin is suspicious of sound film because it has difficulty achieving sufficient "fluidity" between its parts—especially between the recorded image and the recorded sound. Compounding, for Potamkin, is a means by which art intensifies, concentrates, and condenses the multiple components into the unity of the conception, the plan. In the case of cinema, montage, the execution of the assemblage according to the plan, is the method by which "the cinema establishes the compound out of the hybrid" (1977, 44). An ineffective or premature compounding occurred, on the contrary, wherever "a unity is not creatable of the diversities" contained in the compound (1930e, 470). Essentially, this is the case when the material proves difficult to work and so is resistant to stylization, that is, to technical (or technological) reworking. Stylization of elements (the "structural conversion of the ordinary," 1930d, 291n) and planning (the "first necessity of adequate aesthetic form," 1930a, 18) are key to making effective compounds.

Generally, methods of stylization serve merely to render the material flexible enough that it can be shaped. The basic principle is dialectical and organic: "The whole disciplines the detail, the detail disciplines the whole" (1929e, 28). The detail cannot stand out as an isolated effect, as a moment of unintegrated spectacle, which close-ups often did even in silent film. Shots are not autonomous units, are not really units at all except insofar as they articulate a rhythmic structure. Neither psychology nor drama is sufficient to ensure the integrity of the detail within the whole. Only the artistic form is capable of this task, and Potamkin's usual term for artistic form is rhythmic structure (28).

Unlike many theorists of the time, Potamkin recognizes that sound recording is as much a representation as the image. Whereas Gilbert Seldes wants to insist on the stable placement of the microphone as opposed to the roving mobility of the camera and to draw certain conclusions about the nature of sound film from that essential difference, Potamkin forthrightly points out that the recording of sound and image do not constitute a necessary difference. "The camera need not be mobile (that is only a *kind* of camera use)" (1930b, 107), and "the microphone need not be immobile" (1929j, 497). Insofar as the microphone remained fixed as a practical matter during the early transition period, that was only a temporary limitation, which, Potamkin argues (correctly), technology and experience would soon overcome. "As we learn more and more about the nature of speech in the talkie, we will find the microphone can be freed" (1930b, 107). He also notes that the audiovisual figure forged by mimetic synchronization is a produced effect, in fact, a constructed relationship, and to get the effect it is "not necessary to record both sound and image simultaneously" (107). He observes that sound effects were already being added in postproduction and quite often bore little relation to the sounds they represented, since the actual sound was difficult to record or did not record well (1930f, 115). Potamkin welcomes these sorts of substitutions because they suggest that sound, far from being mimetic, is already well on its way to being stylized. "Cataloguing and indexing of sounds [into production libraries] is a step toward conventionalization" (114).

Potamkin wants dialogue treated analogously. "Speech," he argues, "demands analysis (conventionalization) as much as non-verbal sound" (1930b, 110). There is nothing inherent in speech that prevents it from being "stylized, harmonized and unified into an entity with the visual image" (1930e, 465). Filmmakers working on the talkies, however, had generally opted to perfect the literal level of recording as mimetic synchronization, to produce the effect of speech as a vehicle for meaning, rather than to construct stylized utterances that could intensify the structure and convert that speech into form. In particular, filmmakers concentrated on faithfully capturing and reproducing a promicrophonic speech that accompanies the moving lips of the profilmic actor. Although mechanically linked together, image and sound remain conceptually apart, as the mechanical process of mimetic synchronization rather than planning and intention locks them together (1929b, 35). Dialogue rendered this way butts up against the requirements of form. As Potamkin writes about character acting, "it is mimetic in its intention rather than structural" (1930b, 294).

Many writers on the early sound film argue that early talkies generally seem too much like theater. Potamkin suggests that the drive toward the literalness of mimetic recording confuses the issue. He thinks that recording needs to be stylized to be reworked into the film, but he also recognizes that theatrical speech is stylized at a different level from the recording. Moreover, a stylization appropriate to the stage, with its direct presentation of dialogue in performance, is not necessarily or even likely appropriate to the sound film, with its indirect representation through recording (1930e, 465). Potamkin instead advocates speech as "utterance," as "abstracted sound" (1930b, 110), stylized and converted to film form. Utterance is not a mimetic duplication of reality but an analytic reconstruction that must pass through a level of abstraction and conventionalization. "Speech as utterance is stylized speech. Its basis lies in a variety of sources: explosive speech, uniform pitch, monotone, etc." (1930e, 467). Just as the filmed image is "more concentrated, more condensed, always starker" and so also resulted in "closer intimacy" than the stage, "the speaking film enhances this condensation and this intimacy. For the bolder, the more concentrated the image, the more exact is the synchronization" (1930e, 467). Dialogue becomes plastic and workable when speech appears as utterance.

3

Theories of the Classical Sound Film

GRAMMARS AND TYPOLOGIES

Introduction

As we saw in chapter 2, the concerns of the transitional era focused on the specificity of the sound film, on what distinguished the talking film from the closely related forms of recorded theater and silent film, and on what constituted the actual authentic forms of sound cinema. For writers such as Sergei Eisenstein, Vsevolod Pudovkin, and even Rudolf Arnheim and Béla Balázs, counterpoint and asynchronous sound were often taken as synonymous, and these concepts proved influential because they pointed to possibilities of the sound film that were unique to it—or if not unique that were difficult to achieve in other media. In alternation with synchronized sound, asynchronous sound would indeed become fundamental to the sound film. Alfred Hitchcock (1937) noted its use in the reaction shot, a basic element of sound film technique: "This overrunning of one person's image with another person's voice is a method peculiar to the talkies; it is one of the devices which help the talkies to tell a story faster than a silent film could tell it, and faster than it could be told on stage" (9).

As the practices of sound film codified in the early 1930s, theorists came to recognize an essential distinction between counterpoint and asynchronous sound, with counterpoint designating sounds that ran counter to the narrative or thematic point of the scene (whether through irony, duplicity, or whatnot) and asynchronous sound indicating sounds that did not have their source visible in the image. Synchronized sound could run against the emotional tenor of a scene, as when a popular number played by a band in a nightclub accompanied some kind of heartbreak, and asynchronous sound could be in agreement with the emotional tenor, as in a reaction shot or background music. In chapter 2, we saw that theorists were already extremely attentive to how sound, especially asynchronous sound, could be used to construct space, both as a realistic extension of the visible space and as an unrealistic creation of a space for commentary on the principal narrative.

These concerns shifted the focus from defining and exploring the specificity of sound film and toward constructing typologies that mapped the potential of formal relations between image and sound. The specificity doctrine continued to be honored, however, in the relative autonomy ceded to the two domains of image and sound, especially in a worry that the soundtrack not simply be redundant with the image. The grudging acceptance of the talking film also did little to displace the theoretical prejudice, inherited from the silent film, that film was (primarily) a visual medium. Thus, from the standpoint of theory, a properly cinematic soundtrack needed to be both deferential to the images and nonredundant with them. These were conditions that dialogue had difficulty satisfying, since it was often both central to the conception and wholly redundant, whenever the dialogue was synchronized. Music, on the other hand, could satisfy these conditions fairly readily, so music often held a privileged place when theorists wrote about sound. Vice versa, because the conception of film as (primarily) a visual medium elevated the status of music and because music competed with dialogue and effects for room on the soundtrack, composers who wrote about film such as Aaron Copland and Hanns Eisler were often all too willing to accede to the visual dominance of film. Music was also an intriguing theoretical object because its background status was nebulous and often difficult to reconcile with the terms of realistic representation that theorists argued were fundamental to the sound film. Film music as background score had a unique ontological status that had affinities with other forms of dramatic music (theater music, opera) but could not be reduced to them.

This situation led to theoretical peculiarities that extended into the 1970s. From the 1930s to the 1970s, dialogue and sound recording received little critical attention from film theorists, and what attention they received was largely negative. Film narrative was conflated with the image, even though a good portion of it was carried by the dialogue. Sound recording was also taken to be ontologically distinct from image recording in problematic ways. Such authors as Balázs (2010b, 192), Stanley Cavell (1979, 19–20), Christian Metz (1980, 29n7), Gerald Mast (1983, 216), and Jean-Louis Baudry (1986, 304–5), who otherwise occupied fairly distinct theoretical positions, nevertheless all held that, whereas a camera recorded a representation (an image of something not present), a microphone recorded the thing itself and presented it directly to us (the recording of an oboe presents to us the sound of an oboe itself rather than its sound-image).[1] Siegfried Kracauer's rejection in 1960 of the still photograph as the basis for the ontology of the motion picture was therefore a

---

[1] For a summary of scholarship on this issue through the 1970s, see Williams (1980).

useful corrective to this line of theorizing: "We believe [moving pictures] to be not so much photographs as reproductions of life in its fullness" (1997, 114). Although problematic in its own ways, Kracauer's understanding had a distinct advantage in not positing an ontological divide between our reception and understanding of the recorded moving image and the recorded sound. The movement of the motion picture does in fact feel present (if not replete) even as we are aware that it is a recording of a past action, and sound film, perhaps due to the commonly held ontology of recorded sound as faithful representation, enhances this effect of immediacy.

Sound, Balázs among others recognized, is crucial to the representational effect of realism, as scenes lacking appropriate sounds appear by contrast highly stylized. "We accept scene space as real only when it contains sounds as well, for these give it the dimension of depth" (1970, 207). But these sounds, Balázs noted, need to be true only to the fictional world depicted, not to what the profilmic, photographed world—which was most likely a flimsy set—actually sounded like. That is, Balázs was advocating the concept of what today would be termed diegetic sound. The contemporaneous terms were "actual," "logical," or "realistic." The classical system depends on the soundtrack helping to construct the fictional world, and on sound, especially music, that stands outside that world to comment on it or to add to it what the realistic depiction itself cannot easily represent: mood, feeling, psychology, and so forth.

Second-generation theories of the soundtrack were produced after sound film was codified into the classical system and reflect that fact. If the question of sound film had largely been answered with the commercial success of the talking film, other questions lingered and new ones arose: What is properly cinematic sound? How will sound and music relate to the screen action? Do films need music? What functions does music perform? What precisely is film music and how, if at all, does it differ from other music?

In this chapter, I examine several theoretical accounts that touch on these questions. I examine in particular typologies invented to account for the relation of image and sound in sound film. I start by returning to Sergei Eisenstein and look at the concept of vertical montage that he developed in the late 1930s during his work on *Alexander Nevsky* (1938). Eisenstein's typology consists of explicating what he calls "modes of synchronicity," which are themselves based on a typology of montage that Eisenstein had developed earlier. Unlike the other typologies in this chapter, these modes are conceptually graded, in the sense that they are ordered from the most elementary to the most sophisticated.

I next consider two accounts that specifically address music. Aaron Copland offers a typology of functions of film music. Although not aiming to be comprehensive, Copland's typology does capture most of the major functions, and it is largely commensurate with the specifically musical functions contained in Claudia Gorbman's (1987) canonical seven rules. Besides the typology, Copland also expresses several reservations about the conventions of music in the classical system. I then turn to *Composing for the Films* (1947), where Hanns Eisler and Theodor W. Adorno offer a response to Eisenstein while presenting their own critical account of film music in the classical system. Similar to Copland's reservations, they compile a typology of "bad habits" of film music.

Finally, I examine three formal typologies of sound and image relations, all of which seek to map the overall conceptual space of image–sound relationships. Raymond Spottiswoode (1935) developed his typology just as the classical system was being codified, and his typology therefore is somewhat more flexible than latter ones will be. Siegfried Kracauer (1997) originally published *Theory of Film* in 1960, and his typology systematizes that of Spottiswoode while bringing it in better accord with the categories of narrative fiction film but at the cost of being somewhat less flexible. Like Copland and Eisler and Adorno, Roger Manvell and John Huntley (1957) wrote their text specifically about film music, and their typology is therefore most concerned with sorting out the potential relations of music to the film.

Sergei Eisenstein and Vertical Montage

Starting with the publication of the "Statement on Sound," Eisenstein continually pushed two propositions for sound film: first, that the basic principle of film is montage; and second, that the soundtrack should not be bound by mimetic synchronization but should instead be placed in a contrapuntal relationship with the image. Initially, Eisenstein hoped to combine these two propositions by extending the principle of montage vertically to the relation between sound and image. Just as two pieces of film edited together form an opposition across which meaning could leap, so too the coordination of image and sound could likewise form complex audiovisual figures. By the time he was working on what has come to be known as *Toward a Theory of Montage* in the late 1930s, Eisenstein had become much less sanguine. Political circumstances had changed in the Soviet Union, and dialogue had altered the constructive potential of sound film in ways that Eisenstein had not anticipated. Or perhaps he did anticipate—the "Statement on Sound" had accurately identified the inertia of the dialogue shot—but had not understood the difficulty in overcoming this inertia, which is not simply ideological but is deeply bound up with sound film's anthropocentrism, the representation of the human figure.

In any case, from its first pages, *Towards a Theory of Montage* is a defensive text, even as its point of departure is to understand how montage functions in sound film, to think montage beyond its elementary application of the join and the soundtrack beyond the rule of mimetic synchronization but without adopting the classical system of representation, which had become dominant in the 1930s through its adoption by Hollywood. Eisenstein commits to a realism that derives neither from the mimetic properties of synchronization nor from the representational scheme of the classical system based in perceptual realism.

> A truly realistic work of art, deriving from the fundamental tenets of realism, must contain as an indissoluble whole *both* the representation of a phenomenon *and* its image; by "image" is meant a generalized statement about the essence of the particular phenomenon. They are inextricably linked by their present, their appearance and the way they merge with one another. (1991, 4, emphasis in original)

By the time he was working on *Towards a Theory of Montage*, Eisenstein recognized that mimetic synchronization had become the dominant mode of representation in the sound film, but he also struggled for ways to turn synchronization into a dialectical rather than mechanical principle while avoiding what he saw as the pitfalls of the representational scheme of the classical system. And he continued to believe that montage was the key to filmic construction, its function to provide "a coherent, consistent exposition of the work's theme, plot, action and events" (1991, 296). But the montage of sound film also had to pass through the audiovisual figure of mimetic synchronization, which altered it in fundamental ways. "In sound film the role of montage lies basically in the internal synchronization of sound and picture" (4). Vertical montage, if it exists, cannot be a simple extension of silent film montage: this is the conclusion Eisenstein drew from his film work during the 1930s, especially his success with *Alexander Nevsky* (1938). Montage needs to be thought back into the basic cells of film technique. Hence, Eisenstein turns more and more toward understanding the internal dynamics of the shot and to a lesser degree how sound affects those dynamics.

Perhaps because the synchronized shot has so much inertia in sound film, Eisenstein thinks that the shot is a much more problematic element in sound film than it was in the silent film—far less plastic, more compounded—so its structure needs more analytical attention. At the same time, any shot, especially when extended, contains a latent rhythmic quality that can be revealed through synchronization. By synchronization here, Eisenstein has in mind less mimetic synchronization or even a gestural synchronization of individual moments and more a kind of rhythmic affinity between sound and image that allows it to display an "inner synchronicity," closer perhaps to Maurice Jaubert's (1937) idea of rhythmic synchronization or even the latent connections that Jean Cocteau's accidental synchronization reveals (Manvell and Huntley 1957, 75–76).

As is true of many theorists of the sound film, Eisenstein prefers to theorize the soundtrack in terms of music, even beyond his central concept of counterpoint. Music is both generally more compliant with an image-based theory and an art in its own right; it therefore offers both prestige and a submissiveness that dialogue does not.

> Thus the basic key to mastering montage along with the other disciplines within sound film—a new degree of mastery of montage in the new stage of cinema—remains (along with all of its previous depictive and narrative functions) the problem of mastering internal synchronicity, made up from the integrity of the sound (of the image) and the integrity of the picture (of the image) in the film as a whole—until, broadly speaking, the inner synchronicity of a "piece of music" and a "piece of photography" is achieved. (1991, 253)

Music and photography become the basic artistic elements of soundtrack and image, respectively. Eisenstein acknowledges that sequences of shots almost always have various lines or series that can be traced through the sequence and that music (or sound) can play to, or draw a line through, any of them (377).

> In cinema, the selection of "correspondences" between picture and music must not be satisfied with any one of these "lines," or even with a harmony of several employed together. Aside from these general formal elements the same law has to determine the selection of *the right people, the right faces, the right objects, the right actions, and the right sequences*, out of all the equally possible selections within the circumstances of a given situation. (1975, 172, emphasis in original; 1991, 378 in a different translation)

Eisenstein specifically uses the term "vertical montage" to describe his working procedure in *Alexander Nevsky*. He calls it "a new form of montage" (1991, 329), and he theorizes it as akin to a musical score (330).[2] "Polyphonic structure," Eisenstein writes, "basically works by creating an overall perception of a sequence as a whole. It forms, as it were, the 'physiognomy' of a sequence, summarizing all its separate elements into a general perception of the sequence" (332). Vertical montage is essentially like two orchestras (image and sound) treated polyphonically themselves then treated polyphonically in relation to each other. It is like the superimposition of images, a montage of simultaneity, which fits with Eisenstein's general theory of montage as an all-encompassing artistic technique for (potentially) bringing everything into contact with everything else (332). Vertical montage requires some kind of relationship or "congruence" between image and soundtrack (370), and it is concerned not with the depiction (a presentation of explicit content) but with an "awareness of the inner movement" (373). In this sense, music is the dominant conceptual category of vertical montage, the underlying "gesture," for

---

[2] Eisenstein's article on Prokofiev's score for *Alexander Nevsky* has generated an extensive secondary literature. For an excellent recent discussion, see Lea Jacobs (2015).

both image and soundtrack. "For music—the 'gesture' which underlies both sound and picture—is not something abstract and unrelated to the theme, but is the most generalized expressive embodiment of the image through which the theme is articulated" (376).

Eisenstein writes of a particular scene from *Alexander Nevsky*, the lead-up to the famous battle on the ice, that "the same gesture, common to both, is the basis of both the musical and the graphical structures" (1991, 381). Eisenstein famously uses his analysis of this scene as a model for conceptualizing the relationship between image and music rather than something to be taken literally; in particular, the way the analysis insists on reading the image from left to right and also the graphic image of the music in the same direction seems a peculiar constraint since the gestural correspondence would obviously work if the graphic image was reversed as well. (This is a common criticism of the analysis.) It seems that he chose this particular scene because the direction of the notation reinforces the gestural relationship he locates in the images and so makes that relationship palpable, rather than because he means for this to set down any dictates for how to proceed analytically in general. Eisenstein indeed acknowledges the issue (387), without addressing it in a convincing way, except to note that it requires a linearization of the image through the "path of the eye." Eisenstein argues that his images in this case have been constructed to encourage a reading from left to right (388–89). "It is obvious that the method of 'reading' the shots horizontally and 'lining them up' in our perception one after another along the horizontal is not always used" (393).[3]

MODES OF SYNCHRONICITY

Sound film, for Eisenstein, is "specifically a scheme of linkage" (1991, 334) of picture and sound:

> The essential problem becomes that of finding what makes picture and sound compatible, and of finding, for this purpose, the relevant indices, units of measurement, techniques and methodology. This will be primarily a matter of finding an inner synchronicity between picture and music that is sharply perceptible to us as it already is in our perception of examples of outward synchronicity (we have already learned to be keenly aware of the slightest failure between lip movements and the spoken word!). (334)

The idea of "inner synchronicity" is a goal of vertical montage; it does not consist in searching for obvious relations, sounds that belong to the image like the creak of a boat, but rather for those that "aspire to 'that "mysterious" inner

---

[3] Kia Afra (2015) argues: "The relations governing this correlation between image and music may be artificial and constructed, but they emerge as formal relations by virtue of their inclusion in a single phenomenon in the cinema: vertical montage" (35).

synchronicity' in which the visual principle merges wholly with the tonal" (334). This is very much a musical conception, and "inner synchronicity" is more an affinity than a direct relationship, such as found in mimetic synchronization, the zero state of synchronicity. The primary link between picture and sound is movement, and this movement can be mechanical as in mimetic synchronization, or it can suggest a more tenuous connection, one that is evocative and expressive. "In our subject, art actually begins from the moment when the combination of sound and picture do not simply reproduce a connection existing in nature but establishes a connection demanded by the expressive requirements of the work in question" (334).

A first method for moving beyond the "inherent synchronicity" of mimetic synchronization (the zero state) involves "subordinating both spheres (aural and visual) to one and the same rhythm, a rhythm corresponding to the content of the scene" (1991, 334). This is Eisenstein's first kind of audiovisual synchronicity, which he calls "metrical" (335). Metrical synchronicity can be complicated through a kind of syncopation, where movements in image or soundtrack are set at odds with each other, and this yields a second stage of "rhythmic synchronicity," where individual figures take shape. The next stage Eisenstein identifies with melody, where it is no longer metrical and rhythmic patterns that dominate the conception, but instead a line formed (335). The final stage of synchronicity Eisenstein called "tonal," which involves complexes, intervals, and "oscillatory movements" (335). The point of tonal synchronicity is not synchronism or its opposite but rather the combination of and play between image and soundtrack elements in a manner that is "structurally purposeful" (336). These stages of synchronicity constitute the modes of vertical montage.

In his work on visual montage, Eisenstein distinguished "montage by semantic sequence" (forms of parallel montage) from "montage by kinetic sequence," and the latter yields a series that resembles the modes of vertical montage. His series of kinetic montage is metric, rhythmic, tonal (melodic), overtonal, and intellectual (1991, 228; see also 1988, 181–94). The duplication of terms in the two series suggests that for Eisenstein, vertical montage governs the relationship of the image and sound, much as the montage of kinetic sequences governs the image segments. In 1929, when he first proposed his schema for visual montage in "The Fourth Dimension of Cinema," Eisenstein had believed that "the contrapuntal conflict between the visual and sound overtones will give rise to the composition of the Soviet sound film" (1988, 186), but a decade later when he was working on the modes of vertical montage, the overtones had evidently become more obscure, at least at a level of regulating synchronicity (1991, 336). In any event, the overtonal disappears from his modes of synchronicity except as a designation of the whole: "This totality is the sensory factor which most immediately synthesizes the principal image of the sequence" (336). Overtonal synchronicity evidently resides at the (perhaps imaginary or ideal) end point of audiovisual montage: "the *ultimate inner synchronicity, the image and the meaning of the sequences*" (336, emphasis in original). Elsewhere, Eisenstein hints that all of vertical montage is the development of overtonal montage for the sound film (236). The concept, however, remains obscure.

Aaron Copland and the Functions of Film Music

Aaron Copland composed a number of scores in Hollywood and won an Academy Award for his score to *The Heiress* (1949). His concert, ballet, and film scores from the 1930s and 1940s served as a resource for other film composers of the 1940s and 1950s, as they developed a broad pastorale style of Americana, one variant used for westerns, another for representations of traditional, small-town American life (Lerner 2001).

Copland wrote from the perspective of a working composer. Film music, he says, offers "a new form of dramatic music" (2010b, 321), and film is in desperate need of music. "By itself the screen is a pretty cold proposition. . . . [M]usic is like a small flame put under the screen to help warm it" (2010a, 86). At the same time, he agrees with most authors that music needs to be subordinate in film. "Film music only makes sense if it helps the film; no matter how good, distinguished, or successful, the music must be secondary in importance to the story being told on the screen" (86).

Like most composers, especially those who worked in Hollywood, Copland's writing about film music tends to be more practical than theoretical and speculative. But he also has a penchant for identifying, sorting, and describing the problems of composing for the screen. In an essay reworked from several shorter pieces and that appeared in his collection of essays, *Our New Music*, Copland proposed a concise typology of functions for film music. Here, he identified three basic functions of film music—intensifying emotions, creating the illusion of continuity, and providing neutral background. He also offered three reservations about the contemporary practice of scoring—the romantic symphonic style, leitmotifs, and mickey-mousing. In a later piece, he expanded the functions to five basic ones for accompanying music and also recognized music incidental to the scene as an additional function. The typology that he generated consists of some of the more important practical rules of thumb, and he does not aim to be exhaustive. Combining the two accounts results in the following typology of functions and reservations.

FUNCTIONS

Establish place and time. Copland claims that in Hollywood, marking place and time is not often bothered with except for westerns, which make frequent use of cowboy songs and so forth. Hollywood scores, he says, are often "interchangeable; a thirteenth-century Gothic drama and a hard-boiled modern battle of the sexes get similar treatment" (2010b, 322). What he means here is that the intensified chromaticism and heavy symphonic scoring characteristic of the late nineteenth century (and early twentieth century) has become a kind of lingua franca of film scoring. This general style certainly also deploys conventional representations of musical topics for establishing the setting or time, but the scores always revert to the stylistic base of intensified chromatic symphonic music. Although Copland does not think all films require a treatment sensitive to the historic specificity of the setting, he does argue that the musical setting should "reflect the emotion and reality of the individual picture" (2010a, 88). In this respect, a conventional score represents not the particularity of the emotion but its generality and conventional character.

Signifier of interiority. One of the most familiar claims for film music is that it helps articulate the feelings of the characters and the mood of a scene. Copland argues similarly, that music serves to intensify "the emotional impact" of a film (2010a, 87). Copland recognizes this function as belonging to "an old tradition of theater music" (87). Music is frequently used to draw out a dominant feeling in a scene, such as using a love theme to underscore a romantic encounter, but Copland is more interested in emotions and feelings that run counter to the prevailing mood and so suggest a deeper or less evident emotion at work. "A well-placed dissonant chord can stop an audience cold in the middle of a sentimental scene, or a calculated wood-wind passage can turn what appears to be a solemn moment into a belly laugh" (2010b, 322). Such interventions suggest that there is more to the scene than meets the eye, and so they posit another level (an unsettled interiority or some kind of exterior knowledge that troubles the seemingly placid surface of the story). Copland notes that one difficulty with using music in this way is finding a convincing way to introduce music into the scene "without making the audience suddenly aware of its entrance" (2010a, 87).

Neutral background. One way to introduce emotional music into a film scene is to have it evolve from other music that is already present. This is one function of neutral music: it allows music to be already present in a scene so that it can be called on to perform other duties. Neutral background music also serves to fill time and aural space in scenes that would otherwise be awkward, especially in dialogue scenes, where the delivery of lines and pauses can be mistimed. Music can frequently fix such timing issues while also providing a composed aural background to cover up the hiss of an optical soundtrack. Although useful to the film and a genre of music novel to film, neutral background music is, Copland says, "the movie composer's most ungrateful task" (2010b, 323), but it is also "something very special" (2010a, 87). Even when neutral in tone, as it often is when used in underscore, it provides a kind of underlying warmth. As Copland notes, it serves to remove "the deathly pallor of the screen shadow" (2010b, 323). Because it serves to underscore dialogue, it is music that is often not much noticed in and of itself, though "it undoubtedly works on the subconscious mind" (2010a, 87). Copland attributes to Max Steiner the development of the most effective realization of the style: "for certain types of neutral music, a kind of melodyless music is needed. Steiner does not supply mere chords but superimposes a certain amount of melodic motion, just enough to make the music sound normal and yet not enough to compel attention" (2010a, 91).

Continuity. Montage in film is often rougher than is ideal, and the logic of the shots is not always self-evident. "Pictures, jumping from episode to episode, from exterior to interior, have a tendency to fall apart" (2010a, 87). Music, Copland says, can help such scenes by smoothing out the rough spots and making the whole scene seem to belong to a single continuity. "The use of a unifying musical idea may save the quick flashes of disconnected scenes from seeming merely chaotic" (2010b, 323). In a sense, film borrows the impression of continuity from the accompanying music: because the music sounds continuous and because the music fits with the images, the sequence of images also seems continuous, like they belong together.

Dynamic shaping of a scene and giving film a sense of finish. Copland does not actually talk overly much about the dynamic shaping, but he notes that music that leads to "The End" card is nearly ubiquitous. Films during the classical era occasionally went without much music, and some even avoided music for the opening credits, "but I never saw or heard of a picture that ended in silence."

Source music. Besides the five functions mentioned previously, Copland also notes that music is common as part of the scene. A nightclub will feature jazzy foxtrots for dancing, a parade will have the sound of a military band playing a march, and so forth. Such music is similar to the first function in establishing place and time, but here the source of the music emanates from the depicted scene rather than sounding as a comment from an exterior source like a narrator painting the scene from outside.

RESERVATIONS

Idiom. Film composers have developed the intensified chromatic symphonic style of the late nineteenth century into a kind of lingua franca, where the same basic style is used for "every type of story, regardless of time, place, or treatment" (2010a, 88). While Copland finds the style distasteful, both pompous and outdated, he also thinks it has the effect of making all film scores sound much too similar. Copland prefers a more austere, modernist style, partly because it better fits contemporary artistic sensibilities, but even more so because it gives films more options for scoring. Copland effectively makes an argument against the ubiquity of the intensified symphonic style, but he does not really mount an argument against it in general (other than taste), nor does he address the communicative utility of a conventional style.

Leitmotif. Like many critics of film music during the 1930s and '40s, Copland thinks the device of the leitmotif is more a crutch for the composer who needs to score a film quickly than an aid for the audience's understanding. Copland's primary criticism is that film composers apply the leitmotif mechanically, resulting in a patchwork of music. "In a high-class horse opera I saw this method reduced to its final absurdity. One theme announced the Indians, another the hero. In the inevitable chase, every time the scene changed from Indians to hero, the theme did, too, sometimes so fast the music seemed to hop back and forth before any part of it had time to breathe" (2010a, 88). Copland may have had in mind something like the lead-up to the big attack in *Stagecoach* (1939). As the coach moves along a road in Monument Valley, it is accompanied by upbeat "traveling" music that emphasizes the mobility of the machine and the optimism of the passengers. With a cut to the "Indians" grimly watching the stagecoach from the cliff, the music turns ominous, abruptly interrupting the music with a blast of brass stating a motive that evokes an Indian musical topic. The sequence then repeats with a return to the stagecoach music and back again for the Indians. The juxtaposition of the music is bald and unmediated, and the repetition emphasizes the juxtaposition and the coding that accumulates with the alliance of image and music: the stagecoach is civilization, modernity itself moving across the landscape; the Indians are villainous, intent on using their power to reclaim the land. The sequence then moves into a long, spectacular attack, with the Indians ultimately defeated by the arrival of the cavalry. Instead of leitmotifs tagging the situation in the most obvious way, as perhaps in this sequence, Copland argues for music that is broadly representational and fitting to "the underlying ideas of a picture" (2010a, 88). Yet the treatment in *Stagecoach* points to a difficulty with Copland's critique. He complains about how the cutting of the music leads to a kind of breathlessness in the music, as though that were always a negative thing. The initial juxtaposition of motives is undoubtedly jarring in the sequence from *Stagecoach*, and the music of the stagecoach does seem curtailed, but the sequence also prepares the conflict to come. At that level, the four shots and four breathless musical statements serve to articulate an "underlying idea" of the film.[4]

Mickey-mousing. Copland thinks film music too often tries to closely mimic action, like a cartoon, rather than play for broader significance. The basic issue with this method, Copland suggests, is that it aims to draw out details of action and imbue them with too much interpretive weight. "An actor

---

[4] It is also worth noting that Copland dropped his objections to the leitmotif when he expanded his list of functions from three to five.

can't lift an eyebrow without the music helping him do it" (2010a, 88). As a result, music seems overly manipulative.

Copland's typology of functions has proven very influential, and several of them are incorporated in one way or another into Claudia Gorbman's (1987) list of seven rules. Perhaps one reason Copland's list remains a reasonable summary of functions is that, while he drew on his experience as a film composer to formulate his functions, he was writing for a general audience. Thus, he lucidly explained what the music did in line with his aesthetic values rather than trying to work out a larger theory about how music and film interacted or a more exhaustive list of functions.

Hanns Eisler and Theodor W. Adorno and Critical Theory

CONTRA EISENSTEIN

In *Composing for the Films* (1947), the most influential book on the theory of film music until the publication of Gorbman's *Unheard Melodies* (1987), Hanns Eisler and Theodor W. Adorno criticized Eisenstein for seeking formal correspondences between music and film of the sort he identified in his modes of synchronicity that underlay the concept of vertical montage. Introducing the concept, Eisenstein (1991) had noted a difference between Offenbach's famous Barcarolle serving as an accompaniment of a scene of lovers in Venice and finding an "inner movement" between the ebbing and flowing of the Barcarolle and the play of light on the water (372–73). Eisenstein claimed that abstractions of the latter made it a different and more advanced stage of vertical montage than the former. According to Eisler and Adorno, however, even the latter case still posits a "pseudo-identity" between music and image, albeit at a more abstract level (1947, 67). It is doubtful that Eisenstein would have disagreed completely with this assessment, since his concern with vertical montage was to classify different kinds of synchronicity and so also to get a handle on the range of potential open to vertical montage.

Eisler and Adorno, on the contrary, seem intent on allowing only the higher orders of relation that are not direct and so do not posit an identity or morphology. "The unity of the two media is achieved indirectly; it does not consist in the identity between any elements, be it that between tone and color or that of 'rhythms' as a whole" (1947, 70). The injunction here is essentially moral; and it seeks to preserve a measure of music's autonomy, to exempt music from performing a redundant service. The basic problem for Eisler and Adorno is that any relation that suggests an identity between music and the picture would necessarily be false and so serve to "camouflage the incompatibility" between the domains (72). For Eisler and Adorno, this "incompatibility" is itself a figure that reflects a social truth, and so to disguise it is to acquiesce to ideology. Nevertheless, they concede that "there must be some meaningful relation between the picture and the music" (69), and they link the two along the plane of movement. "The photographed picture as such lacks motivation for movement," and music "intervenes" as "a stimulus of motion, not a reduplication of motion" (78). Music here is a kind of complement to the pictures, and the points of contact, the way music motivates the image without reduplicating its gesture, seem similar enough to the higher stages of Eisenstein's modes of synchronicity to think that they were working at a similar problem from a somewhat different angle. In any event, it is hard to know what to make of Eisler and Adorno's call for "musical planning, the free and conscious utilization of all musical resources on the basis of accurate insight into the dramatic function of music" (80), if planning does not include an array of options for coordinating music and picture according to dramatic function and other considerations that Eisenstein discusses under vertical montage.

THE NEGATIVE THESIS: SHAM IDENTITY

Composing for the Films was written by Eisler, a German émigré composer who worked occasionally in Hollywood and was a frequent collaborator with Berthold Brecht, and Adorno, a musically trained philosopher who was one of the founders of the Frankfurt School critical theory. The book was drafted while both lived in Los Angeles during World War II but originally appeared under Eisler's name alone, since Eisler became a target of the political right in the United States shortly after the war. At once a diatribe against classic film music practices and a perceptive sociological analysis of the Hollywood production system of background scoring, the book was quickly recognized as an important contribution to the theory of film music, and, despite being somewhat outdated with respect to the industry practice, the book can still be read profitably for its keen insights into contradictions endemic to producing and consuming commercial art.

The basic thesis of the book is largely negative: that music is mostly redundant in film; that film music rarely if ever exploits even the most rudimentary critical possibilities open to it; and that the presence of music is largely effaced in film so that any critical involvement that it does obtain goes mostly unheard (Eisler and Adorno 1947, 3–19). If much contemporary film music scholarship continues to accept this critical thesis largely intact (often without acknowledging the source), the positive suggestions they offer for how film music might be reformulated into a more self-reflective practice have proved remarkably ineffectual.

Gorbman (1991), for instance, shows on this count just how closely Eisler's score for the *Spanish Main* (1945) accords with standard Hollywood practice. In a later piece, Gorbman (2004) also questions the effectiveness of Eisler's use of atonality in *Kuhle Wampe oder: Wem gehört die Welt?* (1932), arguing that the score would most likely result in audience puzzlement.[5] Then too, Eisler

---

[5] Neumeyer and Buhler (2008) make a similar point about Eisler's music for *A Scandal in Paris* (1945).

and Adorno never clarify how ideology and art are to be weighted in evaluating film music. They conclude, for instance, that Eisler's score for *Hangmen Also Die* (1943) is effective primarily because it ensures that the audience identifies with the Czech people, "the real hero of picture," rather than Heydrich, the Nazi collaborator and villain (1947, 25). Yet such identification would hardly be novel even in a standard Hollywood film (e.g., *Casablanca* [1942]), and the melodramatic deployment of music for the purpose of a rather simplistic demonization seems open to a critique similar to the one they raise against Eisenstein. The problem with their analysis of the film in the terms set out in the book is that music winds up being evaluated more on the basis of its overt ideological stance, its conventional melodramatic power to encourage proper audience identification, than on its contribution to the work as art (27).

In fact, it is not at all certain what Eisler and Adorno think film music is, and they largely deny it a separate ontological status. They famously declared that film music was a music without history (1947, 45). "It would be ludicrous to claim that motion-picture music has really evolved, either in itself or in relation to other motion-picture media" (49). Its eclectic practice, low status, dramaturgical needs, commercial base, and technological determinants mean that it is essentially impossible for music in film to develop a practice distinct to the composing for the films. At best, it can appropriate historical currents from outside film and follow a course of "haphazard development" (46). During the period when Eisler and Adorno developed their critique of Hollywood film music, their description was more or less apt, if one-sided, and it revoiced in more strident terms a common criticism of the time that film music was a degraded commercial form with little new to offer musically other than a steady paycheck for composers. For Eisler and Adorno, even the marked changes in approach to composing for the films that accompanied the transition to sound seemed driven not by the musical problems posed by film and recorded sound but by basic technological and economic considerations.

A real history of film music, they argue, can only be understood in terms of the transition from "more or less important private capitalistic enterprises to highly concentrated and rationalized companies," a transition that the changeover to sound film had accelerated (1947, 51). "Improvements" in music for film, therefore, occur largely on the industrial side of production (50). Hollywood business practices, which opt for streamlining and standardization, also have the effect of neutralizing any advances in compositional technique appropriate to the cinema, since they are deemed overly experimental. The resulting process of codification locks in a series of "bad habits" that conventionalizes film music to enhance its communicative efficiency. Evolution of a musical technique appropriate for the films is therefore constrained to those aspects that can be attributed to improvements of technology, as with recording that improves the fidelity and "sound" only so that music can more easily sit unobtrusively unheard in the background.

If Eisler and Adorno find film music to be without a history where its status as music for film does little to affect its status as music, they do recognize its importance in the cinema. Earlier, I noted that they understand music as crucial to motivating the movement in the image. This importance was evident in the silent film, where they argue that music had been introduced

> as a kind of antidote against the picture. The need was felt to spare the spectator the unpleasantness involved in seeing effigies of living, acting, and even speaking persons, who were at the same time silent. The fact that they are living and nonliving at the same time is what constitutes their ghostly character, and music was introduced not to supply them with life they lacked . . . but to exorcise fear or help the spectator absorb the shock. (1947, 75)

In their account, film music originates as a protective screen that distracts the spectator from fully recognizing the allegorical import of the image and the threat of universal muteness that it embodies.

> Motion-picture music corresponds to the whistling or singing child in the dark. The real reason for the fear is not even that these people whose silent effigies are moving in front of one seem to be ghosts. The captions do their best to come to the aid of these images. But confronted with gesticulating masks, people experience themselves as creatures of the very same kind, as being threatened by muteness. (75)

If audiences take comfort from the fact that sound film has untied the tongue of film, Eisler and Adorno insist that "the sound pictures have changed this function of music less than might be imagined. *For the talking picture, too, is mute.* The characters in it are not speaking people but speaking effigies" (76, emphasis in original).

Dialogue in the sound film, for Eisler and Adorno, is an aural rendering of the intertitles. But just as the intertitles dissociated words from bodies so that they floated in the black space between images, the spoken words of the talkies also do not seem to belong securely to the bodies that speak them. Mimetic synchronization is in that sense always already something of a sham.

> Speech in motion pictures is the legitimate heir to the captions; it is a roll retranslated into acoustics, and that is what it sounds like even if the formulation of the words is not bookish but rather feigns the "natural." The fundamental divergencies between words and pictures are unconsciously registered by the spectator, and the obtrusive unity of the sound picture that is presented as a complete reduplication of the external world with all its elements is perceived as fraudulent and fragile. (1947, 77)

The sham of mimetic synchronization is concealed through an enforced redundancy that has the effect of congealing movement, which in turn compounds the problem. Because the images no longer move as they did in the silent era, the words, Eisler and Adorno claim, lose effectiveness, and the film regresses to a state of muteness that the actual spoken words only barely conceal.

> Speech in the motion picture is a stop-gap, not unlike wrongly employed music that aims at being identical with events on the screen. A talking picture without music is not very different from a silent picture, and there is every reason to believe that the more closely pictures and words are coordinated, the more emphatically their intrinsic contradiction and the actual muteness of those who seem to be speaking are felt by the spectators. This may explain—although the requirements of the market supply a more obvious reason—why the sound pictures still need music, while they seem to have all the opportunities of the stage and much greater ability at their disposal. (77)

Even as they excavate the traumatic core of dialogue—its resemblance to the superfluous intertitle—Eisler and Adorno here are also typical of theorists of the time in arguing to maintain the repression of dialogue and offering music as a model for an alternative practice to mimetic synchronization where music served many of the same functions it did in the silent film because the talking film resembled the silent film more than it did the theater.

BAD HABITS

Eisler and Adorno open their book with a typology of the "rules of thumb" of "standard practice," which they call "a kind of pseudo-tradition" (1947, 3). Their typology does not seek to be exhaustive and its presentation is not systematic. Instead, they focus on some of the more obvious traits to demonstrate the basic issues with the practice.

Leitmotif. Like Copland, Eisler and Adorno find that the organizing of film scores around the leitmotif results in a "patchwork" structure that exasperates the discontinuity of the film (1947, 4). Eisler and Adorno agree with Copland that the leitmotif is more a benefit to the composer than to the audience, since it means the composer "can quote where he otherwise would have to invent" (4). They note the leitmotif's similarity to song plugging, which uses repetition to create familiarity, but more important they find that the film form is not suitable to what is artistic in the technique. To the extent that the leitmotif succeeds in Wagner's music, it does so because the conciseness of the leitmotif is there set in the large temporal canvas of the music drama (5), and "it requires a large musical canvas if it is to take on a structural meaning beyond that of a signpost" (5). The motion picture, by contrast, is comparably brief, and rather than being constructed out of scenes of significant duration, it is constructed out of disconnected shots that are assembled to form relatively short sequences. When a film score deploys leitmotifs, the discontinuity of the picture is answered by a similar and problematic discontinuity of the music; and the musical cues tend to be relatively brief. "Musically, also shorter forms prevail, and the leitmotif is unsuitable here because of this brevity of forms which must be complete in themselves" (5). The leitmotif also serves a mythic significance that endows "dramatic events with metaphysical significance" rather than tagging the arrival of characters and things. Because for Eisler and Adorno films seek "to depict reality" (5), they think that films must necessarily lack this mythic dimension of the music drama. This claim is considerably less well founded, though it was a common view during the era in which they were writing. Nevertheless, it was (and still is) a common idea that the leitmotif is essentially a signifier of a character, thing, or idea, and it has received significant criticism from many different perspectives despite its ubiquitous use (Bribitzer-Stull 2015).

Melody and euphony. Most film scores feature themes and harmony of a conventional nature. This conventionality allows them to appeal to the public taste, but it is not clear that this makes for the most dramatically effective music in a film. The lyricism at the heart of melody, they say, runs contrary to the idea of the cinema, which requires a music that is subordinated to the picture. Film also lacks the symmetries of a tuneful melody. "Visual action in the motion picture has of course a prosaic irregularity and asymmetry. It claims to be photographed life" (1947, 8). What is required instead is a music that freed of "conventional fetters" can complement the asymmetries of the motion picture action (9).

Unobtrusiveness. One common assessment of music during the era of the classical sound film was that if audiences were aware of the music, then it was not good film music. Eisler and Adorno dispute this claim in two ways. First, they argue that scenes that are dialogue heavy should use sound effects rather than underscore the scene with music as an accompaniment (1947, 10). Unobtrusive underscore results in a musical sound that isn't properly music. (Here, they come to the opposite conclusion to Copland's defense of neutral music.) Second, they say the use of music should be planned so it can serve the picture and remain music at its essence (11).

Visual justification. This occurs when the screenwriters go out of their way to introduce a visual source for music, by, for example, having a character walk over to turn on a phonograph. Eisler and Adorno acknowledge that this practice is no longer common in 1947. Even so, their complaint that "music becomes a plot accessory, a sort of acoustical stage property" (12) remains odd. We can agree that forced additions of diegetic music are problematic without calling into question the use of diegetic music in general, which need not "hinder the use of music as a genuine element of contrast" (12).

Illustration. Music frequently serves to establish the mood of a scene, and often enough it fixes on a detail in a scene to give some motivation. Eisler and Adorno note the formula "birdie sings, music sings" as one instance of this general tendency (1947, 12). The issue is not so much the mimicking of birdsong, however, as an approach that would scan the scene for musical opportunities rather than for narrative pertinence. Eisler and Adorno also complain about stereotyped music for nature scenery—majestic mountains or the boundless prairie—without noting that those settings themselves are as hackneyed (13). They do recognize that the musical illustration is an effective tool of film composition, but claim that it is a solution that is too often opted for when something better might have been devised (13). "Musical illustration should either be hyperexplicit itself [like the image]—over-illuminating, so to speak, and thereby interpretive—or should be omitted" (14).

Geography and history. Eisler and Adorno claim that Hollywood composers prefer to find music appropriate to a time and region and rework that rather than devising something themselves (1947, 14). In this, they again come to almost the opposite conclusion as Copland, who says composers are likely to devise a tune in generic nineteenth-century style. Eisler and Adorno perhaps come closer to Copland in advocating for music that uses "advanced musical resources" (15), since this would be music that was composed for the particularities of the film.

Stock music. Although by the time Eisler and Adorno were writing only low-budget pictures used extensive amounts of music from the classical repertory, the authors are very critical of the practice because it seems to trade on the value of the music from the domain of concert music. The result is music that signifies in unpredictable ways, and often at odds with the needs of the picture (1947, 15–16).

Clichés. Too much film music consists of standardized accompaniments to typical situations. The problem is that a scene needs a particular effect, but because music has been so stereotyped, it cannot achieve the needed effect. "The powerful effect intended does not come off, because the listener has been made familiar with the stimulus by innumerable analogous passages" (1947, 16). They make the important point that genre pictures should be given more leeway in using standardized patterns, because in essence those films achieve their effect through their "play" with conventions and standardization. Pictures that seek an individualized statement, however, must avoid the standard patterns if they are to be true to their aim: "What is objectionable is the standardized character of pictures that claim to be unique; or, conversely, the individual disguise of the standard pattern" (16–17).

Standardized performances. Eisler and Adorno complain that music is all recorded and reproduced in a very standard way that tends to dull anything novel about the sound. "The main purpose here is the production of a comfortable and polished euphony" (1947, 18). The result is a music that disappears into the background.

The "Statement on Sound" by Eisenstein, Pudovkin, and Alexandrov and *Composing for the Films* are undoubtedly the two most influential documents of classical film theory that address the soundtrack. Both were formulated as critical responses to Hollywood practice, and each outlined an oppositional practice along with its critique.

The Classical System and the Typological Analysis

The codification of the sound film into the classical system in the first half of the 1930s encouraged typological thinking. The introduction of the sound film had required the creation of new categories and distinctions, but the uncertainty of the transitional period seems to have discouraged exhaustive classificatory schemes for image and sound relations. Eisenstein had developed typologies of image montage during this period and introduced the general concept of counterpoint, but it was only in the later 1930s that he developed the elaborate modes of synchronicity to classify potential relations between sound and image. Although *Composing for the Films* was not generally typological in its structure, its introductory chapter outlined nine "prejudices and bad habits" that the classical system had codified, and Aaron Copland devised a brief typology of film music functions that has proved influential.

For technical reasons, the early practice of the sound film had been dominated by the rule of mimetic synchronization, which insisted that every sound have a source in the image. The concept of "counterpoint" had been introduced and admitted as a formal alternative, but its deployment in the mode of conflict insisted on by The "Statement of Sound" proved perplexing, even as the rule of mimetic synchronization proved overly limiting. Somewhat in hindsight, Raymond Spottiswoode, an influential British film theorist, wrote in 1950 of the potential opened up by refusing the rule of mimetic synchronization:

> There is no reason whatever why the sound track should reproduce the sounds usually made by the objects represented in the band of images, of which the spoken word is the most obvious. Even here, in fact, a person who has never sung a note of music can be gifted by the film with the most divine voice, men can be made to speak as women, an actor whose lips move in English may be heard in Italian or French. Anything can be made to happen. Expected sounds (doors banging, bands playing, feet shuffling) can be suppressed, unexpected sounds substituted. (1950, 7–8)[6]

---

[6] The pagination and content of the 1935 and 1950 editions are identical, aside from a new preface. Only the text on pp. 1–13 and the arrangement of the chart at the end of the book differ between the two editions.

Indeed, counterpoint in a less overt conflictual mode of a generalized asynchronous sound allowed filmmakers to operationalize offscreen sound, to treat it not simply as an addition to and extension of the image but as a dynamic representational space that underscored lack, the incompleteness of a particular shot, and that could therefore draw the sound film beyond the image of one particular shot to another (also incomplete) shot and on and on. This conception was absolutely crucial to reconciling sound film with the continuity editing of the silent era.

The opposition between mimetic synchronization and counterpoint, or more generally between synchronous and asynchronous sound, was a basic conceptual distinction that engendered a series of further oppositions—foreground/background, diegetic/nondiegetic, objective/subjective—and an ordering of these distinctions became the foundation for the classical system, which used them to organize the functions of the soundtrack (Neumeyer 2015). That original opposition, though initially cast as different models for governing the relationship of image and sound, was generalized and incorporated into a representational system, which drew on the particular power of each, turning the soundtrack from a recording of a scene and toward narrative representation. The issue was now framed in terms of a direct or indirect relationship between image and the soundtrack, a relationship that was in turn mediated by the narrative and open to psychological representation, an incipient psychological realism. The relationships that emerged from this new conception were parallel and contrastive. Parallel meant the soundtrack related directly to image and, more important, that it ran with the grain of the narrative, whereas contrastive meant the relationship was indirect or even oblique and often ran against the grain of the narrative.

Raymond Spottiswoode and Film Grammar

The extent to which such oppositional thinking facilitated the codification of the soundtrack can be seen in Spottiswoode's influential scheme, a typology of "film grammar" that was first published in 1935. Spottiswoode, a British film theorist who wrote *The Grammar of Film* as a student at Oxford University, deploys two primary oppositions to analyze the relations of the soundtrack: realistic/nonrealistic and parallel/contrastive (1935, 174). He conceives these oppositions as poles of scales, that is, as realized in continuities rather than dichotomies. The first opposition (realistic/nonrealistic) can be realized along two different scales, the numeric and the intensive. The numeric scale deals with the extent of the realism with respect to figures in the image. The pole of realism under the numeric is just the rule of mimetic synchronization itself: all sounds correspond exactly to sources in the image (174). The pole of nonrealistic sound, by contrast, consists either in the removal of all sounds or in their complete replacement with sounds that seem not to match their sources (175). Either option results in a fully stylized rather than realistic representation of the sound. The limit of realism for the intensive scale consists of the volume of sound precisely matching that expected from the image scale. This limit can be breached on either end, with a sound of greater or lesser loudness than the image implies (176).

A further opposition, this one dichotomous rather than continuous, establishes whether the source of the sound lay inside or outside the frame, that is, whether the sound is synchronous or asynchronous. Spottiswoode (1935) called the latter situation "contrapuntal," borrowing the familiar term from Eisenstein and Pudovkin (176). The ordinary situation, oddly enough, is "noncontrapuntal." Thus, "noncontrapuntal realistic sound" is sound that corresponds in a realistic way with an onscreen source. "Contrapuntal realistic sound," by contrast, is sound that seems to come from the world of the image but whose source is offscreen. To classify the unrealistic pole of the opposition, Spottiswoode introduces another opposition, this one distinguishing between subjective and objective renderings (178), which seems designed as a measure of what narratology would call narrative focalization (see chapter 6), that is, whether the unreality of the sound is attributed to a character within the film (subjective) or to an entity such as the director or narrator outside the world depicted (objective). This opposition has intermediary stages, but these stages are better conceptualized as discrete points between the poles rather than as falling on a continuous scale. Ordinary sound treatment, which usually falls nearer the realistic pole, is also usually construed as more or less objective, inasmuch as, like the ordinary image, it is taken as neutral, that is, not strongly anchored in a particular subjective point of audition. (Spottiswoode does not mention this, but ordinary sound treatment is more likely to take the point of audition of the camera, or at least be theorized as doing so, but even this is usually adjusted to ensure clarity of the dialogue through a high ratio of direct to reflected sound.) Subjective sound, like subjective images, usually involves the introduction of some sort of distortion from that ordinary, objective sound—a movement along the numeric or intensive scale—toward the unrealistic pole. In that respect one signification of unreality on the soundtrack is subjectivization. But unrealistic sound can also be more or less objective. Such objective, unrealistic sound is often realized as a commentative function, such as voiceover or accompanying music. (Spottiswoode only implies but does not specifically state that accompanying music can also shift focalization and so also the subjective cast of a scene through its evocative and contrastive modes.) The parallel/contrastive opposition is less concerned with the source of the sound (as counterpoint is) than with the relation of sound and image to the idea of the film, what we today would normally call its narrative. When both sound and image correspond to this idea, the relationship is parallel; when sound and image "present or evoke different concepts and emotions," the relationship is contrastive (180). The absolute poles of this particular opposition, Spottiswoode notes, are rarely encountered (181).

The more common solutions of the classical system—its ordinary practice of rendering some sounds, especially dialogue, realistically and not rendering others unless they are narratively pertinent—tends to fall on the continuum between poles when an opposition is continuous. Thus, in terms of the opposition of realistic and nonrealistic, the usual solution is partly realistic, partly nonrealistic, but in a way that uses the value of narrative clarity to establish a hierarchy between foreground and background. This can be done (through mixing) both on the numeric scale by rendering some sounds but not others and on the intensive scale by boosting principal sounds such as dialogue and lowering other sounds such as ambient noise or music.

With this in mind, we can understand that the numeric and intensive scales are closely related in that every sound in the numeric scale can have its intensity adjusted rather than it being a simple binary choice of presence and absence (1935, 176). The conception is rather like a contemporary mixing board with each potential sound source in an image miked and patched to its own fader and with other unrelated sounds patched to other faders that might be used as supplements and substitutes. The unrealistic pole, then, allows for unrealistic deletions on the numeric scale and unrealistic modifications of sounds on the intensive scale in order to functionally separate foreground and background either to enhance clarity or to force the sound to model the attention presumed by perceptual realism but confused in monaural reproduction. (The microphone, as the saying goes, is undiscerning and records everything, both essential and extraneous sound, with the same fidelity.) The unrealistic pole can also be used, however, to substitute for or supplement realistic sound, either in whole or in part, and the substitution can be covert or overt. (As an addition, a supplement would necessarily be to some degree overt.) If a substitute is covert, Spottiswoode classifies it still as realistic "since the audience firmly believes it to be so" (175); if a substitute or supplement was overt, then the sound would be what narratological theories call extra- or nondiegetic. With respect to the opposition of parallel and contrastive, the classical system favors parallelism, because parallelism strengthens the presentation of the idea, but it recognizes that contrast offers potential for irony and, especially with music, psychological complication not easily obtainable through other techniques (10).

Although realism does not always line up with parallelism or unrealism with contrast (1935, 181), realistic contrast—lively street noise indifferent to an unfolding tragedy, for instance (183)—is less common than unrealistic contrast, and Spottiswoode found unrealistic (i.e., nondiegetic) music particularly suitable for conveying contrast (184). Spottiswoode also classified nondiegetic music according to the following functions:

1. *Imitative*—music resembling other sounds usually in distorted fashion.
2. *Commentative*—music reflecting on the film, usually objectively as with voiceover.
3. *Evocative*—music bringing along associations of emotion (moods) or thoughts (leitmotifs); this usually has a subjective inflection inasmuch as the moods or thoughts belong more to one character of a scene than the others.
4. *Contrastive*—use of commentative or evocative music in a contrasting way to the images. This is not an independent mode but reminds that comment and evocation can run with the film or against it.
5. *Dynamic*—music correlating with rhythm of cutting and action. (49–50)

Spottiswoode's classificatory schema is thorough but complicated, often overly so, and it is not always clear how the various scales he proposes articulate and interact with one another. His musical functions, while helpful as a starting point for thinking about musical treatment, are vaguer and less supple than those proposed by Copland.

Siegfried Kracauer and the Types of Cinematic Sound

Spottiswoode's classificatory scheme was simplified and systematized to a great extent by Siegfried Kracauer, who, writing in 1960 as the classic studio era was coming to an end, likewise maps the terrain with a set of two primary oppositions. For Kracauer, these oppositions are synchronism/asynchronism and parallelism/counterpoint, and these divide the uses of sound into four "types" (1997, 113–24). Kracauer's scheme is therefore less overtly but more thoroughly oriented according to narrative. His first opposition aligns with Spottiswoode's secondary opposition of contrapuntal and noncontrapuntal sound and is purely formal: it tracks whether the sound is synchronized to the image so that the image appears to be the source of the sound. Taken literally, this opposition reduces to onscreen/offscreen, which specifies whether the source of the sound lay in the field of vision shown by the image. But asynchronism in particular has a somewhat broader application that also allows it to relate to departures from realistic sound, what Kracauer, like Spottiswoode, also identified as its commentative function (112).[7] That is, asynchronous sound can either be actual or commentative, whereas synchronous sound is necessarily actual. Asynchronous sound is thus sound not directly motivated by or whose source is not evident from the image, whether it belongs to the world of the image or not, whereas synchronous sound follows

---

[7] Kracauer attributes the opposition of actual and commentative sound to Karel Reizs (1953, 278–79).

the rule of mimetic synchronization and is simply redundant with the image. Kracauer's scheme therefore places much greater weight on finding an operational theoretical distinction between actual and commentative asynchronous sound than does Spottiswoode's.

Much like Spottiswoode's parallel/contrastive opposition, Kracauer's other opposition of parallelism and counterpoint tracks whether sound and image are consistent with respect to an idea being expressed. Parallelism then specifies a sound that runs with the narrative implications of the images, whereas counterpoint specifies a sound that runs against the grain of those implications. This set of oppositions allows Kracauer to divide sound, as mentioned, into four basic types, with each asynchronous type being subdivided, depending on whether its sound is actual (offscreen) or commentative (belonging to a different dimension). One of the primary objectives of the typology—this is true of Spottiswoode's as well—is to break the conceptual identity that would equate asynchronous sound with the contrapuntal (or in Spottiswoode's terms contrastive) relationship between sound and image and synchronous sound with the parallel (1997, 115). For Kracauer, it is perfectly possible to have a synchronous treatment of sound but have sound and image pursuing different aims. A face, for instance, might reveal that speech is hypocritical (113), or the image might draw our attention away from the words of speech and toward what would otherwise seem incidental noises on the soundtrack. Although this typology maps the entire terrain of the soundtrack, Kracauer curiously restricts the use of parallelism for effects to synchronism, allowing exceptions of parallel asynchronism only for certain "symbolic" uses of sound. "Sound there substitutes for language, up to a point" (129). In the case of music, he concentrates on the parallelism and counterpoint of the commentative function (139–44), though he recognizes that with the addition of what he called "actual" (his term for diegetic) music, music that has its source in the world of the image, music can, like dialogue, express any of the types.

Characteristic of theorists who experienced the transition to sound first-hand—Kracauer was an important cultural critic in Weimar Germany and wrote frequently on film for the *Frankfurter Zeitung*, where he served as an editor for its feuilleton—he was also very concerned with the specificity of sound film and so took pains to distinguish cinematic and uncinematic usage of sound and music, the cinematic naturally being the only ones proper to film. Cinematic usages are those that acquiesce to the visual nature of the medium. "For sound films to be true to the basic aesthetic principle, their significant contribution must originate with the pictures" (1997, 103). This does not mean that films are best silent, that talking should be eliminated, or that synchronized sound should be avoided; instead, speech needs to be "de-emphasized" or "undermined," or the emphasis shifted from "meanings of speech to its material qualities" (106–11). The idea is "to play down dialogue with a view to reinstating the visuals" (106).

At first glance, this would seem to make Kracauer opposed to the classical system and its emphasis on dialogue, yet nowhere does he in fact question the centrality of dialogue for sound film. Indeed, he acknowledges: "The bulk of existing talkies continues to center on dialogue" (1997, 104). He only insists that cinematic uses of speech require the subordination of dialogue to the images; in fact, read carefully, he only insists that dialogue and soundtrack *not* subordinate the images. Insofar as he is willing to accept the dominance of dialogue when it "undermined itself from within" by running away from sense, as with Groucho Marx, or dissolved back into its "material qualities," as with Eliza's speech in *Pygmalion* (1938), Kracauer's professed insistence on visual dominance yields whenever sound or voice serves to reveal in its own way the materiality of physical reality, its resistance to submitting to form, so long as dialogue does not then assert itself to impose anything more than its own accidental form back onto the images. (His well-known celebration of the drunken pianist similarly valorizes the potential unruliness of music [137–38].) At any rate, Kracauer's theory of the sound film recognizes the importance of narrative—indeed, when writing about music, Kracauer notes that the primary affiliation of the music is with the narrative, not the visuals (142)—and that dialogue holds a privileged place on the soundtrack. This is the principal reason he needed to counter the attack from Eisenstein and Pudovkin on synchronous sound: its theoretical reduction had been influential but left too much of sound film unexplained.

Roger Manvell and John Huntley and "Functional" Music

Roger Manvell and John Huntley (1957) follow a similar typological scheme to Spottiswoode and Kracauer, albeit even more simple and formalistic. Manvell was a prolific author and film historian, as well as the founding director of the British Film Institute (BFI). Huntley was also a prolific author, and, before likewise joining the BFI, he was trained as an assistant to Muir Mathieson, who worked as a music director and conductor on many high-profile British films. Manvell and Huntley begin with a threefold division of the soundtrack into the usual components of speech, music, and effects (1957, 60). Each of these is then divided in turn, with the first term being realistic, the second more stylized. This is more or less Spottiswoode's scheme of realistic and unrealistic sound. For effects, this division is "spot" and "library." Spot sound is sound recorded at the time of filming, whereas library sounds are those added after the fact.[8] In this case the distinction does not actually coincide with realistic

---

[8] In the text, the authors note that reverb and other artificially produced effects generally belong to the second type of effect, but almost as a separate category.

and stylized, since library sounds often sound more realistic than sounds re-corded on set, but library sounds are constructed, added after the fact, and so are rendered rather than real.

Manvell and Huntley's treatment of sound effects reveals that their scheme is based in production rather than function or aesthetics. Whereas Spottiswoode would claim that the difference between spot and library is in-significant so long as they both sound realistic, Manvell and Huntley require an opposition that stretches from actual to stylized, so they turn to produc-tion rather than aesthetics to locate it. This way of constructing the opposition also suggests a confusion between reproduction and representation that the authors have not effectively worked out. For dialogue, the division is "realistic" and "stylized or poetic." Here, the manner of delivery or construction of the dialogue marks it as "normal" or something other than "normal" speech.

The division for music is "realistic" and "functional," and each of these is in turn divided, the "realistic" into song performance, dance, and musical (or opera). The difference between song performance and musical (or opera) is that in the first case the performance belongs to the world of the film, whereas in the second case characters express themselves through singing without being aware that they are doing so. Dance can likewise be either a perfor-mance or more akin to the situation in musical or opera where characters are not aware they are dancing. "Functional music" has a number of types, mostly related to mood and scene type, and this is their term for the nondiegetic score. They dislike the term "background music," because they think it is a misnomer. Good film music, they argue, does not recede into the background but instead "move[s] audiences to believe in [the] living reality [of a scene] by playing insistently upon their emotional responses" (1957, 72). Functional music "'points,' underlines, links, emphasizes, or interprets the action, be-coming part of the dramatic pattern of the film's structures" (73).

Although more systematic than Spottiswoode's scheme, Manvell and Huntley's typology is less grammatical. The formalism also leads more toward a scheme of identity than to function. Manvell and Huntley's scheme moves away from realism as stylizations, but they are not as able to account for the representation of realism itself, at least not as well as Spottiswoode.

On the Difference between Realistic and Nonrealistic Music

Spottiswoode distinguishes realistic and nonrealistic uses of sound, and Kracauer offers actual and commentative to mark a similar divide. Manvell and Huntley follow Spottiswoode's terminology and note that filmmakers gen-erally observe this distinction for music and sound. For Spottiswoode, the cat-egory of the nonrealistic is akin to stylization that can be accomplished in a variety of ways. Manvell and Huntley also recognize an element of stylization, especially for dialogue, but their focus on music and the fact that they wrote well after the codification of the classical system mean they have a more difficult time recognizing a continuum. "Realistic" both for Spottiswoode and for Manvell and Huntley designates more or less what we would today call diegetic; "actual" serves the same purpose for Kracauer. This is music motivated by the narrative situation and that belongs to the world represented, that is, music that is "part of the action," "realistic" to the narrative representation. Spottiswoode (1935) speaks of film in terms of illusion, the "means by which the film is made independent of a realistic recording of events and objects." Illusion in this sense is essentially the way the diegetic emerges as a fictional world from what appears on film. In this way, Spottiswoode argues, films "achieve illusory ends by means not purely illusive" (47).

Although all these writers are describing the classical system, they nevertheless have somewhat different emphases. For Spottiswoode, realistic also means that the recorded sound on the soundtrack accords with the naturalistic expectations of what we see. His conception, though consistent with the diegesis as an imagined reality drawn from the recordings given on film, is not yet firmly wedded to representation and narrative. For Manvell and Huntley, however, narrative representation looms large, as is quite apparent in their discussion of nonrealistic sound and music. The same can be said for Kracauer (1997) and commentative music, "an artificial ingredient" (138), music "not belonging to the world presented" (118). For Spottiswoode, "nonrealistic" simply designates a formal departure from naturalistic expectations; the result is a stylization that can be interpreted in a wide variety of ways, one of which suggests a commentative function and the narrative distance expected of commentary. For Kracauer, "nonrealistic" has disappeared as an articulated concept, and "commentative," which favors a conception of narrative distance over stylization, has assumed its place as opposed to "actual." In this way, Kracauer essentially folds Spottiswoode's other functions of evocation, contrast, and dynamics under the commentative. Manvell and Huntley proceed similarly. For them, nonrealistic treatment is dichotomous with realistic sound and is marked though special production techniques: stylized speech, library sounds, and functional music. "Nonrealistic" music is functional, "part of the background effects for the establishment of atmosphere" (1957, 41), and it does not require a source in the world depicted on the screen.

In this respect, Manvell and Huntley's functional music is a descendent of pit music, the music of silent film. But in the classical system, nonrealistic music ultimately receives its warrant from its indirect relation to the narrative world. It is characterized not so much by stylization as by its construction or positing of a space apart from the narrative, its status as nondiegetic. Manvell and Huntley point out that a "controlled use" of the distinction between realistic and nonrealistic music distinguishes music in the sound film, and it was a hard-won distinction. Not just any deployment of nonrealistic music, even music loosely coordinated with mood, can effectively establish nondiegetic space: Manvell and Huntley complain that many composers in the early sound era followed the procedure of the silent era of a "blind use of a continuous background score" (1957, 41). The metaphor of blindness is worth attending to, not just because it seems a displacement of the deafness of the silent film, but also because they attribute it to the music: this is music that can evidently not "see" the picture, that, therefore, falls out of harmony (synchronization) with it. "Blind" also evokes a kind of primitive uncontrollable emotion—blind passion or blind drive—one that follows a compulsion untempered by reason. In terms of the classical system, we can say that this music is also, like the silent film apparatus, somewhat deaf to talk. In silent film, this is understood to be beneficial: music substitutes for this missing voice. But when the voice is present on the soundtrack and the music still chatters on, then there is a potential for crosstalk, for an indifference to actual dialogue no longer in need of substitution; this music is "blind" because it cannot "see" that the picture talks, and if music's presence is nevertheless deemed appropriate or even necessary, its role is now as supplemental support rather than substitute. And this change also leads to technical solutions, such as the "up and downer," a piece of automated mixing equipment that ensures that dialogue remains intelligible and music subordinate.[9]

From the foregoing discussion, we can surmise that silent-era methods evidently did not accord well with the narrative dichotomy of diegetic and nondiegetic music, and by 1957, when Manvell and Huntley were writing, the sound film clearly required something other than a silent film score. Still, Manvell and Huntley do not distinguish the narrative status of the music (whether it belongs to the representation) and its function (forming a background to the situation). Moreover, they do not adequately specify the function of the background, whether it is to be one of supporting the other elements of the soundtrack or the general narrative, at least in part because they understand "background" not as a narrative function of setting, atmosphere, and attention but as an evaluative criterion of artistic status. In particular, they do not fully recognize that diegetic sound can, and often does, perform this function so the choice for filmmakers is not just between diegetic and nondiegetic music, but representationally between a realistic background sound (which might be diegetic music) and a stylized, "nonrealistic" one (which would almost certainly be nondiegetic music).

The conceptual problem here is not simply the "nonrealistic" grounding of nondiegetic music in the narrative world; the problem also follows from

---

[9] Alberto Cavalcanti (1939) agreed with Manvell and Huntley that "in early talkies [music] ran under most of the action and even went so far as to point it with synchronized effects which were derived from the manner of the 'silent' orchestra—and were just about the last word in outrageous absurdity" (34).

an incomplete analysis of the representational properties of the soundtrack, which can extend from either of two poles: (1) the realistic mimetic synchronization found in early sound film practice and (2) the unreal stylized but also "blind" treatment found in silent film practice. This conceptual lacuna seems to have been a product of internalizing the classical system and the proto-narratological dichotomies it fosters. Writing just as the classical system was codifying, Spottiswoode is subtler in his understanding of narrative and representation, allowing a wider range of potential solutions. Writing long after the codification, Manvell and Huntley (but also Kracauer) cede much of this subtlety for a crisper narrative conception. Or we might wonder whether they no longer know what to say about more amorphous alternatives that do not fit neatly into the conception. In any event, the finer continuities of stylization disappear under the blunt dichotomies of narrative, and later theorists recall the possibility of stylization primarily in embarrassed and defensive remarks about mickey-mousing and peculiar allowances made for animation and comedy. Manvell and Huntley dismiss both poles as being either antiart or overly indifferent to the film, and perhaps they were: in terms of the sound film, the poles did represent archaic practices less commonly encountered when the classical system was at its zenith.

4

Language, Semiotics, and Deleuze

The Linguistic Analogy

Raymond Spottiswoode's *The Grammar of Film* (1935), discussed in the previous chapter for its typological insights into the codification of the continuity system of sound film, is explicit in grounding constructive elements of film on an analogy with language. During the time he was writing, it was relatively common to consider film a universal language and to conceptualize the techniques of continuity editing as forming a grammatical syntax for film. At the end of the 1950s, Roger Manvell and David Huntley (1957) no longer explicitly imposed a grammar but focused instead on the narrative conventions, and this too was in keeping with a temporary turn in film theory away from the linguistic analogy as leading to unwieldy typologies. Nevertheless, buttressed by the rise of structural linguistics in the academy and its offshoot of semiotics, the idea of grammar and the relation of film (and its music) to language again became an important trend in theories of the soundtrack after about 1960.

The linguistic analogy has proved tempting for theorizing the logical and senselike construction of music and cinema, both of which have been frequently celebrated as universal languages that are easily able to transcend linguistic difference. And music and cinema do share a certain proximity to verbal language. Kathryn Kalinak opens her treatise on film music, *Settling the Score* (1992), by noting an association of music and language:

> Music is a coherent experience, and because it is a system passing internal logic, it has frequently been compared to language. While fraught with difficulty, a linguistic analogy does, at least on a preliminary level, help to reveal something fundamental about how music works. Like language and other systems of communication, music consists of a group of basic units, a vocabulary, if you will, and a set of rules for arranging these units into recognizable and meaningful structures, a grammar. (4)

Yet the analogy is also uneasy. It's not clear, for instance, what Kalinak means by the claim that the basic units constitute a vocabulary; theorists like Deryck Cooke (1959) have argued that the tonal conventions working on melodic shapes constitute something like a vocabulary that allows music to articulate a figure like "joy"; but *pace* Kalinak individual pitches are closer to phonemes or syllables than to words, and the far more usual way of theorizing music's relation to language is to say music has a syntax but no definable content. It is also somewhat remarkable that Kalinak opens her discussion of film music with a discussion of "the language of music," but, while she notes that the linguistic analogy is "fraught" (1992, 4), nowhere does she mention that film similarly has a long and fraught tradition of being theorized in relation to language. Indeed, this shared fraught relationship with the linguistic analogy marks an affinity that offers a point where music and cinema can be productively compared and contrasted.

The formal analytical systems developed to describe both music and film also have strong linguistic underpinnings. And for both the resemblance to language has been located in grammar. Although music theory usually deploys its terms descriptively, almost all of them originate in theories that model (rather than simply describe) musical structure and syntax. For instance, phrase structure, which is basic to musical form theory, follows the linguistic analogy closely, going so far as to borrow much of its terminology from the divisions of classical grammar. Harmonic theory is likewise clearly based on linguistic models of grammatical syntax. With respect to cinema, film grammars, such as that proposed by Spottiswoode, which served to establish and legitimize the rules of continuity editing, form the basis for elementary film analysis. Spottiswoode's "grammatical" approach has been expanded in two directions in the years since its original publication in 1935—to production manuals and film appreciation textbooks. Continuity editing is to film theory more or less what harmony is to music theory, with the labeling of shots being akin to the labeling of chords. Similarly, David Bordwell's (2006) theory of "intensified continuity" stands in much the same relation to classical film editing as does the theory of extended chromatic harmony to diatonic harmony (117–89, esp. 121–38). Both continuity editing and harmonic theory address issues of continuity and logic of small-unit succession.

The languagelike qualities of both film and music made both attractive areas of study for the newly emerging field of semiotics, which developed out of structural linguistics and became an influential interdisciplinary methodology in the 1960s. The issue of film's relation to language has been even more fraught than music's, and clarifying its status has historically been the project of film semiotics, the subject of the first part of this chapter. Film semiotics is itself a reaction to earlier attempts at codifying the film language, which struggled to uphold the notion that film was organized along different lines than verbal language while also identifying its distinctive organizational principles. Prior to semiotics, most considered the concept of a film language at best a vague analogy. In the early 1960s, Jean Mitry reopened the question by insisting on a fundamental difference between film and verbal language at the level of syntax and grammar. Christian Metz followed Mitry to a certain extent, but Metz grounded his semiotic approach to film in structural linguistics, and he shifted the focus from grammar to signification. The result was a formulation that brought cinema extremely close to the conception of music as a language with a syntax but without a semantics. Film, Metz (1982) asserts, "possesses a grammar, up to a point, but no vocabulary" (213). Evidently, film and music each have a characteristic syntax that resembles that of language but a semantics that differs substantially from it. For music, this content is abstract to the point of being nugatory, syntax without a discernible content. For cinema, this content is concrete and mimetic to the point that it cannot dissolve into arbitrary signs, syntax without an arbitrary content. Thus, while both music and film are commonly called universal languages, they have also both been assessed as deficient when compared to actual verbal languages.

Although semiotics no longer holds the status in film theory it once did, its insights continue to inform thinking about film, and its importance for the soundtrack is perhaps even greater, since musical semiotics offers analytical methodologies aimed at musical semantics and signification that are well suited for understanding music's role in the soundtrack.

After a discussion of semiotics and its application to the soundtrack, I conclude this chapter with a discussion of Gilles Deleuze's work on cinema. Although not a semiotician and in many ways very critical of Metz's project, Deleuze's approach to the image draws heavily on semiotic and structuralist modes of analysis, and his goal of creating a taxonomy of images fits as well with a general semiotics approach—Deleuze is in fact explicitly guided by Charles S. Peirce's tripartite analysis of the sign—as it does with philosophy.

Jean Mitry and Language and Rhythm

Jean Mitry is a transitional figure, who worked to mediate the many disputes in classical film theory, especially between realism and constructivism—that is, whether film was fundamentally a reproduction of reality or a representation of it. Although Mitry accepts that the photographic basis of the image ties film to a depiction of reality, he does not believe that film reveals reality in the way André Bazin or Siegfried Kracauer do. "Film images form an arbitrary reality altogether different from 'true' reality." For Mitry, film is an artwork, something made, even if the image is recorded automatically on film. "[Cinema] replaces continuous reality . . . with a series of discontinuous fragments. It selects the framing, angles, and setups and arranges them according to their relative durations, giving them meanings outside the 'global' future time of the universe from which they have been taken" (1997, 168). Reality, in other words, does not simply occur in film. It always comes marked with a vision as a perspective among other perspectives. And that perspective does not consume the world.

> What is unspoiled, what the image really does reveal, is not reality-in-itself but a new appearance correlative with the direct reality of the world and its objects and with what might be called metaphorically the perception of the camera, which, above and beyond the wishes and choice of the director, automatically applies this segmentation of space and therefore the reconstruction of reality, which, by that fact, stops being objective and direct. (169)

Mitry began writing about film in the silent era, witnessed the transition to the sound film, was a founder of the Cinémathèque français (which became a major research center for film history), and then, after World War II, became one of the first professors of film. Mitry was also interested in a variety of approaches—psychological, semiotic, cultural—that would be developed at length by others. Yet his methodological eclecticism and emphasis on film materials and aesthetics place him closer to the first generation of theorists of the classical system like Eisenstein, Pudovkin, Balázs, and Arnheim than to the typologists or to the semioticians and critical theorists that would follow in his wake. Mitry's concern is ultimately with the film and the art that organizes it rather than all that impinges on that process or makes it possible. At the same time, Dudley Andrew (1976) notes an important shift of perspective that places him in greater proximity to later theorists. "With Mitry," Andrew writes, "one feels that 'ideas about film' have replaced 'film' as the central focus of investigation" (181). Mitry, Andrew notes, has a penchant for synthesis and mediating disputes, and his general approach is to present a problem, consider a set of authors' responses to it, and then propose his own solution, which usually involves finding a middle ground (187–88).

Mitry's explication of the concept of film language is typical of his procedure. Mitry is troubled by older conceptions of cinema as a universal language, and he finds grammars and typologies that classify shots and mandate proper procedures for continuity editing to be especially wrongheaded. If cinema is indeed a universal language, it is not due to such rules but because the language of film uses images to express ideas, much as verbal language uses words to express ideas. Although he states "categorically that the cinema is not a language" (1997, 38), he means by this not what he seems to say—"cinema is not a language"—but only that cinema is not a language like verbal language: it does not use words as its principal medium of expression. For Mitry, the affinities of film language with verbal language have been misconstrued; the analogies in particular have been drawn in the wrong places. Film and verbal language both relate to thought, but thought is not, Mitry says, linguistic in structure.

That is, "language" in the most general sense is any way a thought is expressed, and verbal language is but one way—the most direct way, perhaps—of doing so. Film is another way: it expresses thought in images.

> Language implies different systems, each of which has its own set of symbols but which *combine in the formulation of ideas* of which they are merely in the formal expression (in whatever form they appear). Thus verbal language and film language express themselves by using *different* elements in *different* organic systems. (16, emphasis in original)

Unlike verbal language, film language is not a semiotic system based around the organization of arbitrary signs. "A film *first and foremost* comprises images, images *of something*. A system of images whose purpose is to describe, develop, and narrate an event or series of events." Images differ from words in that they do not have arbitrary significations. They are always "images of something." Mitry here recalls Husserl's account of consciousness as "consciousness of" to pursue a similarity between images and thought. Mitry continues:

> However, these images—according to the chosen narrative—become organized into a system of signs and symbols; *in addition* they become (or have the possibility of becoming) signs. They are not uniquely signs, like words, but first and foremost objects and concrete reality, objects which take on (or are given) a predetermined meaning. It is in this way that the cinema is a language; it *becomes* language to the extent that it is *first of all* representation and by virtue of that representation. It is, so to speak, a language in the second degree. (15, emphasis in original)

By "language in the second degree," Mitry means that film is an artwork and so its language is more akin to the expression of literary language that fuses the unique form of the artistic work with language per se. Verbal language presupposes a distinction between lyrical and discursive uses of it, but film does not have this distinction—it has no mundane form—which means that the structures and forms of the film language are not organized as a general or universal grammar. By grammar, Mitry means "a series of rules applicable to all (with rare exceptions) constructions of whatever kind specific to language" (2000, 26). Films do exhibit the appearance of syntactic regularity, but the "rules" are immanent to the film; they flow from the narrative logic of the particular film rather than from any kind of general syntax or grammar, as there is no external rule that obligates one image to follow another. Shots are linked by nothing other than the order required of them by the narrative (28), and it is therefore the logic of the narrative rather than some a priori syntax of film that determines their sequence.

Mitry's conception of the film language is image based. Like most of the classical theorists, he presumes that film is primarily a visual medium. He does not, however, object to sound film and is even open to dialogue, which he recognizes as the most important element of the soundtrack. At the most schematic level, sound film, he says, develops two series: one of images, the other of dialogue, the latter of which he calls "text." These constitute two axes connected through synchronization. Shot 1 occurs at the same time as dialogue segment 1, shot 2 with dialogue segment 2, and so forth. As Mitry notes, there are a variety of ways this system might be ordered. The dialogue segments might be determined by the series of shots, the shots might be determined by the series of dialogue segments, or the two series might in fact develop in a relatively autonomous way. (Mitry considers this third option obliquely during his discussion of voiceover in *Hiroshima, mon amour* [1959].) While he acknowledges that a film can be constructed around either axis, he claims that only a sequence formed around an image axis is properly filmic. The situation where the dialogue axis dominates is characteristic of theater and results in an illustrated sound recording, not a film. "This is dialogue fleshed out with images. The images may well be pretty enough in themselves; they may provide a pleasant enough spectacle. But it is not what might be called film expression—which is what we mean when we say of a film, 'it's not cinema'" (1997, 235). For films constructed on the image axis, the important thing is that

> continuity is based in essence on the visual development which forms the framework, the *structural axis* of the film. This does not mean that the text [dialogue] cannot serve as a hinge, altering or constantly deflecting the continuity, since this is precisely the purpose of its continual interventions. But the logical development and principal significations are based on the development of the images, not on verbal associations. (234–35, emphasis in original)

The situation described by the two axes is basic, even for dialogue, and it ignores sound and music entirely. Few films, even those structured primarily around the image axis, follow the schema closely. Dialogue is frequently presented against a reaction shot; and cutting of image and dialogue together as implied by his supporting diagram is actually somewhat rare because it gives undue emphasis to the edit point. The reaction shot is an instructive audiovisual figure, not just because it places image and sound into potential counterpoint, but also because it shifts the focus from the delivery of the words to their effect on a listener, and this effect is visible, represented in the reaction. In that respect, the reaction shot does emphasize the image axis as the basis for construction. And yet this visual emphasis only appears by virtue of the continuity of the dialogue on the soundtrack. Reaction shots do occur in silent film, but they are deployed differently, as the reaction follows from the previous image (or by implication in reaction to something offscreen), not from a response to dialogue.

With respect to sound and music, Mitry has little to say, and this is in part because he does not have much to say about aspects of film that are not central to the logic of narrative. The narrative is carried primarily by the image and the dialogue, so Mitry's concern is ensuring the subordination of dialogue to image. As long as the subordination takes place, Mitry is willing to grant dialogue a place; and the same presumably goes for noises and diegetic music as well. In these cases, dialogue, noise, and music all become properties of the image. In semiotic terms sound is indexical, in the sense that diegetic sound, whether dialogue, noise, or music, is understood to be caused by bodies in the world of the film. And the signification becomes properly indexical when the sound is offscreen.

Mitry does in fact develop an account of indexical (or what his translator calls "indical") signification that can be productively extended to the sound. Drawing explicitly on American semiotician Charles S. Peirce, Mitry (2000) identifies three types of indexical signification: the indical, the allusive, and the symbolic. "In a shot showing the corner of a garden, a doll can be seen lying on some stone steps. Inevitably, the toy suggests the presence of a little girl. It is an *index*" (103, emphasis in original). The doll is an index to the extent that it signifies not an imaginary play friend or pretend baby, but the little girl. Mitry then proceeds to develop a tripartite typology of the index. The properly indical sign is indirect; it presumes a unity that we infer rather than something given, so it requires only the sign itself. "But it is only an index if we have not yet seen the little girl. In fact, her presence is not guaranteed, at least in the immediate context" (103). The contrary case where the unity was first presented but is now withheld is a different type of index. "On the other hand, if we have observed the doll during the preceding shots, it would be *allusive*" (103, emphasis in original). Finally, a third case occurs when the index signifies from within a further relation. "But, if we learned that the little girl has disappeared and if we were shown, after a wide-angle showing the parents looking for her, a close-up of the doll, then this object becomes a *symbol*" (103, emphasis in original).

Although Mitry doesn't mention it, this schema follows a typical analysis of Pierce with a firstness (index), secondness (allusion), and thirdness (symbol) of the indexical sign. The index proper and the allusion are both indices of absence. The first marks an absence where we do not recognize the referent (it is indefinite) except in a general way; the sign comes before reference is complete. We see smoke and presume fire; we hear a knock at the door and presume a visitor on the other side. The second marks an absence where we recognize the broken link; the sign comes after we have observed an indexical pair. We see fire and then we see smoke from a distance; the smoke now alludes to that fire. We hear a familiar voice from another room. The allusion introduces a distance or gap between sign and definite referent. The symbolic index is an index of lack. Here, the index signifies through a relation: the missing girl. In the case of fire, smoke in the distance might signify that a feared attack has occurred. The famous pince-nez dangling from the mast in *Battleship Potemkin* (1925) signifying that the aristocratic doctor has been thrown overboard is another famous example.

Mitry does not extend this schema of indexical signification to the sound-track, but it is productive to do so. Indical sound would be sounds that precede an image or that are stated without an image. Earlier, I mentioned a knock at the door. Other examples include offscreen nature sounds and ambient sounds, but also the introduction of a character through offscreen sound, such as a monster. The important aspect of indical sound is that the referent remains indefinite. Allusive sound is offscreen sound that occurs when we know the identity of the sound because we have seen a depicted body emit it. Perfectly ordinary instances of offscreen sound such as the dialogue of reac-tion shots are typical of this allusive sound. Here sound alludes to a world that is more than can be shown. Indexical sound that is also symbolic is a more difficult case, as it is both symbolic and an index of lack. Higgins listening to the phonograph record of Liza's voice near the end of *Pygmalion* (1938) or *My Fair Lady* (1964) would qualify. In a more complicated way, "As Time Goes By" in *Casablanca* (1942) also serves as an index of lack: the relationship between Ilsa and Rick in Paris.

The situation with accompanying music is more complicated. Mitry gives it more attention than noises or diegetic music, but he is uncertain about how to deal with it and mostly confines it negatively through prohibitions rather than positively through functions. Partly this is a product of his synthetic method where he defines the problem, examines the positions on the problem, and then finds a middle ground. With respect to music in film, the primary problem is why it is there in the first place. In fact, Mitry admits that sound film can often do without music.

> The tiresome orchestrations supposed to bring out the highlights in the drama and create an apparently essential atmosphere are more of a hin-drance than a help. A film can quite easily dispense with their acoustic adornments, particularly when its action deals with psychological or so-cial realities which create their own duration. Only dreams, fairy tales, or fantasy films—being in a sense more in line with silent films in any case—can benefit from a *continuous* acoustic background. (1997, 249, emphasis in original)

Mitry does not discount music altogether. He does, however, take issue with the usual functions attributed to music. "[Music's] place is not to comment on the imagery, to paraphrase the visual expression, to sustain its rhythm—except in one or two exceptional cases—or to have value or significance of its own" (249). Instead, Mitry draws an analogy with dialogue. "Good dialogue need not have any meaning, any logical dialectic—especially when it is divorced from the images which might give it meaning. Good film music can do without musical structure provided that its intrusion *into the film* at a specific moment should have a precise signification" (249, emphasis in original). Because its primary responsibility is to the film, film music can sacrifice its own coherence and gain an appropriate form and meaning from the film context. But Mitry is not clear what a "precise signification" is. He tells us what it is not: "Film music is not explanation; nor is it accompaniment; it is an *element of signification* (no more no less) but from which it gains all its power once [it is] associated with other elements: images, words, and sounds" (249, emphasis in original). This is very obscure, but we can take from it that music belongs to the signification of the film and that music's place in the signification grants it power as it comes into relation both with the image and with the rest of the soundtrack. Music becomes an "element of signification" when it can draw something specific or unusual from the relation. "Placed in a visual context, it must establish the signifying reactions through contrast or unusual association" (249).

Mitry explains the power of music with a short explanation of how the theme is used in *Stagecoach* (1939). This theme, Mitry says, is "a simple folk song"—"Bury Me on the Lone Prairie"—arranged for the film.

> At the beginning of the film, we follow a stagecoach in a series of tracking shots, with the folk song playing behind; then we see the stagecoach only at the start of each successive part of the journey, this time in much shorter shots. Now, while our attention is drawn to action inside the stagecoach, the theme tune (which we are still hearing) translates the movement of the coach, giving the film the dynamic lift it needs. By overlapping the story-telling, the music first of all signifies through its relation with the images, and then, through a kind of symbolic transference, it assumes the descriptive role originally assigned to them. (1997, 252)

The music for the stagecoach does not really comment on the scene, paraphrase or explain the action, or serve as a mere accompaniment. The arrangement instead captures the dynamic quality of the coach in motion but without replicating in direct fashion the rhythm of the journey or the action. The "precise signification" here then occurs on two levels:

- First, that of mobility, where a background of traveling music— more visceral and concrete than the scenery provided through back projection rolling past the windows—is set in contrast to whatever dramatic action plays out inside the coach. Mitry does not mention it, but the music frequently departs from the coach music to register dramatic actions inside for reasons that are not always altogether intelligible except that it moves the signification from the external dynamism of the mobile stagecoach to the interior dynamics of character psychology.
- Second, that of "symbolic transference," where music does not describe the scenery but instead places the moving stagecoach in

the context of the landscape, where the concept of "civilization" is conveyed by the stagecoach, which by turns moves through its contrary (a land seemingly vacant and brimming with exploitable potential) and opposite (a land seemingly inhospitable and even hostile).

The coach music thus associates a buoyant optimism carried by the arrangement (a buoyancy at odds with its grim lyrics) with this dynamic mobility, and the trail the coach traverses becomes the thinnest of threads binding the civilized world together. Interruptions to this music from without—the intrusion of the primitivist "Indian" motifs especially but also of other obstacles encountered along the way—reinforce the larger ideological schema, based on an oscillation between civilized outposts such as forts and towns and the desperate time in the stagecoach on the uncivilized trail, on the one hand, and an awareness of the internal fissures and ironic reversals that structure civilization and make it possible, on the other. The stagecoach too is overflowing with these rifts and reversals: the banker is trying to abscond with the money, the gentleman is a gambler and a scoundrel, the doctor is a drunk, the wife is prejudiced, the prisoner is the hero, the sheriff has arrested the hero not to punish him but to protect him, the prostitute has a heart of gold, and so forth. As is typical in westerns, the peace of civilization is maintained through a cultural violence that purges difference (the doctor and the prostitute are both driven from town for their violation of social mores) and insists that the originary violence be turned outward toward the expansion of civilization through the appropriation and domestication of land.

In any event, along with the title of the film, the score emphasizes the stagecoach over any of the fixed places it stops at. Although the places are all introduced with music, the music is different in each case, despite framing and cinematography that emphasize the similarities. Each departure of the stagecoach, by contrast, is underscored by a variant of the theme. At a structural level, the recurrence of image and music, even varied, has the effect of bestowing on these sequences an initiatory function. The appearance of the theme thus helps articulate the formal rhythm of the film, where the stagecoach or trail is not a transition between situations that take place in forts and towns but instead an initiating action where fine differences yield new situations, some of which occur in the coach, others in town.

This reading of *Stagecoach* through its music goes further than Mitry to tease out implications of what he might mean by "precise signification." It also attends to the relation of music to film rhythm, an important concept for Mitry, recurring throughout his *Aesthetics and Psychology of the Cinema*. Mitry approaches rhythm much in the same way as he does language. Just as film language needs to be disentangled from verbal language, so too film rhythm needs to be separated from musical rhythm. For Mitry, musical rhythm entails both the cyclical repetitions of meter and the more particularized rhythmic formations. And it takes place as a musical development that allows the expression of symmetry and other formal figures. Rhythm is in this sense essential to music, and music often seems to emerge from rhythm. Visual rhythm, by contrast, is more a product of the narrative sequence. "Film rhythm is linear. It is the rhythm of narrative, whose continuous flow never repeated itself" (2000, 221). It "organizes significations" rather than the material itself as in the case of musical rhythm (1997, 272). In this respect too, film rhythm is akin to film syntax. "To all intents and appearances, film rhythm is not free, whereas musical rhythm (the rhythm of sounds with no concrete reality to further and, therefore, no static qualities) has no other referent than its formal needs" (2000, 221). Mitry points out the difficulty when musical and film rhythms are simply subordinated.

> Music becomes "deformed" if it tries to follow the image and the image becomes stiff and "mechanical" when it becomes subordinate to the music. It is therefore vital to ensure that, through the music, the internal reality is directed outward to the external world, providing it with the basic units of rhythm crystallizing either into relative tempi or static spatial dimensions. (1997, 253)

In the case of *Stagecoach*, the musical rhythm of the theme serves primarily to emphasize the motion of the coach. Music does not follow the image so much as its association with the coach in motion articulates larger filmic rhythms that would be less sharply defined in the absence of music.

For Mitry, the rhythmic quality of film music is most apparent in the silent film, where the rhythmic structure of music gives the audience "the sensation of duration actually experienced" (1997, 248). Silent film, Mitry believes, provides little measure of passing time, and without sound the temporal flow lacks strong direction. The image spools off at an arbitrary speed and becomes unhinged from felt time.

> The "unrealistic" nature of silent film makes it incapable of allowing the audience to experience a real feeling of *duration*, of *time passing*. The time experienced by the characters in the drama, the relationship in time between shots or sequences, may be perfectly well recognized—but it is *understood*, not *experienced*. (248, emphasis in original)

Although sound film is more realistic, the function of music does not change. "Its role in 'realistic' films is pretty much the same as it was envisaged in the silent era: to provide the audiences with a feeling of duration, an idea of time relative to which the psychological time is defined" (253).

Semiotics of Film/Semiotics of Music

Although Mitry drew on semiotics and appreciated many of its insights, his resistance to the idea that film could be structured like a verbal language separated him from film semiology proper, which understood semiotics to be a form of general linguistics. As Christian Metz (1974a) notes, "The film semiologist tends, naturally, to approach his subject with methods derived from linguistics" (108). Methodologically, this understanding means that se-miotics examined film in terms of its analogy to language. Whereas classical film theorists had also pursued an analogy to language, they conceived this analogy in terms of grammar and syntax; semiotics, by contrast, examines the analogy in terms of structure and signification.

Semiotics is generally defined "as the study of signs, signification and signifying systems" (Stam, Burgoyne, and Flitterman-Lewis 1992, 1). It emerged as part of the so-called linguistic turn, but it sees its methodology as "scientific" compared to impressionistic, literary, and philosophical approaches of earlier methods. Film semiotics is also fundamentally concerned with "the study of the mechanics of films themselves" (Andrew 1976, 217). It involves taking apart things, isolating what signifies or bears signifying functions, and usually entails discerning the various codes that are operating to produce the complex signification of the object. Under semiotics, the object appears as a wholly constructed object. The object also appears as a site of conflict, where varying codes vie to articulate and determine the signification of the film.

As a methodological approach, semiotics is common to both music and film studies. But there are significant differences in how the method has been developed in each discipline. Partly this has to do with intellectual tradition. The semiotics of film, originating in France, grew from the structuralist school of Claude Lévi-Strauss and ultimately from the Swiss linguist Ferdinand de Saussure. Saussure understood the sign as binary in structure, being divided into the sign and its referent or signifier and signified, and his key claims in-cluded the requirements that language use signs that are arbitrary and that language is a system of double articulation. The semiotics of music, by con-trast, has been more influenced by American philosopher Charles S. Peirce than by Saussure. Peirce understood the sign as ternary in structure, adding the interpretant, the particular way we form a relation between the signifier and signified, to the binary structure of Saussure. Beyond the basic conceptual differences in terms of the construction of the sign as binary or triadic, the emphases of the two semiotics are also somewhat different. Those from the Saussurean tradition tend to stress codes and language systems, whereas those from the Peircean tradition tend to be concerned more with the classification and operation of the signs.

The semiotics of film emphasizes reflections on methodology as a basic part of the method, so much so that many critics of the approach often complained that the development of analytical tools took precedence over insights the tools provided into actual films. As Francesco Casetti (1999) writes,

> The identification with methodology exposed semiotics to controversy. Its will to being scientific was perceived by some as a turning point, by others as a sign of its aridity and asceticism. Its attention to the instruments more than to the objects of analysis was for some a sign of rigor, while for others it was an excuse for abandoning the concrete reality of cinema. (132)

Metz's work from the 1960s and early 1970s, though always intriguing and insightful, often seems curiously apart from either cinema or film as he defines the terms. In his writing from this period—for example, *Language and Cinema* and *Film Language*—methodological concerns dominate, and the object, whether emphasis falls on film or on cinema, seems selected to serve as a means of reflecting on the semiotic method. For this reason, the nature of the questions Metz explores, especially whether and to what extent film is in fact a language or language system and how semiotics therefore might apply to it, often seems to position his writings more as contributions to general semiotics than to the semiotics of film.

Ultimately, Metz concludes that film is not in fact a language system. Although film does have systemic elements including codes, these are structured quite differently than those of natural language. Filmic signs are all at least partially motivated rather than being wholly arbitrary. The primary signification in film is thus mimetic; it works by analogy, determined by resemblance (1974a, 108–9). Because the image was not itself coded but only analogical, Metz therefore refuses a semiotics of the image. Shots cannot be the equivalent of phonemes or even words. Instead, they are more akin to sentences, with montage serving as a punctuating means of articulation rather than the fine control of meaning through signification that comes from the double articulation of language (115). On his refusal of the semiotics of the image, Metz follows Roland Barthes's reversal of Saussure. Saussure believed that linguistics was an aspect of general semiotics, whereas Barthes thought semiotics was a part of general linguistics. (Mitry's approach to semiotics followed a more strictly Saussurean basis.) For Metz, then, semiotics could only apply to film to the extent that film had a language system, and it could be shown to be open to linguistic modes of structural analysis. This is one reason Metz spends so much time and effort looking for an arbitrary level of articulation in film, the analogue to the second (phonemic) articulation in language: without it, film cannot be a language, and if it cannot be language, it also cannot have a semiotics. With the recognition finally that film was indeed not a language, Metz turned to narrative and psychoanalysis to make sense of it, and I will return to these developments in chapter 6 and chapter 8.

The semiotics of music has confronted a situation somewhat different than the semiotics of film. If the semiotics of music was similar in posing a basic question like whether and to what extent music is a language system or a language and even ultimately in the kinds of answers it gave (Nattiez 1990a; Agawu 1991; Lidov 2005), the semiotics of music has developed a niche within the discipline of music theory, while its concern for meaning has also allowed semiotics to participate fruitfully in the general musicological turn toward hermeneutic studies, which have become as much a regular part of scholarly production in the discipline of musicology as they are in film studies.

Those working in applied semiotics, whether film or music, have not generally approached the soundtrack as a distinct entity, and these applications have come rather late. On the music side, this research has come mostly in the study of what are called musical topics—conventional musical codes. Philip Tagg's doctoral dissertation (2000) presents an expansive study deriving from the close semiotic examination of fifty seconds of television music. A book he wrote with Bob Clarida (2003) discusses a set of ten pieces of television music. Each discussion triangulates between a semiotic analysis of the text and an analysis of listener surveys. Tagg (1982) also devotes a long article to examining collections of mood music, which contains some six hundred items, of which he analyzed forty-four in detail. His research goal was to specify what music signified when it was explicitly presented as signifying nature. Ronald Rodman (2010) explicitly adopts an applied media semiotics model derived from Uberto Eco (1979) to understand television music. His premise is the conventional character of television and its music, and he too focuses primarily on locating, classifying, and interpreting musical topics. He examines their traditional uses such as signaling setting, mood, and character type, but also how genre organizes musical topics into codes that correspond to it, and finally how individual shows rework the conventions in characteristic and sometimes even original ways.

As we will see when we return to musical topics in chapter 7, semiotics has continued to be an important field of research on the soundtrack, but along with the weakening of linguistics as the dominant strand (and a recognition that semiotics was the general field so that not all semiotic systems needed to be languages), the applied aspect became much more prominent.

Christian Metz and Aural Objects

The semiotics of film has a strong visual bias, and it most typically considers the soundtrack only at the level of describing the whole film. Metz, for instance, divides film into five channels or "sensory orders," three of which concern the soundtrack: image, written text and graphics, dialogue, sound effects, and music (1974a, 58; 1974b, 16). The bulk of his commentary and analysis, however, concerned the signifying code of the image, even though it constituted only one of those five orders. Metz did contribute an important article on "aural objects," which argues that sounds in film are more extensions, characteristics, or components of the image than something that has sufficient autonomy to set up a real parallel or contrapuntal track. Metz does not ontologize the relation—mimetic synchronization is not necessary for film or an intrinsic property of it—but he does see the audiovisual figure of synchronization as rooted at a very deep ideological level so that it can assume an appearance as the natural state of film, which is akin to the Soviet directors' claim (Eisenstein, Pudovkin, and Alexandrov 1988) that a piece of sound film possesses a significant degree of "inertia" because of the mimetic relation. Metz (1980) writes that "ideologically, the aural source is an object, the sound itself a 'characteristic.' Like any characteristic, it is linked to the object, and that is why identification of the latter suffices to evoke the sound, whereas the inverse is not true" (26–27). As noted in the discussion of Mitry, sound conceived in this way is an index in Peircean terms. Seeing the source, we identify the sound because of the relation of causality: the body makes the sound. Semiotically, recognizing the sound, we identify the source; the sound becomes the index to the source. But concealing the source and engaging the indexical mode can cause ambiguity, because many noises sound other than they seem. Unlike the visual domain, where we recognize the object of vision as the thing itself, with sounds, "the recognition of a sound leads directly to the question: 'A sound of what?'" (25). The indexical signification of sound opens onto a hermeneutic. When we hear a sound, we do not fully apprehend it until we identify its source. The aural object without a representation of the source is underdetermined, and "if one of the two indicators [sound and source] has to be suppressed, it is curious to note that it's the aural indicator that can most easily be suppressed with the least loss of recognizability" (26). Moreover, we lack strong conceptual categories for classifying sounds so they can signify the general class of source object rather than the particularity of a certain object. A dog bark, for instance, signifies a dog object, but without the audiovisual figure of synchronized sound, it is often difficult to know that the bark came from a particular dog.

The indexicality of sound, moreover, means that sound can detach from its source object, and this makes sound both semiotically mobile and less substantial as a characteristic of the object. Another way of saying this is that the bond between sound and its source is looser than for other kinds of characteristics the object possesses. According to Metz, "the primary qualities are in general visual and tactile" (1980, 28). Sound, by contrast, is a secondary quality closer to an attribute than a substance of an object.

These observations lead immediately to issues of offscreen sound, which Metz calls one of the "classical problems of film theory" (1980, 28). The term, Metz notes, is a misnomer. It is not sound that is offscreen but rather the visual representation of its source. Metz reminds us that sound itself is never offscreen; it is, he says not quite accurately, "never 'off'": either it is audible or it doesn't exist." It is, in fact, sometimes absent, does sometimes fail to sound, and produces the desire for us to be brought closer so that we may hear that sound. The absence of a sound does not imply that the sound does not exist, only that it is not heard, or not heard clearly. In *On the Waterfront* (1954), Terry and Edie converse in a park near the docks where the horns of the ships obscure much of their dialogue. The absenting of sound here works through masking, where dialogue is obscured by the horns and is only brought occasionally into focus. Such a staging of sound works very much like the fluctuations—the concealing and revealing of sound sources—that give rise to the concept of offscreen space. We might agree that the geography mapped by the play of sound sources within the image differs from that of offscreen space, and it would undoubtedly be a worthwhile project to map out the peculiarities of that geography, but to deny sound an existence in its absence is to deny very real representational capacities of the speakers vis-à-vis the screen. Here, the image stands as an index to the missing sound, and in the reversal of the indexical signification we recognize that the voice is not the simple attribute of the image that we thought.

We might also note the inverse to Metz's claim that sound is never off: sound itself is never properly "on." Metz remarks how sound envelops:

> When it exists, it could not possibly be situated within the interior of the rectangle or outside of it, since the nature of sounds is to diffuse themselves more or less into the entire surrounding space: sound is simultaneously "in" the screen, in front, behind, around, and throughout the entire movie theater. (1980, 29)

To the extent that sound is "on," it is, in fact, "on speaker" (or rather "from speaker"), not onscreen, and its "diffusion" occurs from the sound system, not from the screen, even when the loudspeakers are located behind the screen. Nevertheless, Metz's point that the technical language used to talk about sound in film reveals the priority of visual representation in film's conceptual framework is certainly on mark, and it is worth considering the ideological stakes of this particular reduction that privileges the representation of the source over the representation of the sound, which therefore comes to appear as pure reproduction, as a faithful copy of the world.

Gilles Deleuze and the Movement-Image

Before he published *Cinema 1: The Movement-Image* in 1983, Gilles Deleuze was a highly regarded philosopher known especially for his antipsychoanalytical writings with Félix Guittari. Although Deleuze wrote occasionally about art, literature, and music, there was little to indicate that he harbored a keen interest in cinema (Bogue 2003, 1). Deleuze's cinema books recapitulate many themes from classical film theory—he calls his work on cinema "a taxonomy, an essay in the classification of images and signs" (1986, iv)—and he often questions the state of film theory at the time he was writing in the 1980s. At the same time his theory, although drawing on Peircean semiotics, is not really formal or structural. He has written instead a philosophy of cinema that works to deduce the concepts of cinema from its basic materials. He sought to devise "concepts proper to cinema, but which can only be formed philosophically" (quoted in Bogue 2003, 2).

In *Cinema 1*, Deleuze offers an intricate typology of what he calls the "movement-image" based on Peirce's semiotics, and in what follows I will extend his analysis of the movement-image to the soundtrack. The movement-image is basically the realistic image of classic film that appeals to an analogy of the sensory-motor schema that we commonly use to negotiate the world. The soundtrack can be analogously divided on the basis of its usual components and sorted into the Peircean triadic categories: firstness (music: icon of feeling), secondness (effects: index of object), and thirdness (dialogue: symbol of language). While there is much to be said in favor of this particular ordering, Deleuze actually maps out not three but six categories in his semiotics of the movement-image. He begins with the perception-image, which stands outside the Peircean framework as its zero point. He then moves on to defining images of firstness (affection-image), secondness (action-image), and thirdness (relation-image), as well as two intermediary images, the impulse-image, which falls between affection and action, and the reflection-image, which falls between action and relation.

Because Deleuze considers the soundtrack to be a component of the movement-image rather than a separate track or another image, he does not discuss the function of sound in the movement-image in much detail. His six divisions of the movement-image can, however, be productively mapped onto various aspects of the soundtrack: perception-image as point of audition and rendered sound; affection-image as nondiegetic music; impulse-image as naturalistic sound effects; action-image as dialogue; reflection-image as musical and/or theatrical performance; and relation-image as difficult soundtrack figures such as the acousmêtre, wandering dialogue, voiceover, and fantastical gap. In the following sections, I will consider each of these types in turn with special emphasis on extending the types to the soundtrack.

ZERO-POINT: PERCEPTION-IMAGE

The perception-image is basically the framing of a perception, that is, an image that offers the perception of a perception. The operation of selecting and isolating images in order to act on them in a purposeful, or at least interested, way is "framing" (Deleuze 1986, 63). The perception-image is other than the image of the thing; it is that image framed by another special image, one that reflects our interests. "In perception thus defined, there is never anything else or anything more than there is in the thing; on the contrary, there is 'less.' We perceive the thing, minus that which does not interest us as a function of our needs" (63). This defines subjectivity as "subtractive."

In terms of sound, the perception-image would consist first of all in instances of overt character focalization and point-of-audition sound. Secondarily, it consists in any device that establishes a consciousness of recording on the order of the camera consciousness that follows from techniques such as obsessive framing. Examples might include instances of overt rendering, where an attempt is made to reconstruct the impact of a sound, how it sounds to and affects the observing subject, rather than the sound as it would sound in itself, and hyperacute hearing, where details are signaled out that indicate a perceptual framing. Rendering is an addition that seeks to appear as a subtraction: it gives emphasis to the pertinent elements of the object, and it yields a perception-image insofar as it represents the impact, the incoming perception given by the object as it is selectively framed by the subject rather than an expression that has absorbed the impact in the body.

FIRSTNESS: AFFECTION-IMAGE

If, according to Deleuze, the movement-image in general is structured by an incoming perception-image that is extended into an outgoing action-image, the affection-image appears as just that interval between the perception-image and the action-image, a zone of indeterminacy that is the mark of freedom and that also allows movement to appear as expression. In terms of images, Deleuze connects the affection-image to the close-up of the face. "The affection-image is the close up, and the close up is the face . . ." (1986, 87). If all close-ups resemble one another to such a degree that the identity of the actor in close-up can be obscured, this means only that the affect does not pass through the individuality of the actor. The face in close-up nevertheless has moments of "singularity" that accrue to the affect, and particular faces and parts of faces seem predisposed toward the expression of particular affects.

The affection-image, Deleuze says, "relates movement to a 'quality' as lived state (adjective)" (65); it is "a motor tendency on a sensible nerve," as Henri Bergson puts it (quoted in Deleuze 1986, 66). As no longer perception but not yet action, the affection-image lies outside the normal spatial-temporal coordinates of the sensory-motor schema. Because it occupies the gap between perception and action, the affection-image also construes space in terms of what Deleuze calls "any-space-whatever." As David Rodowick (1997) explains, "An any-space-whatever is a space that is not yet situational. Sometimes it is an emptied space, sometimes a space whose parts are not yet linked in a given trajectory of movement. Any-space-whatevers are figures of indetermination, but this does not render them abstract universals" (64). In essence, the any-space-whatever of the affection-image occurs wherever place recedes into space, but not space as an abstract universal form spreading out continuously in contiguous segments. In this latter scientific reduction of place to the grid of space-time, particularity is obliterated by the general, universal form to reach the abstract and continuous coordinate system of a homogeneous space-time. Instead, in any-space-whatever, the particularity of the place, what Deleuze calls its "singularity," is isolated and detached from its immediate context, from everything that integrates the singularity and particularity into a larger continuous whole. Any-space-whatever is not, then, the generalized or universal space of science, but rather ordinary, singular space that has lost its homogeneous quality, in particular, the way it connects to adjoining space to produce the impression of continuity. Places like airports, ruins, and shopping malls are all instances of any-space-whatever. What distinguishes the any-space-whatever is the connection to virtuality, possibility, and potentiality, as opposed to actuality. The impression of continuity allows the singularity of any-space-whatever to link up with other singularities in innumerable ways so that new continuities are forged. "It is a space of virtual conjunction, grasped as pure locus of the possible" (1986, 109).

In the affection-image, movement assumes form as expression. Expression, though related to a cause, is not reducible to it and is indeed comprehensible without appeal to a justification by cause. This relates to the abstract character of the close-up, which appears detached from its spatial-temporal context without seeming therefore to be a fragment, a partial object. One of the characteristic aspects of the close-up is that it turns the part into a thing of its own. The affect itself is similar in this respect or follows a similar logic of decontextualization. As Béla Balázs notes, the expression of fear on the face does not require knowledge of the cause to explain it or make it comprehensible: "Expression exists even without justification, [and] it does not become expression because a situation is associated with it in thought" (quoted in Deleuze 1986, 102). What is left is an abstract coordinate system of expression, coordinates determined by potential and virtuality rather than actuality. Power and quality, intensity and reflection are the poles of expression in the affection-image. In any event, the familiar points of orientation have disappeared. It is a space empty or disconnected.

This explains the emphasis on the face in the affection-image, as well as its division into poles of faceification and faceicity, one turned toward thought, the other toward feeling. Unlike the face, which divides into thinking and feeling, with one pole or the other prevailing but both present in a continuum, the voice bisects into meaning and tone, and this difference is one reason the voice cannot be equated with the face in quite the way Michel Chion (1999) suggests when he proposes theorizing the voice on the basis of the face (6). The relation of voice to meaning tends to overwhelm its affective pole, and indeed the voice of meaning belongs more to action than to affection. If these moments of the voice are not separable, they do offer distinct faces to the voice. Sound is more detachable as quality from the body than qualities of the image. It is also more difficult to say, "It's not blood; it's red" in sound (Godard, quoted by Deleuze 1986, 118). Sound, as Metz (1980) argues, passes through its image source and aside from musical tone does not generally abstract in the manner of redness. One can say, "It is not a gunshot; it's a bang." But even "bang" does not possess the cultural range of abstraction that red does. Certainly, sound can produce a line of bang (Neumeyer 2015, 112–16) just as the line of red that engenders a "virtual conjunction" of all objects with that quality (Deleuze 1986, 118), but the sound rarely abstracts to the same extent, and when it does it tends to be taken as a musical sound.

In terms of the soundtrack, the affection-image would seem to align most closely with background music. "There are," Deleuze says, "two sorts of questions which we can put to a face . . . : what are you thinking about? . . . or what do you sense or feel?" These are questions that can be profitably put to the film through music as well. That is, music often underscores—tells us—whether the face is presenting a pensive or an affective self. Then too, the face, Balázs (1970) remarks, "abolishes space" (96), and music likewise dissolves, or rather abolishes, ambience. Music is ambience as pleasing bokeh. Fundamental to both the close-up and music is the effect of "tearing away" from realistic spatial and temporal coordinates to emphasize expression of affect. Byron Almén (2008) notes music's advantages in presenting a narrative, and they correspond remarkably to the attributes of the affection-image: "The relative freedom from descriptive specificity in music allows the dynamic interactions between events to be foregrounded, interactions that are fruitfully homologous with psychological and social dynamics and emerge all the clearer and with greater force in the absence of a descriptive milieu" (13). If for psychological and social dynamics we substitute potentiality, the power and quality of music as an expression analogous to the face, we can recognize in this quote music's affinity for the affection-image, an affinity most apparent in the virtuality or idealism of music but also in its fluidity, its flow, the way it connects qualities and potentials into intensive and reflective series.

Music, like the close-up but even more so, is decontextualized from its space of production, and if music is neither disconnected nor empty in itself, its connections to the image are, as Deleuze notes, generally the thinnest of all soundtrack components, and it frequently serves to give sound to silence but also to open up to the absolute out-of-field, that is, to the nondiegetic.

FIRST INTERMEDIARY STAGE: IMPULSE-IMAGE

If the world of the affection-image is, like music, virtual, largely imaginary and fantastic because it occupies "a space that does not yet appear as a real setting" (Deleuze 1989, 33), the world of the impulse-image is naturalistic. It gives rise to "symptoms of an originary world operating below the setting" (33) and extends the virtual, imaginary world of affection into the real world of action. "An impulse is not an affect, because it is an impression in the strongest sense and not an expression" (1986, 123). It is impression, then, not expression. The impulse-image is also not exactly a transitional stage between affection-image and action-image. Although an intermediary image, the impulse-image nevertheless has a consistency and a logic that sets it apart. The fundamental element of the impulse-image is the "formless character" of the milieu. Because in an impulse-image a milieu is recognizable as such, it is no longer an any-space-whatever; because the milieu consists of a background of "unformed matter" where cultural distinctions are not yet fully operative, this originary world resembles any-space-whatever, especially in the way it retains access to potential or virtual forces. We might also say that the originary world actualizes the power and quality of affect but in a naturalistic way rather than the realistic manner of the action-image. In an impulse-image, moreover, the forces of the originary world are too strong to be contained by the actualized milieu, which is why the impulses or drives appear as symptoms and run through the milieu, overturning it until the force has exhausted itself.

Though a kind of unconscious of the milieu, the impulses and drives of the impulse-image are not psychological, that is, a mechanism of the subject that provokes an action, even a violent one; they are instead forces operating under and from within the milieu, forces that the milieu must suppress and channel in reproducing itself but that burst forth as antagonisms when the order of the milieu proves inadequate to the task. Subjects in whom an impulse awakens are shattered by it and ripped from the milieu; but they are propelled by the force from the originary world that seeks to return rather than by the reaction to the inadequate milieu. The monstrosity and violence they exhibit is the force of the originary world acting on the subject in the milieu rather than the subject's confrontation with the milieu. Understanding an impulse-image leads not to a psychoanalytic interpretation focused on character motivation but to tracing the drive of the impulse, which leads outside psychology.

The impulse-image constitutes a unified world that encompasses everything, but it is a world without organization, or rather its organization is that of "the steepest slope," where natural discontinuities are forced into continuities by following the impulse along a path of least resistance, like a river finding its natural course. Deleuze speaks of radical beginning and absolute end being linked by the steepest slope that closes the world off and drags everything down the slope. Nevertheless, because there is a gap between beginning and ending, there is also the time and qualitative change required to traverse it, however steep the slope, even if that time, under the press of destiny, hurtles toward catastrophe, where it disperses and degrades, a reflection of entropy. If this approach to what Deleuze calls the time-image ultimately fails to reach it, that is because the law of the steepest slope itself represents "the temporality of decline" (Bogue 2003, 83); it subordinates time to the movement of traversing the slope, of following the impulse to the point that entropy degrades it.

The characteristic impulse-image is the fragment, a partial object ripped from the milieu. It differs from the affection-image close-up in retaining a discernible connection to the milieu. Where the close-up of the affection-image decontextualizes and so delivers a discontinuity that can enchain in an indefinite variety of ways, that of the impulse-image retains its context and appears as a fragment, a part. The fragment, whether as symptom or fetish, is also represented as revealing deformation. The world of the impulse-image is a world of monsters. The deformation of the symptom or fetish tends to spread across the entire milieu, until the milieu is universally degraded. It contains "the desire to change the milieu" (Deleuze 1986, 129). Impulse is about connecting, enjoying in whatever fashion, whereas affect is about "intrinsic qualities of the possible object" (129).

In terms of the soundtrack, the impulse-image would seem to align most closely with sound effects. This is most apparent in the naturalistic world that sound effects create wherein sounds pass freely from one source to another, being embodied by each in turn but settling definitively in none. Effects in this sense are like the originary world seething beneath diegetic representation. We encounter this world in moments such as the dream sequence from *The Artist* (2011), where the silent film with its music gives way to the world of effects and the things seem to spring alive. Here, the presence of the dream assimilates the originary world. But the silent film itself is, in Deleuze's terms, a naturalistic medium compared to the sound film, which is realistic.[1]

In films that receive their soundtrack definition from sound effects, say, certain cartoons, but also many action and horror films, an impulse-image draws on the status of the sound effect as a partial object. Finally, the early sound film that operated under the rule of mimetic synchronization constructed a naturalistic world, and the "inertia" of a piece of synchronized sound film may have contributed to this character inasmuch as it had the tendency to yield fragments whenever the image cut.

SECONDNESS: ACTION-IMAGE

The action-image is the most important of the movement-images, as it forms the basis of classical sound film. The poles of the action-image are sufficiently robust that each can support a distinct form of action-image.

---

[1] In this respect the scene from *The Artist* might also be interpreted as a relation-image. See "Thirdness: Relation-Image."

Large Action Form

The large action form, which Deleuze presents schematically as S-A-S', consists in an initial situation (S) contracting into an action (A), which then expands out into a modified situation (S'). Deleuze delineates five laws for the large action form, and I have glossed each of them in terms of implications for the soundtrack, especially dialogue, the primary soundtrack component of the action image.

First law. The large action-image is organized as an organic structure, and this structure is the first law. This law has two parts, which state (1) that the world of the action-image is fully encompassing and (2) that the initial situation is a microcosm of that encompassing world. This means that parts are functionally differentiated and hierarchically ordered, and nothing is superfluous. The narrative of the film follows from the tensions already at play in the initial situation. As David Rodowick (1997) summarizes, "The milieu and its forces construct a situation that englobes the protagonist, defining the challenge to which he or she must respond" (68). When we pick through an action-image we find the forces that shape the milieu—the situation and behaviors—spread throughout the image. The initial milieu contains the situation and motivates the behavior that sets the whole in motion.

With respect to the soundtrack, the first law is essentially that the soundtrack is structured in the first instance by the placement of the voice.[2] The centrality of the voice in this sense represents the realization of the sensory-motor schema on the soundtrack. This does not mean that the voice is always centered or central, only that any use of the soundtrack that does not center or treat the voice as central will nevertheless be understood in terms of that operation of decentering.

The voice is set within a soundtrack that constructs the milieu: just as certain visual elements (sky, land, town) serve to encompass and define the milieu in the visual image, so too noises (wind, cattle, crowd) and music serve to establish the ambience on the soundtrack. The voice then emerges from or intrudes upon that ambience, as a representative of the milieu or as a stranger who stumbles upon it. In any event, the voice enters into dialogue, which is the primary form action takes on the soundtrack.

Second law. The action-image begins with the slow spiral of the unfolding situation but at some point it must contract into definite, purposeful action. The necessity of this contraction is the second law. Deleuze calls it a "binomial," which requires a second line of action to develop and converge in a "decisive action" that is characterized by conflict, prototypically structured as

---

[2] This is essentially the vococentric premise articulated by Michel Chion (1994, 1999) and expounded by David Neumeyer (2015). See chapter 5.

a duel (1986, 152). This second line of action requires parallel montage, and so also an initial separation of the lines of action.

The voice, likewise, acts through meaning and contracts into dialogue. The extent to which dialogue carries actual force as action—that its meaning produces actual effects—determines its actualized power, that is, whether the voice or soundtrack is a central or subsidiary element. In terms of the binomial character of the soundtrack, the voice (and its meaning) may be pitted against something else, either other dialogue or an antagonistic relation to another sound component, which assumes representation of the milieu. The criterion of parallel montage is realized on the soundtrack at the large scale with differentiated soundscapes for the various lines of action (and functions within each line of action) and at the small scale with asynchronous sound, which is the most conspicuous audiovisual sign of the binomial. If the normal configuration of situational speech in classical style is synchronized dialogue, where the editing of individual shots follows the allocation of lines under the rule of mimetic synchronization, the contraction into action is characterized by a disposition of shots not according to moving lips but according to significant action. Such cutting follows the effect of speech, most notably by registering a reaction.

The characteristic audiovisual figure of the binomial is therefore not the synchronized lips of speech, although it accords most closely with the sensory-motor schema, but the reaction shot, a nominal affection-image that registers the power of words and the accompanying music that underscores this power. The reaction shot gives, however, not an affection-image itself but the actualized affect, virtual power converted into actual force, the musical stinger being the auditory sign of this conversion. Asynchronous sound in general has a binomial character, as it serves to open the situation and move it into action. As offscreen sound, asynchronous sound destabilizes the image since it suggests an action outside the current image. As space expands under the force of the relative out-of-field, the action contracts.

Third law. As Deleuze notes, "the third law is the reverse of the second" (1986, 153). Following André Bazin, Deleuze calls this "the law of the forbidden montage." This law states that at some point the two participants in a duel must confront one another within a single image. The forbidden montage ensures that the confrontation is real, that the lines of action have in fact converged in a single image. This is the moment of pure action, the moment of maximum contraction, and it is often reserved for the key moment of the conflict, but it is also used for resolution—a love scene where the shot/reverse-shot structure has allowed each member of a couple to state his or her feelings and the two-shot unites them for an embrace and a kiss—or a reunion, where parallel montage yields to a shot where the distance has finally been bridged.

In terms of the soundtrack, the third law likewise reverses the second: where the second law emphasizes asynchronous sound to move from situation into action, the third law insists on a moment of mimetic synchronization. Some words, some sounds must be shown synchronized with a body to establish the ownership of words and sounds and so also the control over their actualized power. Although asynchronous sound is a common means of expressing the contraction into action, the key moment—the screaming point (Chion 1999) or explosion point (Celeste 2007)—must establish a clear sync point. The telling word, the fatal shot, the decisive blow, or the big explosion must be shown synchronized to its source, and its effects on the milieu or the way it alters behavior must then be shown. Finally, the sync point, though usually concluding an action and opening the expansion into the new situation, can also be used to initiate the action, especially when the focus of the image is on behavior. "Behavior is an action which passes from one situation to another, which responds to a situation in order to try to modify it or to set up a new situation" (Deleuze 1986, 155). In this case, the sync point is a bursting into action, and the action itself assumes form as violent reverberations.

Fourth law. This law establishes that no duel is unique, that conflict constitutes a series. "The binomial is a polynomial" (Deleuze 1986, 153). Even the central conflict of the film does not stand alone but has indeed been prepared by numerous other duels. The contraction into action may be initiated by a duel and concluded by another, with other conflicts intervening. The lines of action are organized around a series of conflicts, so that the central conflict between the lines themselves expresses the final outgrowth. Moreover, the lines of action may converge and diverge at various points in the film even if the decisive encounter is generally reserved for last. The result is that it is often difficult to separate out all of the conflicts into discrete moments, or sometimes even to decide where precisely the conflict lies. "Is the duel that of the cowboy with the bandit or the Indian? Or with the woman, with the boyfriend, with the new man who will supersede him . . .?" (153).

In terms of the soundtrack, the fourth law establishes the general organization by sync points. However remarkable any particular screaming point or explosion point, it is not unique but is instead part of a more or less intricate series of sync points.

Fifth law. This is "the law of the great gap" and it states that the final situation will be a significant transformation of the initial situation. The transformation also takes time, roughly the full extent of the film. The great gap is the action-image's equivalent to the impulse-image's steepest slope. But instead of a collapse into the originary world that swallows up the character, the great gap opens to a world that awaits the character who can answer its challenge and fulfill it. Insofar as the original milieu is buffeted by forces that create the gap into which the spiral of the action contracts, this is because it needs someone who has the power to tap those forces and channel them productively. The milieu in this respect has prepared a place for the hero "long before he comes to occupy it and even before he knows he is to occupy it" (Deleuze 1986, 152).

A similar case might be made for the antagonist who, however, does not so much vie to fill the gap instead of the hero but rather draws power from the forces of disorder and seeks to maintain or increase the buffeting often in the name of false restoration or reaction. Like the hero, the antagonist often seems to have had a place prepared.

Just as the law of the forbidden montage is the reverse of the second, which requires parallel montage, so too the law of the great gap is the inverse of the first law. Whereas the first law had addressed the organic structure, the fact that all the forces that would shape the milieu and operate on the behaviors were present in the initial situation, the great gap indicates that the initial situation is nevertheless lacking, that its strength is in the form of potential rather than actualized power. Simply, the first law establishes that the potential of the initial situation is encompassing; the fifth law insists that this potential is insufficient until actualized.

The centrality of dialogue manifests the first law on the soundtrack and the law of the great gap is the inverse of that centrality: not that the voice ceases in its central role but that, like the hero, its position is imperiled. The hero, unable to muster the words to rally the community or finding the words of the antagonist more powerful, turns against them as ineffectual or unreliable. Words are then displaced by action, and this displacement is itself meaningful as a withdrawal of words into effects and sometimes music. Frequently, the final conflict is preceded by a dialogue exchange where the protagonist is taunted or the antagonist is given the opportunity to reform. But the decisive moment itself—explosion point, screaming point, kiss—is rarely presented in the voice and more rarely still by means of a word. The voice and the word, however, reassert themselves as the action expands into the new situation, and the voice sanctifies the action by endowing it with meaning and the embrace of community. Here, with the re-establishment of the milieu under a transformed situation, speech is again crucial, suitably centered, and with an actualized power it had previously lacked. How the hero responds to speech in this new situation—taking it up as leader or falling silent—defines the hero. But equally important is the relation of effects and especially music to this speech: does music belong to the hero or to the community, and how does speech set within it?

Small Action Form

The small action form is schematically A-S-A', or action-situation-modified action. Despite the tripartite model, actions or behaviors serve to "disclose a situation" (Deleuze 1986, 160), which is never explicitly stated, and therefore the structure of the small action form is more binary than ternary. "The action advances blindly and the situation is disclosed in darkness, or in ambiguity. From action to action, the situation gradually emerges, varies, and finally either becomes clear or retains its mystery" (160). The situation in the small form is therefore more fragmentary, it traces an elliptical rather than a spiral path, and the representation is local rather than encompassing like the large form. Often the small form involves presenting a pair of actions from which a change in situation is inferred. It is therefore based around the sign of the index, of which there are two principal types: the index of lack, where the situation is not given but must be inferred, and the index of equivocity, which is like a pun, with two disparate meanings sharing a sign or a sign that is easily confused. In the latter case, Deleuze writes, "it is as if an action, a mode of behavior, concealed a slight difference, which was nevertheless sufficient to relate it simultaneously to two quite different situations, situations which are worlds apart" (161). Whereas the large form follows a logic of integration, encompassing a larger and larger world as the great gap is filled, the small form follows a logic of differentiation.

Deleuze compares the historical film (large form) to the costume drama (small form) and the crime film (large form) to the detective film (small form). In both these pairs of genres, the large form begins with a general encompassing milieu, whereas the small form emphasizes particular modes of behaviors. The historical drama and costume drama, for instance, treat fabrics in a contrasting manner. In the first case the fabrics fill out the overall conception and verify its authenticity rather than testifying to any sort of lived historicity; in the second case the fabrics belong to the costumes, which constitute a form of action, and the situation follows from the behavior suggested by the costume rather than vice versa. Even more telling is the difference between the crime film and detective film: in the crime film, the milieu of the criminal underworld presents the situation, which then contracts into a series of conflicts and duels that bring the crime figure down; in the detective film, by contrast, the film centers on the reconstruction of a crime, an initial situation that is not given, and the film spends most of its time trying to reconstruct through the actions of the detective.

Unlike the five laws of the large form, the small form only has one basic law, that of the index itself: "the slight difference in the action which brings out an infinite distance between two situations" (1986, 170). In terms of the soundtrack, the small form arises whenever offscreen sound is exploited not to reveal additional space but to allow an ambiguity to unfold. In *The Apartment* (1960), after having rejected C. C. in the restaurant in favor of Jeff, Fran has a change of heart and races back to C. C.'s apartment. As she climbs the stairs, she hears a loud bang. Fearful of the worst, she runs to the door and pounds furiously. The door opens, revealing C. C. holding a bottle of champagne. This sort of ambiguity is the essence of the small form, which exists not to reveal more space to be encompassed as in the large form but to illustrate a particular distance, however near or far.

On a larger scale, the small form is supported by sound or music that emphasizes lack, displacement, disconnection, and equivocation. *Casablanca*

(1942), for instance, starts as though evoking a large form, with music, images, and narration that all point to an encompassing world. Soon, however, it quickly shifts from the literally global perspective of the titles to the fragmented, local perspective of Casablanca itself, whose relation to that larger world is at best fraught. As the grand opening narration suggests, getting to Casablanca—itself part of a "circuitous route" to Lisbon—requires an arduous journey, following a twisted path through Europe, across "the Mediterranean and . . . the Rim of Africa." The journey itself fragments space and scatters those shown in the images that accompany the map into ghostly figures. Leaving Casablanca is similarly treacherous, requiring an exit visa and a seat on the plane to Lisbon. The plane therefore represents the thinnest of lines, what Deleuze calls a "vector," reconnecting Casablanca to the rest of the world; and indeed this vector is so thin, so twisted, and so jagged and traverses so many unknown holes that the forces engulfing the rest of the world in war are presented as curiously disorganized in Casablanca itself, which therefore appears as a series of heterogeneous and rather disconnected spaces.

SECOND INTERMEDIARY STAGE: REFLECTION-IMAGE

The reflection-image is a means of transforming the action-image so it takes on attributes of the relation-image, typically by synthesizing large and small action forms to produce novel configurations. The most typical transformation occurs with the insertion of one type of action for another (in the large action form) or one type of situation for another (in the small action form). For instance, when in the large action form some action foreshadows a latter more consequential action, the first action serves as an index for the second (A'), and this results in the insertion of the sign of the small action form into the large. Vice versa, in the small form, an encompassing symbolic sequence might substitute for an inferred real situation so that this symbol reflects the real situation rather than presenting it. In both cases, the sign (index or what Deleuze calls a synsign) from the opposite action form takes a prominent appearance, transforming the basic action form. Though the small action form dominates in *Casablanca*, the large form has a sufficient presence in the figures of Laszlo and Strasser that it could conceivably be understood as a reflection-image, depending on whether we take Rick as being remade by an encompassing world.

The reflection-image is essentially transformational, wherein "an intervening sign indirectly reflects its object . . . and transforms Large Form and Small Form by injecting an element of one form into a sequence of the other" (Bogue 2003, 94). Dialectical use of montage performs a similar transformational work. In the small action form, dialectics permits what Deleuze calls the law of the "qualitative leap." In such cases, the line of the dialectic causes the small form to take on properties of the large form, as the dialectical line itself becomes the figure of the encompasser. "The broken line [of the index] has ceased to be unpredictable, and becomes the political and revolutionary and 'line'" (Deleuze 1986, 180). Likewise, with the large action form, the dialectic serves to transform the impulse-image into an action-image as a milieu takes form out of the originary world: the dialectic displaces the law of the steepest path and averts its seemingly necessary regression and descent. The dialectic operates on the large form as

> the law of the whole, set and parts: how the whole is already present in the parts but must move from the old to the new, from legend to history, from dream to reality, from Nature to man. It is the song of the earth, which is transmitted through all human songs—even the saddest—and whose refrain returns in the great revolutionary hymn. . . . The large form—SAS'—receives from the dialectic a "respiration," an oneiric and symphonic power overflowing the boundaries of the organic. (180)

The other way that reflection-images arise is through inversion and discursive figures. Inversion introduces "a topological deformation" (166), where, for instance, the large form devolves into mere functionalism that allows the disruptive force to flow from within the interior of the milieu (akin to an originary world) rather than posing the more usual exterior threat. The discursive figure appears when the stakes of the action are a discourse. In *The Great Dictator* (1940), the situations are transformed by the discourse, the Jewish barber taking up the place of discourse and indicating the difference from that of the dictator. The form is a small action form, but the place of the action that reveals the situation is the discourse, thought, a mental image rather than an action per se.

In the last instance, the connection to the soundtrack is clear, as is its relation to dialogue: a discursive figure occurs whenever the status of dialogue is reflected in the image; that is, when discourse assumes form as action, it constitutes a reflection-image because the dialogue is an indirect relation of the action and the situation, presuming that dialogue is not itself action. The soundtrack analogue to such inversion is somewhat more difficult to discern and describe. This might involve the breakdown in boundaries among the sound components, and especially challenges to the centrality of dialogue from within: dialogue overriding itself through overlap, dialogue devolving into noise, noise or music assuming the function of dialogue (as in a scream or performance), or chit-chat or slang substituting for the expected conventional register. The audio dissolve might be another form of inversion. None of these devices overrides the principle of dialogue's centrality per se since the voice or voice substitute remains dominant. But they each subvert the principle because clarity is pushed to the side in favor of something else.

The soundtrack analogue to the small form transformation would involve a displacement of the soundtrack for a situation by another encompassing sound. Here, a contrapuntal use of music is a possible example: elegiac music over the final phase of a battle (such as in the opening battle scene from *Gladiator* [2000]), the substitution of a musical interlude and disconnected images for an expected presentation of a situation, or perhaps a song over a travel montage that represents the traveling situation rather than action might all be instances of this small form transformation. In the case of elegiac music, it only passes from the battle to the elegy by virtue of the intervention of a third, the relation, a mental image, an interpretation of the battle, the battle as viewed from some exterior position outside the basic conflict. The final type of reflection-image is the transformation of the large form by virtue of the index. This will typically be some sort of theatrical action that foreshadows a later action. This is the province of the musical performance insofar as its reference is indexical. In *Casablanca*, the Battle of the Anthems serves as this type of index. Though the film is as a whole of the small form type, the Battle of the Anthems belongs to the large action form by virtue of Laszlo's presence as an encompassing hero.

THIRDNESS: RELATION-IMAGE

The relation-image is the most complex of the movement-images and it is the most difficult to specify concretely. Like the reflection-image, it involves the addition of a third element to the primary conflict and duality in the action-image. Deleuze associates this third element with interpretation and mental activity and identifies it as "relation."

Deleuze follows philosophical tradition in distinguishing two types of relations: natural and abstract. Natural relations form series and are governed by signification. Deleuze points to the relation of portrait to model and to the circumstances of its production as an instance of such natural relational series (1986, 197). Abstract relations, by contrast, presuppose a whole and they are governed by sense. An abstract relation, Deleuze says, "designates . . . a circumstance through which one compares two images which are not naturally united in the mind" (198). Deleuze points to the way distinct geometrical figures, say, an oval and a parabola, are united by both being conical sections.

Although relation-images are mental images, they are not normally images of someone's thought but rather images of how thought orders the world, that is, interpretations: "It is an image which takes as its object, relations, symbolic acts, intellectual feelings" (Deleuze 1986, 198). Framing therefore assumes special importance in the relation-image, since it is the relation that must be framed as object. It is no longer the individual elements or their conflicts that the framing contains in order to present. Instead, it is the changing relation among the elements that is key. Conflict when it still appears now serves to expose the relation, to become thereby transformed, like other actions, into a symbolic act that cannot be reduced to duel, to action in pairs. And this transformation occurs through the framing, which should not, as Deleuze frequently does, be reduced to the visual frame of the screen itself since its logic includes deframings and auditory extensions as well. These can be sorted according to the signs of composition that Deleuze assigns to the relation-image. The "mark" is the ordinary series that forms a well-ordered set. It is essentially an action-image as it appears and has been incorporated into the relation image. It is the framing as frame that typically divides onscreen from offscreen (that generates in turn two series, the onscreen and the offscreen). The "demark," by contrast, is a sign that falls out of that series, that sets itself apart. It is uncanny. Its extraordinary property arises from and in opposition to the ordinary series. "Deframings" and certain kinds of auditory extension into the offscreen are examples of demarks.

A self-reflective musical performance, which belongs more properly to the reflection-image, can nevertheless serve to illustrate the basic configuration. A musical performance does not consist in simply the visuals and sound (or music). Instead, it forges an interpretation of the relation between image and sound insofar as the performance is delivered for an audience. This interpretation can become an object in its own right, at which point it passes over to a relation-image proper. When, for instance, Jo sings "Que sera, sera" at the embassy in the second version of *The Man Who Knew Too Much* (1956), she sings too loudly for the space so that her voice can expand throughout the embassy, an expansion that the camera diligently tracks through a series of cuts revealing empty space in the embassy. Here, the relation of body and voice, their synchronization and separation, enters the image and becomes the object of the image. And the cuts back to Jo straining to hear the reply of her son's whistle, even as she sings and plays, set up again a relation, a distance to be bridged, a distance that only sound that can wander free of the body can bridge.

Similarly, in *The Artist* (2011), the film plays as a silent film with recorded orchestral score for all but two scenes. The most prominent of these is the auditory dream where George is startled to discover that things make synchronized sound, and because of the context of the film the relation of synchronization here is uncanny, a demark. From the standpoint of the image, it is not simply a dream but a relation-image that deploys an impulse-image. What appears in this image is the uncanniness of synchronization; that is, the convention of synchronization is defamiliarized by the encompassing convention of the silent film within which it is embedded. The silent film conventions thus frame the conventions of synchronized sound film as a relation. What might in an ordinary sound film pass as a series of unremarkable marks—sync points—becomes in *The Artist* a demark, as the natural relation passes outside of itself, as though torn from the series. It presents a "clash" in the natural series, the silent film convention of *The Artist*.

Psycho (1960) is perhaps the most telling. Here, the voice grows so unstable that a substitution occurs, one for another, that follows, as it were, Hitchcock's schema: "the criminal has always done his crime *for* another" (Deleuze 1986, 201). Mother for the son, son for the mother. This is the figure that Chion (1994, 1999) calls the acousmêtre, the acoustical being who inhabits the space just beyond the frameline. What distinguishes the acousmêtre is its ability to remain offscreen. In this respect, the figure exhibits camera consciousness generally lacking in filmic characters: it is an acute observer of the situation as it sees what even we as spectators do not: the camera. And the acousmêtre thereby exposes the habitual relation of sound and image, the pull the sound exerts on the image to reveal the source. The acousmêtre thereby serves as a figure of deframing. (And yet the acousmêtre, like the film itself, takes little apparent notice of the microphone, which records its presence, and ultimately foretells its downfall even if the microphone also seems to serve as the source of its power.)

With the relation-image, neither the sound nor its source is given precedence in itself or even by relation of the action-image's causality. Instead, the set of relations of sound and source receives emphasis. "What matters is not who did the action . . . but neither is it the action itself: it is the set of relations in which the action and the one who did it are caught" (Deleuze 1986, 200). Hence, the frame as that which determines the set and establishes the relationship takes on new importance and the offscreen cannot be equated with the out-of-frame in this sense. The frame determines the limit of the relation. But the frame is not restricted to what can be seen. This reveals a significance to Deleuze's claim that the sound is a component of the image. The image is not determined by the visual frame, and the relation-image entails, as it were, the framing of this frame, of bringing the frame into consciousness. Every shot shows a framed relation, and the frame of this relation extends to the soundtrack. If the "single shot subordinates the whole (relation) to the frame" (200), then even the absolutely offscreen (the nondiegetic) must belong to and at some level be subordinated to this frame.

If sound and image always form a relation within a set, these being delimited in the first instance by the onscreen, the offscreen, and the nondiegetic, these relations are not yet relation-images inasmuch as they do not presume or emanate from an interpretation. When these basic relations are disturbed so that an interpretation forms, so that it seems the disposition of the relation is the content of the frame, then a relation-image begins to form. If the visuals reveal the relation-image through the consciousness of the camera, the soundtrack reveals it not so much through a consciousness of the microphone but rather through a consciousness of sound's relation to the image, where we are made aware of the terms of the audiovisual contract. Consciousness of the soundtrack transforms the sounds and music into symbolic acts, but the soundtrack still remains bound to the image.

5

Neoformalism and Four Models of the Soundtrack

Introduction: Semiotics and Formalism

Formalism and semiotics share a number of overlapping concerns. They are both analytical in approach; they both emphasize the objective, scientific character of research; and they are both principally concerned with the distinctiveness of film art. For semiotics that concern centers on film language; for formalism it is understanding the various subsystems that make up a film as a whole. Semiotics focuses more on the general case (what are the structures that film share?), whereas formalism is especially occupied with the close reading of a particular film (what distinguishes the formal practice of this film?). With its disciplinary history in structural linguistics, semiotics seeks to identify and abstract signification, meaning, and communication in film, whereas formalism is interested in the compelling display of craft, filmic ideas articulated in the characteristic devices and artistic form of film. Yet these are only broad tendencies, and in practice semioticians have made detailed analyses of individual films, while formalist scholars have been interested in understanding the logic and historical development of the various subsystems, how individual filmmakers define their characteristic style, and even how the economic structure of the studio system affected the production historically.

Neoformalism

Absorbing lessons from structuralism, New Criticism, Russian formalism, and even musicology, neoformalism emerged as a movement in film studies just about the time Christian Metz abandoned structural semiotics and worked to reconcile his film semiotics with Lacanian psychoanalysis. Metz's new approach, part of the grand theoretical synthesis that came to be known as "apparatus theory," proved as revolutionary but only slightly longer lived than his film semiotics.

Associated especially with the so-called Wisconsin School of scholars—especially David Bordwell, Noël Carroll, and Kristin Thompson—neoformalism labored under the shadow of apparatus theory for much of the 1980s. With the dissolution of apparatus theory in the 1990s, the influence of neoformalism increased to become one of the major branches of the now-diverse field of film theory. Neoformalism would define itself as being against, or at least post-, theory—"theory" at this time being largely synonymous with apparatus theory and those offshoots that would be picked up and developed as critical approaches when apparatus theory collapsed. Carroll (1988), in particular, argued that theory served largely to "mystify the movies" rather than offering clarity or being edifying. Bordwell (1989) slyly suggested that theory served primarily to increase scholarly productivity, an engine for quickly "making meaning" of films in a way that was acceptable to the regime of academic publishing. The difficulty with this interpretive practice, he suggested, was that it wasn't clear what purpose all this publication served (other than ensuring the author's placement and promotion) since the interpretation so often followed predictably from the theoretical premises and rarely challenged those premises in any meaningful way. Thompson, who in the opening chapter of *Breaking the Glass Armor* (1988) wrote the closest thing to a manifesto for neoformalism, argued overtly against the prevailing research paradigm, which involved finding a theoretical method, usually imported from outside film studies, and applying it to a film (or set of films) to produce a reading. "Preconceived methods, applied simply for demonstrative purposes, often end up by reducing the complexity of films" (4). Thompson argued instead for developing research questions aimed at discovering the particularity of the film—what is unusual or intriguing about it—and the development of (analytical) "approaches" designed to answer those questions (5). "Because the questions are (at least slightly) different for each work, the method will also be different" (7).

Neoformalism can also be understood as picking up from classical and contemporary theorists a number of threads that were abandoned in the rush to embrace apparatus theory. From Eisenstein, it takes a delight in formal experimentation, the analytical neutralization of the basic material, and the valorization of craft; from Arnheim, the notion of film as art in the sense of a representation rather than a reproduction but also the grounding of film theory in current research about perception and psychology; from the typologists and semiologists, the importance of crisp analytical categories and a precise descriptive terminology; from Marxism, the attention to how the industry organizes work and deploys technology in the interest of making a profit; from Mitry, the careful analytical attention to the historical grounding and context; and from Metz, the appeal to analytical method as scientific. Neoformalism synthesizes all this into a research program that aims at revealing and reconstructing a "historical poetics." It dedicates itself to close analysis, careful historical work, and an understanding of film as a work of art that rewards study for its own sake. It also shuns speculative theory—especially speculative work that is not clearly bracketed off as such—and eschews the move into hermeneutics, especially the politically tinged interpretations that apparatus theory was designed to facilitate.

Kristin Thompson and the Analytical Approach

As developed by Thompson (1988), neoformalism espouses a belief in the possibility and efficacy of aesthetic theory (3), which entails a theory that art is distinct from other cultural activity on the one hand and a theory of artistic relations for each artistic medium that is immanent or specific to the medium on the other (8–9). "Art," she writes, "is set apart from the everyday world, in which we use our perception for practical ends. We perceive the world so as to filter from it those elements that are relevant to our immediate actions" (8). Art in this view offers an experience like no other, an experience obtainable and definable by contemplating aesthetic forms. Art allows us to perceive what practical perception pushes to the margins, permitting us to see in new ways. Neoformalism begins as an aesthetic theory, a theory of art, only pushing out to social theory from grounding in the specificity—the characteristic devices and practices—of the art.

Thompson indeed rejects the form–content distinction, arguing that anything that enters into the artwork is transformed into a property of form. "Meaning is not the end result of an artwork, but one of its formal components" (1988, 12). Neoformalism also breaks with the communication model in not taking meaning as the final term, its underlying principle. Films have meaning, but this meaning (along with all the particles of meaning that coalesce in it) is only a component of the film. If the film is an artistic whole, the form and meaning of the whole are only themselves moments in the total artwork. Treatment is central, more so than the theme or final meaning.

Suspicious of overt hermeneutic activity, an interpretive drive in search of meaning, neoformalist analysis tends to favor instead identifying and tracking the formal devices that make the meaning and coherence of a film possible in the first place. Although neoformalist analysis is purportedly directed toward recovering what is challenging in a film and developing and refining skills for apprehending the particularity of the film (Thompson 1988, 33), the need for the analysis to have general theoretical validity—"each analysis should tell us something not only about the film in question, but about the possibilities of film as an art" (6)—means that neoformalist analysis has the tendency to "hollow out" film techniques, to generalize and abstract from them the formal properties that remain once they have been emptied of the particular content and signification that any instantiation of a device would have in a particular film. "While many works may use the same device, that device's function may be different in each work" (15). In this way, it becomes possible for the device to be redeployed with a different function and so also for it to assume a different meaning in a different context. It also becomes possible to substitute one device for another on the basis of "functional equivalency" (15).

Neoformalism therefore yields a neutralization of the material and figures, which become arbitrary stylistic choices evaluated in terms of artistic efficacy rather than the figures having immanent ideological content of their own. Noël Carroll (1996a), for instance, writes: "It is vastly implausible to believe that cinematic structures, like point-of-view editing, are inherently or intrinsically ideological. The use of point-of-view editing in a particular film may serve ideological purposes. But the structure itself is ideologically neutral" (258). The selection of shots is simply evaluated aesthetically on the basis of how well the device serves the film's "dominant," which Thompson (1988) defines as "the main formal principle a work or group of works uses to organize devices into a whole" (43). To some extent the neutralization can be attributed to the abstractions endemic to theorization.

One way neoformalism maintains its appearance of neutral, objective analysis is by following the "natural" or immanent articulations of film as a basis of segmentation. That is, it tends to view the film with the grain, the way the film asks to be viewed. Occasionally, it will adopt arbitrary articulation, but in this case it will attempt to make the articulation unbiased, as a randomly selected segment. As an aesthetic theory, formalism is not, at least not primarily, a theory of communication with a message encoded in the film to be passed along to the spectator (Thompson 1988, 7–8; Carroll [1996a, 127], however, dissents on this point). This is one reason formalism of most stripes tends to be suspicious of or at least ambivalent about hermeneutic activity, especially any systematic interpretive method that privileges a priori certain patterns of meaning over others. In particular, neoformalism accepts the intentional fallacy, which presumes that intention matters only to the extent that it has been realized in the material; and if it has been realized in the material, then there is no reason to appeal to the category of intention, or indeed history (Wimsatt and Beardsley 1946).

Consequently, interpretation—at least overt interpretation seeking after meaning—is not the central activity of the neoformalist approach. "Neoformalism does not do 'readings' of films," Thompson proclaims. "The main critical activity," she adds, "is 'analysis'" (1988, 34n25). Music theory has traditionally held a similar view, where analytical activity has likewise been valorized and interpretive readings denigrated, but in current practice the field is more likely to accept the concept of "readings" or "hearings" as a nod to pluralistic values (Lehman 2017b). This nod to pluralism at the same time has the effect of rendering the toolkit of analysis—if not the tools it contains—as ideologically neutral. Music theorists recognize that the analytical tools themselves may have ideological biases built into them, but the presumption is that, if the analyst understands the tool, the bias can be effectively controlled for. Nattiez's (1990a) argument for the neutral level of analysis essentially makes this argument.

David Bordwell and the Music(ologic)al Analogy

Aside from its interest in economic questions and industry history, the historical poetics of neoformalism closely resemble the common concerns of historical musicology, and this resemblance is hardly coincidental. Already in "The Musical Analogy" (1980), Bordwell had proposed treating film along the lines of music scholarship. Given the aim of constructing a field of inquiry around the close study of films, it is easy to see why Bordwell thought musicology a congenial analogy for the emerging discipline of film studies: music scholarship at the time offered an alternative model to the methodological paradigms imported from other disciplines such as sociology, Marxism, semiotics, and psychoanalysis that were dominating the research protocol of the emerging discipline of film studies. These methodologies brought with them elaborate theoretical premises that often seemed at odds with—when they did not completely efface—the element of film as an art form. The scholarly study of music, by contrast, offered a methodology and research agenda dedicated to the explication of an art form in terms of its historical context rather than as an instance of the application of some methodological paradigm whose origin lay outside the art form. The primary advantage that the study of music provided as a model was that it served only as an analogy in the sense that a precise method, which grew from the study of music, was not imported; instead, Bordwell appropriated only the relation of a method to the material under investigation. The analogy also suggested certain classes of questions that could be asked and some guidelines about how a researcher might go about answering them. The irony was that Bordwell was proposing this musical analogy just as the scholarly study of music was beginning a profound change that would take it away from the formalist and positivist moorings that Bordwell found so appealing (Buhler and Neumeyer 1994, 367).

If early classical theorists of film had also been interested in a musical analogy, that was, Bordwell noted, at least in part because the analogy forced attention to the constructive element in film; the connection to music helped underscore that however much film seemed driven, by its investment in mechanical reproduction, along a path of realism, it was also irreducibly a construction, a product of human choice and intelligence. "Music has become a model of how formal unity can check, control, and override representation" (Bordwell 1980, 142). Although the term "representation" in film studies is usually opposed to recording and reproduction and so associated with those who see film as a constructive art, Bordwell seems troubled by the term because it includes the presence of a structuring narrative, something that, interestingly enough, formalist studies of music have also traditionally eschewed along with hermeneutics, another scholarly trend within film studies that Bordwell finds problematic (Bordwell 1989). In this programmatic essay, Bordwell therefore set up the formal properties of film, like those of music, in opposition both to the recording of reality and to narrative.

More than simply the musical abstraction from reality and narrative recommended the musical analogy. Bordwell points to a shared structure. "What has made the analogy attractive are the ways in which a musical piece can be analyzed as a *system of systems*" (1980, 142). Although the ostensive concern of Bordwell's article is to define and explicate the appropriation of the musical analogy by filmmakers and theorists along organic and dialectical lines, he seems equally concerned with preserving the analogy as the basis for current film scholarship. Music scholarship has a rich tradition of theorizing music's formal systems, especially with respect to pitch relationships and form, and the entire subfield of music theory is devoted to developing, refining, and applying such systems to musical works. Bordwell concludes the essay with the following statement: "If we want to know how cinema may work upon the social and the suprasocial, the musical analogy must persist, for it crystallizes the drive of film form toward multiple systems. But these systems must be situated within the process of cinema's heterogeneity" (156).

Noël Carroll and Modifying Music

Despite the fact that Bordwell looked to a musical analogy to ground neoformalism, the soundtrack has not received as much attention as the rest of the filmic system in neoformalist studies. In this respect, neoformalism has accepted a visual bias to film and shaped its research agenda accordingly. When the soundtrack is considered, music and sound are approached as formal elements that offer filmmakers choice in how to assemble a film. The soundtrack may perform functions particular to it, but primarily it serves to convey information that might have been presented in other ways. Spoken dialogue replaced the dialogue card during the transition to sound, and dialogue, sound effects, and music offer alternatives along with visual action to providing narrative information in sound film. Character motivation, for instance, might be shown through action, reported through dialogue, or hinted at through music, and the particular choice of the filmmakers will bear on the style and form of the film.

Consistent with this functional approach, Carroll (1996a) devotes a short essay to what he calls "modifying music," music that "serves to add further characterization to the scenes it embellishes" (141). Carroll begins with Copland's typology of five functions discussed in chapter 3 and suggests he is going to develop a further function, although instead he offers a function that cuts across Copland's typology, combining parts of Copland's first three functions: establishing time and place, signifying emotion, and creating a neutral background. Drawing an explicit grammatical analogy, Carroll proposes that music in film often functions like an adjective modifying a noun or an adverb modifying a verb. Music, in other words, modifies a film narrative by imparting a new quality or power to the representation. Carroll therefore posits "two different symbol systems": music is a semiautonomous symbol system that runs alongside and affects the rest of a film's symbol system. These symbol systems are not determined by the material properties of the media—that is, image track and soundtrack. Music is instead that symbol system consisting of sounds on the soundtrack that are organized musically. The two symbol systems—music and film—work as an effective pair in film, Carroll says, because they are complementary: "each system supplies something that the other system standardly lacks, or, at least, does not possess with the same degree of effectiveness that the other system possesses" (141). The advantages of music, Carroll says, include that it "is a highly expressive symbol system" and offers "more direct access to the emotive realm than any other symbol system." Curiously, Carroll is much more interested in identifying the lacks in music's symbol system and bolstering the strengths of the film's symbol system than in assessing any actual complementation. He is particularly quick to avoid any suggestion of the ultimate inadequacy of film's symbol system, noting that we should neither oppose the two systems absolutely nor take music as necessary: "it is not the case that the movie is pure representation to be supplemented by means of musical expression" (143).

In point of fact, Carroll treats music more as supplement than complement, since music for Carroll is one means— though not the only one— film uses to clarify "the expressive quality" and "emotional significance of the action" (1996a, 144). Music, it turns out, is deployed not so much because the filmic system is in itself inadequate but because films "are aimed at mass audiences. They aspire for means of communication that can be grasped almost immediately by untutored audiences." Modifying music is a mark of easy consumption: it primarily offers film a means of clarifying expression, making the film easier to understand. "Modifying music, given the almost direct expressive impact of music, assures that the untutored spectators of the mass audience will have access to the desired expressive quality and, in turn, will see the given scene or sequence under its aegis" (144). The clarity that music offers—the way it makes the world screened "much more legible than life"—belongs to and is a prominent marker of the economy of mass art. By emphasizing this clarifying function and restricting it to a popular appeal, Carroll insulates the general filmic system from any particular symbolic need for music. Film "needs" music only to the extent that film "needs" emotional clarity; and even if a particular film does require such clarity, film's symbol system has other means of providing it.

Strictly speaking, then, music's value to film lies primarily in the way it can increase the efficiency of existing modes of communication rather than in the way it might potentially open up new modes of artistic expression. Carroll does not specifically deny that music can perform radically different functions, but his analysis of music's symbol system continually underscores its inadequacies, as though the idea of music having a coherent symbol system posed some sort of unspoken ontological challenge to that of film. In particular, he emphasizes music's deficient capacity for focusing or "particularizing the feelings it projects" (1996a, 141). This deficiency derives ultimately from instrumental music's lack of a body—what Carroll also calls "the logical machinery"—on which to project the emotions and thereby individuate them (142). The film's symbol system supplies this body. "The music tells us something, of an emotive significance, about what the scene is about; the music supplies us with, so to say, a description (or presentation) of the emotive properties the film attaches to the referents of the scene" (142). Ultimately, Carroll seems to argue that if film exploits music to give its narrative the appearance of emotional depth, music benefits in turn because its symbol system gains a particularity, a relation to concrete meaning, that normally escapes its purview.

As Carroll's account of modifying music illustrates, neoformalist film theory can approach the soundtrack both in itself, as a relatively autonomous system with respect to the conventions of its construction and the formal relationships that obtain among its parts, and more generally as a system that articulates and is itself articulated by the similar system governing the image track or narrative. If neoformalist theory has tended to follow the general (and questionable) bias of film studies in granting the image precedence—the actual constructive precedence of commercial filmmaking lies in the narrative system, and devices that generally maximize narrative clarity at that—nothing in the precepts of neoformalism demands that this precedence be followed. Carroll's account of modifying music renders music external to the rest of the filmic system in a way that, while perhaps ordinary and normative, is not generally tenable. If the soundtrack gains much of its power from its ability to represent what the film cannot otherwise show, whether that be music that registers the emotional depth of a character's interior or offscreen sound that registers a world that exists beyond the edge of the frame, that power is purchased only by otherwise deferring to, or seeming to defer to, the centrality of the image.

Formal Models of Music and Film

Although modest in scope, Carroll's "Notes on Movie Music," which was originally published in 1986, was the most extensive neoformalist theoretical treatment of music and the soundtrack until Jeff Smith's critique of the psychoanalytical basis of Claudia Gorbman's theory in 1996 and his *The Sounds of Commerce* in 1998.[1] Neither of these contributions really laid out a theory of the soundtrack along neoformalist lines, and Smith's main subsequent theoretical emphases have been on the use of popular music, music and narrative theory, and the soundtrack of contemporary cinema. His writings on these topics will be considered in chapters 6 and 9.

With its keen focus on the determinants of the style of the classical-era film score, Gorbman's *Unheard Melodies* (1987) was in many respects a good fit with the historical poetics of neoformalism; but Gorbman was also committed to the prevailing apparatus theory in a way that was difficult to disentangle from her other claims, and this posed challenges to reconciling her theory with neoformalism, as the sharp critique of Smith (1996) suggests. Gorbman's theory has nevertheless proved very influential indeed, and I will return to it at length in the next chapter, which deals explicitly with narrative theories. One of her major contributions was to show why film music in particular deserved special scholarly and critical attention, and after Gorbman it has become common for scholars to offer models and theories focused on music's particular role in cinema, especially as it relates to narrative.

In the remainder of this chapter, I consider four formal models of music and film offered by Kathryn Kalinak (1992), Nicholas Cook (1998), David Neumeyer (2015), and Annabel Cohen (2013, 2014). All of these theories follow a formalist tenet in assuming the concrete existence and semiautonomy of the musical subsystem and are concerned specifically with identifying the formal characteristics, functions, and properties of this subsystem. Kalinak, Cook, and Neumeyer develop their models as a framework for analytical understanding, whereas Cohen, a psychologist, develops hers to provide an account of the cognition of film music.

Kathryn Kalinak and *Captain Blood*

Kathryn Kalinak published *Settling the Score* (1992) in a series edited by Thompson and Bordwell, so her book can in some ways be understood as a reworking of Gorbman's theory in a way that the analysis of music in film better fits the strictures of neoformalism. In particular, Kalinak uses cognitive

---

[1] Carroll (1978) also published an early article on early German sound cinema.

studies and the generative music theory of Fred Lehrdahl and Ray Jackendoff (1983) to replace much of the psychoanalytic framework that Gorbman relies on. But Kalinak's approach is broadly similar to Gorbman (but also to Copland) in delineating a set of functions for music, most of which relate to narrative. Kalinak is concerned with developing a working model for analyzing music in film more than developing a tight general typology of functions, as Gorbman did.

Kalinak (1992) is refreshingly aware that the framework of classical film theory includes a visual bias that limits its observations. In particular, she notes that this bias figures an inferior position for the soundtrack in the very vocabulary we use to describe it (20). Much as onscreen and offscreen in Metz's account of aural objects already frame sound in terms of its physical source in the image, so too parallelism and counterpoint, two terms that classical theory evolved to discuss the relationship between image and soundtrack, likewise assume the precedence (and hierarchical superiority) of the image. "Such nomenclature," Kalinak notes, "assumes that meaning is contained in the visual image and that sound can only reinforce or alter what is already there" (24). "Modifying music" of the kind that Carroll discusses works similarly because it presumes that music qualifies an image or narrative situation that is already there. In general, Kalinak says, any "language that suggests music reinforces, emphasizes, contradicts, or alters the image falls into this trap" (30).

Kalinak notes that this conception often neglects the way music fully participates in the construction of meaning. "Narrative," she writes,

> is not constructed by visual means alone. By this I mean that music works as part of the process that transmits narrative information to the spectator, that it functions as a narrative agent. Mood, emotion, characterization, point of view, even the action itself are constructed in a complex visual and aural interaction in which music is an important component. Thus when tremolo strings are heard, the music is not *reinforcing* the suspense of the scene; it is a part of the process that creates it. (1992, 30–31, emphasis in original)

Indeed, the entire soundtrack contributes to the creation of the narrative. When string tremolos are added to a scene, they do not just modify a feeling of suspense that is already there. In a very real way, the scene would not have the sense of suspense without the tremolos. The tremolos are not so much modifying "suspense," in other words, as they are creating it. The suspense of the scene derives, at least in part, from the music. Kalinak, like Carroll, retains music as a separate subsystem with formal attributes of its own, and these remain distinct from the other elements of the filmic system. Kalinak's understanding of music therefore goes quite a bit further than Carroll's modifying music in defining a distinct set of functions for music to perform, ones that go beyond qualification, and she does not require the strange assumptions about mass consumption that Carroll does.

A WORKING MODEL OF FILM MUSIC

Rather than providing a typology or general overview of her theory of film music, Kalinak instead presents her theory implicitly as a "working model," which she develops through an extended analysis of *Captain Blood* (1935). She explicates her analysis in ten sections, each of which discusses an element of the model. The approach is similar to that presented by Aaron Copland in chapter 3, and Kalinak also draws on the functions that Claudia Gorbman developed in her work on narrative functions that I will discuss in chapter 6. In what follows, I have reorganized Kalinak's order of presentation to some extent to better draw out what I think is the latent theory behind the working model.

GENERAL CONSIDERATIONS

Spotting. This concerns where music appears in a film. In sound film, music is generally intermittent rather than ubiquitous, and so music will structure a film simply on the basis of a binary logic of presence and absence. Music required in the action such as for a diegetic performance sequence is obvious and will often mark off the represented space as musical and so liminal. Usually, the kind of music in such a scene will also be apparent from the setting as well (a jazz band at a nightclub). There are a few instances of diegetic music in *Captain Blood*, such as at the beginning of the sequence in Tortuga. Most historical films will attempt some sort of matching of diegetic music to the time period of the film, but action-adventure films draw heavily on fantasy and so they have more leeway in this respect than do historical dramas. Films centered on fantasy and adventure emphasize exoticism, while those of a historical bent focus on authenticity.

Nondiegetic music is not motivated by the action to the same extent, even when it is modifying music, and so most scenes could play either with or without it. This is not to say that nondiegetic music simply adds to, alters, or reinforces what is already there. Kalinak notes that music can also be an element in the basic construction such as with suspense. But music can modify, construct, or simply be absent, and music can be more or less overt in terms of its treatment. Most of the music in *Captain Blood* is nondiegetic, and the decisions about which scenes should have music (and what kind) determine the tone and representational practice of the film.

Structural unity. Music is an important force of coherence in film: it binds otherwise disparate elements together. It can do this across the film where, say, repetitions of a theme help convince us that the film has a thematic core (Kalinak 1992, 104), or a cue with a continuous form or a broad melody can make it seem like a series of shots cohere into a sequence. It is in this sense that film music is an "arbiter of narrative continuity" (80). That is, music tends to appear at those moments in a film when narrative is most tenuous: "transitions between sequences, flash-forwards and flashbacks, parallel editing, dream sequences, and montage" (80). As an example, Kalinak offers the music that accompanies the time from Peter Blood's conviction to his arrival as a slave in the Caribbean (81). Kalinak notes how the integrity of the musical form in this case overrides the temporal and spatial dislocations of the sequence itself. "The reliance upon an established form, the use of continuous music, and the dependence on extended melody rather than short phrases creates the effect of unity reinforcing the narrative at a potentially disruptive moment" (82).

Leitmotif. As noted, a repetition of themes can draw connections across the film, and when it does so it serves the goal of structural unity (1992, 104). But when those themes are also associated with specific characters, objects, or ideas—and they almost always are—they encourage us to make interpretive connections, since each statement brings "with it the associations established in earlier occurrences" (104). Music that makes such associations within a film is a leitmotif. "The leitmotif," Kalinak writes,

> operates on two levels simultaneously: in terms of the narrative it helps create the heroism of the protagonist; in terms of the music it creates both a thread of repetition and variation which binds the score, and also, through anticipation of a return to the original version, a climactic center for the score's overall design. (107)

Although common in film scoring, the leitmotif has come in for some criticism, and, as mentioned in chapter 3, Copland and the authors of *Composing for the Films* both had reservations on the appropriateness of the technique for film. In most films, the system of leitmotifs is fairly rudimentary, with a main theme perhaps associated with the hero, a secondary theme with the love interest, and perhaps a third theme for the villain. Kalinak mentions Max Steiner's maxim that "every character should have a theme" (quoted in 1992, 104), but such thematic proliferation is rare. Although Steiner's scores often feature more leitmotifs than most, his practice nevertheless leans on two or three principal themes for a score's structure. The recurrence of the leitmotifs across the film then sketches out something like a main axis of action with the main theme, which captures the essence of the hero's character, and the secondary axis of romance with the love theme, which characterizes both the heroine and her relationship to the hero. The nature of the film determines whether the villain's theme appears only on the main axis or if it also threatens the axis of romance.

Captain Blood adheres somewhat to this basic schema, though Peter has three leitmotifs rather than one, the love theme derives from one of Peter's leitmotifs (1992, 109), and the villainous characters do not have well-marked leitmotifs, being characterized more by malevolent mood music than strongly marked recurring themes. Kalinak claims that Korngold deployed "leitmotifs for Peter Blood as well as for King James and King William; for all the important locations . . . ; for the love between Peter Blood and Arabella Bishop; and for the torturous slavery on Colonel Bishop's plantation (which doubles as a motif for Colonel Bishop)" (105). Characterizing music exists for each of these items to be sure, but most of this music is deployed as musical topics or mood music rather than leitmotifs because it is not often repeated dramatically so as to become detached from its generic reference. Kalinak recognizes this emphasis to some extent when she focuses her analyses on the three motifs for Peter, with brief comments on the love theme. These are in fact the leitmotifs that most structure the score.

Idiom. This category explicitly addresses style and tone and implicitly the communicative efficacy of music. Of all the categories that Kalinak explores, idiom seems the most contingent, lacking on first impression a solid theoretical foundation. Kalinak follows common descriptions of film music as based on a nineteenth-century chromatically intensified symphonic style. (Copland and the authors of *Composing for the Films* both make this claim as well.) Although true in a broad sense for the film scores of the 1930s, actual practice was eclectic from the beginning, including popular styles such as jazz (associated with the urban milieu) and a considerable amount of the kind of dissonance characteristic of contemporary concert hall composition of the time (such music was useful in grotesque, "screwy," and horror scenes and any situation that depicted abnormal situations). If the style of Hollywood film music from the 1930s can nevertheless be broadly characterized as in a late romantic, intensified chromatic, symphonic style, this has more to do with a general ethos than the particulars of the style.

Kalinak offers several explanations for the adoption of this style: two historical reasons (the training of the composers and the tradition of the silent film), two ideological rationales (Caryl Flinn's [1992] idea that the romantic idiom allowed composers to believe that they were individual artists in a corporate world and the idea of uplift, namely, that the musical style imported the Vienna Opera House to Hollywood), and a structural explanation (the dominant melody and accompaniment texture of late romantic style was highly suited to the hierarchical organization of film, which attempts to sort all elements into foreground and background). The last explanation especially is somewhat dubious. Although symphonic style frequently deployed the melody and accompaniment texture, this was more common for vocal-like melodies, andantes, dances, marches, and other music that invoked popular or nationalistic genres and topics. Properly symphonic themes, on the contrary, were more likely to be built through motivic work allocated contrapuntally throughout the texture. Kalinak is quite right that melody and accompaniment was (and continues to be) the dominant texture of film scoring, however.

Still these explanations do not seem theoretically robust. Was it a mere fluke of history or quirk of ideology that resulted in the late romantic symphonic style becoming the lingua franca of Hollywood? Putting the question this way is actually more clarifying than it might seem, for the symphonic idiom offered a well-articulated repertory of meaningful devices (codes, musical topics) in a traditional, if slightly out-of-date, style that formed the basis of the operatic and concert programming of the time. In this respect it was indeed akin to a musical "mother tongue," and so its conventions offered a musical basis for efficient expression and communication. Kalinak notes, for instance, how meaningful orchestration could be, where the brass fanfare that Korngold wrote as *Captain Blood*'s main theme deploys "the power of the horns to suggest heroism" (1992, 101). Even more telling in this respect is the scoring of the pirate theme for Peter, which uses French horns to construct a musical trope that combines the hunting musical topic with the musical topic of the fantastic. Moreover, the late romantic symphonic style was an idiom that was flexible enough to assimilate many of the newer currents of style, including the impressionism of Debussy and Ravel, the primitivist nationalist style of early Stravinsky, popular styles like jazz, the American pastorale style of Copland, and even aspects of the atonal style of German expressionism, so long as the music could be classified as meaningful musical figures.

EXPLICIT RELATIONS OF MUSIC TO NARRATIVE

Kalinak notes that music has various ways of relating to the sequence or situation, but these can be classified into two broad categories: whether music plays to what is explicit in the scene, especially action or spectacle, or to what is implicit, like feeling or thoughts (1992, 84).

Modifying music. Music that has an explicit motivation in the scene will normally be a form of modifying music in Carroll's sense, and its primary function is accompaniment. *Captain Blood* opens *in medias res* with Jeremy Pitt riding furiously on horseback as bombs explode all around him. The music, a rapid hurry (a theatrical genre to accompany action), captures and reinforces the tempo of the frantic ride (1992, 84). Here music does not really create the desperate nature of the ride, which is evident enough from the scene, but music does seem to qualify the desperation.

Mickey-mousing. A second, more extreme realization of playing explicitly to the action in the image is the device of mickey-mousing, where music closely mimics an action rather than simply trying to qualify it (1992, 85–86). Because it draws attention to the music, mickey-mousing is used very judiciously in dramatic scoring during the classical era, but its use is commonplace for punctuation of a significant action, whether as a stinger to emphasize a startling dramatic moment (such as when the prisoner is branded with the mark of the "fugitive traitor") or a short passage to mark a longer action (as when Colonel Bishop is tossed off the ship) (86).

Spectacle. A third kind of explicit motivation is spectacle, which is usually marked by privileging of music (1992, 97). "The creation of spectacle in the classical narrative model afforded music this [elevated] position, where virtuosic technical display was heightened by the substitution of music for sound" (97). The virtuosic technical display could consist of musical performance, sublime cinematography of landscapes, or special editing patterns as with montage. Kalinak includes main and end titles under the category of spectacle as well. Credit sequences feature a special mode of extradiegetic address but also a transition into the film (as with a dissolve from the main title into the opening sequence) or out of the film (from the final scene into the credits).

In *Captain Blood*, the title music, which offers the regular varied alternation of two leitmotifs associated with Peter, ends with a segue to the hurry that accompanies Jeremy Pitt's furious ride. A transition shot showing the king's decree posted on a building serves as a narrative hinge to the depiction of the ride, and musically the static image of the decree is accompanied by a tonally unstable fanfare derived from the main theme that dissolves into hurry music on the cut to the ride. Once the ride starts, the music defaults to its common role of modifying music, that is, as accompaniment, with the image (and even sound effects) dominating the musical treatment, which simply establishes a rapid tempo and a frantic mood. But from the opening Warner shield up through the tonally uncertain fanfare that marks the decree, music dominates, and the tonal slips of the fanfare, desperately seeking firm tonal ground, seem to foreshadow music's loss of autonomous representational power once the narrative work of the film begins. The title music's indefinite evocations of an epic world of grand adventure—now brashly heroic, now lovingly tender—give way to something far more specific and much more of human scale with the plunge into narrative. In the brief main title, music associates with spectacle to paint this world as it wants to be, and the film will reach for music and spectacle whenever it approaches this idealistic conception, which marks not so much an external point to narrative as the horizon of its all-encompassing world.

IMPLICIT RELATIONS OF MUSIC TO NARRATIVE

Besides playing to action explicit in a scene, music can also draw out what is only implicit (1992, 86). Kalinak's account of how a string tremolo can create suspense that is not otherwise in a sequence is an excellent example of this. With respect to implicit content, film music is "expected to perform a variety of functions: provide characterization, embody abstract ideas, externalize thought, and create mood and emotion" (86). In general, thought, emotion, and feeling are properties internal to the characters and so not visible in the image. Our experience of our own world allows us to recognize that people have a private side that they may keep hidden, and this assumption of an interiority that is at least partially occluded is basic to the aesthetic of psychological realism that is most commonly used in the classical system. Of course, we can discern aspects of this interiority from a character's actions, demeanor, and speech. Emotional intensity is conventionally cued visually through close-up, lighting, mise-en-scène, and vocal delivery. But music seems to reach deeper than the image, divining what is otherwise hidden in the interior of the character; it can convince us that an otherwise innocuous facial gesture bears emotional significance. Indeed, it can convince us that a character has an emotion that could not be deduced otherwise from the image.

Emotion. Music is commonly associated with emotion, and film music often underscores emotional and affective states, using its referential codes to assign emotion so that the music sounds like the character feels. As noted, film also developed a number of visual devices to suggest a heightened emotional state, and an actor's bearing and vocal delivery could be tapped as well. "The focal point of this process became the music which externalized these codes through the collective resonance of musical associations. Music is, arguably, the most efficient of these cases, providing an audible definition of the emotion which the visual apparatus offers" (1992, 87).

Subjectivity. Emotion is an aspect of subjectivity, but Kalinak also emphasizes the role that music plays in marking point of view, that is, establishing what narratologists call focalization (see chapter 6). When several characters are present in a scene, music (but also other elements of the filmic system) usually selects one of them for special treatment, and it is as though we are hearing through the music what that character is feeling. "Music encodes not only emotion but point of view. The classical narrative model developed a number of conventions for internal thought including voiceover, specific editing patterns (the eyeline match especially combined with the dissolve), and musical accompaniment. Together or separately, these techniques offered an analogue for a character's consciousness" (1992, 90).

In *Captain Blood*, there are several scenes where camera technique and music combine to conjure a vision, as if we have entered into the mind of a character. When Peter leaves port in his new pirate ship, "a dolly-out on Blood aboard ship is positioned as the object of [Arabella's] eyeline match" (1992, 90), even though the scale of the match is impossible. This makes Peter appear as if in Arabella's thought. Such visions are often coupled with fantasy. When, after a period of successful pirating, Peter receives word that there is an English ship on the horizon, his crew declines to give chase. Looking out over the sea, Peter seems to be thinking of Arabella as first we hear her leitmotif, and then her image seems conjured as the match to his eyeline. The scene on Arabella's ship, however, briefly takes on a life of its own, as it is played as a distant reverse-shot, a massive expansion in the knowledge of the film's narration, with a report of a pirate ship, and Arabella's eyeline calling up Peter and his leitmotif. But of course nothing other than the crossing of visions here establishes the ship Peter sees as Arabella's, and indeed the whole scene aboard Arabella's ship may well be imagined by Peter. Such giddy narrative confusion of improbable coincidence and fantasy was common in these kinds of action-adventure films (and the novels on which the films are based), so deciding between the alternatives was never really the point, but the use of Arabella's leitmotif in the sequence ensured that the fantasy element would be as prominent as the coincidence.

COMBINING IMPLICIT AND EXPLICIT RELATIONS OF MUSIC TO NARRATIVE

Mood. Where emotion and subjectivity are implicit but centered on a particular character, mood is implicit but with a more generic level of signification. In the language of narratology, its focalization is external even though its reference is implicit, whereas that of emotion and subjectivity is internal with implicit reference. When music creates a general sense of suspense, agitation, dread, and so forth, and these feelings belong to the setting and not the characters, then the implicit relation of music and narrative is one of mood. Mood can also sometimes fit with the explicit relation of music and image inasmuch as it can reference time and place. "Mood music tapped the power of collective associations to create the time and place represented in the image" (1992, 90). Of course, this is an explicit relation of music and image, not an implicit one. When the ship makes the passage from England to the Caribbean with its cargo of condemned men, for instance, the passage of the ship is marked by music that evokes a ship at sea, but it also has a doleful quality that carries the grave tone of the narrative situation but that is not fully evident in shots of the ship.

Underscoring. This is a peculiar function of film music—only radio dramas have anything like it and then only when music is added to a prerecorded reading of the lines—and, like mood music, it can fluctuate between explicit and implicit relations to the image. Sometimes it is quite neutral, as Copland noted. In fact, it rarely if ever relates to the image directly and is more dependent on the speech of the character than actions. "The conventions of underscoring developed to bring the expressive possibilities of music to the human voice" (Kalinak 1992, 94). Explicitly, underscoring responds to tempo, pitch, and breaks in the dialogue. Because dialogue is given priority (93), the first function of underscoring is to avoid adversely affecting the intelligibility of the dialogue. The music will often, however, try to emphasize the emotional drive of speech, becoming more impassioned as the speech becomes more riled up, and so forth. Another effective device for underscoring dialogue is for music to punctuate the speech with stingers, which can produce an effect similar to accompanied recitative in opera. Kalinak analyzes the moment when Peter and his men get ready to sail off as a pirate ship for the first time to illustrate the technique. Peter's line, "Break out those sails and watch them fill with the wind that's carrying us all to freedom," is accompanied by

> a rising sequence in the violins, which create a sense of anticipation. At the pause after the phrase "Break out those sails," an orchestral chord punctuates Blood's speech, almost as if it were the equivalent of a comma. The next phrase is "punctuated" similarly, with chords after "and" and "watch" speeding up the delivery of the line and lending an urgency to Flynn's intonation. The final two chords punctuate the line after "the wind." A drum roll culminates on the last word in the line, "freedom," obviously drawing attention to its importance. The tension set up by the drum roll is resolved when the full orchestrated version of the Blood motif returns at the conclusion of Flynn's dialogue. (95)

Besides the explicit relation to dialogue, underscoring can also play against the words to indicate an implicit layer. In *Captain Blood*, many of the early scenes between Arabella and Peter work this way, as music disregards their bickering words to focus on establishing a romantic mood.

Nicholas Cook and Multimedia Systems

As Kalinak notes, classical film theories have a visual bias, and this bias has infiltrated many of the terms we use to talk about sound and music in film. In particular, much of the language understands music as qualifying a meaning that is already there. This is the basis of Carroll's modifying music, which is fully in line with classical film theory in this respect. Nicholas Cook (1998) accepts Kalinak's analysis of the issue and extends it: the problem, Cook says, is less the primacy of the image than a hegemonic structure that requires one medium to be the source of meaning and all others to be only qualifications of it. In such a structure, "there is nowhere that such an approach can locate the emergence of new meaning" from interaction among media (115).

Cook, a trained music theorist, works to develop a theory that can account for such interaction in a meaningful way. Cook's theory is not specifically directed at film music but rather at music in the general multimedia situation, that is, any system that combines music with at least one other medium in a single artwork. He does not deny that the "hegemonic" situation occurs; in fact, he argues that this is the way that most theories have erroneously understood interactions. For Cook, such interaction does not normally yield a situation where one medium is hegemonic and another submissive; nor do the media generally interact in a way that is simply additive. Rather, media more commonly interact in a way that produces emergent properties, that is, where the meaning that arises from the interaction cannot be predicted from the media assessed separately. Cook considers the sequence from *Psycho* where Marion drives through the rain and then pulls over.

> Herrmann's angular, repetitive music does not connect in a literal manner with anything that is visible on the screen: it does not obviously synchronize, for instance, with the regular rhythm of the wiper blades, or the irregular rhythms outlined by the lights of the oncoming cars. And whereas its busy quality, its high level of activity, could be seen as corresponding to the speed of the car and the rain, the music continues at its own pace as the car slows down and stops. Rather than corresponding to anything that is visible music jumps the diegetic gap, so to speak, "seeking out" and uncovering the turmoil in Marion's mind, and thus transferring its own qualities to her. Its angular contours embody her unease; the repetitions and constricted quality of the orchestration create an obsessive quality, rather like when you go over the same thing again and again in your mind. The process works the other way round, too; heard in the context of the film sequence, the music acquires a specifically sinister quality that it does not have by itself. And the result of these reciprocal interactions is to create a bond of empathy between audience and film character. (1998, 66–67)

By "jumping the diegetic gap," Cook means that the music shifts from being a kind of external commentary like providing general mood or describing the rain and shifts to being an internal representation like interior thoughts and feelings. In this case the music seems to sound like Marion feels. In any case, as Cook notes, this is not a situation where music imitates the narrative or even amplifies something already there or vice versa but where music participates at a basic level in the construction of the scene. Music plays the role of indirect discourse.

> This account of the familiar working of music in the narrative cinema illustrates the principle of difference. . . . The music is not simply more or less similar to the pictures, in the static manner of Eisensteinian correspondence. Instead, the relationship between music and pictures has a dynamic, processive character, passing from difference at one level to similarity at another; by virtue of jumping the diegetic gap . . . the music signifies in a manner that is qualitatively different from the pictures, and the issue of parallelism or counterpoint accordingly takes on a quite different aspect. (67)

Cook presumes that each medium is a relatively autonomous system, so, for instance, the soundtrack and the filmed image would form two mediums. Indeed, Cook's definition of medium is not bound to mechanical reproduction, so it is not the two physical mediums of soundtrack and film, say, that is key to making film multimedia, but the existence of multiple media systems: music, dialogue, and sound effects are in this sense not simply components of the soundtrack but separate mediums that are then combined on the physical medium of the soundtrack, which is therefore already an instance of multimedia.

As noted, the compounding of these systems into instances of multimedia does not produce sums of effects but rather emergent properties, which Cook sees as operating by the logic of metaphor, a logic that is also, he thinks, the means by which musical meaning emerges in general. Music and the other media share an "enabling similarity," and the potency of metaphor is evaluated by "what the similarity enables, which is to say, the *transfer of attributes* from one term of the metaphor to the other" (1998, 70, emphasis in original).

Following Kalinak, Cook is especially concerned with the constructive aspect of music, seeing most theories of music and cinema, for instance, as restricting music to a subsidiary role of "expressing" aspects of the narrative, such as characters' feelings, already presumed to be there.

> To see the music as expressing the characters' inner thoughts is to naturalize the latter, to suggest that they have some kind of priority over the music. It is to reduce the music to a kind of supplementary role, underlining or projecting something that already exists. It is, in short, to collude with Hollywood in its creating of the "transparent or invisible discourse" of which Gorbman spoke. (1998, 86)

This case is more complicated than Cook portrays it inasmuch as such feelings are, as Kalinak notes, usually only implicit in the image. The priority in this case runs not really to the image or to the character as depicted but to the narrative that allows us to believe that these characters have thoughts and feelings. "In reality, music—like any other filmic element—participates in the *construction* of cinematic characters, not their reproduction, just as it participates in the construction, not the reproduction, of all cinematic effects" (1998, 86, emphasis added). The thoughts and feelings in the scene may not precede the existence of the music, which does the main work of constructing them, but the image, the music, the dialogue, and so forth all shape the scene under the presumption that these characters have thoughts and feelings.

The insistence that music is a constructive force in film means that although Cook questions whether music's autonomy is ever anything more than "an aesthetician's (or music theorist's) fiction" (1998, 92), he nevertheless must uphold the notion that music is a relatively autonomous system among other filmic systems in order for it to do its constructive work. Indeed, he mostly agrees with the proposition inherited from formalism that music itself is only form, not content, the difference being that he believes music rarely if ever exists in such a state (i.e., as music itself). "Music," he says, "is never 'alone'"

(23). "Music alone"—he borrows the term from Peter Kivy (1990)—is not a real state of any existing music but only a structuring ideal that serves to ensure that its subsystem remains relatively autonomous and that music is empty but capable of absorbing meaning when it is inevitably incorporated into multimedia. Music in media, Cook says, is usually "empty of meaning, but ready to accommodate any meaning that is aligned to it, or even to create meaning where there was none" (1998, 96). Music combines easily with other media, and meaning is always emerging from these encounters. To the extent that this meaning cannot be reduced to that of the other medium, it is constructed by the interaction between the media.

Cook aims to consider music and the other media—text, dialogue, image, and so forth—independently so as "to provide an inventory of the ways in which different media can relate to one another" (1998, 98). By applying two tests, Cook sorts the relationships according to three potential models: if a similarity test shows that the two media are consistent, the model is "conformance." If the test shows that the two media are coherent rather than consistent, on the other hand, he applies a further "difference" test, which finds the two media either contrary, in which case the model is "complementation," or contradictory, in which case the model is "contest" (86–106). Cook also divides conformance into three subtypes: triadic, where each media relates to the others through a third term (e.g., emotion); dyadic, where each media relates to the others in a pairwise fashion; or unitary, where one media is dominant while the others conform to it. As Cook notes, unitary conformant relationships are "vanishingly rare" (102) in practice, but it has also been the most common way of theorizing interactions in part because it establishes a clear hierarchy between them. In classical theory, parallelism is usually presented as music (or sound) being subservient to the image or as being redundant. In practice, parallelism is more generally an example of triadic conformance, where both music and image conform to the needs of narrative, and the individual component media slide in and out of conformance, complementation, and contest with each other. This was the situation I described previously with music relating implicitly to thought and feeling, a situation that in turn has some affinities with Annabel Cohen's congruence-associationist model discussed later.

David Neumeyer and Vococentrism

Whereas Kalinak presents a working model for understanding classical Hollywood film music that does not presume at every turn a visual bias toward film and Cook develops a theory of the emergent properties that result from musical multimedia, David Neumeyer (2015) is concerned with developing an analytical toolkit for understanding music's place and work in the soundtrack.

He begins with two premises—"the integrated sound track is basic, and the cinema is vococentric" (3)—and extracts three principles from them:

> the first of which recognizes that the sound track is the film's audio system and asserts that, as such, the sound track has priority over any of the individual elements. The second acknowledges that the sound track is constructed—the overriding priority in the classical system being narrative clarity, not acoustic fidelity—and it is hierarchical, with the voice (speech, dialogue) at the top, music and sound effects below. The third follows directly from the second: film music is stylistically plural. It is in fact any music used in a film. (3)

Compared with the other theorists we have considered in this chapter, Neumeyer is most explicit in confronting the hierarchical structure of sound film. His distinctive contribution is placing film music within a framework of vococentrism, a concept he develops from Michel Chion (1994 and especially 1999; Chion's theories will be treated later in chapter 8 on psychoanalysis). Music may form a semiautonomous subsystem in film, but the vococentrism of sound film ensures that music must always confront a hierarchy where the voice is assigned priority. This does not mean that the voice is always dominant but rather that any displacement of the voice is heard as such. For Neumeyer, vococentrism reflects the reality of filmic structure; understanding that begins from the premise that vococentrism "yields results that are truer to film as an art. Furthermore, it is both richer and more nuanced with respect to music than the all-too-common approach in which film is seen as a backdrop for interpretation of its music" (5).

Along with the assertion of vococentrism, Neumeyer retains, perhaps unnecessarily, the usual bias from classical film theory that film is a visual medium, and he transforms it into a hierarchy:

> In the classical model, narrative-image-sound may be a set of relations, but it is first of all a hierarchy. Narrative unfolded by images—the fundamental property of a film—is supported by sound: most directly (and one can argue necessarily) by speech, more indirectly (and one can argue incidentally) by music and effects. (2015, 12)

This is debatable. Although narrative clearly stands above image and sound, the actual hierarchy between image and sound is more nebulous. As I documented in chapters 2 and 3, classical film theory certainly agrees with Neumeyer that narrative is principally image based. The practice of the films, however, does not. Early sound film was if anything dominated by dialogue, which determined everything from lighting to mise-en-scène to shooting schedule to editing patterns. This dominance would be mitigated as the practice of sound film was codified, but dialogue remained, as the term "vococentrism" suggests, central to the conception of narrative. We can also recognize the uncertainty as to hierarchical status in Neumeyer's classification of the two basic formal structures of dialogue and spectacle. Dialogue is, as Neumeyer says, the ordinary basic filmic structure, and he attributes agency in these appropriately to the soundtrack. By contrast, spectacle, which are the moments of antinarrative or narrative inefficiency that narrative film deploys against itself to tap the power of intensity and memorability (30), is also the basic structure in which image (but also music) has agency. This classification of basic structures is persuasive, but it runs against the idea that dialogue is hierarchically subordinated to the image. This is not to say that image is subordinated to the voice, even if the voice has principal agency in most dialogue scenes. The voice, like most sounds, is a property of the image in the classical system; that is, the image reveals its source, and the status of voice as an index to the body in the image rebalances the hierarchy so that it is not weighted in favor of the voice. We can say then with confidence only that both image and dialogue are subordinated to narrative; that the figure in the image, especially the face, subordinates other visual elements; and that the voice subordinates other soundtrack elements. The actual hierarchy between voice and figure remains uncertain and depends on whether structural subordination follows from the logic of dialogue that guides the construction of the sequence or from the source of the voice that roots dialogue in a body of the depicted world.

Not insisting on a visual bias leaves interpretive options more open, and this seems more in keeping with Neumeyer's ecumenical bent. In general, Neumeyer constructs his theory to allow as much interpretive latitude and diversity as possible. The viewpoint he constructs to survey the theoretical terrain is panoptic and reminiscent of semiotics, especially with his invocation of the "author-text-reader tricolon" as the basis for the initial articulation of the field. His aim is only to develop a map of the full theoretical terrain and insist that we, as interpreters, be responsible about locating our position within the field of possibilities rather than placing prohibitions on certain positions or movements. "I assert that the interpreter must always be clear in locating the focus and . . . be willing to acknowledge its limitations" (2015, 6). Thus, although he draws heavily on Bordwell's work and finds Bordwell's appeals to both cognition studies and careful historical study congenial, Neumeyer does not share Bordwell's general skepticism of hermeneutics, and believes that a hermeneutics can be forged that accepts Bordwell's insistence that interpretation be grounded in historical specificity (conventions of style) rather than conventions of interpretation (6). Analysis and interpretation are almost impossible to disentangle in practice since both rely on both implicit and explicit meanings, and the general drift in the humanities from analysis based in structural models and close reading to interpretation underwritten by critical practices has been part of a historical corrective.

> By the late 1960s, the opposition closed system/infinite meaning began
> to shift criticism into its poststructuralist phase, and with that change
> attention swiftly moved away from the text to the reader (or viewer,
> audio-viewer . . ., critic), most directly through interpretive models of
> deconstruction in literary studies . . . and reader-response theory, but
> also through cognitivist analytical models, most prominently . . . for film
> studies through Bordwell's narrative theory. (6)

Neumeyer is less concerned with which position within the tricolon a researcher chooses to occupy than that the position be recognized in a self-
conscious way. "Separating textual effects from interpretive practices—at least
provisionally—has greater heuristic value for the study of films, and sound
and music integrated within them, than does insisting that they cannot or
should not be separated" (6–7). More important than policing the boundaries
of analysis and interpretation is separating meaning, which belongs to the text
and is unpacked using stylistic knowledge, from interpretation, which belongs
to the reader (audio-viewer) and the critical practices that regulate it (5).

Neumeyer's own interpretive concerns center on classical Hollywood
films and the vococentric model that evolved to govern its practice; he is
especially interested in understanding how music functions in the classical
system. "Music's first allegiance is to narrative" (2015, 29). His approach is
both structural and functional, and he develops a set of five functional binary
oppositions to guide his analysis (64): (1) clarity/fidelity, (2) foreground/
background, (3) diegetic/nondiegetic, (4) synchronization/counterpoint, and
(5) empathy/anempathy. The first binary, he says, is really an opposition of
aesthetic principles, and clarity is the principle that "guarantees the functional priority of the other four binaries" (64). He includes it among the other
binaries because the opposition "can sometimes have expressive effects" (64).
The ordinary, unmarked shot in the classical system embraces the first term of
each binary (65), and collectively they constitute the terms of vococentrism;
yet the other binaries are not really derived from the binary of clarity and
fidelity. Indeed, fidelity often means an erosion of these binaries if not an
actual subversion of them. That is, a faithful recording might emphasize mis-
cellaneous background noises that distract from the dialogue because in real
life the world is largely indifferent to the needs of conversation; it might fail
to keep the talking subject in the frame so that the sound becomes asynchronous because in real life the subject knows nothing of the position of
the camera; or it might include whatever sound or music that happens to
occur, whether it is appropriate to the emotional tenor of the scene or not.
The binary of diegetic/nondiegetic, however, simply disappears under fidelity
since there is no outside of the faithfully reproduced world. (There is really
no inside—that is, depth—to this world either since a faithful reproduction
simply shows the world as it appears.)

I would expand this set of binaries to include two others that Neumeyer develops apart from the basic five, because they are also central to the articulation of the diegesis in the classical system: (6) onscreen/offscreen and (7) exterior/interior. The first term of each of these binaries likewise represents the unmarked situation in an ordinary shot. Neumeyer presumably excludes the onscreen/offscreen binary from the basic set because he sees it as classifying attributes of the diegesis from the standpoint of the narration (what is shown versus what is not shown) rather than being filmic elements themselves (2015, 77). That is, the distinction between onscreen and offscreen ordinarily belongs to how the diegesis is represented rather than being part of the diegetic representation itself—though subjective and semisubjective shots can confuse the issue. The binary of exterior (real) and interior (psychological) concerns the representation of character depth within the diegesis, and so belongs to the psychological dimension of "constructed realism" (23). Neumeyer's working out of these binaries in his analysis of *Rebecca* (1940) indicates the important role these binaries play in constituting diegetic space (77–95).

The premise of constructed realism is that sound film is not a recording of the world, but instead its world is built into an imagined diegesis. "In the classical synchronized cinema, onscreen space and diegetic place are made to coincide so that the character or object appears naturally unified, the representation of an organic body, whatever sort of world that body may seem to occupy" (2015, 23). Important bodies are synchronized bodies, and the sounds of these bodies, especially dialogue, is given special treatment that ensures its foreground status. In our world, dialogue would simply be one sound among others, a part of the world, but in film it is raised up, given emphasis, much like the figure of a main character is distinguished from people in a crowd. "The background, by contrast, defines that world and need not be synchronized even when it is motivated" (23). Objects in the background, even when they are people, are marked as background through a lack of synchronization. On set, extras in crowds silently mimic chatter, which is then replaced in postproduction with appropriate crowd noise, and the fact that we do not find synchronization cues between image and the background chatter allows us to recognize the speech as noise rather than significant dialogue. Music works similarly, its background status also signaled by a lack of synchronization. If it also lacks motivation in the image, as is common for film music, this nondiegetic status is not usually problematic even though it may be unrealistic. "Traditional nondiegetic music . . . can be understood as a stylized background—like stylized sets or lighting" (23). This pairing of foreground dialogue (diegetic and synchronized) and background music (nondiegetic and nonsynchronized) is the ordinary situation of the vococentric cinema, and it marks out what Neumeyer calls an "axis of psychological realism" (80) that typically governs the classical system. Departures from this axis then become expressive deviations that can be deployed to do things like create an overwhelming sense of malevolent presence of the title character in *Rebecca*. Even though we never see her in the film or hear her voice, both the pictures and the soundtrack register her almost ubiquitous presence (85–86).

According to Neumeyer, synchronized speech secures a place for the rest of the soundtrack. Music works by iconism, mimicking "the voice's functions and modes" (2015, 31). Music in film doesn't quite work like music outside of film, and music's resemblance to speech in film is both a distinctive element and a limitation. Neumeyer identifies three primary functions music performs: "(1) referentially (supplying or reinforcing identifying markers of time place, social status, ethnicity, etc.); (2) expressively (as a marker of emotion); (3) motivically (that is, in the manner of the motif in literature or motive in music, supplying recurring elements that help to clarify the process of narrative comprehension)" (11). These functions all involve ways of music becoming stuck to meaning in a way that impedes the music's "flow." Neumeyer here draws on Carolyn Abbate's idea (2004) that music is "sticky." For Abbate, words, images, and physical gestures stick to music. But for Neumeyer, music sticks to images, and is carried along by them. Music's relation to meaning therefore often clogs up the works, and music ceases to flow as music. "Music that is 'stuck' to organized meaning pays homage to the vococentric nature of cinema. The more music participates in supporting, advancing, or commenting on narrative, the more it loses the integrity of its diachronic flow" (13). Here, Neumeyer seems to be describing a species of modifying music in Carroll's sense of the term. In any case, the invocation of referential and expressive codes suggests a semiotic. "Like the insert in the image track, a topical reference or motivic recall in the music element of the sound track particularly pulls the audio-viewer out of the diachronic flow" (15).

The conception is both powerful and monstrous. "Music's curiously subversive power: the voice that cannot be a voice speaking a well-defined body of codes that cannot be a language" (2015, 31). Film music's lack is not so much its sacrifice of flow for meaning or a failure to transform codes into "real" language, but a "voice" that would relate music to narrative and ensure that its "first allegiance" really was to the film's narrative rather than its own peculiar meaning or its own flow. "Music needs the voice—or to put it another way, music needs the hierarchy of sound and links to image and narration guaranteed by the voice. Speech mediates for a music that, except in performance and perhaps in spectacle in mute emotion, really has no place in the cinema except by the historical coincidence of certain theatrical conventions" (24). In and of itself, this assertion is somewhat peculiar, and, as a matter of fact, it is questionable as the case of silent film suggests. And "music's curiously subversive power" derives from its ability to mimic the voice, on the one hand, yes, but also to follow its own flow, on the other.

That said, Neumeyer's key insight here is that the presence of the voice creates a need for its setting, that is, a background plane, and this background plane authorizes in a sense any approach that subordinates the background to the voice. He summarizes Altman, Tatroe, and Jones (2000): "The significant historical event was the development of background sound, in relation to which a distinct and effective role for nondiegetic music could be found" (2015, 24). During the transition to sound, a surprising technological finding was that silence did not generally make an effective background for the voice because the variability of recording from shot to shot, the sound edits, and the ground noise of the disk or soundtrack drew attention to the apparatus. A positive background sound, whether music or ambience, greatly mitigated these issues, and music was generally the easier to control once rerecording processes were developed to an acceptable quality. The unreality of a musical background, moreover, helped facilitate the stratification of representation required to articulate the diegesis into exterior and interior.

> What music *did* contribute was some of the elements of stylization that were required if the talking film was to be construed as something other than a recording of the world. The principle of psychological realism governing narrative film requires such stratification—that is to say, the audio-viewer must be given a means to discern that the world depicted is not simply what is seen and heard but something more or other than what it appears to be. (24)

The stylization of music thus both served a background function that established the continuity of the aural space and opened the representational plane to the interior of the image.

Annabel Cohen and the Congruence-Association Model

Annabel Cohen begins a recent summary article on film music and cognitive science with a brief description of a scene from *Avatar* (2009). On Jake's first visit to the planet, his team is attacked and Jake becomes separated, jumps off a cliff into a pool of water, and pulls himself out. As he forms a weapon, Neytiri is about to shoot him when a wood sprite appears. A helicopter that arrived to extract Jake's team departs, stranding Jake. Following the music, Cohen (2014) divides the scene into four segments.

> In this short sequence of barely a minute, four contrasting music cues parallel distinct activities in the film—the orchestral music associated with the chase, the heart-beat music foretelling danger [when Neytiri is about to shoot him], the delicate music associated with the wood sprite and Jake's goodness, and the ponderous diminished triad music associated with the departure of the helicopter. (99)

For Cohen, this short sequence is unequivocal proof that music adds meaning to a film, and indeed its rapid changes suggest that music plays a reactive role to the narrative situation. At the same time, once placed in a narrative situation, music also facilitates memory of that situation, and played alone it can also immediately conjure images of situation.

The psychology of film music is interested in the perception and cognition of film music, how people make sense of film and how music in particular facilitates this process. Cohen chose the sequence from *Avatar* not because it is particularly rich or interesting, but because it is exemplary of how music ordinarily functions in film. She notes that a cognitive scientist or experimental psychologist would extract three claims from our ordinary experience of the sequence to examine: "(1) music interprets and adds meaning; (2) it aids memory; (3) it engages the audience" (2014, 101). That is, a psychological (or cognitive science) theory of film music would need to offer a convincing explanation for these three claims, and Cohen has proposed what she calls the congruence-associationist model (CAM) to do so. The current version of CAM is quite complex, and it is perhaps best understood by examining its genesis, since some of its attributes are more easily comprehended in their earlier, simpler form.

CAM began as a simple framework for explaining the first claim (Marshall and Cohen 1988), and Cohen has expanded it to encompass a fairly robust model that addresses all three claims (summarized in Cohen 2013, 2014). In developing the initial framework, Cohen and her student Sandra Marshall began with the idea that music simply added a meaning to the film. What they observed, however, was that music does not add meaning in a simple fashion, but that it in fact interprets the image as well. In particular, music evidently has the capability to draw out and color elements of the image differentially. This led them to the important conclusion that associations of music accrued with the congruence of internal structure between music and image. Any structures that did not find congruence were ignored by the audio-viewer. That is, the congruence of internal structure marked a visual element for attention, and the full associations of the music could then pass to the structurally congruent elements in the image. It was thus possible for certain figures in an image (rather than the whole image) to accrue the associations of the music. A figure whose structure was congruent with the music could seem sad (while other characters did not) when the music was sad (2013, 19–28). The early iterations of CAM assumed visual dominance, and, although Cohen has weakened that assumption in later formulations, the visual remains the dominant stream even in the latest versions of the theory. This is to say that the auditory channels always modify the visual. Congruence also affects attention, so congruence/incongruence becomes a means of establishing a hierarchy of foreground and background. (Cohen implies this without explicitly stating it [23].) Congruence, moreover, has the strongest effect if meaning is underdetermined or ambiguous in one of the channels (26–27).

Subsequent modifications to CAM have worked to address points 2 and 3 on memory and audience engagement. Cohen first modified CAM to encompass audience engagement to provide a more plausible cognitive model of the audio-viewer. Her main concern here was to devise a model that included the active cognition of the subject, where the subject negotiated the bottom-up incoming perception and the top-down expectations formed in long-term memory to construct a "visual narrative." As the term "visual narrative" suggests, this version of the model continued to accept that film was dominated by its visual channel. This version of CAM also increased the input channels from two to three, adding speech to music and visuals, without, however, considering the degree to which the speech channel was itself narratively dominant. In the context of speech, it becomes clearer that congruence is closely aligned with the traditional category of synchronization (2013, 29), and one of the main things that CAM was devised to explain, namely, the differential effect music had on objects within an image, applies even more to speech, where common sense would suggest objects synchronized to speech are marked for attention far more than are objects congruent with music. Synchronization (or, in the parlance of CAM, congruence) is the basic device of the sound film for distinguishing figure and ground. The formulation just stated also prioritizes the visual inasmuch as it presumes that synchronized speech distinguishes a visual figure—marks it for attention—much more than synchronized speech distinguishes the voice, although it is not clear this is actually the case. (The face may dominate any image it belongs to, but images often feature multiple faces. With the soundtrack it is relatively rare for multiple voices to vie for attention in the same way, and when it happens, as in overlapping dialogue of screwball comedy, it usually occurs with both bodies in the image so that the overlapping dialogue upends hierarchical distinction much the same way that the narrative does.) The voice differs fundamentally from music in that it is normally attended to whether or not it is diegetic, and this complicates CAM's explanation of music's inaudibility since the internal structure of the voiceover does not disappear in the way music's does, even though neither is "generally part of the reality of the film story" (29). It would seem that noncongruence must be coupled with a condition of hierarchical subordination for it to disappear from consciousness in the way music in film often does. In addition, this version of CAM included the top-down processes from long-term memory, which fed expectations of narrative and proper channel formation. The visual narrative was thus a result of information from the film feeding up through the perceptual channels (bottom-up) and expectations from long-term memory feeding down into it (top-down).

This second iteration of CAM was criticized, once again, for its assumption of visual dominance and for its limited number of perceptual channels. It was also incoherent on how top-down processes affected the processing of music, which seemingly bypassed music short-term memory to work primarily through structural congruence of music and visuals, on the one hand, and through passing associations by means of leakage or short-circuiting directly to the visual narrative, on the other. Cohen responded to these criticisms with a third iteration of CAM, which usefully shifted from the concept of visual narrative to working narrative and increased the number of channels to correspond to Christian Metz's analysis (1974a): music, speech, noise (sound effects), visuals, and text. Each of these channels was subject to an initial brute-level analysis into structure and meaning. Congruence operated on structure, with congruent patterns marking prominent figures in the working narrative and associations carrying meanings from the channel into the working narrative. The mechanism of congruence means that the channels are especially susceptible to leakage in the bottom-up processes when structures in the channels synchronize, and in this way meanings can also appear cross-modally, with the associations synthesized in the bottom-up processing rather than in the working narrative. Of the channels, music seems especially prone to such cross-modal influence, especially when it is serving a background function but is congruent (but not fully synchronized) with a figure. This model also has a more coherent representation of how long-term memory affects the working narrative since expectations are recognized as having been primed in long-term memory along all channels with those expectations and then feeding down into the working narrative back along those channels. Finally, the model no longer assumes that the visual channel is dominant, and it becomes possible to consider narrative in terms of fluidity that might better explain the fluctuating quality of offscreen sound and nondiegetic music.

The most recent iteration of CAM is shown in Figure 5.1, and it addresses a problem of image analysis. While Metz had distinguished the image of things from the image of text, Cohen notes that empirical research has suggested that we process objects differently than movements, especially those that mimic the movements of the human body. She therefore added a kinesthetic channel to the model, though inexplicably she separated it from the visuals.[2] In terms of music, this channel seems especially important, as musical structure is more likely to be congruent with the motion of an object than with an object per se. On the other hand, music is more likely to form distinct semantic associations

---

[2] Cohen notes that technology allows seats in some theaters to shift with images, mimicking movement, but she also recognizes the motor neuron phenomenon, where watching someone else perform an action will activate motor neurons in our own brain. These seem to describe separate perceptual channels, one belonging to the visual stream, the other to the registering of bodily sensation. This suggests that, like the aural stream, the image stream might in fact be divided, with the latter falling into separate channels for objects and movements. The movement of seats to mimic filmed actions would in turn seem to belong to a separate channel yet.

with objects and to elicit images of those objects in memory. This is the common work of the leitmotif, and in general music is semantically sticky (Abbate 2004; Neumeyer 2015), whether music sticks to the images or vice versa. If "music marks images for conscious attention" (2014, 108), it would seem that this happens more as object than as movement. In such situations, there would also seem to be a semantic reversal as the affective quality of the music seems to pass to the movement often as a property or visual extension of feeling: any musically congruent movement registers as the object feeling like the music sounds. These final points are my extensions of the logic of CAM into a speculative synthesis.

Besides adding the kinesthetic channel, the current iteration of CAM also inserts a level between long-term memory and the working narrative where narrative hypotheses and expectations form prior to being integrated into the working narrative. Overall, CAM "conceptualizes a process of optimal synthesis whereby the physical elements of sound and light presented by the film, along with the mental memories and story grammars that the audience brings to the film situation, culminate in a 'working narrative,' or one's conscious experience of the film" (2014, 101). Cohen outlines a number of explanations that follow from this model. It gives an account of how music contributes

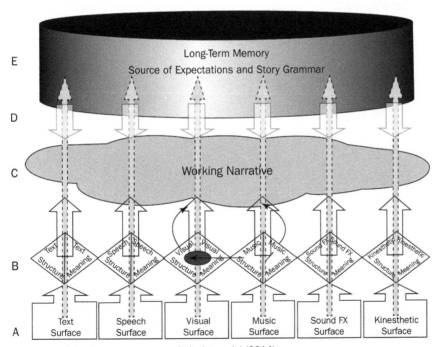

FIGURE 5.1 Cohen's congruence-associationist model (2014).

meanings and associations to the narrative. It describes how music can influence structural articulations in other channels and how it can affectively color the information in other channels (or indeed an element in another channel). It explains how music can make these contributions without being consciously noticed. It accepts that music can perform much of this work whether or not it is diegetic, nondiegetic, or some place in between. But the model also generates anomalies not mentioned by Cohen. First, it does not explain novelty very well. Level D in Figure 5.1 generates hypotheses, but when these are thwarted in clever and unexpected ways, it is not clear how the system responds, since the model insists that information from level B not consistent with level D is discarded. It must in fact be the case that information from level B is at some level retained so that it can be drawn on if the hypotheses from level D do not ultimately pan out. Second, the model presumes that music is basically additive, in the sense that music adds information to the primary visual channel. This is why the model says music can provide meaning without being consciously heard. But there are many instances in film where music dominates and even more instances where we are fully aware of the music. This is trivially the case in performances, but many sequences of scenic spectacle also feature music prominently and in a situation where most filmgoers consciously attend to the music. There are also instances where music runs contrary to the surface visuals, for example, elegiac lyrical music that sounds over images of an intense battle. In this case, it is the very incongruence that is affectively charged (and we often are very aware of the music in such cases as well).

6

Narratology and the Soundtrack

Introduction

No category has been as central to thinking about film and its emergence as an art form as narrative. As early as 1910, by far the greatest number of commercial films were narrative films, and thus, no matter what the specific issue that an early film theorist might be focused on, the connection to, or implications for, narrative and storytelling has always hovered over the conversation. Recall that Aaron Copland (2010a) insisted that film music be subordinated to story: "no matter how good, distinguished, or successful, the music must be secondary in importance to the story being told on the screen" (86). And often when classical theorists insisted on the visual dominance of film, they were instead advocating for narrative dominance and presuming that in sound film the image was (or should be) primarily responsible for carrying the narrative. In this way, "image" became a shorthand for narrative itself, even though it was actually carried primarily by image *and* dialogue.

The previous two chapters addressed primarily the immanent materials of film, how film structures them, and models for making sense of them. The several theories and models for analysis that we examined in the previous chapters all touched on narrative in one way or another, often quite explicitly. As we saw in chapter 4, semiotics systemically explored the analogy of film to language, and ultimately Christian Metz would, as we will see, locate the languagelike quality of film in narrative. Metz (1974a), indeed, saw narrative as more significant than the image. "The role of 'story' is so powerful that the image, which is said to be the major constituent of film, vanishes behind the plot it has woven . . . so that the cinema is only in theory the art of images" (45). In chapter 5, the predilections and preferences of the formalists and those doing related work led inevitably to questions of narrative even when the analysis was focused on shot composition, editing, modifying music, or the oppositions structuring the soundtrack. Narrative organizes the films at the highest level, so the needs of the narrative also affect style and technique at the most basic level. The broad framework for analysis was always going to be narrative.

Narratology and Film

The systematic scholarly study of narrative, narratology, developed out of structuralist approaches to semiotics and a return to the work of the Russian formalists. Scholars, especially those working on folklore who had been inspired by the writings of Claude Lévi-Strauss, inferred that stories were structured grammatically, much the same way as the sentences they were constructed with were. As befits its origin in semiotics, the basic methodology of narratology is structural and formal in nature. Gérard Genette's *Narrative Discourse* (1980), a study of Proust, established much of the formal terminology for the field of narratology. Proust's elaborate narrative style placed extreme pressure on both language and narrative structure, and Genette's study has both the advantages and disadvantages of that for a foundational text. Proust's challenging narration allowed Genette to catalogue a large number of exceptional narrative procedures, but it also left the more quotidian narrative elements less explored or serving only the instrumental function of explaining higher-level operations, deformations, and transformations. Besides favoring complexity, Genette's study also has a literary bias, since as a close study of Proust Genette had to attend to the subtleties and peculiarities of French novelistic discourse. Both issues became more significant with work that attempted to apply insights from Genette's work to other media and in attempts to derive from it a general narratology.

Narrative theory typically begins with a basic temporal distinction between the time of the story and the time of the narration. These two levels usually correspond to story and plot, although the terms can differ. Because much of this part of narratology derives from the work of the Russian formalists, the distinction of *fabula* (story) and *syuzhet* (plot) developed in various works by Viktor Shklovsky and Vladimir Propp is often used, as the Russian words have the advantage of clearly making themselves technical terms. Terms differ and occasionally migrate categories, but the distinction between the chronological order of action and the actual order in which it is told is basic to the conceptualization. (The *fabula* is actually closer to the material for the story than the story itself and includes aspects that do not appear in the story.) Most frequently, literary narratives mark this distinction with the past tense, which allows the narration to represent the appearance of something past; in that way both levels appear simultaneously in the narrative discourse of the narrator. Hence, "plot" is sometimes called by the form it takes in narrative, namely, "discourse" (Chatman 1980); that is, the story is plotted in discourse. This foregrounds narrative as an interpretive act, as a telling of some story that precedes the narrator's account of it. Story therefore has the appearance of truth, and the narrator can efface its own presence (attempt to make the narrative appear identical to the story), intervene to reveal some other truth or concern not apparent in the chronological story, or distort the story as a lie.

Greek philosophy already distinguished between poetic modes, with the epic using a voice to report (diegesis) acts from another time in present time and the drama using a body to imitate (mimesis) past acts in present time. Mikhail Bakhtin (1981) distinguishes in turn epic narration from the novel in terms of the distance of the narration: the epic relates to origins and national myths and presumes an absolute, inaccessible distance between the narrator and the story, whereas the novel is a secular form of narration that relativizes the distance in an almost pragmatic manner; it can draw the narrator and the reader close to the story, even into the interior of its characters in one scene, and then push away to a greater distance in another.

The variability of distance in the novel, which can at times virtually collapse into dramatic and lyrical effects, is significant inasmuch as it calls into question the necessity of distance—or even the existence of a narrator— for narration (see, for instance, Banfield 1992; Martin 1986). Distinguishing levels through some means is perhaps normative for narrative, at least literary forms, and when drama recounts stories instead of playing them out, it seems to be shifting modes and staging a narration. Film presents more difficulty still, combining, as Hanns Eisler and Theodor W. Adorno (1947) suggest, epic form in the classical sense but with dramatic action. This action is in turn cut and assembled in editing, and the tone and distance are often more novelistic than epic. Although film narratologists disagree on many particulars, they do concur that film narrative differs in fundamental ways from literary narrative. If editing distinguishes film absolutely from drama, positing a narrative agent who is calling the shots, the moving image, especially when coupled mimetically to the voice, on the contrary creates the impression that the movement is real, that it is happening as in a drama. Moreover, although editing clearly marks a different narrative level than action, editing also often seems to disappear—not because it is unobtrusive, though it is usually that too; not because viewers are passive and inattentive; but because editing is inseparable from the experience of the moving image that the cut ended and brought into being. We will return to the issue of film narration momentarily.

If the narration of film is frequently sufficiently effaced that it is lost in the experience of the real time of the film, art forms like music or painting do not have a reliable way of indicating narration at all, and some have questioned whether they generally allow for narrative forms. Carolyn Abbate (1991) suggests that instances of musical narration are rare and strange, like stage narrations. Jean-Jacques Nattiez (1990b), on the contrary, argues that listeners' experience of musical narration belongs not to the music but to listeners' accounts of their experience of it. These positions are difficult to refute if we accept the premise that narrative must necessarily be structured like a literary narrative, and that a musical narratology should be an aspect of a general literary narratology (Almén 2008, 11–12). The analogy fails just as a semiotics of music that requires itself to be a general linguistics fails: because music is not structured just like a verbal language. But as Byron Almén notes in his study of musical narrative, nothing about narrative presupposes the precedence of literary narratology. He argues instead for developing "a set of foundational principles common to all narrative media and principles unique to each media" (12). Almén understands "narrative as articulating the dynamics and possible outcomes of conflict or interaction between elements, rendering meaningful the temporal succession of events, and coordinating these events into an interpretive whole" (13). Narrative, in short, is effective storytelling, and the medium of narrative—whether music, film, literature, or drama—simply determines the specific advantages the storytelling might exploit or the constraints it must negotiate in accomplishing its task.

As with music, film also struggled with the linguistic analogy, and I discussed this issue in the opening of chapter 4. Christian Metz (1974a) ultimately located his solution to the problem of film language in narrative. "*Now, it was precisely to the extent that the cinema confronted the problems of narration* that, in the course of successive groupings, it came to produce a body of specific signifying procedures" (95, emphasis in original). Film becomes cinema and is able to develop a languagelike character, Metz thinks, because it is structured like a narrative. Film has a form, a beginning and an end, Metz says, because it is ordered according to the principles of narrative. In this respect, cinema cannot exist without narrative form. Until it is structured as a narrative, film is simply shots that have been joined together. The principle of montage, of ordering shots so that something new appears from them, therefore derives from the prior needs of narrative. Before montage, film was not a "means of expression" but only a "means of mechanical recording" (94), and montage is simply the development of a syntax to govern the assembling of shots into a narrative line. It is therefore narrative that turns film into cinema, and it becomes cinema precisely by becoming semiotic, by finding an essentially arbitrary means of articulating its signs into meaningful groupings.

As noted in chapter 4, film semiotics is the study of film as a system of signs; film narratology, by contrast, is the study of film as the representation of a story. They are brought together because, as Metz noted, the production of a distinctive means of telling stories led film to produce its own set of signs rather than simply reproducing those that it recorded. Moreover, narrative implies, if not fiction, at least a working of the imagination, a construction. The space of the diegesis and the story are not in that sense "real," not simply given, but must be constructed by the spectator from the film. "The 'reality' of fiction (the concept of the diegesis) [is] a reality that comes from within us, from the projections and identifications that are mixed in with our perception of the film" (10). The diegesis, construed semiotically, is an imagined signified, the film containing the signifiers that denote it. This is the sense of Metz's definition of the diegesis in terms of denotation.

If film semiotics eventually gave way to a narratology, neoformalism has also found narratology to be an important aspect of its project. In chapter 5, we looked especially at neoformalism's commitment to close analysis, and narratology provides important analytical tools for understanding how films are organized to tell stories. David Bordwell's (1985) point of departure for narration is the spectator, a position that, he claims, is not adequately considered by other theories of narrative such as proposed by Metz. "I adopt the term 'viewer' or 'spectator' to name a hypothetical entity executing the operations relevant to constructing a story out of the film's representation. My spectator, then, acts according to the protocols of story comprehension" (30). Bordwell draws on Genette and Russian formalism in devising his theory of film narration and grounds his theory in cognitive science, which he sees as a better foundation for an account of filmic narration than the prevailing methodologies drawn from Marxism, psychoanalysis, and semiotics. The spectator in those theories, he says, is constructed as "relatively passive" and "pointillistically" (31). This is only partially true inasmuch as the spectator in these theories is, as Bordwell notes, ideal or imaginary. "A film . . . does not 'position' anybody. A film cues the spectator to execute a definable variety of operations" (29). This is a misapprehension of "positioning," since the claim of positioning is film immanent; that is, it applies to the implied spectator, the spectator presupposed by the film, not the real, empirical one. The analogy here is to perspective in painting or classic theater design: the perspective defines a point from which the picture (or scene) is presumed to be observed. One can and often will, however, look at the picture from other, less ideal points. Generally, the empirical viewer will adjust for the skewing and so attempt to view as if from the ideal position. This is what is meant by "adjustment." At the same time, such "skewed" viewing means that the empirical viewer sees not just the picture but also that the viewing point is not ideal, not the one presupposed by the representation. These are the symptoms of the picture that Bordwell wants to discount, though they appear by virtue of distinguishing the empirical spectator from the implied one. Occasionally, these skewed views lead to insight, to seeing something about the representation that the ideal viewer must suppress to understand the picture as represented. Sometimes, a film constructs a secondary implied spectator, where irony or "looking awry" is also built into the text, as it were (Žižek 1991a).

Bordwell also does not make clear how "cueing" spectators differs materially from "positioning." He concedes that his "spectator" also does not coincide with any real spectator. Likewise, it is an implied spectator that the film positions, not an empirical one; any empirical spectator is at best invited or encouraged to see the film from this position or, in the terminology of the theory, to occupy the position that has been reserved for it. These theories, in other words, posit the spectator as a function, position, or agent presupposed by and constructed in and by the filmic text. Both positioned and cued spectators are therefore theoretical abstractions. They both deploy this theoretical abstraction in a similar way: as an implied figure to which the film encourages empirical subjects to conform by an appeal to internal coherence, the way the film wants itself to be understood. Bordwell deploys cognitive science in essence to depoliticize or neutralize these terms of understanding, to exempt "narrative comprehension" from the point of ideological critique by naturalizing Hollywood narratives by claiming that they conform to the way the brain works. The idea is to render the machinery as unbiased and the cognition it requires as natural. It seems doubtful, moreover, that those he opposes would dispute the claim that Hollywood narratives are constructed to conform to a habitual cognition that has all the appearances of something natural. They simply see the naturalized form of this habitual cognition to be ideological through and through.

Edward Branigan (1992) also makes strong appeals to cognition in his narrative theory. He sees the shift to narratology as part of a large movement in film studies from ontology to epistemology (xi). At the same time, it is instructive that Branigan finds it necessary to supplement narratology with other methodologies, including linguistics and especially cognitive science. This proliferation of methods is a sign of a new organization to film studies that was taking place in the 1990s. Branigan is not a narratologist turning to film to refine his general theory of narrative or a cognitive scientist hoping to use film to study the workings of the human mind. Instead, he turns to narratology, cognitive science, and linguistics to develop a set of narrative principles for film, principles that might indeed feed back into a general theory of narrative, but his aim remains focused on understanding the narrative organization of classical Hollywood sound films (xii). However interdisciplinary his narrative theory is in conception, in other words, the resulting text is firmly grounded in the study of film, which is now a discipline capable of containing, organizing, and productively utilizing the centrifugal forces that determine the field.

Narrative, for Branigan, "is a fundamental way of organizing data" (1992, 1), indeed, "a perceptual activity that organizes data into a special pattern which represents and explains experience" (3). Its primary operation is to align what he calls "spatial and temporal data" into "a cause-effect chain of events with a beginning, middle, and end" (3). He therefore sees it primarily as a mode people use to capture and make sense of their experience. For this reason, narrative is a mode of comprehension that lies more in the attitude someone brings to an object or experience than in the thing itself. Things do bear marks, however, of narrative organization, so narrative comprehension is not merely imposed but is in a sense negotiated, and the utility of applying the mode of narrative comprehension must be evaluated according to the questions someone wants to ask (1–2). Nevertheless, Branigan's focus falls more on how organization facilitates and encourages a particular comprehension than on the act of comprehension itself. In this respect, it remains oriented toward the filmic text.

One useful intervention is Branigan's concern with tracking and identifying levels of narration, each arranged in a series reminiscent of the communication model that distinguishes sender, message, and receiver. Figure 6.1 shows eight intersecting but hierarchically arranged levels, labeled according to the form of the message that determines the "epistemological context" of that level: text, fiction, story world, event/scene, action, speech, perception, and thought (1992, 87). The model allows for considerable play among the levels (this play is indeed one way narratives represent complex causal chains), and it allows him to integrate the concept of focalization, the way characters provide

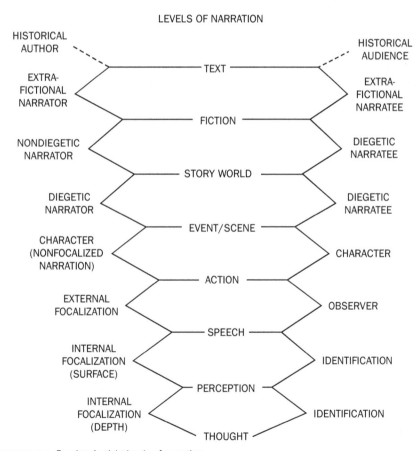

FIGURE 6.1 Branigan's eight levels of narration.

information about the narrative world they inhabit, into his basic framework. Characters say and do things, of course, but they also experience their world, and focalization is the means by which narratives relate interior experiences such as what characters see or hear or what they feel, dream, or think (101). It is narrative's attempt to render a "consciousness of" (106), as the narrative shifts a character from being "a focus of a causal chain to being the source of knowledge of a causal chain" (101). Narratives can indicate focalization through point-of-view editing or point-of-audition sound; often that involves some disruption to "normal" representational strategies (103–4). Though Branigan doesn't mention it, music is also an important marker or even medium of focalization inasmuch as it represents interior states.

Introduced by Gérard Genette, the concept of focalization has been extensively developed by Mieke Bal (2009). "Focalization is . . . the relation between the vision and that which is 'seen,' perceived" (145–46). Branigan notes that Bal allows focalization to occur at the level of both the narrator and the character, which he finds somewhat nonsensical and pointless, because it threatens to collapse a functional distinction between narrator levels and character levels in his schema. Guido Heldt (2013) points out that Branigan's own account confuses narration and focalization in a way that is contrary to Genette's conception. For Genette, Heldt writes, "narration organizes the narratees' access to story information, while focalization describes the access the narration itself has to information" (23). Even on Branigan's own ground, it can matter a great deal whether a feeling reported by a narrative belongs to the narrator or focalizes a character.

Focalization is one of the principal means by which narration manages points of identification, and because of music's relation to feeling, music is one of cinema's most powerful focalizing tools. Yet music reports feelings at various levels of focalization, and it is possible for music also to convey a feeling, such as suspense, that may belong to none of the characters. It is surely possible to deal with such music as narration rather than focalization, except insofar as it is taken as feeling, as an affective response—instead of something else it remains a report of that feeling or response; in other words, it reports an experience. Branigan can only see Bal's extensions of focalization as pointless because he rarely attends to the narrative work of music, and he does not integrate it into his theory.

Narratology and the Soundtrack

CLAUDIA GORBMAN AND NARRATIVE FUNCTIONS

Branigan's omission of music is telling and disappointing inasmuch as music was among the first subsystems of film to have its theory rewritten in terms of narratology. Claudia Gorbman (1987) combined narratology with psychoanalysis, a common combination when she was writing, to theorize how music worked in the classical system. She identified a set of practices or principles for music and sound mixing, and she understood these "principles" as descriptive rather than prescriptive, based on mixing practices during the period. These principles, or "the Seven Rules" as they are sometimes called, are here generalized to the soundtrack as a whole:

1. "Invisibility"—the means of production are not shown;
2. "Inaudibility"—all aspects of the soundtrack should be subordinate to the narrative and the work of sound editing or music should not be consciously heard;
3. Signifier of emotion—music testifies to the presence of emotion;
4. Narrative cueing—music and sound effects draw attention to pertinent elements in a scene, make formal articulations, and draw connections among otherwise disparate events;
5. Continuity—sound editing and music draw scenes together, dissipate the disruptive force of cuts, and cover up gaps by giving a consistent aural background;
6. Unity—the structuring principles of music (repetition, contrast, and return) complement and reinforce the narrative structure;
7. Breaking the rules—any of these rules can be broken in the service of another rule (73).

Gorbman's rules are neatly segmented functions, almost like each of the first three pairs forms an opposition that serves as a spine upholding the narrative structure: the first two designate professional competencies that relate to sound's subjugation to narrative; rules 3 and 4 speak to the signifying work of the soundtrack and concern the synchronization of sound to narrative in the broadest sense; rules 5 and 6 address issues of continuity and unity, the "connective tissue" that binds disparate shots, sounds, and musical themes to the narrative structure. The final principle guarantees that the principles are evaluated in terms of the general narrative system. Gorbman's principles, especially rules 3 through 6, have strong affinities with Copland's five functions of (1) establishing place and time, (2) signifier of interiority, (3) neutral background, (4) continuity, and (5) dynamic shaping that were discussed in chapter 3. Copland's first function is part of music's cultural and filmic codes that constitute narrative cueing, the second aligns with signifier of emotion, the third and fourth with continuity, and the fifth to narrative cueing and unity. Similarly, Kalinak's working model is in essence an elaboration of Gorbman's principles, especially rules 3, 4, and 6. In chapter 5, I divided the ten attributes of Kalinak's model into four large categories: general considerations, explicit relations to narrative, implicit relations to narrative, and combinations of explicit and implicit relations to narrative. The general considerations mostly relate to rule 6; the explicit relations to narrative elaborate rule 4; and the implicit relations to narrative and the combinations together develop rule 3. One reason Gorbman's principles have proved so durable is that the list is very concise with minimal overlap among rules while also mapping out a fairly complete inventory of narrative functions for music.

Along with the seven principles that guide the soundtrack in relation to narrative, Gorbman also points to another important principle that does not fit neatly into this list. Scenes of spectacle and grandeur that do not bear directly on the narrative often disregard the inaudibility rule but without clearly invoking another rule or indeed submitting to the narrative under the terms of the exceptions allowed by the seventh rule: music in such scenes, she notes, is often consciously heard, as "it is helping to *make a spectacle* of the images it accompanies" (1987, 68). In these cases, spectacle serves as a counterorganizational principle to narrative, and many film historians have identified a tension between narrative and spectacle as fundamental to classical style. Since music helps underscore spectacle, music has sometimes been classed as an antinarrative and potentially subversive force in film.

Besides articulating the seven principles, Gorbman also introduced a number of technical terms from narratology to help explain the function of music in narrative film. Of these, none has been more influential than the binary distinction between diegetic and nondiegetic music; and the distinction has proved as dissatisfying as it is indispensable (Neumeyer 2009; Taylor 2007). The distinction rests on determining what music belongs to the primarily narrative level (diegesis), that is, the representation of the world in which the story takes place—roughly, what music the characters hear (Gorbman 1987, 22ff.)—versus the other music that belongs to the level of narration, that is, music that the characters do not hear, and that went generally under the name of background score or more narrowly commentative music in earlier theories of the soundtrack. The dissatisfaction with the terms begins, in fact, with Gorbman herself, who practically launches her discussion of the distinction by reflecting on the frequency with which it is evaded and blurred, and her explication of the concepts throughout the book gives more attention to exceptional cases that challenge the boundary than those that sit neatly within the categories. As she notes in her preliminary discussion of the distinction, "the only element of the filmic discourse that appears extensively in nondiegetic as well as diegetic contexts, and often freely crosses the boundary line between, is music" (22). Gorbman sees this fluidity as one significant advantage music enjoys over other elements of the filmic system because it allows music to perform a wide range of narrative functions and often at the same time. In that sense, the distinction marks poles of a continuum rather than a dichotomy.

No doubt one reason Gorbman approaches the distinction from problematic cases is to keep the distinction from hardening into stiff categories that would leave the tool inflexible. Much of the extensive scholarly literature inspired by her book has followed her in looking at instances where the distinction seems less than stable and so opens up logical puzzles that can be filled with hermeneutic speculation. Woody Allen's gag on the harpist in the closet in *Bananas* (1971) (Brown 1994, 68; Biancorosso 2009, 12–13) and Mel Brooks's similar deployment of the Count Basie Band in *Blazing Saddles* (1974)—Jeff Smith (2009) calls the latter "the paradigmatic exemplar of this technique" (20–22)—are frequently mentioned examples, and a film like *Laura* (1944), where the theme often floats nebulously between diegetic and nondiegetic status, seems to encourage us to interpret this lack of stability in the distinction as part of the film's dreamlike idea (Kalinak 1992). (The latter point is complicated, however, by a film such as *Rebecca* [1940], where similar effects are achieved while strictly maintaining the distinction between diegetic and nondiegetic, suggesting that the erosion of this distinction is not the primary source of the effect.)

Besides the central distinction, Gorbman also appropriates Genette's category of the metadiegetic, which concerns narration within narration, such as a character telling a story. But it can also be extended to situations such as dreams, thoughts, and memories (1987, 23), in which case it is also an example of internal focalization. Gorbman offers the hypothetical example of music associated with a romance early in a film recurring as one of the characters remembers it. The music in this case seems a product of the memory and so both metadiegetic and nondiegetic (23). A good example of metadiegetic music occurs in *Brigadoon* (1954), where Tommy has left the mythical village and returned to the city but is finding it hard to readjust. In an attempt to put it behind him, he goes on a date, but words and situations trigger aural memories of his time in Brigadoon.

SARAH KOZLOFF AND THE NARRATIVE FUNCTIONS OF DIALOGUE

Sarah Kozloff (2000) proposes to do for dialogue something similar to what Gorbman accomplished for music: theorize the subsystem of dialogue with respect to narrative. One of Kozloff's principal claims about film dialogue is that "film dialogue has been purposely designed for the viewers to overhear" (15). In this respect, it is doubly addressed: on the one hand, its audience is diegetic, and the speech is addressed, within the film, to the characters who are being talked to; on the other hand, the audience is the audience for the film, and here dialogue serves to fill gaps in spectators' knowledge (19). Well-crafted dialogue solves this issue on the terms of Gorbman's inaudibility rule: the audience is provided the information it needs to know but in a way that the audience will likely not take notice of it.

Like Gorbman, Kozloff focuses on isolating distinct narrative functions, and she draws on work of narrative and drama theorists in particular to formulate these functions. (For some reason, the principle of overhearing and its corollary of an inaudible double address are not included among the functions.) She identifies six fundamental narrative functions and three related aesthetic effects. The narrative functions are:

1. Anchorage of the diegesis and characters—when characters speak about where they are, where they have been, or where they are going, they create the place by identifying it. The same applies to identifying characters by naming them (2000, 34–37).
2. Narrative causality—dialogue sets up a subsequent event, announces a deadline, and so forth (37–41).
3. Verbal events—dialogue supplies missing information, such as a motive, or it becomes an important event like a confession of a crime or a declaration of love (41–43).
4. Character revelation—dialogue tells us about the character's personality, motivations, and ambitions, and distinguishes one character from another (43–47).
5. Adherence to the code of realism—people speak in real life, so seeing characters speak on film in ordinary conversation assures us that the world we see resembles our own (47–49).
6. Control of viewer's evaluation and emotions—dialogue controls pacing that information is delivered; it can also cue us to pay attention to something we might not ordinarily take as significant (49–51).

The three aesthetic effects include:

7. Exploitation of the resources of language
   a. Poetically—devices such as rhymes or alliteration can shift the dialogue into a different register (52–53).
   b. Jokes—humor can be used either as a principal attraction as in comedies or as a means of contrast (53–54).
   c. Irony—dialogue often emphasizes different levels of meaning and knowledge (54–55).
   d. Metadiegetic narration—dialogue is occasionally used to tell stories, especially to fill in backstory without a flashback (55–56).
8. Thematic messages/authorial commentary/allegory—dialogue can be used to deliver moralizing message (56–60).
9. Opportunities for "star turns"—dialogue serves to highlight talents of stars (60–61).

A comparison to Gorbman's seven rules is instructive. As noted earlier, Gorbman's rules are neatly segmented functions, with the first three pairs forming a set of oppositions that establish three broad narrative commitments for the soundtrack: subjugation, synchronization, and continuity. Kozloff's functions are, by contrast, organized in a much less tidy fashion. She provides two large divisions into functions proper and aesthetic effects, but after that the principles of division are not well articulated. It is not clear if Kozloff intends her functions to be independent of one another or whether she considers her list exhaustive. Kozloff's first function serves to situate the action; in that respect it is a kind of narrative cueing: "this is France." The second function relates more to unity and large-scale form; causality serves to bind smaller units into larger ones. The third function either is another instance of narrative cueing: "this is what you should know," or relates to emotions or inner thought: "here is my declaration of love; this is why I acted this way." The fourth function similarly involves emotions and thoughts, but rather than more private expressions, here the expressions are public, the revelation not of intentions but of personality. The fifth function relates somewhat to narrative cueing insofar as it establishes the reality of the diegesis but also indirectly to the first two rules concerning subjugation. The sixth function presents the most direct form of narrative cueing as it tells us what to pay attention to. The seventh function concerns idioms, address, and styles, and they belong more to the principles of composition than narrative functions per se. In terms of Gorbman's rules, they relate most closely to unity, especially in the first three types, but metadiegetic narration pulls out of these functions altogether, as it is a mode of narration. The eighth function is similar, also suggesting a modal shift more than a new function, and it is most closely related to nondiegetic music. The ninth function is also more a principle of composition than a narrative function. This would most likely be covered under the rubric of rule 7, as it violates the spirit of rules 1 and 2.

By comparing Kozloff's functions of dialogue to Gorbman's rules, I do not mean to imply that the narrative functions of dialogue would be better explained by Gorbman's rules. Those rules are optimized for nondiegetic music, which most often must play in the background; dialogue, by contrast, almost always occupies a foreground position. I mean to show instead that Kozloff's functions are more difficult to generalize in practice. Only the distinction between verbal events and character revelation, between dialogue that reveals a private self and dialogue that reveals a public personality, seems to have the kind of analytical power for dialogue that Gorbman's rules have for music. The others are all certainly things that dialogue does. But do anchoring the diegesis, setting up causal connections, and adhering to the rules of realism, for instance, offer sufficiently distinct and generalized functions to warrant defining as individual functions?

MICHEL CHION AND THE AUDIOVISUAL SCENE

Writing around the same time as Gorbman albeit retaining a stronger tie to the traditional grounding of the soundtrack in the image, Michel Chion (1994) incorporates the central distinction of diegetic and nondiegetic into a rudimentary model of film sound that in many respects updates the early models of Raymond Spottiswoode and Siegfried Kracauer discussed in chapter 3. He calls this model the "audiovisual scene." In it, the frame, rather than the image per se, is now the fundamental unit: the frame serves as a container for the image, obviously, but also extends to the soundtrack so that the status of each sound element is decided through its relation to the frame. "We classify sounds in relation to what we see in the image, and this classification is constantly subject to revision, depending on changes in what we see" (68). Thus, to the basic distinction between diegetic and nondiegetic, he adds the familiar distinction between onscreen and offscreen, and indeed grants it priority. The priority of the frame then serves to establish the priority of the image. He also notes that nondiegetic and offscreen sound share the property of being acousmatic, that is, of being without visible source. In semiotic terms, sound is most typically construed as indexical, and so the basic hermeneutic that any sound in film unleashes, Chion thinks, is the search for the source, the enigma of offscreen sound and what converts it into an active force that shapes the film form. "Active offscreen sound [is] acousmatic sound that raises questions—What is this? What is happening?—whose answer lies offscreen and which incite the look to go there and find out" (85). This results in a tripartite model with three sets of boundaries, and the visual representation of the model, at any rate, suggests that each of the boundaries is roughly equivalent.

As Chion notes in his discussion of it in *Audio-Vision*, this model, which he introduced in an earlier book, was criticized for being overly rigid (1994, 73–74). It is easy to see why. Like the more basic diegetic–nondiegetic distinction of Gorbman but without its flexibility, Chion's tripartite model leaves many cases difficult to explain. Chion himself points to the omission of what he calls "on-the-air" sound (i.e., acousmatic sound from loudspeakers), internal sound (i.e., sound that belongs to the interior of some character encompassing a perspective not available to other diegetic characters, i.e., focalization), and ambient sound, and he included them in a revised version of the diagram, reproduced in Figure 6.2 (78). Both on-the-air sound and ambient sound are generally localizable in the diegesis—we presume characters hear it—but the source is neither securely inside nor outside the frame. On-the-air sound he understands as occupying the outer regions of the diegesis, presumably because the source of the sound in a loudspeaker can accommodate the sound to the frame (when the loudspeaker, phonograph, or radio is shown), but the ultimate source of that recorded sound is itself acousmatic within the diegesis. He notes that this positioning gives it an ambiguity that allows it to easily shift into the nondiegetic realm as well. Ambient sound, by contrast, is conceptualized as a kind of membrane that serves as a buffer between the diegetic and the nondiegetic. This is a curious placement, since as a formal entity ambient sound seems more pertinent to bridging the distinction between onscreen and offscreen sound—ambient sound points to a reality that extends beyond the frame—or to questioning the efficacy of the frame as the ultimate

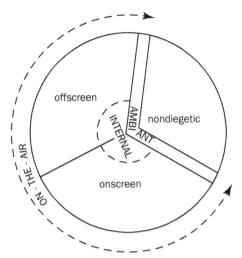

FIGURE 6.2 Chion's audiovisual scene.

Credit: From *Audio-Vision*, by Michel Chion, translated by Claudia Gorbman. Copyright ©1994 Columbia University Press. Reprinted with permission of the publisher.

container of the film than to buffering the boundary between diegetic and nondiegetic space.

Nevertheless, this function of establishing the continuity of diegetic space is one that ambient sound shares with nondiegetic music. Its hermeneutic neutrality—the way it does not produce curiosity to uncover the source of the sound but instead creates an "atmosphere that envelopes and stabilizes the image" (1994, 85)—is another quality that it shares with a certain, common register of nondiegetic music. The other category, that of internal sound, begins to move toward recognizing what narratologists call "internal focalization," but Chion does not ultimately have much to say about it even though it ends up occupying the center of the revised diagram of the audiovisual scene.

All three types of sounds, however, are difficult to accommodate within Chion's model of the audiovisual scene, not so much because they embody a problematic relation to source in the image, as he seems to believe, but rather because, like nondiegetic music, they concern relations to, are justified by, and open up perspectives on levels of narration and focalization. Chion's model is in essence an attempt to deduce narrative relations from the priority of the sound source and the relation of that source to the visual field of the frame, but the difficult placement of these sounds in the visual representation of his model suggests that the image as framed does not fully determine narrative levels, relations, and functions. Indeed, it seems to misconstrue semiotics for narratology. His concept of "extension" is a good example: it plots a continuum from highly limited extension (i.e., internal sound focalized in one character) to vast extension (i.e., external diegetic sound encompassing the sound of the narrative universe beyond the actual capacities of any diegetic character to hear), but the concept of extension measures the expansions and contractions of narrative space, not a relation to image per se, which in this case is also a function of narrative (1994, 87–89).

In the concept of extension, then, we begin to glimpse a second audio-visual scene taking shape, one based in the fundamental constructions of narrative representation and that go under his general rubric of rendering. Rendering for Chion is also intimately related to source sound, and at first pass therefore seems a concept that applies only to diegetic sound. But, like extension, rendering involves moving beyond diegetic sound construed in terms of strict correspondence to the diegesis. Rendering, Chion says, "does not attempt to reproduce the real noises of the situation, but to render the impact of the blow or the speed of the movement" (1991, 71). If it is not bound to being a reproduction, rendering is also not simply a code that transmits a meaning. Rendering seeks to represent not how a sound sounds in itself but how the sound feels.

> The term rendering implies that, because there is a transposition, a channeling via at most two senses, and with pretty poor sensory defi-nition, of much more complex perceptions, to recreate the impact, the very appearance of an event, it is not enough to film and record it. Live perceptions are never purely auditory and visual. (71)

There remains an ambiguity in this formulation, however, as to what precisely is being recreated. Common sense, which I would caution does not make it true, would dictate that the visceral impact of rendering is a movement of identification, of positioning the audience within the diegesis, so filmgoers seem to have become absorbed into the scene they experience, even if it is done using methods that violate the strictures of fidelity. It is in this sense a kind of intense focalization, but often without a clear diegetic anchor for the focalization. With rendering, filmgoers feel themselves moved inside the film and have a distinct overall sense of being there. This approach of iden-tification is, of course, fraught, and it violates other attributes of common sense—above all, that we know that when we attend a film we are attending a film so that the identification is never complete however lost in the film we might become. It also violates our sense, which we need to retain for the film to remain narratively intelligible, that the scenes are being selected and presented to us. Full identification with the diegesis necessarily involves the disappearance of the narrator unless we want to claim, like an intensified version of apparatus theory, that the narrator is somehow narrating into the story itself an empty position for the filmgoer to occupy. Rendering is a cru-cial concept in theories of the soundtrack and we will return to it at length in chapters 8 and 9.

GIORGIO BIANCOROSSO AND THE CINEMATIC IMAGINATION

Giorgio Biancorosso (2001) provides an excellent overview of the theoretical complexities of diegetic music, which is more typically taken as matter of fact, simply an attribute of the image. Biancorosso argues that diegetic music is in fact always doubled:

> Like a face in a picture, diegetic music is the object of twofold perception. The spectator is confronted with a real sound—the recorded sound of the music via the loudspeakers—as well as a virtual one—the music as the imaginary product of agents and causes internal to the movie world. An immense, unbridgeable gulf separates them, both ontologically and psychologically. It is because they are so incommensurable that the real and the virtual (or imaginary) sound do not exclude each other in our perception. They act upon two different areas of the psyche. They occupy adjacent yet distinct spaces. That is why one actually hears both. (¶19)

This doubling is characteristic of diegetic sound in general, but it is not characteristic of nondiegetic music inasmuch as nondiegetic music does not require concrete representation in the image. If nondiegetic music were in fact similarly doubled, it would require a placement outside the loudspeaker but not in the screen. Nondiegetic music might in this sense be mysterious when approached from the standpoint of diegetic representation, but its mystery from the standpoint of what Biancorosso calls "a (real) sound in a (real) space," that is, as a sound from the loudspeaker in whatever room the film is reproduced, is no mystery at all, since we are confronted with music that frames space in this way all the time. Nondiegetic music, Biancorosso writes,

> can be both frame and object, sometimes simultaneously. Like credits music, and like the muzak we incessantly hear in stores, bars, shopping malls, it reminds us where we are and what we are there for, especially when it plays profusely as in certain Hollywood films of the 1930s and 1940s, for instance, or most contemporary Hindi films. When this happens, nondiegetic music provides an acoustical frame through (and not just before and after) the film, thus bridging the gap between the beginning and end credits. (¶25)

Nondiegetic music is thus like glass or perhaps a varnish or even exterior lighting that continually helps frame the film as film, that keeps reminding us or calling us to imagine. Its ubiquity serves to divert attention from the fact of reproduction, in that respect allowing us to forget the doubling of real and virtual in the representation of sound (¶41–42).

Biancorosso suggests that whereas diegetic music is semiotic in that it "stands for" something else, that it becomes a property of the image or an index to the absent source that caused it, nondiegetic music, on the contrary, has the indexical capacity of pointing, indicating in a different semiotic register of the index of the deictic "this" or "that." The musical stinger is prototypical in the way it urges an audience to pay attention to this thing, this word, this facial expression that it accompanies. Nondiegetic music can point to something in the image in a way that diegetic music cannot. (Or if diegetic music does this, it must inevitably be a coincidence or be granted the power of divination.) Still, Biancorosso is not particularly clear about how this indexical mode operates. The example of the shark motif in *Jaws* (1975) seems to "stand for" the shark in a similar way to diegetic music. Many leitmotifs have a similar property. This is as much as to say that it is not the semiotic principle of indexical signification, or "standing for," that separates the two but a belief in the sound's place in the diegetic world. Diegetic music is not just indexical of its source but also iconic with the sound that the musicians might play, and so we have no trouble believing that we hear the music the characters do. With the shark, the relation differs: the nondiegetic music of the shark is not iconic with the sounds of the shark unless we take the world onscreen to be quite different from the world that we experience. The music may be iconic to the feeling that the shark is meant to represent in the sense that the music resembles that feeling, but that is another question and another level of analysis. In general, leitmotifs and much nondiegetic music carry a symbolic signification, relatively arbitrary cultural codes of musical moods and topics, along with their indexical pointing signification. In fact, Biancorosso also recognizes that nondiegetic music frequently represents mood, and in this case he speaks of this capacity as "a vector." As vector, nondiegetic music "directs our attention toward a certain element or a particularly meaningful aspect of a scene, guiding us to a certain understanding and a certain emotional response to it" (2001, ¶27).

ROBYNN STILWELL AND THE FANTASTICAL GAP

Robynn Stilwell (2007) argues both for the efficacy of upholding the distinction between diegetic and nondiegetic music and sound and for a recognition that the boundary is fluid and highly permeable. "The border region—the fantastical gap—is a transformative space, superposition, a transition between stable states" (200). Sometimes this fluidity is used rather mundanely to facilitate the passage from external mood music of a night club, say, to the internal music that underscores fantasy, dream, and romance. In *The Lady Eve* (1941), Jean and Charles are introduced in a ship's dining room, with music playing. Although the orchestra is never shown, it seems to function at first as simply diegetic background music appropriate for the space. Over the course of the scene, the music conforms more and more to the action while retaining its character as diegetic background music, and when Jean and Charles leave the space the music accompanies them as they go to his room. There is nothing especially remarkable about how the music crosses from diegetic to nondiegetic in this scene, as it follows the strategy of "diegetic withdrawal" in compressed form (Slowik 2014). At other times the fluidity could be dramatized and turned into a region of the "fantastical gap."

These are the situations that most interest Stilwell, and she devotes the bulk of her article mapping its geography. She notes the fantasy space constructed in many backstage musicals of the transition and early classic sound era, especially those with musical numbers staged by Busby Berkeley (she cites *Dames* [1934]), which used a more or less diegetically anchored music against an image that dissolved theatrical space into a fantastic, impossible configuration (2007, 188). She also explores the overlap of diegetic and nondiegetic music in *Silence of the Lambs* (1991), where nondiegetic horror music is overlaid on a diegetic recording of Bach's Goldberg Variations, a procedure that she argues causes the point of identification in the scene to constantly slip and shift (191–92). In *I Know Where I'm Going!* (1945), the story of crossing class divisions is thematically recapitulated in the boundaries of diegetic and nondiegetic music. She also notes that the boundary often gets especially fluid and porous when films turn to an explicit internal focalization that seeks to represent a character's interior state (194–97). The movement from nondiegetic back to diegetic music can also have disorienting effects, as the origin of the music in the nondiegetic sphere can color its diegetic status, destabilizing the space that would serve to anchor it. In the opening of *Holy Smoke* (1999), the device creates "a liminal space where [Ruth] will become transformed" (198).

JEFF SMITH AND FILM NARRATION

Jeff Smith (2009), although willing to accept the distinction between diegetic and nondiegetic music as a heuristic, thinks that the deployment of the distinction in the study of film music has tended to elide a more important distinction, fundamental to the narratological project, between narration and narrative (2). This charge is somewhat misleading. In the narratological study of film music, the distinction between narrative and narration has not in fact so much been ignored as it has been presumed.[1] But the implicitness of narration is indeed a problem that has led to a certain important confusion that I will address later. Before I do, however, let me address other aspects of Smith's contribution.

---

[1] David Neumeyer's (2009) definitions run thus: "diegetic sound means 'sound in the universe in which the story takes place' and nondiegetic (extradiegetic) sound means 'sound not in that universe and presumed to belong to the level of the narrator'" (28). Note that there is nothing in this definition that would place nondiegetic music outside the narrative (as produced by the narrator) unless we take Neumeyer to be saying that nondiegetic sound is not a product of the narrator but actually occupies the same position, that is, that it speaks itself next to, rather than as a part of, the rest of the filmic narration. I find no evidence in the text that this is the meaning that Neumeyer had in mind.

To the basic distinction of nondiegetic and diegetic music, Smith, drawing on David Bordwell's (1985) work on film narration, adds the distinction, inherited from the Russian formalists, of *fabula* and *syuzhet*. As discussed previously, the *fabula* is the underlying chronological temporal order of the narrative reconstructed from the text in terms of cause and effect, but also the totality of the universe, the diegesis, from which the story draws its material. This term is usually translated as story, though it actually consists of the materials for the story. *Syuzhet*, which narratology usually translates as plot, discourse, or even text, is the way the narrative orders its material into a text and includes certain stylistic elements of the narration. This distinction between *syuzhet* and *fabula* is helpful insofar as it allows Smith to refine the definition of nondiegetic music as music that "belongs solely to the syuzhet," or the discursive or storytelling level of the narration (2009, 2). More specifically, nondiegetic music, for Smith, is music that is absent from the *fabula* and so it is not subject to diegetic representation. Smith helpfully points out that the *fabula* contains all sorts of music that does not appear in the story, and this nonrepresented *fabula* music, though usually inconsequential from the standpoint of film analysis, is a useful reminder that the *fabula* is not a subset of the *syuzhet* any more than *syuzhet* is a subset of the *fabula*. They are distinct narrative levels that cannot be reduced to each other, and much of narratology is concerned with examining how narration mediates between them (and in many theories other narrative levels). At the same time, it is apparent that the *fabula* is presumed to contain the full "reality" of the diegesis, whereas the *syuzhet* is only a partial representation of it in narration. *Syuzhet*, by contrast, can contain aspects such as reflections and knowledge of the future and the significance of the *fabula* events that fall outside the reality of the *fabula*'s here and now. Given that Smith is willing to allow a definition of nondiegetic music in terms of its absence from the *fabula*, it would seem that he posits a strict relationship between diegesis and *fabula*: the diegesis is the world of the *fabula*, which is the "reality" of the film.

It is this notion of the "reality" of the diegesis that stands behind concepts such as Christian Metz's spatial anchoring that Smith finds problematic. The connection between realism and being in the diegesis refers to how the diegesis specifies its own "reality" and defines the reality of the narrative and nothing more. It says little about fidelity, how the representation of the diegesis in a text conforms to the actual being of that world or indeed to our own world. An appearance of and appeal to realism is nevertheless built into the narratological project, into the very divide between *syuzhet* and *fabula* that Smith himself accepts as unproblematic: however stylized the representation in the storytelling, narratology's search for temporal developments stratifies the text in a way that produces a world divided into appearance in the *syuzhet* and the more extensive and unmasterable world of the *fabula*. Elements of spectacle and stylistic excess adhere to the discourse (either at the level of story itself or in the translation of story to the medium of discourse), allowing *fabula* to retain its position of the kernel of the real. The concept of a diegesis in effect implies a realist ontology.

This is not to defend Metz's idea of spatial anchoring or Smith's more proximate target, David Neumeyer (2009), who draws on the concept in building his model for interpreting film music (which is summarized in chapter 5). But I do want to point out that Smith's challenge to realism undermines his own placement of the diegesis in the *fabula*. It may well be the case that "nowhere else in film studies is the notion of 'diegetic' wholly equated with the concept of realism. Elements of mise-en-scène or cinematography, for example, are often treated in highly stylized fashion, but a film's departure from realism does not disqualify spaces and objects from being considered a part of the film's diegesis" (2009, 4). From a strict narratological standpoint, however, this loosening of the concept of diegesis to include stylization would seem to require confusing the story's appearance in a film and *fabula*. Stylization generally belongs to the level of *syuzhet* and discourse; if the stylization belongs to the *fabula*, it is not really a stylization at all but simply a property of the *fabula*, perhaps a distinguishing attribute of a particular region within it, say, a dream from waking reality.

This explains a situation such as *The Cabinet of Caligari* (1920). Smith argues that "it would be strange indeed to argue that Caligari's asylum exists outside the world of the fiction" (2009, 4). But this is not what is generally being claimed when someone says of music that it falls outside the diegesis. The claim is that the music belongs to the level of narration, to the discourse of the filmic narrator, rather than to the world narrated, to the *syuzhet* rather than the *fabula*. So in the case of *The Cabinet of Caligari*, the parallel claim would be that the stylization of the asylum belongs to the level of the narration as well, either to Francis or his auditor if internal, or to the higher-level narrator who visualizes Francis's tale and renders it if external. An interpretation that started from either of those premises would not be particularly implausible, even if *The Cabinet of Caligari* poses a difficult case. The more perplexing question in a sound film would be whether a narratological interpretation would ever permit the music that would inevitably accompany such an internal narration to be a product of the internal narrator that we would have little issue ascribing the images to. Scholars of film music generally resist making a definitive attribution of the music in a dream, say, to the dreamer, unless something in the dream explicitly authorizes it, even though most film dreams are accompanied or at least initiated by music. It is also not so clear whether the difference of interpreting music in this respect is a product of something that inheres within the musical register or whether it is a product of the narratological theory brought to bear on explaining it.

We might, nevertheless, take Smith at his word and consider the alternative explanation that the asylum in the *fabula* looks just like the asylum we see in the film. That's certainly a possibility, one the film does seem to ask its audience to entertain (which is one reason the definition of diegesis in the film also seems more unstable than most); but embracing it entails a number of problematic consequences: first, it posits a diegetic world quite different from our own (or suggests that our own world is far stranger than we imagine); second, it erodes the distinction between *syuzhet* and *fabula* on the one hand and narration and narrative on the other, and so calls into question the efficacy of narratological analysis; third, it prevents us from easily reading the stylization of the asylum as a sign of psychological deviance, which is also what the film encourages us to do; fourth, the interpretation of the film world as a consequence becomes more obscure because the boundaries of the diegesis have become unmoored. None of these objections is insurmountable, but each poses a real difficulty to forging a convincing and generalizable interpretation of the film.

BEN WINTERS AND THE NONDIEGETIC FALLACY

When we broaden the concept of diegesis to include stylization on the musical end, the diegesis also becomes very different from our world indeed, as all music now becomes potentially audible in the diegesis. Although Smith does not seem willing to embrace the full consequences of such stylization, Ben Winters (2010) sees little sense in insisting that any music should necessarily be construed as inaudible in the diegesis. "To assume that music the characters do not seem to hear does not belong in their narrative space, and must therefore be the indicator of an external narrative level is perhaps . . . to deal with cinema as an overly realistic medium" (228; see also 226). Winters (2012b) goes on to propose understanding film as producing a "musicalized narrative space" (48). This antirealist position results in a diegetic world quite different from our own where characters apparently encounter, as a natural property of the world they inhabit, distinctive lighting, set design, or mood music that would ordinarily be ascribed to stylistic excess of the narrative discourse. Under these terms, Winters (2010) says,

> it is not whether or not the characters can "hear" music that dictates whether the music is part of the fictional world . . ., but whether the music appears to exist in the time and narrative space of the diegesis, or whether it appears to "narrate" at a temporal distance from that space. (236)

Winters outlines an intriguing antirealist position. But using music's temporal relation to the diegetic action seems problematic, as it is inattentive to the function of music's temporal coordination. Most important, it is not clear whether music is supposed to be construed as a sign, that is, as a bearer of meaning, or as something else. If we take music to be miming some aspect of the narrative content as Winters suggests, say, the temporally proximate feeling of the character, the mimetic relationship is still in the position of being a signifier of the feeling unless we are also willing to admit that the characters of a film feel musically, that is, that they, rather than the filmic narrator, express their feelings in music, in which case, music would not really be miming that feeling but would simply be that feeling.[2]

To understand some of the advantages and disadvantages of Winters's formulation, it will be useful to chart the terms of antirealism. Philosopher Jonathan Dancy (1991) defines antirealism as an epistemological position that refuses to acknowledge a distinction between the world of appearance and a world shaped by forces beyond our recognition. For the antirealist, the world is simply as it appears; it possesses no hidden depth; it conceals no essential secret behind appearance.

> The anti-realist does not believe in the existence of a further "real" world which lies behind the world that we know and which may come apart from our world in ways which of course we could not recognize if they occurred. For [the antirealist] our world, the recognizable world, is the only world. So for the anti-realist the enterprise of epistemology is easier, since the objects of knowledge are brought closer to us; and there is no yawning gap between evidence and truth, since there can be no evidence-transcendent properties. (19)

Because it denies the split between appearance and essence, exterior and interior, surface and depth and is also deeply suspicious of explanations appealing to hidden, ultimately unknowable causes (such as intention), antirealism is a profoundly counterintuitive position. We all "know," for instance, that we do not display our full selves to the world; from this "knowledge" we infer that others are similarly reserved and so we cannot "know" another person fully, know his or her mind, from only the appearance of that person; but an antirealist would deny this possibility, arguing either that this split is apparent and so not hidden at all or that it is a subjective delusion. The power of antirealism therefore comes not from its appeal to common sense, as Winters suggests, but, as Dancy notes, from its utility, its capacity to solve certain sets of otherwise intractable problems, especially skepticism, that seemingly stem from realist epistemological presuppositions.

We can see the stakes of antirealism in Winters's analysis of the music to the early scene in *The Best Years of Our Lives* (1946) where the soldiers arrive home. He writes that this music offers "the characters a musical vision of home" (2012b, 48) and argues that it is absurd to claim that "the clapboard,

---

[2] Heldt (2013) notes that Winters's conception "confuses narrative and diegesis. The music is essential to the *depiction* of the fictional world . . . not to the fictional world *as depicted* in the film" (61, emphasis in original).

New England-style" houses of the scene belong to the diegetic reality of that vision in a way that the music does not (49). The comparison, however, is strained. We can easily grant the appearance of the houses to the reality of diegetic vision because it accords with the way we experience our world on the one hand and with the way the characters seem to respond as if they see their world the same way we do on the other hand. The same cannot be said of the music, where the film provides no direct or indirect evidence of the characters' musical hearing. Such music may sound to us like home (it does sound like a musical vision of home); it may sound like home feels to the characters (and so be a musical representation of the characters' vision of home); and music may well register subtle shifts in a character's feeling (so that music traces the unfolding of a character's feeling, especially Homer's trepidation as he nears his house). But it seems a leap to say this music belongs to the world of the characters' hearing as Winters describes it. The aspect of that music which belongs to the scene is the feeling that the music indicates. The feeling the music conveys in this instance surely belongs to and is intended to belong to the characters, but music remains a sign, and it comes to serve as an elaborate metaphor that allows the film to provide the audience with a picture of interiorization; this scene is an example of how film uses music to establish an interior focalization.

It is also simply not the case that in a literary narrative "we would not suggest that the 'look' belongs at one narrative level and the 'feel' at another" (2012b, 51). In fact, insofar as the look of the houses belongs to a general description (external focalization) and the feel belongs to a character (internal focalization), a narratologist might well make precisely this distinction. Moreover, a narratologist would certainly separate the actuality of the house, which belongs to the diegesis or *fabula*, from how it is described in the discourse. That is, narratology would presume not that the house was only discursive but that the discourse was describing a house that extended beyond any description of it. That is its commitment to realism, and although the house may be wholly fictive and discursive in (our) reality, and although it may make sense and be productive to approach it by insisting on its irreality, that is not how anyone would ordinarily take it in. In any event, we can attribute—rightly, I think—music to the film's discursivity; we cannot, however, infer from this its place in diegetic space. At best we can say that it offers a perspective on that space, a point of view, a means of focusing or focalizing and that that perspective, that point of view, that act of focalizing belongs to the space and so it is diegetic. I would add that the same is true for the more problematic case of musicals, where the distinction between what we hear and what we see, and what we take the characters to be hearing and doing, is, like the fantastical gap, crucial to understanding.

In any event, Winters's suggestion that a musical theme belongs to a character in the same (diegetic) sense as a distinctive piece of clothing or a dialogue quip seems even more problematic, because, unlike musical feeling, it is not at all clear how a character would generate such music diegetically. Musical themes in film usually relate to being, identity, or essential character and so lack a correlate to temporal mode of expression in the diegesis. That's why they belong to the narration. A closer analogy would seem to be an epic formula, where the recurring character attribute belongs clearly to the discourse of the narrator, however proper the epithet might be. If anything, musical themes seem to reflect the film's perspective on the character; they are an element of filmic tone that coincides with decisions such as how to frame and light a character, or what film stock or lens to use. If we know Indiana Jones by his theme, it is because it is an apt description that tells us all we need to know about him. But in itself, it is precisely a description, an epic formula. Likewise, in the case of the zither music to *The Third Man* (1949), the ostentatious music lies closer to the level of the black-and-white cinematography and distinctive lighting choices than to the level of the Ferris wheel in the Prater per se (Winters 2010, 224). (It is how the Ferris wheel appears in the film that is akin to the work that music of this sort performs in film, not that it appears in the film.[3])

To counter Winters's position, we should ask: does the world we see screened seem like the sort of world where the characters hear the music the way that we do? If he is saying that the music (rather than the feelings it indicates) belongs to the narrative space, he is saying that this fictional world we see is quite different from the world we live and experience (since we do not generally walk around the world with cinema music underscoring our actions or broadcasting our feelings) and that our tendency to see the world screened as fundamentally like our own is really a delusion that refuses to take the fiction at face value. There is undoubtedly merit to this position despite its violation of common sense, and I will return to it, but for the moment we should ask what evidence we have, what evidence does film present, that the music belongs to its narrative space. At the least, we need to acknowledge that most film characters, at least those outside of musicals, do not respond to the music in the underscore at all. To all appearances—and to an antirealist recall that appearance is everything—the screened world is a divided world, with characters confronting a world that seems structured very much like our own however that world might seem to us, and so film music belongs to the

---

[3] Oddly, Winters (2010) seems to believe that film is more indifferent to its presentation through editing and cinematography than its presentation through music. "One might be able to detach the editing or cinematography from one's construction of the *fabula* relatively easily . . ., but removing music in this way appears far more problematic" (231). As any filmgoer at all sensitive to film will attest, this is simply a bizarre claim. Although I would not, as many film scholars would, place cinematography and editing above music, I would certainly not follow Winters's musical essentialism. In fact, music is frequently changed—indeed, whole new scores written—suggesting that on the contrary any necessary connection between music and film is extremely fragile, if not nonexistent.

representation of that world rather than to the world itself. The realism of film, we might say, is precisely the appearance of this divide between the world that the film presents and the intimation that this presentation is not all, that film holds something in reserve that must be divined.

Surely, the commonsensical viewpoint—which I again add does not make it true and which I will not ultimately advocate—is that, because the film world looks very much like our own, any film world will be assumed to be like our own unless and to the extent that the filmic discourse somehow specifies that it is not. And nothing that we perceive in film normally suggests that background music is typically "part of the narrative world we see on-screen" (2012b, 45). We know this, at least in part, because of the way that film handles violations, makes jokes out of its musical conventions, as Biancorosso (2009) shows at length. These jokes work because music in film can always, with proper recontextualization, be revealed as diegetic, but underscoring is generally understood not to be. *The Truman Show* (1998), far from being the contrary example Winters believes it to be, confirms this: the film presents us with the conditions under which we should interpret the reality of its music.[4] I will return to these issues in the section on focalization later.

GUIDO HELDT AND LEVELS OF NARRATION

Guido Heldt (2013) develops a thorough account of musical narratology, focusing on levels of narration. The basic framework is borrowed from Branigan (1992), though Heldt is critical of many of the particulars in Branigan's theory and makes suitable adjustments mostly in terms of the conception of focalization. Heldt shows the efficacy of this model through a large number of examples, ranging from logos and titles (extrafictionality), to direct audience address (extrafictional narration), to a wide variety of options falling across the continuum of diegetic and nondiegetic music, to instances of mental representations of music (focalization or metadiegetic narration). The result is a kind of topographical map of musical narration, or rather of the functions that music can perform at various levels of narration. This map is extensive and well illustrated. Heldt is especially clear on the importance of separating level from function and content.

---

[4] Winters's better examples for his case involve diegetic sound that is used in physically unrealistic ways, such as sound in the vacuum of outer space. Here, we have to believe either that this world differs from our own in substantive ways or that these sound effects, which really do seem to belong to the objects depicted, are in fact nondiegetic, that is, addressed to us as the audience rather than something perceived (or potentially perceived) by the characters. These impossible sounds are rather like certain impossible shots or impossible geometries that film occasionally indulges in. As Biancorosso (2009) points out, Allen's gag with the harpist in *Bananas* also works only because the music on the soundtrack is not presented realistically (13).

The question of what level of narration the music is on has to be kept apart from the question of what it says and does. Nondiegetic music can function as a distancing comment but also evoke mood or give insight into the inner state of a character; diegetic music can provide "realistic depiction" . . . but can also be blatantly unrealistic, and can structure and inform a scene as well as nondiegetic music. (2013, 62)

Heldt's biggest contribution, however, is to the theory of musical focalization, which he develops from Gorbman's concept of metadiegetic music. I will discuss these topics in the next section.

Music and Focalization

Narratology defines focalization as a limiting of perspective within a narrative level, not a change in narrative level. This limiting of perspective allows an experience of a character (as opposed to an action) to be reported in the narration. According to Gerard Genette's (1988) formulation, focalization allows us to divide the question of who speaks in the narration (who is responsible for the narrative representation) from who sees or perceives in the story (64). The basic formula for narrative focalization, given by Mieke Bal (2009), is: the narrator (N) says that the focalizer (F) sees the object (O). Bal adds the position O to distinguish focalization *through* F from focalization *on* O. The distinction is important because it tells us not just who is doing the focalizing but what the object of focus is. Heldt (2013) argues that the distinction is especially helpful for interpreting the focalizing work of film music (122).

Ordinarily in fiction, especially in film, we are presented with a somewhat abstract perspective on a scene. It is the scene in the subjunctive mood: this is what anyone whatsoever would have experienced had they been there. The focalization is external because this perspective does not have direct access to the internal experiences of the characters in the scene. F occupies the position of a general observer, what I am terming "anyone whatsoever." With external focalization, the narration allows us to read characters' faces, hear their voices, and see their actions to be sure, but we must draw inferences about psychology from outside, from observation. The characters are in position O. This ordinary focalization is also diegetic because the perspective (F) is located in the world that the story plays out in, although, being subjunctive, it exists there only as a possibility.

Focalization can also be internal, and in this case what was O under external focalization now becomes a focalizing subject in its own right. The filter is now not the knowledge and awareness of anyone whatsoever but precisely that of the character. The perspective, however, is here limited to seeing and hearing the world more or less as that character does. That is, the character occupies position F. This provides some gains in that we now have access to the exact perception of the character, but it also has losses because our perspective has been reduced from the general to the particular: we see and hear just what that character does. In addition to point-of-view shots and point-of-audition sound, many metadiegetic effects, like dreams; some forms of internal narration, such as triggered flashbacks, imagined scenes, and soliloquies; and other subjectivizing effects belong to the category of internal focalization. Many of these move beyond reports of simple perception of point of view and point of audition to the representation of thoughts and feelings. At the inner limits of internal focalization, the awareness moves into the unconscious, that is, past the point of the focalizer's ability to understand or perhaps even recognize the perceptions or experience as his or her own. This is the space of absolute internal focalization, of the blind unconscious drives and feelings that, although existing within the diegesis, are so cut off from normal experience as to almost constitute a separate domain.

Heldt (2013) notes that this concept of focalization leans heavily on a literary model. Film narration doesn't speak but primarily reports by assembling images and sounds (123). Heldt points out that narratology usually follows Genette in distinguishing focalization as a mode of narration rather than a level, and he finds Branigan's model problematic, in part, because this confusion is a central facet of the model. Focalization in Branigan's terms is not a mode of narration but the form that levels of narration take when narration crosses the boundary of the subject to report on internal states. This allows Branigan to present a stratified view of narration that extends in a strict hierarchy through eight levels from the historical author creating the text at the highest point and furthest remove to internal focalization at depth (the reporting of thoughts) at the base. Heldt rightly points out that, according to Genette's definition, focalization and a metadiegetic narrator should all exist at the same narrational level of the diegesis as modes. For Genette, levels are marked by the "voice" (who is representing) and focalization by the grammatical "mood" (who is perceiving). Heldt therefore usefully reduces Branigan's basic model to narration and convolutes it, as shown in Figure 6.3, in line with Genette's definitions to show the modalities of narration at the diegetic level (120).

One issue, however, is the confusion itself. If there are systematic and interpretive advantages to keeping focalization distinct from levels of narration, Branigan's model nevertheless shows that focalization is often confused with narrational levels, can even be productively confused with them, and it is worth asking why that should be the case. Then too, how is it that the metadiegetic, a level of narration, is apparently so similar to focalization that it can be mistaken for it, that Gorbman's initial example of metadiegetic music, for instance, is actually an example of focalization, as Heldt claims (2013, 119)? Heldt's own example of metadiegetic music, "The Broadway Melody"

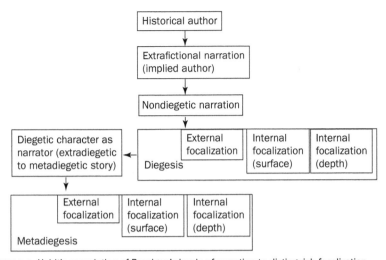

FIGURE 6.3 Heldt's convolution of Branigan's levels of narration to distinguish focalization.

sequence from *Singin' in the Rain* (1952), is only marginally better, since, although the sequence itself involves a diegetic narrator and so is metadiegetic, the narrational level of the music and visuals in the sequence is not as clear since Don tells his idea, and the image and sound are purely imagined, internally focalized evidently through Don (119–20). The difficulty with attributing such music to a metadiegetic narration is evident in an example from earlier in the film when Don, again as a metadiegetic narrator, tells the story of his rise to fame, while the images and music ironically counterpoint his story. A better example of music that combines the metadiegetic level of narration with focalization would be Catherine's final narration from *Suddenly, Last Summer* (1959). In this scene, Catherine describes "a music made out of noise," and the soundtrack reports this sound, focalized through her. Another example might be the music accompanying the newsreel that opens *Citizen Kane* (1941), which would be nondiegetic with respect to the newsreel, diegetic with respect to the world within which the characters watch it, and metadiegetic to the audience watching *Citizen Kane*. Here, the focalization is external at each level.

With metadiegetic narration and focalization, confusion abounds and cannot always be successfully disambiguated. It is therefore worth asking whether this confusion is in fact inherent to the situation, that is, whether it is in the nature of what the account of narration and focalization attempts to model, and whether the confusion can be put into play to productive ends, either in forging narratives on film or in analyzing them. That is, there is no particular reason to think that clarity on the issue of level and mode is either necessary or an analytical advantage. The situation resembles in many respects the distinction between diegetic and nondiegetic, which are frequently blurred in practice. Many of these analytical issues stem from a basic ambiguity in the material, where the same figure shifts meaning depending on context. Asynchronous sound works this way too, since it can mark a mode of diegetic representation (offscreen) or a level of narration (nondiegetic).

Although it is often a challenge to keep the distinction between metadiegetic and focalization crisp, focalization remains a useful addition to a narratological account of film music because focalization permits, as Heldt argues, "a more integral discussion of the representation of subjectivity through music in film" (2013, 124). Heldt's model distinguishes four different types of focalization, but he discounts nonfocalized narration characteristic of traditional literary omniscient narration as being difficult and unusual in film. The remaining three he arranges, much as Branigan does, in a series from external to internal, with internal being subdivided into two types, surface and depth. Heldt subdivides "internal focalization (depth)," arguing that there are two distinct ways to represent the deep interiority of subjectivity. For music, external focalization usually entails diegetic music and it involves the way conscious musical selection can reveal the taste and identity of characters (124). Internal focalization (surface) is essentially point-of-audition sound, hearing the way a character does. Besides Chion, who popularized "point of audition" (1994, 89–94; 2009, 85–86), Anahid Kassabian (2008) discusses benefits of using focalization for understanding point-of-audition sound in her discussion of *The Cell* (2000) (299–305). Heldt (2013) discusses one of Chion's examples, Abel Gance's *The Life and Loves of Beethoven* (1936), as well as *Beyond Silence* (1996) (125–26). Both use point-of-audition sound to render deafness. Alex Newton (2015) argues that point-of-audition sound frequently serves to render subjective isolation, such as Benjamin in his diving suit in *The Graduate* (1967) or headphone sound in the opening to *High Fidelity* (2000) (104–41). As noted, Heldt (2013) subdivides internal focalization (depth), with one subtype used to denote "a character's internal experience of imagination of it" (126) and the other to figure "a character's inner state" (127). The first subtype overlaps with examples usually explained as metadiegetic, and Heldt demonstrates it with a scene from *The Glenn Miller Story* (1954) where Miller is shown writing music and we hear the sounds (126). Such episodes are common in films centered on musicians: Adam's fevered dream of himself playing and conducting Gershwin's Piano Concerto in F from *An American in Paris* (1951), many of the composing scenes in *Amadeus* (1984), and Julie's struggles with "completing" her dead husband's unfinished oratorio on European unity in *Bleu* (1993) all represent music as imagined. The overlap with metadiegetic narration comes from the fact that the character's imagination in each case is tasked with "playing" the music. The second subtype, Heldt says, is "a more problematic category," because in these cases music does not represent itself but the character's interior state (127). It is not exactly a problematic category from the standpoint of narratological analysis. Gorbman (1987) had offered "signifier of emotion" as one of the basic narrative functions of nondiegetic music. And the ability to represent emotions has been one of the dominant arguments for music's place in the cinema since the silent era. What makes this second type "problematic" is placing it within the category of focalization, since focalization is by definition located on the diegetic, not nondiegetic level of narration. Heldt's (2013) formulation draws out the contradictory aspect: "It is connected to the examples of nondiegetic music not as external 'voice,' but as an emanation of something diegetic" (127). Nondiegetic music here appears to be the figure of thought and feeling, that is, something that is diegetic.

This conundrum may well be one of the reasons stylization is, as Jeff Smith (2009) notes, difficult to separate from the diegesis in film studies and why Ben Winters (2010, 2012b) wants to locate music that characters most evidently can't hear in the diegesis.[5] In becoming an "imitation of a character's mental states or processes" (Heldt 2013, 127), music focalizes diegetic affect; it becomes a kind of point of feeling, allowing us to hear what a character feels. This is an artistic, stylized substitution, an emotion-as-we-hear-it, that compensates for film's inability otherwise to penetrate the surface of its images and represent the interiority of its characters.

Any music understood thus as a stylization, however, is no longer easily positioned outside the diegesis, and this is perhaps Winters's point. Heldt suggests that this construction of music remains ambiguous since it is difficult to say from just the relation of music and action whether the music is describing a character's interiority nondiegetically, in which case "we may experience it as manipulative," or expressing the feelings of that interiority through focalization, in which case "we may experience it as a powerful tool" (129). Focalization thus gives us an option to understand some music as an aspect of the diegesis's stylization, as a psychological sound effect, as an emotion-as-we-hear-it.

When examined in terms of focalization and stylization, Chion's concept of rendering is the name of a wide, porous boundary between diegetic and nondiegetic. In the discussion of rendering in the previous section, I mentioned that how a sound feels under the rendering contains an ambiguity, and it is time now to address that ambiguity in a bit more detail. Does the feeling belong to the diegesis in general, that is, to anyone whatsoever in the diegesis? Is it limited to a specific character within it? Or does the feeling belong to a position outside it, say, to the feeling of an empathetic narrator? These are questions of the focalization of narration. David Neumeyer and I note:

---

[5] Heldt (2013, 127) makes a similar point.

> The proposal that music be understood primarily as a stylized mode of representing the sound world places sound on a par with visual means of cinematic signification. In fact, music has often been theorized along the lines of such stylization — as a signifier of excess used to fill in what would otherwise be absent. Nondiegetic music represents, as it were, something otherwise masked by the screening of reality: how the world feels, say, rather than how it appears. In this sense, music is not unlike stylized lighting and sets. Yet stylization in the visual sphere is taken as how the world screened looks in itself. Though this visual world appears askew to us, the characters inhabit and negotiate it as though that is in fact the way their world is. It appears to us, in other words, as it naturally exists. We see, more or less, as the characters see, but interpret it as a world constructed with an eye turned to the so-called "pathetic fallacy." (Buhler and Neumeyer 2005, 281)

This idea of stylization is consistent with the model of focalization presented here, and it also anticipates to some extent the antirealist theory developed by Winters. But where Winters (2012b) seeks to "restore" music in film to narrative space, so that music is "the product of narration not the producer of narrative" (43), focalization and stylization on the contrary remain committed to the narratological model and presume a realist theory of film representation. Although realist, this model does not reject stylized music or sound as a mark of focalization, nor does it demand that every or even most elements in the story be realistic. It only specifies that the level of reality is defined by the diegesis (*fabula*), that the diegetic world extends beyond the film, and that any stylization as a representational figure that exceeds or reduces the diegesis belongs to the level of the narration. This model, which augments the traditional one, recognizes analytical and interpretive utility in maintaining a category of stylization that is attributable more to narration than to narrative space. The conjunction between focalization and stylization allows considerable play and confusion between the categories of diegetic and nondiegetic.

FOCALIZATION IN *CASABLANCA*

To conclude this discussion, I will apply the concept of focalization to the famous scene from *Casablanca* (1942) where Sam sings for Ilsa, and Rick and Ilsa first see one another in the café.[6] The first part of the scene with Ilsa and Sam features dialogue and what seems straightforward diegetic music with external focalization. And yet this outward appearance is undermined somewhat by the treatment of sound in the scene. To begin with, unlike what we

---

[6] My discussion here summarizes a portion of a study of *Casablanca* that I wrote with David Neumeyer and that appears in Neumeyer (2015).

might expect, throughout the scene the sound of Sam's voice is more prox-imate than is Ilsa's. The scene leading up to Sam's performance of "As Time Goes By" has in fact all been miked to prepare his performance, that is, so that the intimacy of that performance will sound natural. The impression of Sam's relative proximity and intimacy in the scene is precisely an expressive effect, if an extraordinarily subtle one. And yet, once we recognize it, we can also ask to whom this expressive effect belongs. If it is not attributed to only the narrator, then we can attempt to determine its work within the diegesis. It might, for instance, be used to signal a shift in focalization. In this scene, a long close-up of Ilsa, her gaze increasingly turned inward as she listens, seems almost to transform Sam's performance and this hearing into internal focalization. In this scene, Ilsa seems to be using the music to ride an emotional wave: we see Ilsa hearing and see the intensity of her reaction, even if we remain somewhat uncertain about the exact contours of this feeling. Seeing her listen and the intimacy of the sound together encourage us to intensify our own listening, to plumb this music for the emotions that she is apparently finding in it. The effect of all this is that the long-held shot of Ilsa's inward gaze here seems set up like it is preparing an eyeline match. We await the cut that will show what she sees (or rather imagines) and that will turn the implicit internal focalization of this hearing into an explicit internal focalization of the whole perspective. Rick's flashback in the café later in the film will follow precisely this procedure, giving us the definite stylized signs in both image and sound that allow us to confirm the crossing to the explicit internal focalization of the flashback itself. In the case of Ilsa and Sam, the shot that would complete the eyeline match to the interior never comes. Consequently, the scene hovers at the threshold of rendering where diegetic sound relates to the feeling of the scene—here, Ilsa lost in her thoughts and oblivious to anything in the bar except Sam and the music—rather than providing narratively pertinent business, which will emerge again only when Rick appears. But the signs of internal focalization are never made explicit.

The recognition scene that interrupts this performance poses similar questions but from a somewhat different perspective. First of all, if Sam's music is obviously diegetic, the music that accompanies the recognition is, on first analysis, similarly nondiegetic. The characters give no indication, at any rate, that this is music of their hearing, at least until the tune from "As Time Goes By" appears, when the situation becomes somewhat more ambiguous. And yet this music, like the manipulation of the recording to highlight Sam's performance, is music that is bound up with tracing the feeling of the encounter. It paints not the world of objective appearance but the world of felt, lived experience. It is in that sense a rendering. If the music here is akin to feeling in indirect dis-course, if its stylization means that it seems more clearly internally focalized than Sam's performance, if we can agree that this music seems to register a feeling, we can nevertheless ask to whom this feeling belongs. That is, where is its point of focalization? To ask in Genette's terms: Who "speaks" through this music and who "sees" through it? That is, who reports the observed feeling and to whom does the feeling belong? If we just take the moment when the chord appears and for argument's sake grant that it represents the feeling of shock, the situation still poses numerous possibilities. First, it might represent the shock of the audience, or that of the narrator, or the narrator telling the audience that it should feel shock at this encounter (or that this is indeed a shocking encounter). It might similarly be located in external focalization, as the feeling that anyone whatsoever who experienced the scene would register as shock. A variant would be to attribute an external focalization to Sam (Sam does seem shocked). Or it might be taken as the sound of subjunctive empathetic extension: if I had been there and observed this scene, that moment would have felt as shocking to me as this sound. Or once more removed: if I had been there and observed this scene, this chord sounds like the shock I perceive that Rick (or Ilsa) feels. We might then continue to internal focalization. Is this music Rick's or Ilsa's? That is, whose experience does it represent? If we decide it represents Rick's focalization, that still does not answer whether it renders Rick's feeling of shock (the chord sounds like the experience of shock feels to Rick) or Rick's apprehension of Ilsa's feeling of shock (the chord sounds like the shock Rick observes that Ilsa feels). The same analysis could be made, *mutatis mutandis*, reversing the positions of Ilsa and Rick.

Such cases are at root ambiguous, because the focalization remains largely implicit. And such ambiguity is often the case in film, especially where music is concerned. This is not to say that these alternatives are equally plausible. For this chord, the focalization and the shock registered by the music seem to be initially Rick's, at least in part because the chord is accompanied by an explicitly cued eyeline match from Rick to a second close-up of Ilsa. This eyeline match seems to make this close-up the object of Rick's perception, suggesting that the feeling the sound indicates also belongs to Rick as the emotional reaction to what he sees. And yet this disambiguation, even if we accept it, is only momentary, lasting no longer than the cut back to Rick that occurs significantly even before the chord has fully dissolved. Because internal focalization is hard to maintain in contexts like this that are not also metadiegetic (which stabilizes through the presence of the diegetic narrator), focalization often fluctuates (as it will throughout the subsequent dinner scene, circulating with implicit internal focalizations of Rick and Ilsa and a more general external focalization).

Conclusion

As I noted at the outset of this chapter, narrative has been a major concern of theories of the soundtrack. Even when authors do not explicitly address narrative, the concept regulates much of what they say. The Soviet tradition of film theory may emphasize how montage is determined by dialectics, conflict, and theme rather than the immediate concerns of plot, but montage is still understood in terms of effective storytelling and dramaturgy, and Pudovkin, for instance, advocates for a contrapuntal treatment of sound on the basis of dramatic emphasis. The classical system, of course, takes narrative as fundamental and developed the system of continuity editing to facilitate narration even if it was understood as relating to dramaturgy. Comparing Spottiswoode to Kracauer, as we did in chapter 3, we saw how much crisper the narrative conception had become for the latter than the former.

Classical film theorists developed theories of the soundtrack that were either formally descriptive or practical with a focus on dramaturgy. These theories emphasize the foreground/background distinction with respect to position and pertinence. More recent theories specifically geared toward narrative rather than dramaturgy concentrate on the capacity of the soundtrack to contribute to the definition of the imaginary diegesis both directly with diegetic music and sound and indirectly with nondiegetic music and sound. If classical film theory already recognized unreal music and a commentative function that did not belong to the screen, the focus remained in those cases on the function of a background that establishes mood and maintains continuity (background music) rather than its direct or indirect relation to the diegesis. Even theorists such as Eisenstein who valorized music and sound in a contrapuntal relation to the image tended to understand the soundtrack as a complementary strand that set up a particular rhythmic correspondence with the image rather than as something that assumed a certain position with respect to the narrative. Indeed, with the narrative understanding of the music in terms of position and function, the old debates between synchronization and counterpoint often seem beside the point.

In theories such as semiotics and neoformalism, the analysis focuses on the signifying, syntactical, formal, structural, or constructive details, but it is guided by the whole, the classical system, and the classical system has centered on narrative as an organizing principle. It is surely not a coincidence that both semiotics and neoformalism ended up producing narratological theories. Nor is it a coincidence that the formal models produced by Kalinak, Neumeyer, and Cohen and discussed in chapter 5 presuppose narrative, and each of these authors works out their propositions about how music works in film with appeals to narrative structure and order.

In this chapter we first considered the narratological approach to film as it appears in the work of Metz, Bordwell, and Branigan, and then we examined how narratology has been applied to the soundtrack, especially music. Gorbman's book begins this tradition, and nearly every author writing on the theory of the soundtrack since has engaged with her work in a significant way. It neatly summarizes the theory and practice of the classical style, even as it opens a number of areas to productive scholarly development. This is characteristic of narratological theory and is both the strength and weakness of the approach, since the terms, aesthetic aims, and organization of the classical system figure so large within it. It is not in fact always a simple or easy task to repurpose the theory for post- or nonclassical films since such films have different structuring principles and aesthetic commitments, sometimes radically so. The limits of narratological theory, moreover, are the limits of the structuralism or formalism that underlie it. This is one reason that the film narratology that grew out of semiotics (and that Gorbman draws on) would ultimately find it advisable to incorporate Lacanian psychoanalysis and structural Marxism into its model: it opened the study of film narrative to the analysis of ideology and transformed narratology into a form of critical theory.

7

Critical Theory and the Soundtrack

Introduction

Semiotics, neoformalism, and narratology all focus on how film organizes its materials into a text. That is, its materials and organization are considered to be immanent to the film; they belong to the film itself; and analysis seeks to understand what the film is in itself. This focus on what is immanent to film constructs it as a thing apart, and one difficulty that both structuralism and formalism confront is that this emphasis on film as a thing apart also undermines what it is in itself. Like all art, film is something made and something experienced, and the film itself does not really exist without this engagement, which is its very raison d'être.

As already observed in chapters 4 and 6, by the 1970s, Christian Metz's semiotic project had already run into severe difficulties, not simply because he could not convince himself that film's signification was primarily linguistic (so he concluded that film was not in fact a language and the status of film's signification grew somewhat obscure and devolved to the level of narrative), but also because the abstractions required for semiotic analysis seemed increasingly to close off important aspects of filmic signification from investigation. His turn to narrative, discussed in the previous chapter, was a means to overcome some of these difficulties, but narratology's inherent structuralism simply transferred many of the difficulties to higher levels of structure. As Dudley Andrew (1985) remarks, "structuralism and academic film theory in general have been disinclined to deal with the 'other-side' of signification, those realms of preformulation where sensory data congeal into 'something that matters' and those realms of post-formulation where that 'something' is experienced as mattering" (627). Literary formalism confronted similar problems—reader-response criticism was one direct reaction to the austere focus on the text in structuralism and the New Criticism.

Neoformalism has confronted similar difficulties as it bracketed off interpretive and ideological questions to concentrate on aesthetic effects **187** irrespective of content. As with semiotics, another side of the film is closed off from investigation, and many scholars writing about film question whether the aesthetic can be thus separated from ideology. Aesthetics since Kant, whose approach basically opened the formalist epoch, may have sought disinterested contemplation as the ground of understanding art qua art, but a critical practice grew up in its shadow that questions the conditions of possibility that make an aesthetics and the disinterested contemplation that it authorizes conceivable in the first place. This practice, which often goes by the term "critical theory," asks, what is the "ideology of the aesthetic" (Eagleton 1990)?

Although the term "critical theory" first came to prominence in the interdisciplinary work of the Frankfurt School, especially that of Theodor W. Adorno and Max Horkheimer, the term today, at least as applied to film and other humanities, covers a wide range of interpretive methods, including under its rubric many of the most significant trends of recent scholarship: not only the "classic" forms of Marxism and psychoanalysis but also poststructuralism, feminism, gender and sexuality, phenomenology, hermeneutics, postcolonialism, race and ethnicity, deconstruction, and cultural studies among others. Along with semiotics, neoformalism, and narratology, these critical theories form the methodological base of film studies today, and they all have made important contributions to the theory of the soundtrack.

The otherwise rather disparate interpretive methods of critical theory—or critical theories as I will henceforth refer to them—are linked by a commitment to locating and interpreting an ideological substrate of film. The premise of critical theories of art is not only that aesthetic illusion, the surface of the artwork, is a necessary appearance as traditional aesthetics has it, but also that this illusion is bound up with ideology at a fundamental rather than contingent or superficial level; moreover, one of the effects of aesthetic illusion is that it reconfigures this ideological substrate of works into novel aesthetic forms that articulate what Fredric Jameson (1981) refers to as a "political unconscious" of society so that considerable interpretive work is required to understand the relation between aesthetic illusion and ideology. This insistence on the ideological dimension of the artwork has, however, led opponents, generally associated with neoformalism, to label its practitioners as mere "ideological critics," polemically intimating that such "ideological critics" care more about conformity to ideology (or revealing covert ideological structures) than revealing the distinctiveness of film as an art (Carroll 1988, 1996b; Bordwell 1989, 1996). While the neoformalists thus accuse the critical theorists of bad faith and enforcing "political correctness" (Carroll 1996a, 259), these neoformalists also ignore the way in which such interpretive methods, however reductive, admit a dimension of social content, experience, and meaning into the interior of work that neoformalism has difficulty accessing (Nichols 1992).

Hermeneutics of Suspicion

A basic premise of most critical theories is that film means more than it seems (they have a realist ontology), and its excess meaning is structured as ideological figures that serve as foundational cultural myths ameliorating cultural contradictions. Critical theories therefore often engage in what has been called the "hermeneutics of suspicion" (Ricoeur 1970, 32): they read the film not so much for what it wants to say, but for what it attempts to conceal. Film offers a particularly powerful "myth," because its verisimilitude allows it to present its fiction as if it were something real: what is ideological or historically contingent appears in film as something natural rather than the representation that it is. It is for this reason that much critical theory work has involved battling and dismantling André Bazin's (2005) realist "myth of total cinema," the idea that film is a recording of the world, where the appearance of realism now becomes a figure of ideological illusion. Critical theories in this sense take the realism of the myth of total cinema, its drive to reproduce the world, as a mask of idealism, as a cultural fantasy that reveals a will to power. That is, critical theories take issue not so much with the apparent realism of the image as with how the image of that realism has been constructed from codes, stylistic norms, and conventions. It is in this respect that critical theories differ from neoformalism and semiotics, which are likewise concerned with revealing the codes, norms, and conventions of realism. But whereas neoformalism especially wants to take these at face value, as relatively neutral stylistic markers that serve above all to organize technique, critical theories see in such will to style and technique marks of deep cultural ideology. Where neoformalism is content to reveal and analyze, critical theories aim also to decipher, and indeed to unlock doors with keys that the film did not even know it possessed.

Critical theories focus on identifying and interpreting ideological structures that create and reflect power relations as they are constituted in works. The analysis of ideology can take place at three levels: the ideology of content, the ideology of the system, and the ideology of the apparatus.

Ideology of Content (1): Topic Theory

The ideology of content has long been recognized and analyzed, and its identification continues as a practice of film analysis. It is also the least controversial level of ideological critique; Noël Carroll (1996a), for instance, argues that it is both the most pertinent level for understanding pernicious ideological effects and largely consistent with (or at least not antagonistic to) formalist modes of film analysis (268–72).

The musical topic, which I will define as a conventional musical sign with an unusually clear signification due to being an element in the musical

referential code, is frequently deployed by composers for its dramatic efficacy. Musical topic is a term derived from the field of musical semiotics, and,
as such, it relates specifically to the signlike property of music (Ratner 1980;
Agawu 1991; Hatten 2004; Monelle 200; Mirka 2014).[1] Topics consist of musical clichés like fanfares to signal heroism, so-called hurry music for chases,
and jazz to suggest an urban milieu, and they often follow the logic of racial
stereotyping such as the use of "Indian" music in westerns.

As early as *The Birth of a Nation* (1915), one contemporaneous reviewer
criticized the accompanying music for reinforcing the racial characterizations
of the film:

> Music lends insidious aid to emphasize the teaching of the screen, for the
> tom-tom beats from time to time convince us that the colored man, well
> drest and educated though he may be, came from Africa. Why is not some
> Asiatic instrument used to remind us that the Aryan race came from the
> wrong side of the Caucasus? (quoted in Stern 1965, 108)

Here, the writer points to a particularly charged musical content, namely,
"the tom-tom beats," which are musical figures of the primitive serving not only,
as in this case, to insist on an African essence to "the colored man" but also to
point to a non-European essence of the Native American. Similar observations
have been extended to how Hollywood scores women, homosexuals, people of
other races—basically any group or character on which a film deploys music to
make it into an "other," and I will examine a number of these approaches in detail later. What such studies indicate is the ideological force music displays in
film at the level of content, which is, more or less, the level of its signification.

Issues of race, ethnicity, and colonialism have been approached in terms
of the soundtrack from two primary directions: mapping out the development
and deployment of musical topics in background scoring on the one hand
and examining the use of recordings associated with particular ethnic and racial groups (such as jazz or hip hop) on the other. In general, this work has
contributed more to interpretations of particular soundtracks than to the formulation of a general theory of the soundtrack. Nevertheless, scholars sensitive to race and the dynamics of colonialism have offered an especially cogent
critical reception of the theory of musical topics.

As scholars of film music have long noted, scores have deployed musical
topics to gain clarity in signification but at the cost of resorting to and reifying
pernicious stereotypes. Gorbman (1987), for instance, shows how the use of
the Indian motif in *Stagecoach* (1939) represents them as a hostile alien force

---

[1] Some restrict the use of the term "topic" to music citing other musical genres or styles, but this
seems to restrict the topic to what Ratner called "style topics." Although I will not do so here, it would
be worth disentangling the closely related concepts of topics, moods, and melos.

(27–28; 2000, 238–39). I discussed this scene briefly in chapters 3 and 4, and there noted how music lined up with the film's theme about the West. Here, I can draw on Gorbman's analysis to expand that interpretation somewhat. In the set-up to the Indian attack in Monument Valley, a jaunty tune associated with the stagecoach traveling across the landscape is interrupted by the brutal intrusion of fortissimo brass, which is coupled with ominous shots of Indians on a hilltop. The harsh effect is one of jarring semiotic dissonance (although the actual musical materials are less dissonant than bare and modally incompatible), of a primitive music violently cutting into the "normal," untroubled musical unfolding, the latter itself a sign of civilization expanding its influence across the landscape. The music here, as throughout the film, demonizes: "Wordless throughout the film, and virtually invisible until the climactic chase sequence on the plain, the Indians serve as the faceless antagonist, often signaled by music alone" (Gorbman 2000, 238).[2] As David Burnand and Benedict Sarnaker (1999) note in commenting on the same passage, such music "is designed to tell an audience next to nothing about [the Native Americans] as human beings" (7). If demonization was the most common musical representation of Native Americans during the studio era, Gorbman (2000, 2001) argues that the musical codes in the genre of the western changed markedly in the poststudio era, suggesting that the musical codes dissolved along with the genre, albeit at a somewhat slower rate. Michael Pisani (2005) extends these observations, carefully tracing the development and reification of the musical topic of the American Indian in the late nineteenth and early twentieth century. He notes the particulars of the topic, how these conform to a certain cultural image of the Native American, and how resistant the topic became to fundamental modification once it was codified.

Anthony Sheppard (2001) similarly argues that Hollywood composers have tended to score Japanese characters in stereotypical ways that demean and demonize them while also withholding from them the full measure of humanity. Jane Gaines and Neil Lerner (2001) show how Joseph Carl Breil's score for *The Birth of a Nation* systematically deploys topics designating primitivism to demonize each and every assertion of African American subjectivity in the film. Similarly, common musical associations of jazz with the city, whether as a site of urbanity (musicals, romantic comedies) or of dystopic fall (film noir), continue to link race, rhythm, exoticism, and primitivism in ways that are deeply problematic and only rarely problematized (Gabbard 1996; Smith 1998, 72–76).

In recent years, rap music has served a similar, if more overtly racialized function in film (Doughty 2009, 327). If "black music"—whether jazz, blues,

---

[2] Gorbman's description here is not quite accurate. The Indian wife at the fort sings a song before disappearing along with the horses.

gospel, or rap—is a cultural construction with little to no basis in either biology or geography, as Philip Tagg (1987, 2) argues, it is likewise the case that "'black music' is systemically deployed by the film industry to gain swift entrance into the African American condition," as Ruth Doughty (2009, 325) replies. Although Doughty proposes to accept Tagg's nonracialized musical understanding, the logic of her article is one of white appropriation (if not theft) of "black music" rather than of cultural representation and construction of race through music, as Tagg proposes. Among other things, this means that she never interrogates the definition of "whiteness" she deploys (which simply becomes the other of "blackness") and whether and to what extent "Jewish" would have been constructed as "white" (or "passing" as white) at the time about which she is writing, the jazz age of the 1920s. Doughty cites Michael Rogin (1996) on this point but collapses his narrative so that the process by which the Jew becomes culturally white through the othering effects of blackface is all but lost, as are the complex cultural negotiations required of all who stood outside the charmed circle of white American culture—marginals at the time would have included not just Jews, but most ethnic types (Irish, southern and eastern Europeans, even Germans) who have since been accepted as white.

In each of the cases cited previously, the musical topic is heavily marked;[3] it seizes on something that appears to stand outside the standard musical language, and this difference serves both as the ground of its signifying element and as a way to demarcate its exteriority, its resistance to assimilation to the standard in a way that allies these topical figures with exoticism. Mark Brownrigg (2007) summarizes the principles used specifically to signify (exoticized) place:

> the use of a non-Western instrument; the use of Western instruments in imitation of non-Western ones; the use of a melody associated with a specific place; the concoction of a melody shadowing a tune with a specific geographic connotations, adopting the theoretical principles of a music culture in order to produce a simulacrum of it; harnessing rhythms evocative of a certain part of the world; using genuine music and/or musicians from the country the film is interested in evoking. (312)

Brownrigg is particularly concerned with colonizing appropriations of such musical topics, where the exoticism is usually tied to representing a place as distant and governed by customs alien to the "norms" of Western, tacitly white culture.

The American context, with its complicated history of colonialism, genocide, slavery, and immigration, is especially fraught with respect to definition

---

[3] On "markedness," see Hatten (1994, 29–66); also see the summary in Hatten (2004, 11–16).

of its national identity and with respect to its "other." As Kathryn Kalinak (2001) explains:

> In America, the other is nonwhite and constructed through racial difference from that perceived norm. Thus, Native Americans, African Americans, Latinos, and Asian Americans have functioned as points of difference against which American culture defines its essential self. Each of these others has had a specific function in the development of American identity across a variety of contexts defined by historical era, geographic region, and various social and political tensions. (156)

Interestingly, the four "others" of American identity that Kalinak identifies— Native Americans, African Americans, Latinos, and Asian Americans—all have stable and strongly defined musical topics by the time the first film music anthologies were being assembled in the early 1910s, indicating the extent to which these others had been reified into theatrical types and/or stereotypes.[4] Not all topical signification is exotic in this way[5]—for Ralph Locke (2009), exoticism generally includes a will to represent something that is other, to use representation to capture and objectify the other (74)—and not all exoticism is so explicitly racialized,[6] but the exoticism of racialized topics does reveal especially clearly the cultural stakes of topical signification. And it should be noted that a clear separation between the two is not easy to maintain. Kalinak (2001) points out that many of the songs associated with cowboys and the frontier originated in overtly racialized minstrel shows and that their transformation into cowboy songs and western folk music is effected through a process that erases the marks of its racialized history (152).

Locke seeks to distinguish representations of the exotic from works written in a particular style. He recognizes that the distinction is unstable, but it usefully allows him to read the exotic as a mask of power relations. Although this differentiation of modes of stylistic representation leads to sensitive and remarkably insightful analysis, less satisfying is its exemption of works borrowing other "cosmopolitan" styles (e.g., Meyerbeer incorporating Italianate opera structures) from such power relations on the seeming basis of

---

[4] On the unstable relationship between social type and stereotype, especially in works of fiction, see Dyer (1993, 11–18). For an excellent discussion centering on the film version of Rodgers and Hammerstein's *Flower Drum Song* (1961) that explores some of the ambiguities and ambivalences involved in the use of racialized types and stereotypes, see Cheng (2000, ch. 2, especially 36–45).

[5] On nonexotic musical topics, see Shapiro (1984), Buhler (2013), Ringer (1953), and Monelle (2006).

[6] For examples of exoticism that is not explicitly racialized, see Lerner (2001) on the American pastoral; Brownrigg (2007) on the Scottish musical topic (319–22); Schubert (1998) on the *Dies Irae*; Deaville (2006) on chant; Wierzbicki (2002) on the theremin and science fiction; Schmidt (2010) on electronic and atonal music and science fiction; and Kalinak (2001) on cowboy songs and Kalinak (2007) on those songs in John Ford's films.

the exchange of pure, neutral technique. Such commerce simply reflects these power relations at a different level: it signifies the competition and exchange of the great powers, a level at which colonialist and imperialistic exploitation and expropriation (both abroad and at home) that make these exchanges possible can seem to disappear from view because they have been sublated into the power differentials among the various nation-states. This no doubt accounts for a good deal of the instability of the original distinction. Locke's awareness that the colonialist power relations are pervasive surfaces most strikingly in his comments, following Edward Said (1993), on the way sophisticated artistic structures "occlude . . . the functioning of empire" (34), and on what, borrowing terms from Richard Taruskin (2007) and James Parakilas (1998), he calls the "double bind" of "autoexoticism," the application of the colonial will to represent to the self.

Ideology of Content (2): The Table of Knowledge and Communicative Efficiency

Inherited from eighteenth- and nineteenth-century theatrical traditions and codified in manuals and catalogues for cinema musicians in the silent era, topics are structured as a table of figures. From a fairly early date in cinema history, the catalogues take on a tabular form, sorted according to topic and mood and often including fields for other attributes (key, meter, tempo, duration, etc.), as well as cross-tabs to other topics. The most elaborate of these is *Allgemeines Handbuch der Film-Musik* (1927) by Hans Erdmann, Giuseppe Becce, and Ludwig Brav, a two-volume work that includes a huge fold-out table placing each of more than three thousand musical compositions (all listed, with incipits, in volume two) in relation to broad topical categories (x-axis) and intensity of expression (y-axis). As a form of knowledge, a table of topics represents an attempt to catalogue the world, to stabilize knowledge by stabilizing signification. The epistemological project presumes a timeless essence that determines the topic so that it might be efficiently exploited. The "truth" of the signifier, its conformance to the actual thing in the world that it signifies, is less important to this project than the stability of the signification.

Writing in 1951, composer Dimitri Tiomkin freely admits that "much of the [film] music that is accepted as typical of certain races, nationalities and locales, is wholly arbitrary. Audiences have been conditioned to associate certain musical styles with certain backgrounds and peoples, regardless of whether the music is authentic" (21–22). He goes on to note that in the context of films, the use of the conventionalized topic is often "compulsory."

> I have used the "Indian music" that everyone knows not because I am not resourceful enough to originate other music, but because it is a telegraphic

code that audiences recognize. If while the white settlers are resting or enjoying themselves, the background music suddenly takes on that tympani beat, the effect on the audience is electrifying. All know the Redmen are on the warpath even before the camera pans to the smoke signals on a distant hilltop. If I introduced genuine, absolutely authentic Indian tribal music, it probably wouldn't have any effect at all. (22)

Tiomkin's metaphors are telling: they are signs that presume and establish the regime of modernity: the Indian topic, like the telegraphic message, is a code for efficient communication; if the effect is "electrifying," this is so not due to the authenticity of the code but rather because the audience recognizes itself as the addressee of its message (placing the audience on the side of modernity) and because this culturally and arbitrarily coded message can miraculously be transmitted and decoded faster than the image. Moreover, its telegraphic quality is opposed to the smoke signals, reflecting the disparity in the power of modern "arbitrary" (but also electric and digital) communication technologies compared to "primitive" ones assigned to the Indians. If the smoke signals have a seemingly mysterious power to send "the Redmen . . . on the warpath," the musical topic, like the historical telegraph, has the power to warn efficiently of the attack, whereas the message of the authentic tribal music would be as unintelligible to the audience as the message encoded in the smoke signals. Moreover, even if this particular attack proved successful, the music inscribes any victory as temporary that does not manage to gain control over its power of communication, its representation not so much of modernity per se, whose signifiers are largely "arbitrary," but of its particular regime of truth, the "arbitrary" distinctions that it requires for its particular "truth" conditions to appear.

Burnand and Sarnaker (1999), apologists for the practice of scoring on the basis of communicative efficiency, are most forthright and follow Tiomkin's line of argument. Writing of the Indian motif in *Stagecoach*, they state:

This particular musical code stereotypes "Red Indians" as a bellicose enemy rather than a racial or cultural group. It is dramatically essential, therefore, that they *not* be represented through their own music. Indeed the real thing . . . would only be distracting in the context of a narrative attempting quickly and sharply to establish location, culture or provenance. (8, emphasis in original)

The musical topic reveals the formal dramatic function of "bellicose enemy," a function that is indifferent to any particular content (racialized or otherwise), requiring only that some "other" satisfy the role of bellicosity. This functional indifference to the content of the representation is the flip side of the arbitrariness of the signifier. In deracializing the content to reveal the function, however, what is lost is the purpose (if not function) of the cultural insistence of a racialized appearance of the material to fill out the requirements of the dramatic form. The excessively marked content that constitutes the stereotype generally serves to obscure the power dynamic inhering in the dramatic structure that requires the representation and its efficient communication. Also bound to this excess is the particular affective quality of the topic. In this way, although the particular topic may be accepted, condemned, or simply recognized as an arbitrary convention, the structure that reproduces the power relations passes, as in Tiomkin's account or in Burnand and Sarnaker's, without comment into a (natural) property of drama. Doughty (2009), for example, naturalizes dramatic efficiency through the imperative of time:

> Mainstream films look to inform an audience in a concise and unambiguous way. Cues are given to connote location, period, setting, and characterization. These are typically communicated through visual or aural signs. Film as a medium has to rely on such devices, as there is a prescribed period of time in which a narrative can occur. (325–26)

Although Burnand and Sarnaker themselves favor arbitrary convention, presumably because it allows the excess to stand as a mark of representational artifice that underscores the difference of the narrative from the world, it is hardly "dramatically necessary" that the topic be treated this way. Excessive representation, communicative efficiency, and audience address are the key factors, and "authentic" music can easily serve this dramatic function so long as it is readily interpretable as such. As Robert Stam and Louise Spence (1983) note, "In many classical Hollywood films, African polyrhythms became aural signifiers of encircling savagery, a kind of synecdochic acoustic shorthand for the atmosphere of menace implicit in the phrase 'the natives are restless'" (18). This remains true, whether or not the polyrhythms are genuine or fabricated. Indeed, Jean-Pierre Bartoli (2000) proposes that when it comes to exotic musical figures, evaluation of authenticity, either pro or con, bears no logical connection to evaluating the effectiveness of the communication:

> Exoticism in art arrays itself along a continuum that runs from the most realistic possible borrowing of the actual figures [drawn from music of the foreign culture] to the totally fantastic [*onirique*] construction of imaginary exotic figures. Nonetheless, despite what one might think, the question of the [degree of] veracity of the borrowing has no bearing on how one gauges the effectiveness of the communication established between the creator and his public. The question . . . is: What is the most persuasive at a given moment? (65, quoted and translated in Locke 2009, 49)

In any event, whatever the topic used and however real or imaginary it might be, what counts is its ultimate field of signification: Is it deployed to be read, to encourage the audience to read coarsely and simplistically? Or does it instead deepen, problematize, or crystallize a dramatic moment in a way that complicates or simplifies our understanding of the unfolding situation or of the larger world?

Musical Topics: A Postcolonial Critique

Whatever the origin of the material, the topical catalogue remains implicated in a colonial form of knowledge, part of "the nineteenth-century colonialist imperative to conquer other times, other spaces" (Doane 2002, 2–3). It extends what Arjun Appadurai (1999) calls the "taxonomical control over difference" to the realm of feeling, so that musical topics can be efficiently deployed in a "spectacle to domesticate difference" (227). In this respect, the power and legitimacy of the catalogue derives less from a correspondence of the table to the world than from its marshaling of affective states in the service of ameliorating subjects to the social hierarchies and contradictions they encounter. Once catalogued for instrumental effect, music becomes thereby an exquisite weapon of power, at least in part because its affective quality tends to dominate any discursive referent. As Stuart Hall (1999) notes,

> signs appear to acquire their full ideological value—appear to be open to articulation with wider ideological discourses and meanings—at the level of their "associative" meanings (that is, at the connotative level)—for here "meanings" are not apparently fixed in natural perception (that is, they are not fully naturalized), and their fluidity of meaning and association can be more fully exploited and transformed. So it is at the connotative level of the sign that situational ideologies alter and transform signification. (512)

Seymour Stern (1965), whose obsession with *The Birth of a Nation* seems driven by equal parts admiration and horror at the cultural work of Griffith's film, suggests that a great deal of the ideological effect of the film resides in Breil's score, which, precisely because it effectively deploys so much music from the symphonic and operatic repertory, transforms itself into "one of the fundamental weapons of dramatic-emotional power and political propaganda in the annals of art and politics" (120). Perhaps because of his schizophrenic ambivalence toward Griffith's film or perhaps because he focuses on the score's appropriations from the classical repertory and other preexisting music rather than Breil's original compositions, Stern seems less concerned with pinning down the fact of the score's stereotyping than with tracing the score's mythologizing work as ideology. In this way, he moves the point of ideological analysis away from evaluating content and toward how the score mounts its various appeals to persuade its audience of its worldview. In nascent form, Stern anticipates Homi Bhabha's (1983) suggestion that "the point of [postcolonial] intervention should shift from the *identification* of images as positive or negative, to an understanding of the *processes of subjectification* made possible (and plausible) through stereotypical discourse" (18, emphasis in original). Fixation on evaluating stereotypical figures remains caught within the closure of colonial stereotypical discourse, where the stereotype works as a fetish and the only recourse to appearance seems to be moral denunciation that reinforces colonial structures of power (Bhabha 1983, 26). As Ann Anlin Cheng (2000) writes:

> It is clear that we do not yet have a vocabulary, beyond a moralistic one, in which to examine the space between: the ambiguous middle area in the continuum between egregious *stereotypes* on the one hand and the strategic deployment of *types* (tropes by which we recognize ourselves) on the other. (36)

Cheng adds that understanding the play of stereotype and type requires moving beyond an "analysis on the level of moral judgment and instead work[ing] toward an analysis of the way in which the evocations of stereotypes . . . provoke deeper and more vexing problems surrounding the cultural signification of the object of fetish, the racial-ethnic subjects" (39). What is required is a displacement of the colonial structure, the regime of knowledge, that undergirds the stereotypical discourse and produces its social subjects.

In terms of topics, this would suggest proceeding not by identifying stereotypes and/or their dramatic function per se, but by analyzing their operation at the level of structure—both for how the work's structure requires and enables a particular stereotypical discourse as an ideological form and for how that ideological form serves to articulate the larger social structure in all its contradictoriness. Although much basic taxonomic work on moods and topics still needs to be done to understand better their articulating and structuring work, an analysis attuned to revealing such work would resemble Eric Lott's (1995) prescriptions for analyzing blackface:

> Where representation once unproblematically seemed to image forth its referent, we must now think of, say, the blackface mask as less a *repetition* of power relations than a *signifier* for them—a distorted mirror, reflecting displacements and condensations and discontinuities between which and the social field there exist lags, unevennesses, multiple determinations. (8, emphasis in original)

This is not a recipe for producing hermeneutic certainty but instead a call for thoughtful intervention on the level of both practice and critique. The stereotyped musical topic reveals the hegemonic power relations crystallized in the network of musical signification and as such it offers a key not to unlocking meaning, which in the case of the stereotype is all but self-evident, but to deciphering the systemic and systematic displacements by which hegemonic power reproduces itself in representational networks such as music.

Ideology of System

Ideology can also be found at the level of the system, in the choices filmmakers make in terms of commodifying music for cross-promotion (Smith 1998, 24–68); in the systemic insistence that films operate for profit rather than for art (Eisler and Adorno 1947); in the mode of production, especially the characteristic division of labor, for soundtrack production (Faulkner 1971, 1983; Kraft 1996); or in the habits of production, that is, the way music and sound personnel habitually position themselves and define their professionalism in terms of being unobtrusive, not drawing attention to their labor (Doane 1980b). Ideological critique at the level of the system often takes the form of sociological analysis or industry history.

James P. Kraft (1996) argues that a managerial fantasy of control drove the introduction of sound film technology as much as did profit motive.

> Substitution of capital for labor is seldom just a matter of money. Despite occasional breakdowns and problems of synchronization, sound technology was far more reliable than actors and musicians. Talking movies did not demand higher wages, go on strike, or fail to show up for work. Nor did they argue over song selection. Sound movies thus brought rationality to theater operations and made the task of management easier. Such advantages of machinery over human labor always encourage technological innovation, especially when it increases profits as it did in this case. (49)

If Kraft's account recognizes that profit does not provide a full explanation for decisions, even when considered exclusively from the perspective of management, it also conforms to the managerial fantasy of automated production, of labor without workers, and as such it naturalizes the managerial desire that underwrites technological innovation as a hedge against risk. In that respect it is complicit with the ideology of the Hollywood system even if it is sympathetic to the plight of the workers displaced by the technology that serves to anchor the fantasy.

According to Robert Faulkner (1983), the turn to freelance employment after the dissolution of the studio system had the effect of concentrating production in the hands of a few top composers. The result of this reorganization of compositional work was greater inequality of opportunity for film composers; compared to the studio era, where scoring opportunities were relatively equally distributed for those working in the industry, the turn to freelancing in the 1960s and '70s concentrated the scoring of a large proportion of films in the hands of only a few composers. As freelancers, however, composers were hired with more explicit expectations than was the case of studio production, and because as freelancers their employment was contingent rather than secure, they found themselves being hemmed in by these expectations and becoming typecast. "The tendency is to reduce to slogan, and such a reduction severely restricts the possibility of the freelancer promoting his own self-definitions" (1983, 263). Faulkner concludes, however, that the particular network structure that organized freelance composition for Hollywood film did not provide a rational assessment but an arbitrary and capricious one: once it was assumed that almost every composer who landed a job scoring even one commercial film had adequate skills for the business, actual success in Hollywood was essentially random.

> Success or status attainment Hollywood-style is unrelated to productivity; it is unrelated to the dispersion of connections across multiple filmmakers; unrelated to commercial success and visibility of the project in which one's work is embedded or encapsulated; unrelated to the strategy and tactics that a freelancer employs to influence others in this climate of opinion; and unrelated to the networks of collective action one forms and is, in turn, formed by. This weakness-of-everything model assumes that the process of "making it" into the top tiers [of film composers] is random. In any five-, ten-, fifteen-, or twenty-year period of filmmaking and hiring, every extant composer, for example, who scores a film has an equal, constant probability of success. In some lean years it may be a little harder to keep the continuity of activity going; in other years it may be a little easier, but for everyone equally. In sum, nothing that the freelancer does or undergoes really affects his chances in a population-transforming and resource-allocation process. (265)

This model, which Faulkner says represented the self-understanding of many working in the industry when he wrote his book (and continues to be true to a large extent today), ameliorated composers to the gross inequalities of the system since it left open the hope of success even in the face of constant set-backs. If composers devoted time to nurturing relationships despite all evidence to the contrary that it would positively affect the probability of success, this was but "a symptom of the instability of the freelance system," where taking the meaningless action of hustling business served to distract from the nervous fretting of waiting for a call (265). At the same time, what appeared highly unstable from the perspective of the composer might be anything but from the perspective of the industry writ large:

> There is overwhelming evidence that much of what goes on in Hollywood persists regardless of how professional composers, film producers, directors, writers, and cinematographers define it, feel about it and about each other. It may be that the comparatively stable distribution of work preserves a social order where its participants are in flux. (266)

The turn toward electronic and digital music generation has had a similarly disruptive effect. Like the sound film, digital music production is an ambivalent technological innovation because it offers new resources and artistic possibilities even as it disrupts and transforms the existing mode of musical production (see chapter 9). In particular, digital music production in the form of synthesizers and virtual instruments both saves labor costs and offers distinct timbral (and so also symbolic) possibilities from acoustic instruments even when it is used as a substitute for acoustic instruments (Buhler 2009). At the level of social relations, the digital music production, like most technological innovations, destroys existing social networks of musicians (and the cultural knowledge these networks sustain) as orchestras are replaced by banks of equipment, computer programs, virtual instruments, digital audio files, and MIDI and synthesizer programmers. Given the way that digital music production radically disrupts these social relations, it is hardly surprising that the musicians whose livelihoods are threatened should direct hostility toward it or that, along with the usual connotations of utopian rationality that advanced products of technological innovation carry, the cultural signification of the synthesizer and other electronic and digital instruments should absorb and transform aspects of the disenchantment and dysphoria that displaced and alienated labor projects on it (Reyland 2015; Buhler and Neumeyer 2016).

The case is similar with the use of preexisting popular songs. Such songs might indeed be criticized or valorized on a number of grounds (e.g., dramatic pertinence) not immediately connected with systemic ideology, but often its presence in film has been criticized on the basis of profit motive—that its appearance is motivated only to make money for the film even though other musical choices would have been better for the dramatic structure of the film. Irwin Bazelon (1975), for instance, writes:

> Pictures like *Breakfast at Tiffany's* and *A Man and a Woman*, which employ a popular song specifically written for the film and functioning as its music track literally from ear to ear, are seemingly better suited to a songwriter's talents than a composer's. It is a debatable point whether these films and similar types have been "scored" in the strictest sense of the word. Any one of a thousand other songs could serve the identical purpose. (11)

Embittered film composers pushed out of the industry due to changing fashion are particularly prone to this sort of criticism. In general, such criticism reveals more about the resentment of the no-longer-working composer than anything significant about either the industry or the profit motive, although it does have the advantage of reminding us that the music will ultimately be evaluated by the industry in terms of the economic value it adds to the product. The relationship to economics, however, is also often not as straightforward as it might seem. Even during the heyday of the compilation soundtrack album, for instance, it often cost more to license songs than the filmmakers ever expected to recoup in ancillary income, suggesting another logic besides economics guiding the decision making.

Ideology of Apparatus

More challenging is an ideology critique that takes aim not at the content of the individual films or the terms of industry production but at the very existence of film music or sound film. This mode of analysis, which resembles the postcolonial critique sketched earlier and has been heavily influenced by the theory of the apparatus considered in detail in the next chapter, looks at the presence of music or the redundancy of synchronized sound as an ideological figure.

Thus, Rick Altman (1980b), for instance, points to the "ventriloquism" of sound film and notes how the synchronization not only disguises the heterogeneous origins of sound but also serves to single out certain aspects of the image as the soundtrack's "dummy" according to the following "rule": "an individual who speaks will in all probability become the object of the camera's, and thus of the audience's, gaze" (68). Thus the principle of synchronization within the classical system: the synchronized body is an important body, and the use of mimetic synchronization to mark narrative pertinence is absolutely fundamental to sound film practice, as it underwrites the hierarchical division between foreground and background sound. Where a neoformalist will only recognize structuring aspects of sound (for the good or ill of the art of film), Altman underscores how the formal system in fact is deeply and inherently ideological, as it encourages us to ignore the heterogeneous quality of sound and so also the constructed nature of the cinema.

> To say "pointing the camera at the speaker" is to have already been deceived by the ideology of synchronized sound. "Pointing the camera at the (loud) speaker" is precisely what does not happen in this case. Portraying moving lips on the screen convinces us that the individual thus portrayed—and not the loudspeaker—has spoken the words we have heard. (69)

Mimetic synchronization is thus key to representing a hierarchical view of the world (recall Rudolf Arnheim's opposition to sound film discussed at length in chapter 2, as well as the postcolonial critique of topic theory outlined earlier in this chapter, which likewise focused on hierarchy), but mimetic synchronization also serves to "naturalize" this hierarchy, allowing the audience a view of an idealized world that is clearer and more readable than the real one audience members encounter outside the theater (Flinn 1992). The "collusion" between soundtrack and image in the audiovisual figure of mimetic synchronization is thus taken over by members of the audience, who receive confirmation of their own unified selfhood in the cinematic spectacle of synchronization: "If the human audience accepts the cinema's unity, it is because it cannot affirm its own without admitting the cinema's" (Altman 1980b, 71). Although we might dispute the necessity of the audience finding its unity in the identification with the cinema, the point is that even a simple, apparently technical procedure such as mimetic synchronization is not ideologically neutral, is not merely a tool; it is instead a tool that has been forged to reproduce certain ideological presuppositions, which is sometimes classed under the rubric of "bourgeois perception," a concept that dehistoricizes actual perception into a universalized state of "natural perception" (Lowe 1982).

Similar arguments have been made about film music. Synthesizing a point from *Composing for the Films* and Lacanian psychoanalysis, Claudia Gorbman (1987) suggests that, like synchronization, the very presence of music in film is ideological, whatever its content. The fact that it generally goes "unheard," by which she means it is composed to be unobtrusive and so generally to pass without conscious notice, points to its function of lulling the audience into a state of psychic regression, making them more susceptible to confuse the fantasy figures of the screen with reality (50–64). This tendency is furthered by music's narrative functions, which like the stereotypical topics discussed previously normally serve to clarify the narrative. This last point is taken up and developed by Caryl Flinn (1992), who argues that the clarity offered by film music is falsely utopian. Hollywood film music, she argues with specific reference to Korngold, "assuages its listeners, offering a clarity otherwise unavailable to them through the sharply demarcated motifs for 'good guys' and 'bad guys'" (109). (Carroll's account of "modifying music" discussed in chapter 5 effaces this ideological dimension of film music by treating clarity as a basic economic value of mass art.)

Ideology critique at all levels presumes that ideology results in systemic distortion, a false appearance, usually as a product of so-called false consciousness. Film, as a representational medium, is understood by ideology critics as in the business of producing illusion rather than reproducing reality; indeed, the image of reality serves primarily to convince audiences to accept the illusion. Filmic illusion is then tied to the ideological false appearance, but not as an identity.

If film cannot reproduce the real but only offer a representation of it, if film is an ideological instrument through and through, this does not mean that film's illusion is at one with its ideology. A pursuit for a better reproduction of reality, for instance, might lead not to a lessening of the illusory aspect of film but only to a disguising of its inherent representational quality. Vice versa, the most illusionistic film might reveal its representation qualities, and so unmask the very conditions of its own production. Ideological critics tend to valorize such moments of reflexivity, because they almost always require the revelation of the terms of ideological construction at some level of the social structure even if that reflexivity can serve, as in many musicals, to conserve the status quo (Feuer 1993, 87–122). Musicals are often vehicles of social pedagogy (R. Knapp 2006a, 2006b; Buhler 2008), and the reflexive moments are frequently in the service of this pedagogical function of instructing subjects in the terms of the prevailing ideology rather than subverting that ideology.

Gender, Sexuality, and the Soundtrack

Photography, painting, and similar forms of visual art invite the gaze, contemplatively, at our leisure, or more: they invite staring—in some instances to see the human body. The cinema, likewise, frames an image and invites us to look at it. Narrative cinema, because it requires agency, almost always invites the viewer to look at a human body (and anthropomorphizes agents otherwise), and not surprisingly, therefore, the gaze—and its effects on all concerned, from actors to production personnel to viewers—has been a central issue for a critical theory of the cinema from early on. As Lawrence Kramer (2014) puts it, "the cinematic look is structurally voyeuristic, especially in the classic situation of peering through the dark." He goes a step further to assert that "the cinematic image is sexualized by the condition for its perception" (354). This is the starting point for that important segment of critical theory that is based in gender and sexuality and whose overriding aim has been to reveal the systemic oppression that flows from the social structures of power. In the remainder of this chapter, I discuss two main lines of work as they relate to film: feminist theory and queer theory. I also consider the adjustments necessary to these two theoretical positions when attention is brought to bear on the soundtrack. In the next chapter, I examine how psychoanalysis provides a theoretical grounding.

Soundtrack Theory and Feminist Theory

The supplemental status of the soundtrack (and especially music) in much film theory has made it particularly susceptible to analysis based on gender. As Amy Lawrence (1991) bluntly puts it, "in classical film, sound is conflated with the feminine" (111). Mary Ann Doane (1980b) notes that sound technicians from early on used the metaphor of "marrying" the sound to the image to conceptualize the task of sound editing, and the soundtrack was understood as a promiscuous, unruly force that needed to be carefully controlled (50). Caryl Flinn (1992) adds that sound is cast in "the role of an irrational, emotional 'other' to the rational and epistemologically treasured visual term" (6). The "marriage" therefore ensures a "proper"—that is, culturally sanctioned—relationship between image and sound. If sound supplements the image, its "marriage" to the image "domesticates" any threat that sound might pose as it extends the image (43).[7]

Despite this opening for a strong feminist critique of film sound, feminist film criticism has focused primarily on the image.[8] An especially influential article in this tradition is Laura Mulvey's "Visual Pleasure and Narrative Cinema" (1975), which argues that the image of women is structured as a spectacle that rewards a tacitly masculine "gaze." This gaze objectifies the image (of woman) to integrate it into narrative and assert (masculine) control over it at the level of both story and spectator (12). Kaja Silverman (1988) takes issue with this exclusive focus on the image, arguing that, in classic Hollywood, the soundtrack also delimits the representation of women. Silverman claims that a "woman's words are . . . even less her own than are her 'looks.' They are scripted for her, extracted from her by an external agency, or uttered by her in a trancelike state. Her voice also reveals a remarkable facility for self-disparagement and self-incrimination" (31). Indeed, "Hollywood's soundtrack is engendered through a complex system of displacements which locate the male voice at the point of apparent textual origin, while establishing the diegetic containment of the female voice" (45). Silverman's analysis of the voiceover, which she notes is rarely female in classic Hollywood, underscores the stakes of the gendered voice. The male voiceover is, she argues, the prototype of the masculine screen voice in general, because it is granted discursive authority and proximity to the apparatus, whereas the female voice's prototype lies in the embodied voice as an object of spectacle and display (39). "To the degree the voice-over preserves its integrity, it also becomes an exclusively male voice" (48).

The situation with music has been even more explicitly gendered than sound in general, due to the long cultural tradition of coding music as feminine and the convention developed in silent film of associating the primary recurring theme of a film with the heroine (e.g., Rapée 1925, 14). This treatment continued in the sound era, most rudimentarily in the typical doubling of the love theme with the theme for the heroine, suggesting that the heroine existed in the film primarily to be the love object of the hero.

> The fact that the love theme doubles the signification in this way reinforces the male-dominated point of view that characterizes most narrative film— at least in classical Hollywood. This is especially the case where the male character has a well-defined theme of his own. The love theme defines the heroine in terms of the relationship. In a sense, the music suggests that she is essentially identical to that relationship, whereas the theme for the hero

---

[7] For a cogent response to this line of criticism, see Sjogren (2006).

[8] Ann E. Kaplan (1983) provides a succinct, early overview of feminist film theory's concern for image (23–35).

establishes a musical identity for him that cannot be reduced in the same way. (Buhler, Neumeyer, and Deemer 2010, 198)

Such difference in treatment between male and female characters was pervasive. As Claudia Gorbman (1987) notes, music in the studio era rarely failed to register "the presence of Woman on screen. It is as if the emotional excess of this presence must find its outlet in the euphony of a string orchestra" (80). If film theory equates vision with knowledge and rational control, Doane (1987) argues that the very presence of music in film is an acute source of anxiety, since it "marks a deficiency in the axis of vision. Because emotion is the realm in which the visible is insufficient as a guarantee, the supplementary meaning proffered by music is absolutely necessary" to any film genre, such as melodrama or the love story, that depends on the representation of character emotion (85).

> Music takes up where the image leaves off—what is in excess in relation to the image is equivalent to what is in excess of the rational. Music has an anaphoric function, consistently pointing out that there is more than meaning, there is desire. To music is always delegated the task of pinpointing, isolating the moments of greatest significance, telling us where to look despite the fact that the look is inevitably lacking. (97)

In Doane's analysis, music gains this function, however, only by relinquishing all claims to meaning, which makes music's place in film exceedingly ambivalent. "There is always something horrifying about pure affect seemingly unanchored by signification. The heightening effect of music, its straining to direct the reading of the image, is paradoxically highly visible and risks spectatorial repudiation. It is as though music continually announces its own deficiency in relation to meaning" (97). Music is therefore a burden, and it is a burden because it underscores and asks us to look at what cannot be seen and what the film itself cannot show; that is, it is the positive manifestation of a central lack, a concern that will prove integral to the psychoanalytic accounts of the soundtrack that I will consider in the next chapter. In this respect music doubles and is allied with film's other gendered, supplemental, and generally excessive modes of representation.

This burden is not spread equally across film, but falls more heavily on certain characters who are marked out for excessive musical attention much as the camera marks them for gazing upon. Heather Laing (2007), in her excellent study of music in 1940s melodramas, carefully traces the differential musical treatment on the basis of gender. Music, she argues, is not simply a "signifier of emotion" but "a central element of the way in which we actually understand emotion within the construction of gender" (7). This construction and its binding with music were established in the nineteenth century, and the style of Hollywood film music is therefore not accidental, and it comes with real consequences.

> The film scoring style of the 1940s in fact burdens female characters with a Romantic relationship to music that carries with it both psychological and physical implications. . . . The musical representation of their emotions suggests the transcendent nature of women's interiority. At the same time, however, it also demonstrates the inevitable frustration of destructive power of this interiority in the context of contemporaneous—or historical—social mores and/or nineteenth-century ideas of the female constitution. (10)

The pure, unanchored affect to which Doane draws attention is, Laing argues, bound specifically to studio-era cinema's strongly gendered constructions of interiority, and the horrifying aspect of the one seems to mirror the horrifying aspect of the other. Film thus often presses music into an excessively close relationship with the heroine, as Laing notes:

> The sense of interiority usually associated with the female character comes from her specific connection with a theme that can vary to her emotional states with some degree of intimacy, and the frequent combination of statements of this theme with extended, often close-up, shots of her face. It seems that the increasingly familiar and developing music, in a concentrated convergence with her facial expression, allows us to believe that we understand the women's thoughts and emotions to an intimate degree. (141)

From Doane's perspective, we might take issue with Laing's formulation that audiences come to "understand" to the extent that understanding is generally linked to mastery in rational thought. It is more that music allows audiences to believe that they experience moment to moment something like the feel of a character's fluctuating emotions, emotions that are beyond the mastery of rational thought, not to mention language. Doane's formulation has the advantages of mapping the terms more strictly in the gendered categories of classic cinema, but it has the disadvantages of accepting the excluded middle, which simply equates understanding with reason and conceives any emotion unmediated by reason as the expression of irrationality, a configuration that has many negative representational consequences for women. Laing's perhaps less careful formulation is also analytically somewhat more flexible, and it permits conceiving emotion as something other than the opposite of reason.

We can recognize the theoretical stakes and see the extent to which music specifically underscores female interiority by comparing, as Laing does, the musical treatment of male characters.

Men are rarely associated with such intimate themes or shot in close-up to their accompaniment. Although, therefore, isolated emotional moments may be recorded through the combination of a close-up and sentimental music, its lack of thematic relevance seems to register the emotion at a rather more general level than tends to be the case with female characters. (2007, 141)

When it comes to men, music does not, in fact, tend to underscore the image as particularly lacking and so in need of supplementation. Instead, men say what they think, and there is rarely an issue of emotion overrunning the word. When it does, emotion tends to spill over into rash action, that is, exteriorization, rather than remaining in the unfathomable depths of interiority, enclosed within the spectacular but static close-up, typical of female representation. The musical score follows suit: it allows that male emotion is fundamentally comprehensible; however moved a hero may be, his emotion remains contained and mastered and so the music need only express the presence of emotion rather than probing the image to reveal signs of the unmastered interiority that are projected as signs of an irrational interior life. On this point, Laing draws close to Doane's formulation: "in very general terms, we are asked to witness and sympathize with male emotion, whereas our drawing into the woman's musical-emotional trajectory offers the sense of experiencing female emotion" (141). Our inability to say specifically what the music means, the fact that it remains at the level of connotation, reflects the inability to master in words that underlying emotional experience, which is essentially felt rather than understood.

Soundtrack Theory and Queer Theory

If feminist studies of the soundtrack are concerned primarily with exposing and critiquing the ways Hollywood represents and reinforces existing cultural hierarchies of gender, queer studies, a critical theory of sexuality focused primarily in gay, lesbian, and transsexual perspectives, calls into question the very opposition of the sexes that grounds the hierarchy (Butler 1990; Sedgwick 1990). Like feminist and postcolonial theory, queer theory seeks not only to unmask stereotypes but also to analyze their discursive functions to displace and destabilize the social structures and power relations that support them. According to Ellis Hanson's (1999) concise definition of the practice,

queer theory submits the various social codes and rhetorics of sexuality to a close up reading and rigorous analysis that reveal their incoherence, instability, and artificiality, such that sexual pleasure or desire, popularly conceived as a force of nature that transcends any cultural framework, becomes instead a performative effect of language, politics, and the endless perversity and paradox of symbolic (which is also to say historical and cultural) meaning. The very word queer invites an impassioned, even an angry response to normalization. (4)

Focused on revealing the cultural processes and mechanisms of normalization, queer theory is more concerned with transgressing boundaries and/or drawing attention to the arbitrary nature of cultural constructions than it is with establishing, defining, and defending the identities that culture proffers or withholds in either positive (subject) or negative (abject) aspects. For Annamarie Jagose (1996), this means that queer theory "marks a suspension of identity as something fixed, coherent and natural" (98), and Alexander Doty (1993) adds that "ultimately, queerness should challenge and confuse our understanding and uses of sexual and gender categories" (xvii). If queer theory thereby positions itself against the norm, whether as antithesis, opposite, or contrary, it does so to unsettle the norm, to call into question the status of the norm as something natural. In this respect it is perfectly possible to produce a queer reading of a film without "obvious . . . non-straight elements" (Doty 1998, 150), the point being to look for figures that destabilize and denaturalize (or can be used to destabilize and denaturalize) the cultural norms of straightness, what is more militantly called "compulsory heterosexuality" (Rich 1980).

A critical theory of the soundtrack informed by gender and queer theory would be concerned with the "articulation of power and sexuality" on the soundtrack, how desire is made audible on it, for whom, by whom, and to what purpose (Hanson 1999, 1). It might ask whether and to what extent the soundtrack enforces a compulsory heterosexual code, examining, for instance, how the soundtrack imposes normative gender roles and lines of sexual desire on the film's characters and our apprehension of them. (These are general concerns that Hanson outlines for critical queer studies rather than for the soundtrack per se.) One can certainly imagine, at a first stage, analytical studies of how, say, gay, lesbian, bisexual, or trans characters are scored; the way the soundtrack reinforces or resists engaging cultural stereotypes; whether it chooses to demonize, complicate, or valorize the character types the film presents; and so forth (Kassabian 2001, 72–76; Farmer 2005; LeBlanc 2006). Glyn Davis (2008), for instance, provides a brief account of stereotyping of the gay, lesbian, and transsexual voices (179–81). This sort of analysis is similar to the identification of stereotypes in musical topics or examining positive or negative portrayals of women and race on the soundtrack. But queer theory as a field stands in a similar relation to such analysis as postcolonial theory does to the analysis of the cultural field of stereotypes, and as such it is oriented around identifying and analyzing the processes of subjectification embedded within the representations of sexuality proffered by film, at looking at those representations less as reflecting power relations of the society than of signifying those relations.

Queering Asynchronous Sound

Many have argued for treating asynchronous sound—or at least sound that does not settle easily into the body with which it is synchronized—as part of a queer aesthetic. Lucretia Knapp (1993), for instance, offers the example of Marnie from Hitchcock's eponymously titled film. "There are many incongruencies between the film's visuals and its soundtrack, and they create a space for Marnie outside the dualistic economies of patriarchy" (16). Such incongruities, Knapp says, give Marnie a queer voice. Thomas Waugh (1996) likewise notes that more overt deployment of asynchronous sound, especially the offscreen voice and voiceover, is common in homoerotic cinema as a figure of gay desire and that its use is an aesthetic strategy that

> reflects more than its logistic and economic suitability for artisanal and underfinanced industrial cinema. The voice-off or voice-over, emitting from the body of author-subject as he/she retreats once more behind the camera or mixing console, may articulate a level of retroactive self-reflexivity or simply a sportscasting-style simultaneity, descriptive or directive, diegetic or extra-diegetic. This dynamic is at the center of the erotic give-and-take, the tease of the viewer's response by the controlling yet unpossessing author. The apocalyptic moment in the history of the device comes when the forever offscreen Rick X [a 1980s "cable porncaster"] bangs his microphone against his unzipped scrotum, replicating the frenzy of unconsummated desire for both gay subject and gay spectator. Image-sound separation thus cements the irreconcilability of subject and object, exacerbates the tension of the teasing relationship of look-but-don't-touch, touch-but-don't-possess, appear-but-don't-speak, speak-but-don't-appear, and so forth. (57)

Glyn Davis (2008), writing specifically about television sound, likewise suggests that queer disruptions of normal modes of viewing "frequently operate via the aural channel, or, more accurately, bring the aural and visual streams into a dissonant—and dissident—relationship to each other" (173). This formulation, reminiscent of Eisenstein, Pudovkin, and Alexandrov's (1988) call in the "Statement on Sound" for audiovisual counterpoint at the dawn of the commercial sound film (see chapter 2), aligns the queer aesthetic fairly closely with the aims of the old avant-garde, a sort of Brechtian alienation effect, which is perhaps not surprising given that both aim to disrupt a normative social order. Davis (2008) explicitly disavows a connection, however, arguing that, unlike Brecht, who sought to distance his audience from the drama so that they might recognize the mechanisms of social power operating in the drama, the disruptive effects in television often "enhance the relationship with television, producing a purposefully heightened level of attention to the qualities of the text. They may, however, be correctly described as perplexing, destabilizing, perhaps even disorienting" (185). Whatever its relation to Brecht, its similarity to Russian montage theory is striking, except that the unexpected "jolts" of television are, unlike edits in film, often unscripted. More to the point is the interpretive strategy: a queer reading understands such disruption not simply as an attack on the social order but as an opening for a desire not sanctioned by that order to appear.

Queerness and Spectacle

As with postcolonial theory, queer theory often employs an interpretive strategy that reads against the grain. In the case of queer theory, this strategy seeks out figures of camp, "an oppositional reading of popular culture which offers identifications and pleasures that dominant culture denies to homosexuals" (Smelik 1998, 141). Jane Feuer (1993) advocates such a camp approach when she suggests that "'queer' readings of musicals would shift the emphasis from narrative resolution as heterosexual coupling (an emphasis on the comic plot) and toward readings based on non-narrative, performative and spectacular elements (and emphasis on numbers)" (141). Camp readings seize on elements of textual spectacle or excess to bifurcate the film into competing structural levels, one that carries a dominant meaning, the other a secret, subversive, or at least nonnormative one. Figures of spectacle and narrative excess are also sites of filmic artifice, points at which the film acknowledges its peculiar status as a cultural construction. "Mainstream Hollywood images," Lloyd Whitesell (2006) writes, "freely invite queer consumption. Of course, nominal narrative safeguards are in place to maintain the appearance of alignment with prevailing concepts of gender. But the storylines are hardly strong enough to contain all that is going on in the affective and aesthetic realms" (273). Mitchell Morris (2004) argues in similar fashion that the performative artifice common to the musical is especially conducive to queer reading because "artifice is a way of indicating that there is a secret; in the past century's prime cultural texts, if there is a secret, how could it not be that secret?" (152).

The situation is in fact characteristic of much classic Hollywood cinema, since the male hero is always in danger of being treated as a spectacle, as an object to be looked at rather than narratively identified with (Miller 1997, 46–47). The result, Anneke Smelik (1998) writes, is that

> homosexuality is always present as an undercurrent; it is Hollywood's symptom. The denial of the homoeroticism of looking at images of men

constantly involves sadomasochistic themes, scenes, and fantasies; hence the highly ritualized scenes of male struggle which deflect the look away from the male body to the scene of the spectacular fight. (140)

D. A. Miller (1990, 1997) brilliantly analyzes *Rope* (1948) and *Suddenly, Last Summer* (1959) along these lines. These two films, each featuring a prominent level of homosexual thematics, bracket a decade when the Hollywood production code, which had prohibited overt mention of homosexuality, was eroding. Miller's analysis reveals a regime of representation that requires and so produces symptoms of pathology even as the film must attempt (and fails) to contain them. Drawing on Roland Barthes, Miller (1990) says that homosexuality in *Rope* remains at the level of connotation, where the prohibition against allowing it to pass into denotation has its own perverse effect.

> Yet if connotation, as the dominant signifying practice of homophobia, has the advantage of constructing an essentially insubstantial homosexuality, it has the corresponding inconvenience of tending to raise this ghost all over the place. For once received in all its uncertainty, the connotation instigates a project of confirmation. . . . Needing corroboration, finding it only in what exhibits the same need, with no better affordance for meeting it, connotation thus tends to light everywhere, to put all signifiers to a test of their hospitality. (119–20)

What this structure produces, Miller says, is the desire for homosexuality—"the spectacle of 'gay sex'"—to appear as denotation, precisely what the production code forbids. The perversity lies not in "gay sex" or this desire to see it but in the "structure of occultation"—what Eve Sedgwick (1990) describes as "the epistemology of the closet"—that would raise and even require this desire only to proscribe its actual appearance. In this way, the desire to see transmutes into a desire not to see, and the closet becomes the acceptable cultural structure for this "homophobic, heterosexual desire for homosexuality" (Miller 1990, 125), a desire that culture cannot acknowledge as its own.

Suddenly, Last Summer (1959) and the Economy of Sacrifice

Based on a play by Tennessee Williams and directed by Joseph L. Mankiewicz, *Suddenly, Last Summer* is the story of a psychologically traumatized young woman, Catherine Holly (Elizabeth Taylor), and a doctor's attempt to help her. As the film opens, Catherine's rich, domineering aunt, Violet Venable (Katharine Hepburn), has had her institutionalized for telling scandalous stories about her cousin Sebastian's death, and Violet has offered to build a new wing for a run-down New Orleans' psychiatric hospital if Dr. Cucrowicz (Montgomery Clift) agrees to perform a lobotomy on Catherine. The doctor is reluctant to do so unless he is convinced that Catherine's issues cannot be addressed through traditional psychiatric means, and he places her on a rushed course of psychoanalytic diagnosis and treatment. The outcome ostensibly hinges on getting Catherine to recount the gruesome tale of Sebastian's death, which she finally does near the end of the film, where an elaborate flashback reveals that Sebastian was killed in Cabeza de Lobo by a band of local boys from whom he had been procuring sex.

If *Suddenly, Last Summer* was able to obtain official permission to denote homosexuality explicitly, if not by name, it approaches the representation of gay sex, indeed the homosexual body, coyly, by displacement. Sebastian is only ever seen partially, primarily from the rear, and close-ups of Catherine routinely substitute, Miller (1997) notes, "whenever such possibility [of representing gay sex] would be on the verge of realization" (36). The result is "*a homosexual closet constructed for general heterosexual use,* for the indulgence, in other words, of a homosexual fantasy that we must mainly understand as not the peculiar coinage of the gay male brain but the common, even central daydream of the normal world" (37, emphasis in original). The operation of the closet, which is here seemingly underwritten by a desire for literal transparency, is particularly evident in Catherine's final narration, where her voice recounts the story of Sebastian's death but the image, in flashback, never manages to dissolve Catherine's body. Miller comments:

> "Isn't that what everybody wants," Cathy remarked earlier in explaining her suicide attempt, "me out of the way?": and everybody suddenly includes the audience in whom, for this almost statutorily desirable body, the sequence excites no desire, but only a desire to see through it, to watch it once again turn transparent, and so further disclose the phantasmatic scene of gay male sex, "the beach at Cabeza de Lobo," that lies behind it. (39–40)

Yet if the film effects a displacement here, it does so by seeming to desynchronize the image to Catherine's narration: on her mention of the "indecent" white bathing suit Sebastian had made her wear, the image shows instead a man in a white bathing suit, and although Catherine does soon appear, "in a crucial respect, she has arrived too late" (41). In this way, "Cathy's body is implicated in male homosexuality not merely as its sign, or even its analogy, but as its very evidence" (42). Writing about the stage play rather than the film, Robert F. Gross (1995) makes a similar point about Catherine, who "comes to embody a desire as much her cousin's as her own, combining female heterosexuality and male homosexuality in a single vector. Hence, her profoundly threatening advances to Doctor Cucrowicz erase any difference between gay and straight *eros*; a seemingly heterosexual action is permeated with gay desire" (240).

Although persuasive, Miller's interpretation (1997) in particular shows an undeniable visual bias—"the level that, in every film, counts most"

(50)—which, precisely because he recognizes and so adeptly diagnoses the pervasive blindness at the heart of Mulvey's (1975) influential analysis of the look, is most curious. His account simply reproduces the hegemonic status of the image, as though this status were some self-evident property of the medium. Miller does, however, closely attend to Catherine's narration in *Suddenly, Last Summer* and implicitly recognizes the important and complex work that the play of synchronization and desynchronization performs within it; both her lack of visual transparency and the unruly appearance of the man in the bathing suit are, however, irreducibly audiovisual figures whose appearance of uncanniness requires not just a particular joining of sound and image but also the assumption of a representational regime of compulsory synchronization that owns the distinctions by which those particular joins can appear especially uncanny.

Miller also mentions, in passing, the musical score's alignment with a normative heterosexuality, as it celebrates, in a way that otherwise seems outrageously excessive, Catherine's ability to stand up just prior to delivering the full story of Sebastian's death:

> If the musical track salutes her achievement with sonorities befitting the most wondrous miracle, or the most heroic triumph, this is implicitly because, in managing to get upright, Cathy has simultaneously become straight as well. She is hardly on her feet for a second before, throwing her arms about her doctor's shoulders, she begins to cover his face with passionate kisses. (1997, 57)

Although the orchestral score here is typical in asserting access to Catherine's interiority and *Suddenly, Last Summer* follows the so-called talking-cure film in working to express the properly gendered female subject as an object of heterosexual desire, Miller notes that the doctor does not reciprocate. Before she had found the strength to stand, the doctor had pricked Catherine with the truth serum, and it is striking that her reaction to being thus penetrated by the shot is an ecstatic embrace of the role as object of heterosexual desire. If this is indeed music that expresses Catherine's emotions and desire, if the doctor's reluctance indicates that she is "peculiarly unlucky in love" as Miller suggests (58), she also gains in her loss of sex appeal a measure of autonomy that allows her to appear as something other than the role offered by compulsory heterosexuality as romantic object.

Surprisingly, Miller does not mention the other music of the film—the boys' band of home-made instruments—that serves both as the most prominent sign of Catherine's psychological blockage and as the accompaniment for the climactic portion of the flashback, which is otherwise uncannily without diegetic sound aside from her scream that concludes it. In fact, the first time she tries to recount the story for the doctor, she falters when "that awful noise . . . , that awful music" rises up on the soundtrack to overwhelm her voice. When under the truth serum she recounts the story the second time, it is clear why she had earlier failed: not only had the music served to drive Sebastian through the streets of the city to ceremonial slaughter, but also the instruments were apparently used as ritual tools in his dismemberment. Literalizing Jacques Attali's (1985) insight that noise is a simulacrum of essential violence and music its channelization into ritual sacrifice (21–31), this unruly sound positioned between noise and music is no simulacrum here but the actual instrument of ritual murder. Catherine has witnessed a primal scene of essential violence, with Sebastian as sacrificial victim.

According to René Girard (1977), the basic social function of sacrifice is to break cycles of violent retribution. Consequently, if sacrifice meets violence with violence, it must do so in a form that avoids provoking a new cycle of retribution, which is why the scapegoat is usually an outsider or, if not an outsider, an innocent. Designed to end retribution, the ritual must avoid signs of retribution (vengeance is reserved for the divine), which carries the taint of impurity. That Catherine's flashback nevertheless represents Sebastian's ritual murder as a form of retribution suggests that we might take her narrative as a misreading serving her own psychic ends. That misreading would also raise questions as to whether Catherine has in fact misconstrued her role as bait, which, however overdetermined, would therefore be a red herring in interpreting the film.

If the function of this sacrificial rite remains obscure within the social context of Cabeza de Lobo, amnesia of the sort Catherine experiences is usually understood psychoanalytically as a traumatic sign of unconscious recognition and psychic censorship rather than as unintelligibility. Catherine can't remember not because she doesn't understand what she has seen, but because she is terrified by what it reveals about herself: she recognizes in its displaced form the traumatic violence of her own primal scene, which twines a compulsory heterosexuality that uses the fantasy of "perverse" homosexuality to police and uphold its boundaries with a revenge fantasy against a perverse patriarchal privilege that blames her,[9] rather than her rapist—"a very ordinary married man," Violet assures—for her "loss of honor." Catherine's narrative thus makes the scene into an allegory whereby she merges with Sebastian and assumes his face and he her anus, as in Miller's reading, but now this fusion is understood as instrumentalized to surmount the shame of the original sexual trauma she experienced at the Dueling Oaks. In that respect, Violet is not so far off the mark when she claims that Catherine killed Sebastian: Catherine's narrative

---

[9] Siegel (2005) notes that Violet's account of the sea turtles on the Galapagos Islands draws explicitly on Melville's story "The Encantadas or The Enchanted Isles." Melville's story, she says, reads the scene as a revenge fantasy, claiming that most sailors "earnestly believe that all wicked sea-officers, more especially commodores and captains, are at death (and in some cases before death) transformed into tortoises" (quoted on 558).

begins to offer Sebastian as her substitute, as a ritual sacrifice for her sins (or, to be more precise, the sins that society has pinned on her), just as at the social level the homosexual functions in the "economy of sacrifice" as the scapegoat for the regime of compulsory heterosexuality. But if sacrifice demands separation and establishment (or re-establishment) of social marks of distinction as the price of that separation, Catherine's separation from Sebastian is especially violent, traumatic, and laden with guilt sufficient to trigger extreme psychological defenses. Symptoms of this trauma appear not only in the amnesia but also in Catherine's demonization of exploitation as (ab)use, as a perversion of social order: her commitment to the idea that Sebastian used people only for his pleasure and in particular that he used Catherine as bait; that she had been used by her rapist, who warned that saying anything about it would disrupt the social order (as it did); and that Violet used Sebastian as an outlet to live a more interesting life than her husband was willing to provide for her. In negative form, demonization of exploitation also prompts Catherine's suicide attempt by conforming to the brutal cultural logic: because she was of no use other than as the bearer of a social trauma that society could not acknowledge, she was "in the way," expendable, and so also offers herself a potential scapegoat. What this symptom disguises, however, is Catherine's own need to exploit Sebastian as a sacrifice in order to find her place again in the social order.

The band of Cabeza de Lobo rewrites this psychic dynamic into a social framework along the lines of social power that Attali outlines: the band's noise announces the threat to social order; the band's music channels that threat into acceptable social form. Janice Siegel (2005) traces the numerous parallels between Sebastian and Pentheus from Euripides's *The Bacchae* and notes the ways in which the film strengthens these parallels compared to the stage play. She also reads the instruments, which she sees as guitarlike, and other aspects of the costumes as invocations of Orpheus and notes the ambiguity of the boys' call for "pan," which is not only Spanish for bread, as the doctor notes, but also a central figure in the Dionysus myth (556). The word "panic," which Siegel (and also Catherine in her narration) uses to describe Sebastian's flight and many use to describe the film's engagement with its homosexual thematics, also has its roots in this Greek figure. Albert Johnson (1960), in his review of the film for *Film Quarterly*, suggests as well the resemblance of the stringed instrument to "a primitive-looking banjo" (42). If this invocation of the banjo allows the band at Cabeza de Lobo to sound like a distant echo of a New Orleans string band and the costumes of its members to resemble a Mardi Gras parade where the mummers' costumes have been plucked—Catherine herself describes the band as looking "like a flock of plucked birds"—we should recall that Catherine's rape takes place after a Mardi Gras ball. This uncanny resemblance relocates the central trauma to the Dueling Oaks, as does her scream, the only synchronized diegetic sound of the flashback and one that has the power both to silence this music—it is not heard again—and to burst across the narrative frame, collapsing past and present, her roles as narrator and narratee; but the scream—a prime example of what Michel Chion (1999) calls a "screaming point" (75–79)—also has the power to cross another narrative line and to deliver the call for help that she had earlier placed, mysteriously dislodged from herself, at the site of the rape. She can evidently separate the two traumatic events only by renouncing Sebastian, but the music—"if you can call it that," she says—does not offer to her a convincing social order where she can locate herself, since its categories remain indistinct, "a music made out of noise."

In refusing the music and choosing to silence it, she ruins the ritual. Where there is no music, there is no society, no distinction, no social support. As she continues her narration after the scream and recounts the depths of her horror, the lack of music not so much expresses a collapse into stark realism as it underscores a final realization that society is not possible under the conditions being proffered. Strikingly, music returns only after Catherine has completed the story, on a shot of Violet closing the empty book that was to contain Sebastian's summer poem. The music continues as Violet, mistaking the doctor for her son, begins speaking as though she were on a voyage with Sebastian. If, as Attali (1985) says, music is "an affirmation that society is possible" (29), music's appearance here in association with madness suggests that society itself exists in a deluded state. "All great music," Adorno (1996) writes, "is snatched from madness" (71). This is not great music to be sure, but it is music, brilliantly deployed, to sound as serenely mad as the society that it underwrites and that underwrites it. The music continues through to the final shot, where Catherine gently offers the doctor her hand, he takes it, and they both walk to the door. Especially after the attempted kiss before the narration, nothing about the gesture except the overenthusiastic music suggests further romantic entanglement, and the music, we now understand, is party to delusion and not to be trusted, most particularly when it beckons with apparently comforting social roles that refuse to acknowledge the sacrifice they require to occupy and uphold.

It is quite possible to read Catherine's attraction to the doctor prior to her narrative as a defense against Violet, whom Catherine knows is pressuring the doctor to give her a lobotomy. In that respect, Catherine's attempts to encourage Dr. Cucrowicz to take her as a heterosexual object of desire may have more to do with self-preservation than with actual desire to assume that normative social role. Kevin Ohi (1999) argues that Catherine's status as Sebastian's bait and Violet's insistence that the doctor's devotion to his medicine reminds her of Sebastian place the doctor (but also the film) in a "double bind" to the extent that he (but also the film) insists on a "curative heterosexual gaze" (37). Ohi, perhaps persuaded by the deluded music, misses Dr. Cucrowicz's coolness toward romance that Miller points out. The doctor most certainly does not treat

Catherine "as the saving heterosexual object of desire." Aside from the music, the film does not either.

The Hours (2002) and Sacrificial Inversion

The economy of sacrifice that proved so traumatic in *Suddenly, Last Summer* also plays a significant if highly ambivalent role in *The Hours*, a film that entwines three loosely linked stories from disparate time periods around the themes of sacrifice and suicide. The contemporary story involves a lesbian couple, Clarissa (Meryl Streep) and Sally (Allison Janney), and Clarissa's relationship with her former lover, Richard (Ed Harris), a gay writer who has grown embittered as he has been ravaged by AIDS.

Michael LeBlanc (2006) discusses how Philip Glass's music for the film works within and against the economy of sacrifice to support Richard's suicide as an inverted form of sacrifice. Glass's score captures the melancholic repetition that structures and haunts heterosexual romance in all three stories, but that of Clarissa and Richard, LeBlanc says, is particularly fraught because the melancholic attachment to Richard is presented as a block to Clarissa's happiness. The final moments between Clarissa and Richard are "steeped in melancholia, those drawn-out piano notes hanging on a given pitch, clinging tightly to the loss of heterosexual romance. Clarissa, also, is trapped in this place with Richard" (135). The music here then emphasizes the heterosexual ideal as something lost, unobtainable, and so also as a bad object that traps Richard and Clarissa in a cycle of unending melancholic repetition.

By embodying the heterosexual ideal in these last moments, Richard bears the burden of that ideal, volunteering to take it off Clarissa's shoulders. What is compelling here is thus how Richard inverts the conventional logic of sacrifice. If sacrifice is typically performed as a method of abjecting the nonnormative term, so that those bodies that signify otherness are repetitively ejected from the symbolic order, Richard performs the opposite move by embodying heter-onormative romance in his final moments, thereby ejecting that very norm. In other words, if the visionary is typically a form of otherness, Richard becomes a sort of antivisionary, carrying the burden of conventionality so that Clarissa does not have to. By sacrificing himself, he carries with him the ideal of heterosexual romance; he becomes a martyr so that Clarissa might move on from that stifling and melancholic fantasy (LeBlanc 2006, 135).

Richard's suicide, then, becomes a way of ending the cycle and the music traces a similar process. Susan McClary (2007) notes that Glass's "music acknowledges [Richard's] emotional contradictions, but withholds the catharsis both we and the characters so deeply crave." At the same time, in contrast to melancholic repetition of the rest of the score, Glass affirms, by

suspending after Richard's death "his own stylistic rules," the relationship between Clarissa and Sally, which McClary finds "remarkable" since it endows
their embrace with the musical cinematic signs of normal romantic feeling
(61–62).

Even so, if Richard's sacrifice is thus novel in terms of the social forms
and distinctions it is meant to uphold, LeBlanc (2006) cautions that it remains caught within "an economy of sacrifice that demands that abjected
individuals carry the burden of melancholic loss so the rest of us don't have
to" (136). The comparison with *Suddenly, Last Summer* on this point is instructive. Sebastian's sacrifice obviously conforms to the conventional logic,
but Catherine's resolutely melancholic response to the trauma destabilizes the
economy by refusing the exchange.

As the analyses of *Suddenly, Last Summer* and *The Hours* demonstrate, it is
often difficult to neatly separate feminist and queer readings because both bear
on sexuality as it relates to power. This does not mean, however, that feminist
and queer theory can be reduced to one or the other, nor that they will necessarily yield similar or even consistent critical evaluations. Within critical practice, feminist and queer theories carry quite distinct emphases. Attending to
Sebastian's representation in *Suddenly, Last Summer*, for instance, we note that
Sebastian not only is shown primarily from the rear but also is only allowed
to speak through Catherine (and to a lesser extent Violet), exhibiting the split
between image and voice—albeit in negative form—that Waugh (1996) sees
as one attribute of representing queer desire, here almost infinitely displaced
and deferred (55–58). Attending to Catherine, however, we note the extent
to which even in the flashback her voice is only ever momentarily allowed
to leave her body; her narration is anchored to the physical presence of her
body, which, in various degrees of close-up, floats along the right edge of the
frame as the events she recounts play out in the rest of the frame, exhibiting
the unity of image and voice, the compulsory synchronization, that Silverman
(1988) sees as the primary disciplining function of Hollywood sound practice (42–71). The treatment of Sebastian and Catherine in the flashback is in
marked contrast to Dr. Cucrowicz, whose voice passes fluidly from offscreen
to onscreen and back again and so serves as the authoritative norm against
which the representations of Catherine and Sebastian are each understood as
somehow deficient.

Although feminist and queer theory both confront the cultural norm
of compulsory heterosexuality, they are each concerned with analyzing,
unveiling, and dismantling different aspects of power configured under the
norm. It is occasionally the case that a figure, say, the spectacular image of a
woman, may open to the liberatory potential of a camp reading from a queer
perspective but also appear exceptionally regressive from a feminist perspective. Such cases are highly ambivalent, not just in the weak sense that the

critical reception is mixed, but in the strong sense that there can be no real deciding between the alternatives without positing gender or sexuality as the essential category for understanding. Unexamined, this ambivalence therefore easily devolves into exchanging competing charges of misogyny and homo-phobia. What is missed is that the forced choice between alternatives serves primarily to enforce the power of the norm, which gains in virtue of dividing resistance and creating the impression that any gain on one front must be paid for by a more or less equivalent loss on another.

8

Psychoanalysis, Apparatus Theory, and Subjectivity

Introduction

As noted in the previous chapter, one of the aims of critical theories has been to reveal the systemic oppression that flows from the social structures of power, and critical theories have most typically turned to psychoanalysis to provide the theory for how these social structures work and reproduce themselves through the formation of their social subjects. Psychoanalysis, whether derived from Freud or Lacan (and psychoanalysis in film studies and musicology rarely ventures beyond Freud and Lacan), provides this theory of subjectivity, of the formation of social subjects. As such, critical theories generally understand psychoanalysis not as providing a true account of innate psychological drives and forces per se but rather as providing an accurate model for how culture shapes, channels, and deforms those psychological drives and forces to produce the norms that society requires to reproduce itself. In psychoanalytic terms, "normal" individuals are therefore those who fit within the variance that the norm tolerates (or, to frame it from the other side, those who can effectively manage the pressure the norm brings to bear on them); because of its history in the clinical practice of diagnosing and treating mental illness, psychoanalysis has been quite interested in classifying deviance from the norm, which psychoanalysis, at least in its humanistic mode (e.g., ego psychology), generally sees as pathologies to be treated to bring the patient back to mental "health," that is, back within the norm.[1]

---

[1] Lacan and to a lesser extent Freud understand psychoanalysis antihumanistically in the sense that it does not presume a stable ego. As Mitchell (1982) notes,

> Humanism believes that man is at the centre of his own history and of himself; he is a subject more or less in control of his own actions, exercising choice. Humanistic psychoanalytic practice is in danger of seeing the patient as someone who has lost control and a

Critical use of psychoanalysis, by contrast, is unconcerned with clinical treatment and is interested in turning psychoanalysis back on itself to examine how it formulates the norm, what the social norms it posits reveal about the society, and how the pathologies that psychoanalysis identifies are in most cases best considered symptoms of contradictions in the social structure. The pathological in such cases "is the symptom of the normal, an indicator of what is wrong in the very structure that is threatened with 'pathological' outbursts" (Žižek 2006, 555–56). Thus, feminists show that the psychoanalytic model relies on a systematic reduction of gender to sex that allows it to naturalize the social hierarchy on the basis of sexual difference, and queer theorists show that the model deploys homosexuality as a privileged fantasy that serves to domesticate desire to the heterosexual form society apparently requires to reproduce itself. As a theory of patriarchal, heteronormative perversion, of how society produces and manages its distinctive pathologies and regime of damaged subjectivity, psychoanalysis therefore provides real insight into the use of gender and sexuality as levers of power, but psychoanalysis also remains caught within the closure of that society. Ellis Hanson (1999) notes with respect to homosexuality:

> The exclusively psychoanalytic framework also poses a problem, not the least since the definition of homosexuality in these theories almost always relies on dubious Freudian conceptions of same-sex desire as a narcissistic crisis in gender identification. Homosexuality becomes the return, or perhaps merely the persistence, of the repressed in an otherwise anxious and heterosexual narrative. This theory does much to explain the paranoid aspect of homoeroticism in classic cinema, queerness as the monster who threatens the heteronormative coherence of the narrative. (14)

The result, however, is that from within the psychoanalytic theory, nonheteronormative desire can only appear as something perverse. The same applies to the analysis of gender, where, as E. Ann Kaplan (2000) notes, psychoanalysis requires women to "accept a positioning that is inherently antithetical to subjectivity and autonomy" (125). From within psychoanalytic theory, the proper place for woman, as a psychical structure, is as the object of desire of the male subject and so she is denied access to the position of full social subject and to autonomous desire (Mulvey 1975; Doane 1987). Although subject, object, male, and female are socially constructed fantasy positions that actual empirical individuals can never fully—that is, properly—assume (hence the symptoms of homosexuality and, in Lacan, of woman), these positions and the particularity of their heteronormative alignment in the social structure reflect

sense of real or true (identity) and it aims to help regain these. The matter and manner of all Lacan's work challenges this notion of the human subject: there is none such. (4)

the reality of a social demand, its internalization by those who live within the society and who experience it as power.

> The panoptic gaze defines, then, the perfect, i.e., the total, visibility of the woman under patriarchy, of any subject under any social order, which is to say, of any subject at all. For the very condition and substance of the subject's subjectivity is his or her subjectivization by the law of the society which produces that subject. One only becomes visible—not only to others, but also to oneself—through (by seeing through) the categories constructed by a specific, historically defined society. These categories of visibility are categories of knowledge. (Copjec 1989, 55)

In this respect, psychoanalysis seems to reveal the psychic mechanism of ideology, not so much as false consciousness—although inasmuch as it is founded on misrecognition, it is that too—but rather as the means by which the social imaginary works to encourage individuals to accept the symbolic code of society, its regime of truth, as the representation of reality. The terms "imaginary" and "symbolic" in this formulation have a technical meaning in the Lacanian version of psychoanalysis that has served as the basis of the dominant appropriation of psychoanalysis in film theory. In film theory, these terms have also been inflected by Louis Althusser's (1995) theory of ideology (itself explicitly modeled on the psychoanalytic theory of the unconscious), in particular his explication of the concept of the ideological state apparatus (100–140). The so-called apparatus theory was inaugurated with a suggestion from Marcelin Pleynet, at the time managing editor of the influential *Tel Quel*, that the cinematic technology had been treated as a neutral ground instead of as a profoundly ideological instrument (Pleynet and Thibaudeau 1978).[2] "The cinematographic apparatus is a strictly ideological apparatus; it disseminates bourgeois ideology before anything else. Before a film is produced, the technical construction of the camera already produces bourgeois ideology" (155).

Jean-Louis Baudry (1974–75, 1976) developed this idea in a pair of influential articles on the cinematic apparatus. The titles of the English translations of Baudry's articles both contain "apparatus," but the word actually serves to translate two different French terms, *appareil* and *dispositif*, and so an operative distinction is being missed. Both terms in fact derive from Althusser's essay (1995), where *appareil* designates the institutional structure, its support and techniques, and *dispositif*, much less thoroughly worked out, designates

---

[2] The discussion between Pleynet and Thibaudeau was first published in *Cinéthique* 3 (1969), and it prompted a sharp response from Jean-Patrick Lebel, who argued in a series of articles published in *La Nouvelle Critique* and collected in Lebel (1971) that because the camera was a scientific instrument, it sublated knowledge, not ideology, and that ideology could only come from the use to which the neutral instrument was put. On this discussion between Pleynet and Thibaudeau as the origin of apparatus theory, see Comolli (1990).

in contrast "the absolutely ideological 'conceptual' device" that hails and interpellates the subject, that is, produces or prepares in advance a place for "a subject endowed with consciousness in which he freely forms or freely recognizes ideas in which he believes" (126).[3] Each of Baudry's essays therefore focuses on a different aspect of the ideological state apparatus, with the "basic cinematographic apparatus" (*appareil*) concerning the technology and its general institutional support and "the apparatus" (*dispositif*) concerning the specific processes of interpellation and subject construction. Apparatus theory has generally followed Baudry's lead here, with scholarship divided between uncovering the ideological implications of the basic equipment and institutional technical practices on the one hand and revealing how institutional imperatives construct and interpellate the cinematic subject on the other.

The *Appareil*

JEAN-LOUIS BAUDRY AND THE BASIC CINEMATOGRAPHIC APPARATUS

In "Ideological Effects of the Basic Cinematographic Apparatus" (1974–75), Baudry hews closely to Pleynet's suggestion, arguing that cinema technology, even its construction of a camera that adopts a mode of representation as ubiquitous as perspective, is not ideologically neutral in virtue of its scientific basis. Like Pleynet, Baudry therefore also distinguishes between two levels of ideological work: the familiar ideology of the content—that is, the film as a representational text and its attendant features—and the ideology inscribed in its technology, which anyone deploying it can accept or resist depending on the individual case but which in any case confronts the filmmaker as a basic determinant of the media. (These correspond to the first and third levels of ideological analysis discussed in chapter 7.) The camera

> lays out the space of an ideal vision and in this way assures the necessity of transcendence—metaphorically (by the unknown to which it appeals—here we must recall the structural place occupied by the vanishing point) and metonymically (by the displacement that it seems to carry out: a subject is both "in place of" and "a part of the whole"). (41–42)

Baudry then extends the analysis of the camera to the mechanism that allows the illusion of motion. Projected, film creates the impression of reproducing an intentional continuous movement at the expense of effacing the actual differences that obtain between the individual frames. This effacement is symptomatic rather than simply academic in the sense that the

---

[3] To add to the confusion, *Dispositif* is also picked up by Michel Foucault to extend his concept of "discursive formation" to nonlinguistic cultural formations. See Bryukhovetska (2010), Žižek (2010, 416–18), and Agamben (2009, 1–24).

impression of continuity depends on the forgetting of the fact of the technology, so that the technology comes to serve as a kind of unconscious of film. He then extends this analysis to the cut, arguing that the drive to develop principles of continuity editing derived from the same impulse to forget the technology. Baudry concludes the article by drawing an analogy between the screen and Lacan's mirror phase (1968). Just as the young child recognizes a more unified image of itself in the mirror and so begins to construct the function of the ego on the basis of that imaginary identification, so too the spectator in the cinema recognizes the screen as the source of a unified meaning. Unlike the mirror, where the imaginary unity is located in the image, the screen encourages an imaginary identification with the look itself, that is, with the camera, which the spectator takes as a substitute for its own defective organ but which maintains its superiority only to the extent that awareness of the technology that makes it possible is repressed. Here, again, the technological base of the cinema functions as the unconscious of the film, and the ideological work of the apparatus—its superego function, as it were—consists in preserving the imaginary identification from recognizing the repression of just that technological base.

JEAN-LOUIS COMOLLI AND TECHNIQUE AND IDEOLOGY

In his work toward constructing the terms of a materialist history of cinema, which was published in a series of articles in *Cahiers du cinéma*, Jean-Louis Comolli (1990, 1986, 1971–72, 1972) provides a historical account of the transformations of basic apparatus. For Comolli, the unconscious that migrates into technology is that of economic relations. Comolli pays particular attention to perspective, especially as it figures as a celebration of deep-focus cinematography in the then-still-dominant realist theories of cinema descending from classical film theory. For Comolli, authors such as André Bazin (2005) perpetrate an idealist philosophy to the extent that they mistake the symbolic code and conventions of perspective for the natural world, which is a way of naturalizing and so repressing awareness of the economic relations that support it. The move toward an image with a greater depth of field is not a natural tendency of the technology but rather a symptom of ideological deception that extends across filmmaking, film criticism, and film scholarship. "What we intend therefore is a rereading of the idealist discourse from the standpoint of the main area it represses—that complex of economic, political, and ideological determinants which shatter any notion of 'the aesthetic evolution of the cinema' (any claim for complete autonomy for the aesthetic process)" (Comolli 1986, 423).

Like Pleynet and Baudry, Comolli also distinguishes between the ideology of the individual films and that of the basic technology. But Comolli makes the additional point that the overt ideology of the individual films and even more so critics' attempts to sort the films on the basis of quality serve primarily to disguise the basic ideological unity of the institutional apparatus. These films

> are the innumerable realizations of the cinema as an ideological instrument, a vector and disseminator of ideological representations where the subject of ideology (the spectator of the spectacle) cannot fail to identify himself since what is involved is always the communication of "A meaning ever present to itself in the presence of the Subject." (423)

Comolli here is drawing on a long article that he wrote with Paul Narboni in 1969 that announced the change in editorial position of *Cahiers du Cinéma* to an explicitly Marxist one (Comolli and Narboni 1971a, 1971b, 1972). This earlier article included a more detailed typology of a film's possible relationship to the underlying ideology of the institution and outlined a series of strategies for criticizing a film's particular relation to that ideology on the basis of type, but it agreed with the basic claim in "Technique and Ideology" that the vast majority of films, whatever their explicit ideological position, remained committed to communicating a univocal meaning rather than revealing cinema as a site for the production of (multivocal) meaning.

Comolli also opposes the fetish that idealist histories make of tracking the appearance of various techniques (such as the close-up) because they presume that the technique can be isolated from the discourse or signifying chain from which it receives its identity and meaning. (Jean Mitry is his particular target here.) To understand a technique, one has to understand the historical state of the discourse in which it is embedded and the material factors, not all of which are technical, that determine that discourse, as a close-up only means what it does because of the discourse, and the discourse is something other than a list of transhistorical conventions, of technical devices without concrete historical determinants (Comolli 1986, 429–30). Comolli also notes that we must be careful not to let those technologies that are most evident substitute for the whole, in the way that the ideological distortions of the camera can seem to serve metonymically for the whole of the cinematic apparatus. That path is also marked by distortions of its own, in particular the effacement and erasure of all work not directly attributable to the camera (e.g., lab work, soundtrack), and so also raises the visible to the seat of knowledge but at the expense of allowing the invisible to remain the natural ground of film's unconscious and so also its largest ideological threat.

Comolli devotes much of the final two parts (1971–72, 1972) of his technology and ideology series to the issue of the soundtrack, examining in particular how the introduction of synchronized speech interacted with an attenuation of deep-focus photography on the one hand and how speech assumed the indispensable ideological role of figuring subjective depth on the other.

MARY ANN DOANE AND THE IDEOLOGY OF SOUND EDITING

The most thorough English-language account of the soundtrack in terms of apparatus theory is found in the early work of Mary Ann Doane and Rick Altman. In 1980, Mary Ann Doane published two articles on the topic, one (1980b) devoted to technology and institutional discourse and the other (1980a) to the processes by which the soundtrack participates in the construction of the cinematic subject. That is, the respective concerns of these articles divide along the break between *appareil* and *dispositif*. In "Ideology and the Practice of Sound Editing and Mixing" (1980b), the article devoted to technology and technique, Doane investigates both the soundtrack practices and the language that technicians working on the soundtrack use in discussing their work. "Not only techniques of sound-track construction but the language of technicians and the discourses on technique are symptomatic of particular ideological aims" (47). The most characteristic aspect of this ideology is the "effacement of work," the development of a sound editing and mixing practice whose labor is inaudible. If sound is positioned by the industry as a supplement to the image, that is, as something added, the split between image and sound ends up having wider consequences as it "is supported by the establishment and maintenance of ideological oppositions between the intelligible and the sensible, intellect and emotion, fact and value, reason and intuition" (48). Effective sound work is precisely that which coordinates the sound to the image so that the split can signify these distinct but entwined spheres of being. But the split is fraught and liable to dissolve the imaginary unity of sound "properly" synchronized to image back into the "material heterogeneity" of the various sounds and images. The imaginary unity thus conceals "the highly specialized and fragmented process, the bulk and expense of the machinery essential to the production of a sound-track which meets industry standards" (51).

The mixing also gives precedence to the voice, which, unlike background sounds, is not generally faded in or out and which travels with the picture throughout the editing process. This practice allows film "to preserve the status of speech as an individual property right—subject only to a manipulation which is not discernible" (1980b, 52). Speech, unlike the other components of the soundtrack, is therefore also integral rather than supplemental. Yet, with speech, the code of intelligibility comes into conflict with the code of mimetic realism that allows us to recognize the actual ideological priorities and commitments of the institution whatever its statements: moments where realistic mimetic sound would obscure the intelligibility of the dialogue are decided in favor of intelligibility unless the situation is to be read as a threat to the speaking character. Speech, in other words, "*belongs* to the individual, defines and expresses his or her individuality, and distinguishes the individual from the world" (52). The emphasis on intelligible speech indicates a privileging of interiority over exteriority, of the world of intention over actuality—ultimately of what is not depicted over the visible—as the site and guarantee of individual definition. "The truth of the individual, of the *interior* realm of the individual (a truth which is most readily spoken and heard), is the truth validated by the coming of sound" (60). Yet the speaking film character is not a subject of pure interiority but rather one who needs to bear the marks of place, the marks of belonging to just this body depicted in just this way, so that its voice can be converted into a measure of depth while also remaining precisely invisible, and so out of conceptual view. The appearance of a body synchronized to a voice recorded to match thus disguises the profound ideological work not only of the voice but also of sound in general, as sound constructed—edited and mixed—to be "the bearer of a meaning," one "not subsumed by the ideology of the visible" (56). Sound in a sense gains ideological potency the more it figures within the representational system of sound film as a site of repression; but the fact that it must serve as a site of repression means that its power is always going to be, like the unconscious, many of whose processes it models, an uncertain ally. "The ideological truth of the sound-track covers that excess which escapes the eye. For the ear is precisely that organ which opens onto the interior reality of the individual—not exactly un-seeable, but unknowable within the guarantee of the purely visible" (56).

RICK ALTMAN AND THE HETEROGENEITY OF SOUND

Rick Altman's work on the soundtrack begins from a similar place. In his introduction to the 1980 special issue of *Yale French Studies* (1980a), a publication that launched the contemporary phase of soundtrack studies in English, Altman notes the strongly visual emphasis that Baudry and Comolli place on the apparatus.

> According to this approach the spectator is placed, within the film as well as within the world at large, primarily by visual markers; even within the limits of this method of handling spectator placement, however, it is surprising that more emphasis has not been placed on the sound track's role in splitting and complicating the spectator, in contesting as well as reinforcing the lessons of the image tract. (4)

The omission undoubtedly lies in the fact that apparatus theory was initially designed less to tease out the complexities of film spectatorship, even if half of the theory was devoted to the interpellation of the *dispositif*, than to show the certainty of a particular ideological inscription in the basic equipment and formal techniques of the cinema. In this respect, it is perhaps not surprising that soundtrack studies begin to gain traction around 1980: at this point concern for the *appareil*, which had initially received more emphasis, passes, as we will see, to a far more complicated if also highly problematic consideration for the *dispositif*. It is in this context of working out a theory of the cinematic subject, a subject situated between the ideological imperatives of the institution and the particular desires of empirical spectators, that "the sound track's role in splitting and complicating the spectator," of offering resistance to ideological determination by opening up a site of contradiction and contestation, of offering an opening for a deconstruction of the cinematic subject, becomes an advantage.

It is interesting in this respect that Altman seeks to inaugurate critical soundtrack studies with a consideration of the *appareil*, focusing particularly on the representational qualities of the microphone technology in his introduction (parallel to perspective in the camera) and the formal device of mimetic synchronization (parallel to continuity editing) in his larger contribution to the volume. In chapter 7, I noted Altman's analysis of mimetic synchronization as a profoundly ideological figure, and we are now in a better position to appreciate his conclusion that "the sound track is a ventriloquist who, by moving his dummy (the image) in time with the words he secretly speaks, creates the illusion that the words are produced by the dummy/image whereas in fact the dummy/image is actually created in order to disguise the source of the sound" (1980b, 67). The very visibility of the image perpetrates the deception, as it serves to distract from the actual mechanism of auditory production, the loudspeakers, and so also diverts attention from the ventriloquist—now understood as the institution itself—who is controlling the words. Altman assigns the words in the first instance to the screenwriter and notes how auteur theory has served to "repress" the work of scripting (70). Yet it is not the director who "represses" the screenwriter but the institution; these figures of director and screenwriter are ultimately actors the institution mobilizes in a drama to obscure the economic base of synchronized sound. Onscreen, the character seems to speak and own the words, the divided apparatus of synchronized sound simply appearing as the "neutral" technology that makes this possible, just as individuals seem to speak and own their words outside any determination by language aside from the fact that it exists as (again) a "neutral" technology of communication. Mimetic synchronization is therefore a mythic figure, one that forges "a new myth of origins" for the soundtrack (the image rather than the loudspeaker, the character rather than the script) but so also one that indoctrinates spectators into a belief about their own autonomy. Altman recalls Baudry's discussion of the mirror phase but now takes account of sound. What is mirrored is precisely an impression of sensory unity: "If the human audience accepts the cinema's unity, it is because it cannot affirm its own without admitting the cinema's; conversely, the cinema appears to assent to the unity of the human subject only in order to establish its own unity" (71).

Rather than pursuing this analysis into the apparatus as *dispositif*, as a "machine" for the interpellation of subjects through suture, as much film theory at the time would (see later), Altman's later work on the soundtrack continues with a strong emphasis on the *appareil*, with detailed historical studies of the technologies of production and reproduction (Altman 1985, 1986), of sites and technologies of exhibition, usually coupled with careful and insightful analysis of the industry discourse on sound as promulgated through the trade papers and technical journals. Throughout, he remains committed to a concept of cinema always already divided by a representation organized to extract profit from "the material resources that it engages" (1992a, 6). The commercial pressures of cinema mean that homogeneity (standardization) is always driving out heterogeneity wherever it finds it (1999, passim). But heterogeneity, the "noise" in the system, is also irreducible (1) because any substantive change in the apparatus brings with it enough heterogeneity that the basic apparatus is not self-identical as a historical object whether or not it undergoes a name change (Altman 1984); (2) because sound film is a dual system that means a relationship between its parts will always have to be constructed (Altman 1980b, passim); (3) because sound recording always bears the imprint of its original space of recording and is reproduced in another (Altman 1992a, 5); (4) because sound recording is always a representation rather than a simple reproduction (Altman 1984, 121); (5) because theaters vary the conditions of presentation as a means of product differentiation (Altman 1992a, 8); and (6) because heterogeneity is an important source of innovation (it allows the appearance of alternatives) and often a location of pleasure and identification for audiences, who are frequently also its source. Thus, in a quintessential demonstration, Altman (2004) traces the way in which those sound practices in the nickelodeon that specifically addressed the audience, especially the popular illustrated songs and musical accompaniments that parody the film, are replaced by a musical practice addressed to the drama of the film (231–85). But he also notes that theater technology such as soundproofing likewise evolved toward eliminating extraneous sound (Altman 1999, 33); that codes of conduct were created to quiet the patrons and keep them focused on the screen (Altman 1999, 38–43; 2004); that the technology of synchronized sound was developed to standardize exhibition; and that booms and microphones were designed to standardize the clarity of dialogue (Altman 1992d, 58ff.): the whole institutional apparatus has been designed to use representation to reduce material heterogeneity and make profits more predictable (Altman 1999, passim). Film scholarship has, he thinks, been complicit as well: scholars opt to distill neat linear narratives rather than acknowledge the complicated, uneven quality of actual historical development; they use the concept of the "text" to occlude the rich, contradictory context of its production and reception; they focus on the artistic conception and occasionally finance, rarely on the technical workers who execute the needed tasks (Altman 1992a, 6–7); and in terms of the soundtrack, they borrow musical terminology that has the effect of abstracting an idealized musical conception from the particularity of sound (Altman 1992b, 16). While Altman's radical nominalism treats each of these approaches as reductively and ungenerously as he accuses them of treating cinema, his aim is to show that processes of representation, homogenization, narrative, meaning, and ideology are at a fundamental semiotic level all of a piece (Altman 1999, passim); although they operate on different cultural levels, they are all means of structuring and ordering difference hierarchically, of transforming the actual complexity of the world into something simpler, more efficient, and more manageable but without fully acknowledging the loss of doing so—or worse yet they naturalize away the actual arbitrary quality of the differences by reifying them within an oppositional hierarchy of essential and inessential.[4]

The strength of Altman's focus on heterogeneity is the way it allows him to track and give an account of the particularity of the sound and of the contexts of production, exhibition, and reception without the normal hierarchies that culture imposes on it. Its weakness largely derives from the same source: since the abstraction required of theoretical discourse demands a movement from the particular to the general, a theory centered directly on heterogeneity will always be fraught and constantly threatened by incoherence. This threat comes out most strikingly in his otherwise reasonable insistence that

> there is no such thing as representation of the real; there is only representation of representation. For anything that we would represent is already constructed as a representation. The structure of representation is thus that of an infinite mise-en-abyme, with the new apparatus having to represent the old, itself representing the previous one, and so on. (1984, 121)

Under this formulation, the appearance of the real is an illusion; the real, assuming it exists, is of an entirely different and incommensurate order than representation. Representation does not concern it. Where, then, is heterogeneity to be located in this scenario? Heterogeneity cannot be something excluded from representation; it cannot be located in the real, because then neither Altman nor anyone else could discuss it, as it would fall outside representation. But heterogeneity is also not representation, because that is the very figure of hierarchical sense that has excluded the heterogeneous. That leaves the mirroring: heterogeneity evidently appears in the process of representational reflection as nonidentity, as that which falls out of the series. Yet even here, although it is perfectly clear that we can recognize what gets left out of the series, it is not at all evident how any representation along the series can add anything besides another reflection to representation, since what is new could only be something that was not contained in a previous representation. Either the series degrades or the representation is somehow replenishing itself along the way, but neither provides a consistent or coherent account. The

---

[4] Responding to criticism from James Lastra (1992, 65–86), Altman (1992c, 40–42) admits that his defense of heterogeneity leads him to hold a problematically nominalist account of sound.

incoherence suggests that there is something amiss in, or at least something missing from, the model.

JAMES LASTRA AND REPRESENTATIONAL TECHNOLOGY

Although James Lastra (2000) appropriates Altman's concept of "representational technology" and shares an interest in producing a rich empirical history of the sound technology *appareil*, he is concerned more with discourse analysis and identifying broad cultural currents than is Altman. Lastra takes device, discourse, practice, and institution as the four "defining parameters" of his work and produces a "thick epistemology" of sound film technology that offers a self-conscious correction of the *appareil* in the work of Baudry and Comolli (13, 4). Both Baudry and Comolli have a strong current of technological determinism in their understanding of the *appareil*. To disqualify any move that would exempt technology from the point of ideological critique, Baudry and Comolli both insist on locating ideology in the "technology itself." But Lastra notes that this formulation, which insists on a grand continuity from the introduction of linear perspective in Renaissance painting to the grinding of lenses to record perspective in cameras, dehistoricizes the technology, obscures the difference between technological inscription and sensory experience, and so also ignores actual changes in the technology, as well as the ways in which technological change is driven by the representational needs of the institution regulating the technology. "Our specific standards and practices of listening are always a function of particular contextual and often institutional demands and often appropriate only to those demands, hence no *single* context or set of evaluative criteria can—without elaborate justification—provide a reference point for theorizing all others" (132). Thus, attempts to locate the essence of ideological transformation in the device are problematic as they reduce out the necessary mediations of the institution. Ideological effects, in other words, are not uniform and are therefore not stabilized by the device.

With respect to sound technology, Lastra takes issue not only with those who would locate ideology in the device but also with those who champion heterogeneity. Indeed, Lastra sees critics like Altman, Alan Williams (1980), and Tom Levin (1984) who insist on the heterogeneity of sound as radicalizing the ideological critique of the technology itself: for such critics, every representation is an abstraction or sample from some original full phenomenological reality, and so any technology, like sound recording, that presents itself as an undistorted reproduction of that reality harbors a pernicious ideological deception. Lastra counters that this radically nominalist formulation carries its own ideological deception: the concept of the original itself.

> Contrary to the claims of theory, which locates all the significant ideological work in what the device does to the original event, the primary

ideological effect of sound recording might rather be in creating the *effect* that there is a single and fully present "original" independent of its representation at all. (2000, 134)

Instead of tracing how heterogeneity resists representation, Lastra focuses instead on strategies of hierarchization that organize representation. What tends to fall away in Lastra's approach is the figure of ideology itself; ultimately institutionally mediated perspectives determine the significance and adequacy of the representation from the details that it preserves and to which it gives emphasis. Yet these representations are not understood as distortions; that is, it is precisely this sense of representation as distortion that the concept of the original—Platonic or not and however imaginary or unobtainable in itself—preserves.

MUSIC AND THE *APPAREIL*

Music has received little attention under the rubric of the *appareil*, at least with respect to technology. Aside from studies of the early days of sound film, when recording often required special musical instruments (Sabaneev 1935, 56–90; London 1936, 163–210) and technical handbooks and recording manuals (e.g., Karlin and Wright 1990, 103–24, 332–421), little research has addressed in a critical and systematic way the mediations of music and the basic technical apparatus as it applies in film. (The relationship between the phonograph and the recording industry, by contrast, has been extensively studied.) The most thorough work has been done on the use of electronic instruments, such as the theremin, synthesizer, and virtual instruments (Hayward 1997; Wierzbicki 2002; Leydon 2004; Donnelly 2013; Buhler and Neumeyer 2016; Casanelles 2016). But even such basic music production technologies as streamers, click tracks, cue sheets, and temp tracks, though mentioned often in passing, have not received sustained scholarly attention. The grab-bag approach of the final chapter of George Burt's *The Art of Film Music* (1994) is typical (217–47).

The situation with respect to the institutional aspects of the musical *appareil* is somewhat better. Sociological studies by Robert Faulkner (1971, 1983) and James P. Kraft (1996), discussed in chapter 7, have examined the institutional organization of musical labor for both Hollywood musicians and composers. Claudia Gorbman (1987) demonstrates how the institution of classic Hollywood has determined the music for its films. She is particularly interested in the conventions and other habits of thought, conscious or not, that the musical practice of Hollywood presupposes. If "classical Hollywood film works toward the goal of a transparent or invisible discourse, and promoting fullest involvement in the story" (72), Hollywood film music, she says, follows guidelines similar to those that govern the rest of the filmic system. I discussed her oft-cited seven basic "principles of composition, mixing, and editing" that underlay classical film music practice in chapter 6. To recapitulate, Gorbman's well-known rules are (1) invisibility, (2) inaudibility, (3) signifier of emotion, (4) narrative cueing, (5) continuity, (6) unity, and (7) escape clause (73). The first two rules point to the transparency of classic narrative and the effacement of work as a mark of professional competence and skill. As with Doane's analysis of the ideology of mixing, the work of film music does not generally draw attention to itself or its conditions of production. These form the technical manifestation of a principle of subjugation. Gorbman's rules 3 and 4 concern the semiotic capabilities of music and its ability to clarify the narrative, especially in representing the emotional tenor of character, mood, and setting that are otherwise difficult to convey through action or mise-en-scène. These correspond, more or less, to a principle of synchronization that aligns music to narrative. Her rules 5 and 6 indicate music's ability to provide coherence, by providing either acoustical "connective tissue" that ties together disparate shots, sounds, and events or a musical thematic structure that reinforces narrative structure. These are both covered under a principle of continuity. Gorbman's final rule permits that any rule may be suspended "at the service of the other principles" (73), which ensures that all the principles (and so also the musical subsystem) are evaluated in terms of and also subordinated to the requirements of the overriding narrative system. The whole then forms the basis for the classical system. We can now also abstract from these principles a basic set of ideological values that are reproduced in and transmitted by the institutional practice of Hollywood film music: transparency, clarity, coherence, anthropocentrism, and homogeneity.

Caryl Flinn (1992) takes as her starting point the stability of the musical subsystem in the studio era and looks at how this stability was created and sustained. "The classical conception of film music," she writes, "maintains that the score supports the development of the film's story line, that it exists to reinforce the narrational information already provided by the image" (14). Subjugation serves to regulate the musical subsystem according to narrative, and it is this regulative function of subordination that accounts for the appearance of stability. The justification for subjugation was not stability, however, but aesthetic legitimization. The institutional discourse on music in the studio era drew extensively on Wagnerian tropes. Wagner's insistence that drama required music to serve the word in the production of meaning ensured that music could be subservient even as it provided a rationale for music's presence in supporting the drama. The invocation of Wagner also redounded to film, which in virtue of its music could be said to resemble the idea of *Gesamtkunstwerk*, which fit neatly with "Hollywood's own investment in unified, coherent texts, since both maintain that textual components should work toward the same dramatic ends" (34). If in the classical Hollywood system Wagnerian synthesis was reduced to redundancy and overdetermination, as Flinn claims, music nevertheless gained by its subordination a relatively secure place within the filmic system that would allow it to codify its practice, stabilize its position, and reproduce its values in the institution.

Both Gorbman and Flinn also point out that the institutional discourse on music and Hollywood have tended to discount the role of technology, since one of the traditional functions of music has been to mask the presence of technology. In this respect, music is itself a particularly efficient technology for effacing the work of the soundtrack and therefore also the labor that goes into constructing it.

The *Dispositif*

JEAN-LOUIS BAUDRY AND THE *DISPOSITIF*

Whereas in "Ideological Effects of the Basic Cinematographic Apparatus" Baudry considers the way in which ideology is inscribed into the basic machinery of cinema, especially the camera, in "The Apparatus" Baudry examines the way in which the cinema, by structuring a viewing situation reminiscent of a dream, proffers a representational regime that constructs and interpellates a certain kind of cinematic subject. The concern here is not apparatus as *appareil*, that is, as institutionally mediated and ideologically determined technology, but apparatus as *dispositif*, that is, as the general set of institutional devices aimed at preparing in advance the place of the cinematic subject. For Baudry, the cinema presupposes a transcendental subject, which the totality of the cinematic situation, the *dispositif*, uses all its power to encourage us to identify with. In developing the concept of the *dispositif*, Baudry draws on the frequently invoked analogy of the cinema to the scenario of Plato's cave but offers the twist of comparing Plato to Freud: what for Plato is metaphysical delusion becomes for Freud fantasy, dream. The cinema, Baudry thinks, follows the psychoanalytic account of the dream in constructing its subject. "The cinematographic *dispositif* reproduces the *dispositif* of the psychic apparatus [*appareil*] during sleep" (1986, 122, translation modified).

Like the dream in psychoanalysis, the cinema offers the subject a dark place of immobility and passivity, a situation that encourages regression to a state where perception and representation coincide. "Taking into account the darkness of the movie theater, the relative passivity of the situation, the forced immobility of the cine-subject, and the effects which result from the projection of images, moving images, the cinematographic apparatus [*dispositif*] brings about a state of artificial regression" (1986, 119). In the dream, the sleep of the subject serves as a defense against the impression of reality so that the dream state regression is clearly marked as fantasy. In the cinema, on the contrary, the subject is awake, so that, even though perception and representation coincide, the cinematic *dispositif* is "capable of precisely fabricating an impression of reality" (111). The impression of reality is therefore a subject effect prepared by cinema, one that follows a path of regression in the psychoanalytical sense.

JEAN-LOUIS COMOLLI AND THE *DISPOSITIF*

This subject effect remains somewhat amorphous in Baudry's account, as it is focused on immobility and a generalized impression of reality rather than on a specific cinematic figure, but it is given better definition by several other writers of the time. Comolli (1971–72), for instance, notes the way that the impression of reality on the one hand is undermined during the 1920s by increased technical facility with montage, which underscored the constructed quality of the image sequence, but then on the other hand is restored by mimetic synchronization of the talking film. This marked shift suggests that the impression of reality is tied not so much to a technical measure, such as depth of field, as to the ability of spectators to extract meaning from the film. With sound film, the audiovisual figure of synchronized dialogue, especially, allows the film to speak the subject.

> For with the Hollywood talking picture, not only sound and noises are synchronized to the image, an image that invests in those sounds and noises and draws toward them: but also and above all the word, that is to say the interiority, the discourse of the subject, this lack, this hollow space that the word identifies as a full presence and in fact does not cease to fill out the ideological statement that speaks this subject. (100, my translation)

The *dispositif*, then, is "cinema as an ideological instrument" (1986, 423) but also a "social machine, . . . the arrangement of demands, desires, fantasies, speculations (in the two senses of commerce and the imaginary): an arrangement which give[s] apparatus and techniques a social status and function" (1980, 122). The *dispositif* does not concern the particulars of ideological statements, then, but the structure of singular meaning that makes such statements possible. In this way, it prepares a place in the discourse for the subject, and hails this subject with the call of meaning.

CHRISTIAN METZ AND ENUNCIATION

Christian Metz (1982) agrees that cinema is "one vast socio-psychical machinery" (80). Metz, who, as we noted in chapter 4, did much to develop the semiotic paradigm in film studies, worked to synthesize his structuralist film semiotics with insights drawn from narratology (see chapter 6) and the psychoanalytically inflected apparatus theory, especially the work of Baudry. For Metz, psychoanalysis offered a theory of the cinematic subject that had been lacking in structural semiotics, whereas a semiotic orientation offered a way of systematizing psychoanalytic insights to the workings of all facets of the cinematic institution, that is, to the *dispositif*. As befits the application of psychoanalysis to the cinema, Metz emphasized the imaginary and understands film theory as reproducing the tensions of psychoanalytic practice. He opens *The Imaginary Signifier* thus:

> Reduced to its most fundamental procedures, any psychoanalytic reflection on the cinema might be defined in Lacanian terms as an attempt to disengage the cinema-object from the imaginary and to win it for the symbolic, in the hope of extending the latter by a new province: an enterprise of displacement, a territorial enterprise, a symbolising advance; that is to say, in the field of films as in other films, the psychoanalytic itinerary is from the outset a semiological one, even (above all) if in comparison with the discourse of a more classical semiology it shifts its point of focus from the statement [the *énoncé*] to the enunciation [the *énonciation*]. (3)

This shift to enunciation is similar to the shift, discussed in the previous chapter, in postcolonial, feminist, and queer theory, from identification to subjectification—that is, a displacement from an analysis of the statement as an ideological form to a consideration of the social structure that makes the ideological form possible. As Harvey R. Greenberg and Krin Gabbard (1990) note in their assessment of psychoanalytic film theory:

> Research has been deflected away from the meaning of the text, toward the processes through which any assumed meaning is generated. Cinema semioticians focus on how the audience experiences a movie. Rather than psychoanalyzing characters or filmmakers, students of Lacan explore the complex fashion in which the cinematic apparatus invokes the Imaginary and Symbolic orders of the viewer. (101)

The resemblance of enunciation to subjectification should not be surprising, given that postcolonial, feminist, and queer theory have all been greatly influenced not only by the same Lacanian psychoanalytic theory that underwrites apparatus theory but also by apparatus theory itself, especially in those aspects of the theory, gathered under the term "suture," that have been concerned with the construction of the cinematic subject.

DISPOSITIF AND SUTURE

Derived from Lacan's rewriting of classical Freudian psychoanalysis, suture is an account of how filmic discourse renders the subjectivity it constructs as natural, as an "imaginary unity" (Johnston 1976; quoted in Silverman 1983, 222). According to Jean-Pierre Oudart (1977–78), "suture represents the closure of the cinematic *énoncé* in line with its relationship with its subject (the film subject or rather the cinematic subject), which is recognized, and then put in its place as the spectator" (35). In particular, suture concerns the construction of the cinematic subject through the relation to a constitutive absence, that which is excluded in a shot, which gives rise in turn to what Oudart calls "the Absent One." The shot/reverse-shot combination so integral to the syntax of classic Hollywood, for instance, gains its efficacy because the first shot not only presents a field of vision but also asserts a position from which that field is seen. But that position, the place of the camera, is itself not seen. The reverse-shot, by contrast, seems to reveal the excluded field, what was lacking in the original shot (Dayan 1974; Oudart 1977–78; Heath 1977–78; Silverman 1983; Bonitzer 1990). The shots together thus "seem to constitute a perfect whole," which helps "assure" the viewer that "his or her gaze suffers under no constraints" (Silverman 1988, 12). But although the field of the second shot seems to contain the position of the first, the means of that vision—the camera on the one hand and the subject who knows on the other—remains absent from the image, and is indeed displaced to the character whose partial body (over the shoulder) intervenes to stand in for the Absent One, to allow a particular meaning to fill the absence even as the Absent One seems to migrate again out of field. In this way, the Absent One always leaves an empty space that it bids the spectator to occupy as subject and to insert a particular meaning. The obliquity of the representation—the presence of the partial body that displaces the subject—divides the absence into lack and meaning, or rather maps meaning into the empty space of the signifying chain. Through the intervention of the figure of representation, the shot succession becomes interpretable. "This necessary obliquity of the camera," Daniel Dayan (1974) says, "has the function of transforming a vision or seeing of the film into a reading of it. It introduces the film (irreducible to its frames) into the realm of signification" (29).

Dayan also claims that "the system of suture is to classical cinema what verbal language is to literature" (1974, 22), and he therefore understands cinematic suture as a subset of the general suturing effects of language. Nevertheless, a basic difference between language and the semiotic system of cinema makes the comparison problematic. Whereas Dayan admits that language is not reducible to ideology, he insists that because the historical origins of cinema are recoverable, that ideology therefore must play a much more constitutive role in cinema. Although this seems to extend the critique of the ideological determinations of the *appareil* to the *dispositif*, the result is not simply to insist on cinema's ideological substrate and to recognize that its fiction is "a mythical organization through which ideology is produced and expressed" (22). Instead, Dayan uses suture to reduce cinema to ideology in a rather unidimensional way. Because suture is the device that allows film to deny its origin as something made, as a construction, it is also the source of film's primary ideological deception, which constructs the cinematic subject only to deny it. "By means of suture, the film-discourse presents itself as a product without producer, a discourse without an origin. It speaks. Who speaks? Things speak for themselves and of course, they tell the truth. Classical cinema establishes itself as the ventriloquist of ideology" (31).

Dayan's conception of suture, though influential, has also been much criticized. William Rothman (1975), for instance, follows critics of Baudry, such as Jean-Patrick Lebel (1971), who argued that the camera is a scientific instrument and so ideologically neutral. Rothman likewise insists on the basic ideological neutrality of cinematic technique, in this case the point-of-view (shot/reverse-shot) cutting that is central to suture theory, on the basis of content. According to Rothman, such cutting can carry no inherent ideological content because "the point-of-view sequence in itself makes no statement about reality—that is, makes no statement—at all" (48). Although neither Rothman's claim that technique makes no statements itself nor the idea that technique can be used to express a range of ideological statements in fact bears on the ideological level that the theory of suture addresses, Rothman's critique does reveal the profoundly reductive quality to Dayan's conception, one that does not adequately account for the play between subject formation under interpellation and psychoanalytic identification.

Responding to charges that suture is overly reductive and empirically suspect, Stephen Heath (1977–78) offers a more subtle account that attempts to avoid simplistic reduction:

(1) the ideological is not reducible to the imaginary . . .; the ideological always involves a relation of symbolic and imaginary (the imaginary is a specific fiction of the subject in the symbolic);

(2) the symbolic is not reducible to the ideological; there is no ideological operation which does not involve symbolic construction, a production of the subject in meaning, but the symbolic is always more than the effect of such operations (language is not exhausted by the ideological);

(3) the symbolic is never simply not ideological; psychoanalysis, and this is its force, has never encountered some pure symbolic, is always engaged with a specific history of the subject (language is not exhausted by the ideological but is never met other than as discourse, within a discursive formation productive of subject relations in ideology);

(4) the unconscious is not reducible to the ideological; it is a division of the subject with the Other, a history of the subject on which the ideological constantly turns but which it in no way resumes. (73)

Suture remains in this formulation, however, a way of binding ideology and the construction of the cinematic subject to the Lacanian registers of the symbolic and the imaginary. If Heath avoids the reductions and determinations of the early versions of suture in particular and apparatus theory in general, the most pressing issue nevertheless devolves on the hermeneutic imperative, ideological at base, that drives the *dispositif*, the social machine of the cinema: the self-forgetting of the subject in the pursuit of meaning. Heath may admit that it is a mistake to locate ideology in the social forms of direct psychic processes. The social basis of ideology is such that it cannot be reduced to the psychoanalytic concepts of symbolic, imaginary, and unconscious, however necessary it might be for ideology to work on the subject through such psychic processes. Like language, empirical individuals are not exhausted by the ideological. Nevertheless, Heath still presses the cinematic system, the *dispositif*, to reveal the way that it produces an underlying homogeneity, an economy of identity, that is a mark of its ideological project. The lure of the statement, of a particular meaning (or set of meanings) that a film intends to communicate, allows film to appear differentiated, whereas its structure as meaning commits any subject who would understand it to accept the identity proffered by the terms of the discourse. Ideology works on and through the subject so that society might reproduce itself, and, in these terms, psychoanalysis provides a theory of the subject and its construction. Ideology and psychoanalysis thus intersect in the cinematic subject, the imaginary form of the subject presupposed by and constructed in *dispositif*, that is, the cinematic system. Psychoanalysis opens this form and its constitutive figures (suture) to a particular ideological critique focused not on the filmic statement (*énoncé*) but on the system, on the point of systemic articulation of the subject (*énonciation*), and this analysis and critique reveal something of how ideology works through the general psychic economy of drives, desires, repressions, and other processes to interpellate cultural subjects.

As the term "suture" suggests, this place of the subject is conceived as the site of a wound. It is here that the individual acquiesces to its own abstraction to gain coherence as a social subject but with the loss of all particularity that goes along with abstraction. Suture is an act of binding, of tying up, of closing the wound in the name of meaning; but it is also an act of closing off that particularity in the face of the demand to be meaningful. In that sense suture is a process of homogenization aimed at creating the image of a unified subject. In this way industrial standardization of production runs hand in hand with the suturing process of discourse formation that speaks the subject into being. By contrast, heterogeneity becomes what is incoherent, extraneous, accidental, contingent—everything that cannot be made meaningful to the empirical individual as subject. Suture demands that the individual as subject work on film in terms of meaning—learn to distinguish the meaningful detail from that which is merely contingent—so that film can reproduce the subject as just that place in meaning. But the empirical spectator's identification with the subject must remain effaced or that spectator will come to recognize that the unified subject belongs to the imaginary at the expense of the real.

MARY ANN DOANE AND THE FANTASMATIC BODY

Although suture has been applied primarily to shot transitions, with the shot/ reverse-shot syntax as its most exemplary figure, the basic notion also extends readily to the soundtrack, or rather image–sound relations in the classical system's regime of compulsory synchronization, the rule of mimetic synchro- nization, what Heath (1981) aptly terms "the law of the speaking subject" that grounds the practice of commercial film in a particular conception of language and a particular order of sound as a property of bodies (178, 201). Indeed, Doane (1980a) understands mimetic synchronization, rather than the shot/reverse-shot editing, as the key figure to the imaginary identifica- tion of the cinematic subject: "The body reconstituted by the technology and practices of the cinema is a *fantasmatic* body, which offers support as well as a point of identification for the subject addressed by the film" (33–34). This fantasmatic body is, as Doane points out, a figure of unity and subjective co- herence, and it responds, she says, to a threat; or, since it is a product of suture, it might be better to say that the filmic system creates the threat to offer the fantasmatic body as its remedy. "Sound carries with it the potential risk of exposing the material heterogeneity of the medium" (35). Altman's account (1980b) of "moving lips" (discussed in chapter 7), which he attributes to this "ideology of synchronized sound," also presupposes this fantasmatic body, as does, in a slightly different way, the use of offscreen sound to motivate what Heath (1981) describes as "a kind of metonymic lock in which off-screen space becomes on-screen space" (45). If the moving lips of synchronized dia- logue serve as the privileged audiovisual figure of sound film, then offscreen sound functions much like the eyeline match that leads to out-of-field space and it serves an analogous suturing purpose: the offscreen sound momentarily suspends synchronization, which is a filmic emblem of subjective coherence, but the following shot restores synchronization, allowing the viewing subject to claim the prior offscreen space as its own (Silverman 1988, 48). "There is al- ways something uncanny about a voice which emanates from a source outside the frame," Doane (1981a) argues; such sound, she continues,

> deepens the diegesis, gives it an extent which exceeds that of the image, and thus supports the claim that there is a space in the fictional world which the camera does not register. In its own way, it *accounts for* lost space. The voice-off is a sound which is first and foremost in the service of the film's construction of space and only indirectly in the service of the image. It validates both what the screen reveals of the diegesis and what it conceals. (40; emphasis in original)

The risk entailed in offscreen sound is recovered in the continual confir- mation of a wider reality. As is the case with the shot/reverse-shot syntax, offscreen sound calls into question the adequacy of any particular shot, and the movement among shots then opens out into an economy of desire that the term "suture" both names and regulates.

PASCAL BONITZER AND THE VOICEOVER AND VOICE-OFF

Pascal Bonitzer (1986) has given detailed consideration to the signification of both onscreen and offscreen sound. Bonitzer notes that mimetic synchronization seems to fix the meaning of every voice, to belittle it by placing a check on the voice's power. Any asynchronous voice, by contrast, retains a certain power over the image. "So instead of looking, it is necessary to think" (322). Bonitzer notes that sound film divides the asynchronous voice into two different registers (322–23), a distinction that is now usually called nondiegetic (voiceover) and diegetic (voice-off), and that both obtain a power over the image in virtue of the lack of synchronization. The power of the voiceover, he thinks, lies in twining its "absolutely other," that is, its transcendent position, where it "is presumed to know," with an address to someone "who will not speak," namely, the spectator (324).

> The voice speaks *from the place of the Other*, and this must also be understood in a double sense. It is not charged with manifesting in its radical heterogeneity, but on the contrary with controlling it, with recording it (that is, with suppressing and conserving it), with fixing it by means of knowledge. The power of the voice is a stolen power, stolen from the Other; it is a usurpation. (324; emphasis in original)

It silences the "other" so that it might speak for them. Voiceover does not, therefore, present point of view. "Its problem is precisely how to silence a point of view" (331). One of the ways it does this is through mythologization, using the captioning capacity of the voice to extract univocal meaning from the image. "To do violence to the image and to impel its referential reality is to extort a surplus meaning from it, to interdict its ambiguity, to congeal it into a type, symbol, metaphor. . . . This is what makes for propaganda" (326–27). The voiceover in this respect works similarly to montage.

The voice-off, by contrast, is both more mundane and potentially more disruptive insofar as it does not mark itself as coming from a radically other space. This is the uncanny quality that Doane mentioned earlier, and it was one of the motivating factors for filmmakers adopting the rule of mimetic synchronization in the early sound film. Recall from chapter 2 the discussion of Rudolf Arnheim's (1997) resistance to the reaction shot, which he claimed left the voice "floating in the dark void" (37). Normally, the offscreen sound serves to signify the extension of onscreen space and so also to motivate cuts, but the longer the synchronization of the offscreen sound is delayed, the more uncanny it becomes. Occasionally, the exclusion can become systemic, in which case a peculiar power accrues to the voice. That the villain in *Kiss*

Me Deadly (1955), for instance, only ever appears in partial shots for most of the film and so is known visually by his shoes rather than by his face "gives his sentential voice, inflated by mythological comparison, a much greater disquieting power, the scope of an oracle—somber prophet of the end of the world" (Bonitzer 1986, 323). Michel Chion (1994) develops Bonitzer's description here into the figure of the acousmêtre, or acoustical being. Chion defines the figure thus: "a kind of voice-character specific to cinema that in most instances of cinematic narratives derives mysterious powers from being heard and not seen" (221). The powers derive principally from an apparent camera awareness: only a character who recognizes the place of the camera could avoid it so thoroughly. Consequently, the acousmêtre is presented as "one who knows," appropriating the power of the Absent One so long as the character remains without visualization. Conversely, when the character becomes visible, the power dissipates. "It suffices for the subject of this voice to appear in the image . . . for it to be no longer anything but the voice of a man. . . . A gunshot, he falls—and with him, but in ridicule, his discourse with its prophetic overtones" (Bonitzer 1986, 323). This process of de-acousmatization dramatizes suture; it presents dispossession through unveiling: once the monster can be shown, it can be killed.

> The acousmêtre has only to show itself—for the person speaking to inscribe his or her body inside the frame, in the visual field—for it to lose its power, omniscience, and (obviously) ubiquity. . . . *Embodying the voice* is a sort of symbolic act, dooming the acousmêtre to the fate of ordinary mortals. (Chion 1999, 27–28, emphasis in original)

Here, then, through the acousmêtre we understand the suturing effect of synchronization as controlling the imaginary—or rather its threat—by binding it to the symbolic.

SUTURE AND THE SOUNDTRACK

Suture does not require this binding off of the imaginary to ensure identification with the cinematic subject. Indeed, the unity of Doane's "fantasmatic body" is typically obtained through an imaginary (rather than symbolic) identification, and film music likewise generally works through—or is at least theorized as—an imaginary identification. Gorbman (1987) argues that film music is a suturing device that "immerses the spectator" in a "bath of affect." It serves the suturing effects of editing by helping

> to ward off . . . the spectator's potential recognition of the technological basis of filmic articulation. Gaps, cuts, the frame itself, silences in the soundtrack—any reminders of cinema's materiality which jeopardize the formation of subjectivity—the process whereby the viewer identifies as

subject of filmic discourse—are smoothed over, or "spirited away" . . . by the carefully regulated operations of film music. (58)

In this way, film music facilitates absorption and identification with the narrative by "draw[ing] the spectator further into the diegetic illusion" (59). Because of the investment in the imaginary, the suturing effects of film music also entail regression in the psychoanalytic meaning of the term. "The classic narrative film encourages the film subject's return to a primitive narcissism, in which there are no boundaries between active and passive, body and environment, self and other. The cinema simulates not reality but *a condition of the subject*" (63, emphasis in original), the goal of which is to create "an untroublesome social subject" who will more easily accept the filmic fiction and so also, one presumes, the illusion of social harmony proffered by the *dispositif* (57).

Doane (1980a) similarly notes that the soundtrack as a whole, not just music, places the listener in a psychologically regressive scenario. "Space, for the child, is defined initially in terms of the audible, not the visible. . . . The first differences are traced along the axis of sound: the voice of the mother, the voice of the father" (44). Sound, moreover, "is not framed" but rather "envelops the spectator" (39). The "sonorous envelope" in the cinema thus promotes an infantile, narcissistic fantasy of unity, usually associated in Lacanian psychoanalysis with the maternal voice. According to Kaja Silverman (1988), this fantasy of unity can be presented either positively (Kristeva, Rosolato) or negatively (Chion), but either way Silverman finds a gendered relation to the body and the voice structured around "the loss of imaginary plenitude" through which the subject emerges as a recognition that the self is not one with the mother's voice. She explains:

> In its guise as "pure" sonorousness, the maternal voice oscillates between two poles; it is either cherished as an *objet (a)*—as what can make good all lacks—or despised and jettisoned as what is most abject, most culturally intolerable—as the forced representative of everything within male subjectivity which is incompatible with the phallic function, and which threatens to expose discursive mastery as an impossible ideal. (86)

Silverman is particularly critical of Chion, who, she argues, aligns the maternal voice with sound but the paternal voice (tacitly and through displacement) with meaning, so that the conception of the maternal voice comes to dominate and demonize representations of interiority (49). Within this formulation, the representation of subjectivity is obtained by containing that interiority, synchronizing that voice to the female body, the body of the other (74–77). Chion's formulation, she thinks, lies perilously close to that of classical Hollywood film because in both "sexual difference almost invariably functions as a major point of reference" (49) so that "the female body [becomes] the site not only of anatomical but of discursive lack" (50). Silverman's critique of Chion basically follows the lines of the feminist critique of the discursive construction of female as the other of reason discussed in chapter 7. Silverman ignores two points, however: first, that Chion's account presumes apparatus theory, and within the context of the *dispositif*, the place of discursive authority and sense is always already an ideological one, a point that Silverman herself will press in her detailed analysis of classical Hollywood's asymmetrical treatment of the voice along the lines of gender; second, that Chion's account is shaped by his understanding of Lacan, and though Lacan has also been criticized on his theory of sexuality, there are good reasons to think that this critique misses its mark (see later).

JEFF SMITH AND THE CRITIQUE OF THE PSYCHOANALYTICAL MODEL OF FILM MUSIC

Along with apparatus theory in general, the theorization of film music along psychoanalytic lines has come under attack. As noted earlier in this chapter, proponents of feminist and queer theory have long expressed dissatisfaction with psychoanalytic theory because it seems to presume a patriarchal heteronormative subject. Others have found it by turns incoherent, reductive, totalizing, ahistorical, dogmatic, and lacking in empirical support.[5] With respect to the soundtrack, Jeff Smith (1996) takes issue with psychoanalytic theories of film music. He notes that film music assumes "a privileged position within a suture model. Because of its tendencies toward both inaudibility and abstraction, film music is thought to be especially well suited to the process of binding the spectator into the world of the fiction" (233). Smith also points out that a psychoanalytic model that presumes the suturing effect of music through its inaudibility cannot provide a coherent account for how we also come to attend to the supposedly unheard music—to recognize a leitmotif, say, when it recurs within a film, or even more significantly outside the film (236). Whatever unconscious (or more likely preconscious) apprehension of music occurs in the theater, it is clear that we as spectators are not barred from attending to music per se in the manner psychoanalysis presumes that the psychological structure prevents subjects from directly accessing their unconscious drives. In this respect, music is at best a signifier of these unconscious drives, a way of granting us imaginary access to them by representing their force on, their knowledge of, and their determination of the diegetic action. The suturing effect of music resides not so much in its inaudibility, then, as in its ability to clarify meaning for us without quite letting on as to how it

---

[5] See particularly Carroll (1988), Bordwell (1989), and the essays in Bordwell and Carroll (1996), especially those by Bordwell, Carroll, and Prince.

is accomplishing its work. Like the unobtrusive cut, which may pass noticed or unnoticed but whose presence seems supplemental to the basic meaning of the sequence, the figure of inaudibility points not to the fact that music is never consciously heard or attended to but only to the fact that it need not be consciously attended to in order to produce its distinctive effect of clarifying meaning. That is, nothing essential seems to depend on us listening consciously to it (although nothing bars us from doing so either). The point is that the music, when we consciously attend to it, still seems, like the observed unobtrusive cut, merely supplemental, nothing more than a fine artistic touch, a formal mark of stylization. For the psychoanalytic theorist, then, it is this appearance of pure supplementarity that grounds ideology and serves as the basis for musical suture because its status as supplement both neutralizes the otherwise disruptive presence of music and effaces its work in producing meaning.

Neo-Lacanian Theory

THE GAZE AND THE VOICE

The most cogent critique of apparatus theory has come not from those opposed to a psychoanalytic film theory but rather from those committed to a strong interpretation of Lacanian psychoanalysis. Philosopher and cultural critic Slavoj Žižek is the best known and most prolific of the so-called neo-Lacanians, but he tends either to interpret films through a Lacanian lens or, more commonly, to use films to illustrate Lacanian concepts rather than engage specifically at the level of film theory.

The same cannot be said of Joan Copjec (1994), who has taken direct aim at apparatus theory, accusing it of using a Foucauldian misreading of Lacan in a way that empties it of psychoanalytic content.[6] "The relation between apparatus and gaze creates only the mirage of psychoanalysis. There is, in fact, no psychoanalytic subject in sight" (26). According to Copjec, apparatus theory radically misconstrues Lacan's mirror phase: where it understands the screen as a mirror, Lacan understands exactly the reverse: the mirror is a screen (15–16). Todd McGowan (2007) likewise argues that "at its most basic level, [apparatus theory] understands the cinema as a machine for the perpetuation of ideology" (2). Apparatus theory, he claims, urges "critical distance from the scene of cinematic manipulation" to obviate its ideological inscriptions.

[6] Bordwell is extremely critical of both Žižek and Copjec, although Bordwell (1996) glosses over important distinctions between early Lacanian film theory and the neo-Lacanians (23–24). The first chapter of Žižek (2001, 1–30) takes Bordwell to task for this conflation. Bordwell responds twice: in Bordwell (2005a, 260–64) and more thoroughly and more testily in Bordwell (2005b), an essay published on his website. For another cogent critique of Žižek's work, see Harpham (2003).

Neo-Lacanian theory, on the contrary, understands such critical distance as "another way of avoiding the real of the gaze" (14). Instead, neo-Lacanian theory recognizes cinema as a machine for encountering the real.

This revival of psychoanalytic film theory has been concerned especially with reappraising the gaze, which apparatus theory construes as a mastering perspective that delivers meaning. Copjec explains the difference in how apparatus theory and Lacanian psychoanalysis conceptualize the gaze this way:

> In [apparatus] theory the gaze is located "in front of" the image, as its signified, the point of maximal meaning, or sum or all that appears in the image and the point that "gives" meaning. The subject is, then, thought to identify with and thus, in a sense to coincide with the gaze. In Lacan, on the other hand, the gaze is located "behind" the image, as that which fails to appear in it and thus as that which makes all its meaning suspect. And the subject, instead of coinciding with or identifying with the gaze, is rather cut off from it. Lacan does not ask you to think of the gaze as belonging to an Other who cares about that or where you are, who pries, keeps tabs on your whereabouts, and takes note of all your steps and missteps, as the panoptic gaze is said to do. When you encounter the gaze of the Other, you meet not a seeing eye but a blind one. The gaze is not clear or penetrating, not filled with knowledge or recognition; it is clouded over and turned back on itself, absorbed in its own enjoyment. The horrible truth . . . is that the gaze does not see you. So, if you are looking for confirmation of the truth of your being or the clarity of your vision, you are on your own; the gaze of the Other is not confirming; it will not validate you. (1994, 36)

McGowan (2003) likewise argues against an analysis based on uncovering the ideological investment in an imaginary identification with the gaze of the camera, an identification that serves to occlude and naturalize the functioning of the symbolic order, and instead focuses on the gaze as "the site of a traumatic encounter with the Real, with the utter failure of the spectator's seemingly safe distance and assumed mastery. The crucial point is that not only is this failure of mastery possible in the cinema, but it is what spectators desire when they go to the movies" (29). Although problematizing the way apparatus theory discounts the real, McGowan makes the gaze its privileged site and thereby reproduces film theory's long investment in the visual at the expense of the aural. We need not abandon his analysis, however, so long as we continue to recognize its incompleteness and understand this incompleteness as systemic and recognized as such within the theory. If the gaze marks a limit of filmic representation, the point at which the film looks blindly back at us, it also approaches the real, this limit, only from one side, that of the image.

The reason we cannot simply dismiss this analysis as inadequate despite its manifest incompleteness is because approaching the real from the side of the soundtrack—here, the voice will serve as the analogous term to the gaze— would not in any respect complement or complete the analysis. Although Lacan himself includes both gaze and voice as instances of *objet (a)* and though both reveal the real as a failure of the symbolic, they are not fully reciprocal. As Žižek (1996) writes:

> Voice and gaze relate to each other as life and death: voice vivifies, whereas gaze mortifies. For that reason, "hearing oneself speak" [*s'entendre-parler*] as Derrida has demonstrated, is the very kernel, the fundamental matrix, of experiencing oneself as a living being, while its counterpart at the level of gaze, "seeing oneself looking" [*se voir voyant*] unmistakably stands for death: when the gaze qua object is no longer the elusive blind spot in the field of the visible but is included in this field, one meets one's own death. (94)

The terms "voice" and "gaze" are not symmetrical in the sense that hearing and speaking map a different order of distinction than do seeing and looking. (The equivalent distinction to seeing and looking would be closer to hearing and listening.) Žižek's analysis, however, performs something of a short circuit by not fully recognizing the disanalogy that obtains, and so obscuring rather than illuminating the relation between them. Like McGowan, he privileges the gaze both by making it the ground that legitimates the voice (we hear because we cannot see) and by placing it in the position of an agent of sublime terror (seeing what we cannot hear). The voice also relates directly to the symbolic— it is a medium of the production of meaning—in the way that the gaze does not, so that the voice reaches the limit of the real in sense, or rather, in its dissolution. Gaze and voice therefore mark two distinct ways that the subject encounters its internal limit, two distinct ways that its symbolic construction of the world can fail, and these follow in turn the contours of sexual difference as theorized by Lacan.

For Lacan, sexual difference is located in the phallic function.[7] But it is not the absence or presence of the phallic function that determines sexuation— the production of sexual differentiation—but the way a subject positions itself with respect to a set of antinomic statements that relates to the order of meaning and expresses an impasse, the failure of meaning. On the masculine side, this relation is through exclusion and prohibition. On the feminine side, the relation is through nonexistence and impossibility. Thus, with respect to the image, we might formulate the antinomies of filmic representation according to the masculine principle of the relation: (1) at least one image is not an object of diegetic representation; (2) all images are possible objects

---

[7] The following paragraph is based on Copjec's discussion of sexual difference (1994, 212–36). See also Lacan (1998, 78–89).

of diegetic representation. The image track constitutes a universe of diegetic representation, but at least one image cannot be reconciled with that world. Formally, this excluded image serves to mark a limit that makes the field of diegetic representation possible. The frame, for instance, imposes a formal limit; it is, Chion (1999) says, "the place of not seeing all" (121), and creates a place for images, though it is not itself a formal part of the diegesis. In this way, the limit of the frame allows the image track to appear coherent. A similar analysis applies to the shot, whose beginning and end are usually marked by a cut that determines its extent. The gaze is another, more radical type of excluded image, a blank spot that refuses to disclose itself within the visual field. Yet to return to Copjec's previous description of the gaze, we find that the blankness and blindness of the gaze likewise serves to impose a limit: "The subject, instead of coinciding with or identifying with the gaze, is rather *cut off from it.*" The excluded image is also the reason that the theory of the gaze can only ever yield an incomplete rather than mastering account of filmic representation.

MICHEL CHION AND "THERE IS NO SOUNDTRACK"

What, then, might a neo-Lacanian account of the soundtrack look like? Here we return to Chion and his perplexing claim that "there is no soundtrack" (1994, 39–40; 1999, 1–6; 2009, 226–30). Read through the lens of Lacan, this statement now evokes Lacan's notorious statement that "woman does not exist." Because no empirical woman can complete the concept of man, Lacan says, woman is a symptom of that concept. If we extend this idea to the soundtrack, we arrive at the idea that no sound—or set of sounds—can adequately complete the image. The soundtrack is, in other words, the symptom of the image. This conception, however, runs the risk of simply privileging the image, granting it priority. In this case, the soundtrack would register the lack of the image but nothing more. What, then, might the soundtrack be or consist in beyond the registering of this lack?

Here, the concept of the voice becomes important. If the gaze is the blank spot in the image that looks blindly back at us, then on first approximation the voice might be taken as the silence of the soundtrack that speaks to us mutely. "The voice is precisely that which cannot be said" (Dolar 2006, 15). It is that which is in sound that does not communicate, that resists meaning; put more traumatically, it is the sound of the world's deafness, its indifference to us. This formulation, though one suggested by Žižek (1991b, 49; 1996, 92–93), is perhaps too symmetrical,[8] since it presumes that the soundtrack, like the image track, is governed by castration, by the limit of the symbolic. Just as the figure

---

[8] Compare Buhler (2001, 53–55), where contra Chion I proposed a symmetrical reading of soundtrack and image track to locate the audiovisual as the product of a dialectical tension.

of woman appears in Lacanian psychoanalysis and approaches the limit of sense in a different manner than does the figure of man, so too the soundtrack does not find its limit as prohibition but as impossibility, the impossibility of film as a consistent symbolic endeavor.

Chion does indeed align the soundtrack with the Lacanian conception of woman. According to Chion (1994), the soundtrack is an incoherent construction that does not produce a consistent universe. "A film's aural elements are not received as an autonomous unit" (3). The soundtrack is also unruly, overrunning boundaries—sound editing, he says, does not yield "a neutral, universally recognizable unit" like the shot (41)—and allowing the appearance of "sounds and voices that are neither clearly inside nor clearly outside" the image or narrative (1999, 4). Essentially, the soundtrack is incoherent because it does not encounter a limit. "Sound is first of all *content* or 'containable,' with no actual frame" (2009, 226; emphasis in original). If Chion acknowledges that the image track is "no less fictive," he nevertheless grants it priority—sound is interpreted or "triaged," he says, through the image—and coherence that aligns it, analogously, with the Lacanian conception of man. By contrast, the image track, Chion says, remains "a valid concept. The image track owes its being and its unity to the presence of a frame, a space of the images in which the spectator is invested" (1994, 39). The appearance of the frame, then, is crucial for the existence of the image track: "The absence of a frame for sounds inevitably creates a dissymmetry between what we see and what we hear" (2009, 227). The frame gives form to the image; the soundtrack has no equivalent form. Consequently, the phallic function of diegetic representation operates on it in a different fashion.

With respect to the soundtrack, we can formulate the antinomies of filmic representation according to the feminine principle of the relation: (1) there is no sound that is not an object of possible diegetic representation; (2) not all sounds are a possible object of diegetic representation.[9] The soundtrack confronts no limit since it includes nothing that cannot be made part of the diegetic representation, but the sounds themselves are individually delimited and so constitute an indefinite rather than infinite set; each sound can be individually paired with an image source, but not all sounds will constitute the world of diegetic representation. Sound encounters no formal limit—it has neither frame nor shot to delimit it. Instead, sound is subject to the contingencies of filmic unfolding, that is, temporality. If sound's "temporalizing power greatly exceeds the image" (Chion 2009, 266), so that sound can seem to insist upon a vectorized temporal flow, upon the appearance of a temporality not reducible to that captured in the movement of the image, music by contrast is, Chion

---

[9] The first part of this paragraph again follows Copjec's discussion of sexual difference (1994, 212–36).

says, "first and foremost a machine for manipulating space and time, which it helps to expand, contract, freeze, and thaw at will" (409). Music therefore ordinarily serves to veil "the palpability of time" (274), the real of temporality, which emerges, Chion says, at "the decisive moment, the climax, the *alea jacta est* or point of no return, the moment of truth and of real time" (272), where music (but also speech) recedes and allows the sounds of the world to reverberate and form the ground of the real of temporality that renders the figure of silence, the "fundamental noise," audible (453–58; see also Žižek 1996, 93). The conception of the soundtrack cannot therefore be extracted from the representation of temporality, which means that we cannot construct a general concept of the soundtrack.

MIMETIC SYNCHRONIZATION AND THE SEXUAL RELATION

What binds the masculine and feminine principles together in Lacanian theory is the appearance of the sexual relation. The analogous figure in sound film would be mimetic synchronization, the joining of image and sound, which is why, from a neo-Lacanian perspective, the metaphor of "marrying" sound to image is no more innocent or coincidental than it is from a feminist perspective. This "marriage" follows the cultural myth of unity wherein two become one to produce the imaginary diegetic world. According to the Lacanian account of the sexual relation, this joining yields two principles, based on the pleasure and reality principles of Freud. Translated into the terms of sound film, the pleasure principle consists in an immediate satisfaction of the apparatus: sound and image appear synchronized, they follow a coordinated path through the apparatus, and they are mimetically bound to one another in the play of an imaginary world. Classical sound film is constructed along the lines of the pleasure principle: a diegesis appears to exist, it is not troubled by an antagonism between soundtrack and image track, and it therefore seems to promise a "natural," that is, mimetic, synchronization between image and sound. The pleasure principle also lies behind the traditional "rules" of "proper" synchronization—something along the lines of Gorbman's (1987) seven rules—that govern the exchange of sound based on an order or set of common values that have already been laid out in advance. Under this scenario, image can relate to sound only insofar as sound enters the frame of the image and becomes "diegeticized." Jacques Aumont, summarizing this situation, writes: "all the work of classical cinema and its contemporary by-products has aimed to *spatialize sound elements*, by offering them points of correspondence in the image, and therefore assure a bi-univocal bonding between image and sound, what we might call 'redundant'" (Aumont, Bergala, Marie, and Vernet 1992, 35, quoted in Chion 2009, 228, emphasis in original). Although image relates to sound through this redundant effect of spatialization and diegetization, sound is not exhausted in this correspondence.

Even under the system of the classical cinema, sound is split because it is what the lack in the image signifies, and that lack is itself divided: both what the image does not contain, which spatializes sound and binds it to the diegesis as a property of the image, and what lies beyond the image, which opens up the nondiegetic, the absolutely out-of-field, where sound—especially music and voiceover—stands in the place of the Absent One, the other who knows and, because outside the diegesis, can serve to guarantee its existence. Under the pleasure principle, sound complements the image, even as it completes it in the imaginary.

The reality principle, by contrast, consists in the reality of the apparatus: sound and image are separate, they follow different paths through the apparatus, they are materially alienated from one another, and the desire for mimetic synchronization appears only in virtue of this original alienation. The reality principle points to the fact that in Lacan's theory the sexual relation is always a failed relation—the satisfaction of the pleasure principle is always a hallucination—and so long as synchronization is theorized along analogous lines, it should suffer the same fate in sound film. Indeed, under this description there would be two ways for the sound film to fail: through the image and through the sound. As noted earlier, the image fails through exclusion; it is defined by a prohibition, a lack: it cannot show everything. Sound, on the contrary, fails because it has no limit. The soundtrack promises what the image track lacks, what the image cannot show: everything, the continuity of a world that lies beyond the frame line, the interior depths of the characters. But the soundtrack pays for this everything with an indefinite formlessness, a lack of boundary, a lack of containment. Because it has no limit, it is not all, not whole. Conceived in these terms, the question is not how to produce complementary accounts of image and sound, where the lack of the one is compensated for by the other and vice versa, but rather to reveal the fantasy on which such complementarity rests. This shifts the issue from explaining the rules of synchronization to what it means, given the fact of the division that underlies the construction of the apparatus, to speak of the soundtrack at all. Chion (2009) writes:

> There are many consequences of this negative claim I have been making that "there is no soundtrack." First, it necessarily explodes any pretense of establishing an overall theory of film composed of two complementary elements, image and sound, and instead leads us to an incomplete and fluctuating model of cinema that does not allow for simply transposing the technical model (one channel for images and one channel for sounds, distinct yet parallel) and where a radical break is produced between the technical level and the levels of perception, discourse, effects, and theory. (229–30)

If sound serves as the support for the concept of synchronization, it also makes evident the impossibility of actually establishing mimetic synchronization as a consistent system that would uphold the diegesis. Without a frame to contain it, the soundtrack both simultaneously embodies the diegesis in its entirety and denies the possibility of its appearing. The soundtrack is the point at which the impossibility of sound film's diegesis assumes positive form. Because sound is thus simply a fantasy screen of the image—the image in its ideal completeness—the soundtrack does not exist. This does not mean that sounds, music, and voices do not exist, of course; rather, it is that the soundtrack cannot serve to guarantee the image's fantasy of completion.

The relation between image track and soundtrack is therefore better conceived in terms of antagonism rather than complementation, a point that, as we considered in chapter 5, Nicholas Cook (1998) also makes, albeit for completely different reasons. If sound film fails because image and sound do not come together to produce a world, then sound cannot be added to the image; sound can only be differentiated from the image. The diegesis is the site not of unity, but of this differentiation, and the claim that the soundtrack does not exist does not so much deny existence as it asserts that the category of synchronized fantasy is false. The claim that there is no soundtrack therefore carries a perhaps surprising corollary: there is no diegesis. The diegesis is not simply a fiction, but sound film's primal myth, an imaginary projection that uses the audiovisual figure of mimetic synchronization as a barrier against reality, against the recognition of the division into image and sound, projecting a unity—Doane's fantasmatic body—through which the actual split is continually denied. Two does not make one, and yet the sound film exists on the assumption of this one; but this unity suppresses not just the heterogeneity so beloved by the first generation of Lacanian film theorists, but also, for the neo-Lacanians, the gap of human desire. This gap is made manifest in the figure of asynchronous sound and the uneasy feeling that there is something awry whenever we encounter it. The effects are felt as a hole in the fabric of the diegetic representation. We can perhaps now understand why the acousmêtre is such an important figure for Chion: it marks precisely this hole in the diegetic, the opening of desire at the point where the pleasure principle fails. Sound is rendered in sound film to satisfy desire, to signify what sound is not, not to be what it is. "The whole enterprise of sound effects in film," Chion (2009) writes, "consists of hijacking some sounds to express others" (239). The signifier of this desire resides not in the sound but in the way the image signifies its own lack, for it is here, where the image delimits the depiction of the diegesis, that sound addresses itself, locates itself as a property that the image desires. Mimetic synchronization fuses a representation that deprives sound a place in the image with a desire that the image cannot contain. Because it is rendered to satisfy a desire that does not belong to itself and that it does not signify, sound can often be cold, indifferent to the demands of the image so long as it fulfills simply the basic requirements of mimetic synchronization.

As opposed to this frigidity of sound, which points to difficulties inherent in the relation of synchronization that requires sound to be both inside and outside the image, pure asynchronous sound—sound undetermined by its relation to the image—would be psychotic sound, sound that has excepted itself from the symbolic order, the signifying network of narrative. Sound completely unbound from the image in this way would mean the end of the symbolic universe, a sound lost to meaning. Such sound would in fact also presume a place of perfect objectivity with respect to sound choice: that it is possible to get outside the signifying network and make an entirely free choice with respect to sound. As Chion (2009) notes, this is virtually impossible to accomplish:

> If the image had a resistance to being layered with nonsynchronous sounds not anchored spatially or diegetically in the image, this resistance, analogous to harmonic dissonance, would communicate to us something powerful in its very violence. The real problem is that everything "works"; there never is any resistance, only a sort of laissez-faire abandonment of sounds and images to this passive superimposing that generates effects erratically, zinging us here and there with momentary pleasures. (230)

MICHEL CHION AND RENDERING

If asynchronous sound has proven too capricious to reliably tap its traumatic kernel, it has provided something of a map for locating that kernel in the contemporary practice of rendering. A profound uncertainty follows from the attempt to substitute the continuity of the soundtrack, which has no formal limit, for the image as the ground of diegetic representation. In many films today, sound takes the place of the establishing shot, and it loses the promise of plenitude that had always been the opening of desire marked by the frame edge. This loss is compensated for by the rendering of sound.

> In fist- or sword-fight scenes, the sound does not attempt to reproduce the real noises of the situation, but to render the physical impact of the blow or the speed of the movement. . . . The rendering is naturally linked to the texture of the auditory and visual material of the film, to their definition, but not necessarily in the sense in which a sharper and more "faithful" image (a more accurate replication) would ipso facto give a better rendering. (Chion 1991, 71; see also Chion 2009, 237–45)

Žižek (1991) notes how Chion's formulation of rendering, especially the way it supports a shift from the image to the soundtrack as the basic field of orientation, leads to a psychotic conception of the relation of sound and image:

The soundtrack gives us the basic perspective, the "map" of the situation, and guarantees its continuity, while the images are reduced to isolated fragments that float freely in the universal medium of the sound aquarium. It would be difficult to invent a better metaphor for psychosis: in contrast to the "normal" state of things in which the real is a lack, a hole in the midst of the symbolic order (like the central black spot in Rothko's paintings), we have here the "aquarium" of the real surrounding isolated islands of the symbolic. In other words, it is no longer enjoyment that "drives" the proliferation of the signifier by functioning as a central "black hole" around which the signifying network is interlaced; it is, on the contrary, the symbolic order itself that is reduced to the status of floating islands of the signifier, white *îles flottantes* in a sea of yolky enjoyment. (40)

Žižek's description of rendering resembles in many respects Chion's description of asynchronous sound, where "laissez-faire abandonment of sounds and images" is analogous to the "sea of yolky enjoyment," and the "momentary pleasures" of accidental sync points fill the place of the "white *îles flottantes*." Yet the points of disanalogy are worth noting as well: however much the real has intruded upon the scenario of asynchronous sound, however much asynchronous sound asserts the reality principle and opens a gap of desire that it threatens to ignore, the overall structure nevertheless respects the drive of enjoyment. The persistence of the drive of enjoyment—gratification in this case as merely arbitrarily deferred—is why it necessarily lacks resistance.

Rendering, however, is of a different order, and its situation is closer to nondiegetic music inasmuch as it retains a fundamental relation to fantasy. Both present a certain stylized excess over the real. "Rendering," Chion (2009) suggests, falls "somewhere between a code and a simulacrum. And between code, rendering, and simulacrum there may be a certain continuity—one might slip from one into another without necessarily being aware of it" (238). In Lacanian terms, code belongs to the symbolic, and simulacrum belongs to the imaginary (Žižek 1991, 40). The continuity—the slippage—dislocates rendering from the image, which the sound no longer accompanies, and so the image track and the diegesis built upon it threaten to dissolve. Rendering attacks the power of the diegesis, its myth of unity, from within. Nondiegetic music, by contrast, is doubled, serving on the one hand as the sublime extradiegetic counterpart to rendering but on the other hand as an external guarantee of the diegesis. By retaining the anachronistic term "pit music," which is otherwise somewhat inexplicable, Chion is able to emphasize a displacement of music that will anticipate the very dislocations taking place within rendering. Music's passage from the theatrical pit to the apparatus had the effect of obliterating all sense of place and labor of production. Absorbed into the apparatus, music loses all specificity:

From the beginning to the end (or periodically if it's not continuous), the music is emitted from the orchestra pit, the grandstand, from a place beyond all places, that contains all times and all spaces, and leads everywhere: to the past as well as the future, to the sea and the city, to depths as well as to the heavens, a place that has no here or there, neither once upon a time nor now. The place is both a pit, where the elementary principles of these mean streets called life muck around, and a balcony in the sky, from where we can view as detached observers—out of time, through instantaneous cuts—past, present, and future. (412)

But music does not become universal by virtue of this loss of specificity. In that respect, at least, music in film is an allegorical figure. Doubled, it is also divided: pit and sky. Rendering ("life mucking around") is already its lower element. As the movement and logic of rendering raise the pit to the sky, the stars go out, music loses its special fascination—is it anything more than a mode of acoustical stylization, an attribute of sound design?—and the view from heaven now reveals an abyss: "the hole in the Other (the symbolic order), concealed by the fascinating presence of the fantasy object" (Žižek 1991, 86). Music convinces us that the image on the screen is the screen of fantasy; and rendering proves a means of traversing this particular fantasy.

9

Theories of the Digital Soundtrack

Introduction

I concluded the previous chapter with a discussion of Michel Chion's concept of rendering, an approach to realizing sound that not only blurs the distinction between diegetic sound and nondiegetic music but also dislocates the sound from the image. Rendering destabilizes the diegesis even as it seeks to represent the experience of feeling and gesture. This distinctive, and decidedly nonclassical, approach to sound is characteristic of contemporary cinema. Indeed, critics and theorists have remarked on the profound changes to both image and soundtrack since the new Hollywood cinema emerged from the studio system.

As Geoff King (2002) observes, the new Hollywood cinema remains a contested term in film studies—for some it refers specifically to the somewhat experimental American cinema of the late 1960s and 1970s that followed immediately as the studio era came to an end, but for others it signifies the new system of blockbuster cinema that only began to take shape in the late 1970s. The emphasis on blockbuster cinema was particularly important to the technological base of cinema because it created pressure to develop spectacular visual and sonic effects, pressure that encouraged the rapid development of computer technologies to facilitate this work and ultimately led to the wholesale conversion to digital production and exhibition. That in turn has had the somewhat surprising effect of upsetting a host of theoretical assumptions about the ontology of film. "*Cinema is going through a major identity crisis,*" assert André Gaudreault and Philippe Marion (2015, 10, emphasis in original). Gaudreault, a film historian who specializes in how early film practice was codified into the institution of cinema, and Marion, a media theorist who works on how a story changes as it confronts the specificity of a medium, are particularly well suited to comment on these changes, which concern the emergence of a new medium and the transformation of the institution of cinema in response to it. They continue: "One of the signs of this crisis is the questions that film scholars have been asking themselves the past few years, taking up the fundamental question once asked by [André] Bazin and reformulating it in various ways: 'When is there cinema?'; 'Where is cinema headed?'; 'Is it cinema?'; etc." (10). All this unease circulates around the digital image itself: Can we still have cinema without the medium of physical film? Is film without celluloid still film? Lev Manovich had already detected that digitalization was effecting a profound transformation of the cinema in his *Language of New Media* (2001): "Computer media redefine the very identity of cinema" (293). In particular, the digital image no longer relates indexically to the profilmic object; the world screened by the digital image is virtual rather than real.

Because the crisis of the digital image emerged in the 1990s at about the same time that apparatus theory—the subject of the first part of chapter 8—collapsed, the reappearance of ontological questions from classical film theory seems on one level reactionary, a return to an era and phase of film theory when categories of film, if not answers to film theory, were more certain. If film studies has long had a theoretical consensus that the image is constructed, the appearance of digital "film" revealed that the field was surprisingly committed to a photographic reality guaranteed by the indexicality of the image. Still, more recent theoretical attempts to shore up film against the digital image have often seemed half-hearted, perhaps because the digital image has all but retained the conventions of the photographic image that reside in its iconicity even while undermining the ontological moorings tied to its indexicality. Even in the digital age, Gaudreault and Marion (2015) note, "The photographic apparatus is still obsessed with capturing and restoring the world, and its reputation remains that of bearing witness to a recorded reality" (67). Film historian Thomas Elsaesser (2013) writes similarly:

As digital conversion does away with this material basis [of film], such a modification cannot but challenge definitions of what cinema is, and, by implication, must change what we have come to regard as the specific qualities of the medium: photographic iconicity, guaranteeing the cinema's "reality effect," combined with the special kind of indexicality, the existential link with the real, guaranteeing the "documentary" truth-value that makes the moving image such a special kind of historical "record." (22)

He adds a pointed question: "Have we simply misunderstood the meaning of 'index'?" (22).

More robust has been the investment of the identity of the cinema in the rituals of exhibition. Raymond Bellour, for instance, argues:

One thing alone is certain: cinema will live as long as there are films being made to be projected or shown in a movie theater. The day its apparatus disappears (or becomes a museum piece, a machine among many other machines in the cemetery of a film archive museum) will be the day cinema truly dies. This will be a death much more real than its mythical and oft-announced death. (quoted in Gaudreault and Marion 2015, 19)

This formulation posits a hierarchy of screens, with the cinema screen as primary. Film experienced in other ways on other screens is less than cinema, and the digital image threatens cinema in this respect as well because it reduces the friction for a film to move from screen to screen on the one hand and for things other than films—most notably opera performances, but also television programming, especially sports—to appear in the exhibition space of the cinema on the other. Gaudreault and Marion write:

> This generalized equivalence of the digital can also be seen, let us repeat, in the multiplicity of devices across which our images travel. Users consume films on a multitude of screens and receptacles. We might even wonder . . . whether this variety of consumption sites is not in the end more decisive than the loss of the invaluable indexicality that gives celluloid film and recordings by analogue moving picture cameras their singular quality. (69)

The soundtrack has been buffeted by similar forces unleashed by the blockbuster system of the new Hollywood cinema, though without quite so much of the ontological worry (Whittington 2013, 62). For the soundtrack, the most prominent changes came in two waves: first, in the late 1970s with the introduction of Dolby Stereo SVA, which greatly increased the number of theaters that could exhibit films in stereo, and second, in the early 1990s, when digital sound systems were installed in theaters. Each of these changes was accompanied several years later by the introduction of home exhibition technologies that would prove crucial: the distribution of films by videotape and later by DVD. The audio quality of videotape was not especially high, and it supported only two-channel stereo, but it transformed audiences into buyers of films rather than renters of theatrical seats, and it allowed for more or less unlimited screening and—especially desirable for study—the ability to control the programming by replaying particular scenes and comparing scenes within and between films (Gaudreault and Marion 2015, 22–25). The DVD added much higher-quality audio and surround sound, allowing a home screening of a film on high-quality, well-calibrated equipment to reproduce fairly closely (more closely than the image at any rate) the auditory experience of the cinema. Until the widespread adoption of large digital televisions around 2010, the sound of films in home exhibition was often far more impressive and cinematic than the image, even when the films were played back in two-channel stereo. Even now, when films are often screened on phones, tablets, and computers, the sound from a decent pair of headphones compensates in many respects for the small size of the screen to deliver the feeling of a big, cinematic experience.

The most prominent changes in film sound came around 2000, when digital production processes, changing workflows, and difficulties with revenues from soundtrack recordings combined to force a different approach. As with the image, the digitalization of sound has also had a major effect on soundtrack production. The digital tools used for both music and sound production are much the same, and the perhaps inevitable result has been a convergence of sound and music into a new conception of the "integrated soundtrack" (Neumeyer 2015; Greene and Kulezic-Wilson 2016) guided by the practice of sound design. The digital soundtrack, in other words, has resulted in a shift as profound and threatening to established ontologies of music and sound as with the image, even if the disruptions to theories of the soundtrack have not been so overt.

Because we are talking about contemporary practices and evolving critical and theoretical responses, this chapter is organized somewhat differently than the preceding ones. In earlier chapters, I have occasionally inserted close readings of individual films where it was useful to illuminate—or critique— authors' viewpoints and arguments, as with Pudovkin on *Deserter* in chapter 2, Mitry on *Stagecoach* in chapter 4, and Kalinak on *Captain Blood* in chapter 5, and as with my readings of focalization in *Casablanca* in chapter 6 and of homosexuality and gender in *Suddenly, Last Summer* and *The Hours* in chapter 7.

Similarly—but more systematically—in this chapter, I approach issues particular to contemporary cinema through engagement with a series of recent films, engagements that open out to pertinent theoretical questions, most of which relate in some fashion to issues of digitalization and computerization. In the first section, I explore how *Hugo*'s (2011) narrative directly addresses the ontological divide opened up by digital film and then consider issues following from it that relate to sound in the contemporary action blockbuster. I start the second section with an account of the opening of *The Adventures of Tintin* (2011) and then examine how animation and digital techniques have generalized—and radicalized—the concept of rendering. The third section looks at the opening of *Inception* (2010) and explores the effects of digital audio workstations (DAWs), especially how this class of software has fundamentally altered the practice of sound and music production. In the next section, I consider a set of theories of stereo and digital surround sound. This discussion concludes with a discussion of a scene from *Gravity* (2013). In the fifth section, I approach the issue of the oft-noted changes in the scoring practice of contemporary films. This section focuses specifically on music and includes brief analyses of *Raiders of the Lost Ark* (1981) and *Batman Begins* (2005), as well as a more extended analysis of *Man of Steel* (2013). In the final section, I begin with an account of a pivotal scene in *Arrival* (2016) and use it to discuss aspects of postclassical style, especially how the soundtrack works in a film that features a complex narrative structure. In each case, I have chosen the film because it illustrates well a particular theoretical issue or because it already serves to organize a discourse on an issue. One recurring motif is the figure of digitalization, and in the chapter I trace this figure to locate the fragmentary outlines of an emerging theory of the soundtrack for the age of digital media.

The Ontological Divide

Hugo (2011) opens with the sound of whooshing air, at first seemingly produced by the movement of animated stars zipping through the clouds gathering to encircle the Paramount logo; gradually this whooshing reveals itself to be the sounds of a steam engine. As the GK Films logo settles into place, the clicking of train tracks dissolves into a ticking of clocks. This change then calls forth the opening shot of the film proper—a set of gears that recalls a memorable scene from *Modern Times* (1936); this moment also serves to inaugurate the film's score with a string figure evoking the sound of a moving train. A slow dissolve offers an analogy of the gears to automobiles moving through a traffic circle. When the dissolve is complete, it is clear that we are seeing the Arc de Triomphe, the location of Paris confirmed by a pan across the city revealing the Eifel Tower. The image then moves in toward the front entrance of a train station. A cut presents a reverse angle of the train station from behind. As the image tracks toward the station, a descending figure sounds gently in the piano, like a train falling from heaven. The shot then travels along a platform between two trains before moving into the station proper, which brings a musical dissolve to the sound of an accordion that seems to emerge out of a puff of steam momentarily obscuring the image. The shot tracks across the station and swoops up to reveal the eyes of a boy surveying the station from the number 4 on the clock. The coincidence of music and the end of the long tracking shot mark this as an arrival point, and the film moves quickly to exposition and introduction of characters—not, however, in the typical sound film fashion of a dialogue scene but in the silent film fashion of showing characteristic action.

This opening tableau draws its imagery from the age of mechanical reproduction—trains, clocks, electricity, steam, and mechanics—but presents it through the perspective of digital cinema. The central dynamic of the film derives from the opposition of the mechanical and the virtual. In this connection we must not forget that *Hugo* was released in 3D and that several of the process shots at the outset make overt use of digital effects. Silent film, insofar as it is represented in *Hugo*, is both a mark of modernity and a sign of its passing.

Hugo in fact uses digital film to tell the story of silent cinema; or rather it stages silent film's historical recovery by telling the tale of the later postcinematic life of Georges Méliès. One of the primary conceits of film historiography is a founding opposition between Lumière and Méliès, between film as a medium

The soundtrack of the film, beginning with the sound effects—the realistic, indexical world of Lumière—moves into the station and introduces Hugo, silently, with accompanying music. Music stands with Méliès as a mark of rendering and of storytelling. This leads to a curious and unstable configuration: Hugo, silent film, music, and Méliès on one side; Georges, sound film, dialogue, and Lumière on the other. The virtuality of digital film necessarily sides with the first configuration, but its erosion of the mechanical basis of film leaves the silent film that *Hugo* would redeem seem like an ancient and superfluous relic destined to be supplanted and discarded by the digital regime of virtuality.

As we have seen in earlier chapters, a central theme in almost all film theories before the 1970s was the veneration of silent film and the denigration of sound, especially dialogue, and *Hugo* certainly demonstrates that nostalgia for the silent film—and the dominance of the image that it underwrites—is very much alive. From its inception, the new Hollywood blockbuster has leaned heavily on the soundtrack for its effectiveness, and the films were—and still are—often belittled for being nothing more than "big and loud." Writing in 1995, Larry Gross indeed located egregious affronts in the contemporary action blockbuster, but he traced their origin to the spectacle of the early sound film: "The moment there was sound, film-makers recorded the voice of *King Kong* (1933) and the airplane machineguns that would shoot him down, to give huge audiences cheap thrills" (7). Gross's statement is a polemical distortion in that he makes it seem as though *King Kong* inaugurated the sound era, whereas it was in fact released well after sound film had established itself as the commercial foundation of the industry. This anachronism is symptomatic, as it opens the film to an allegorical reading of film history: sound, captured as if in the wild, is a monster that threatens to destroy the civilizing force of the narrative that gives coherence to the sequence of images; and no beauty on Earth has the power to kill (or even tame) this sonic beast.

It is striking that this old lament mourning the passing of the silent film should reappear so forcefully just as the digitalization of film production and postproduction took hold in the 1990s, when technology again threatened to upend the foundations of cinematic sense. Stanley Cavell (1979) reminds us that the coming of sound, far from remedying the deficiencies of the silent drama, opened a cultural wound that sound film—whatever its technological advances and pleasures—was never able to close. Sound film carried within itself a traumatic kernel that constantly unsettled the very terms of mimetic synchronization that it demanded (147ff). Cavell locates the most characteristic response—where sound film comes up against and acknowledges its own limits—in a sound practice that distills the presence of a particular silence, that registers not meaning but the audible sense of the void that separates bodies. As a result, we become aware of the fraught presence of the silence that surrounds characters. Yet he also recognizes that much sound film has preferred not to confront the wound, but instead to skirt the traumatic encounter through distraction. *King Kong* again stands as the privileged example. In Cavell's account, however, the film's unruly sound—its combination of "continuous Wagnerama and almost continuous screams"—is not a monster but rather a displacement of the wound of sound: "the film is more afraid of silence than Fay Wray is of the beast" (152).

These two strategies of approaching the wound—distillation and distraction—converge in what Michel Chion (1991) once called the "quiet revolution," the development of technologies of audio production and reproduction capable of delivering "a micro-rendering of the hum of the world" (71). We have considered implications of rendering several times already, and here I want to emphasize that the turn to rendering—to a re-creation of sound (or image) through imaginative reshaping so that it corresponds not to an actual sound but rather to its visceral emotional impact—initiates a subtle but decisive shift in the status of the image: from the screen as Bazinian "window on the world" to screen as "monitor" (73). The image had once established perspective and promised, in Cavell's words, "a world of immediate intelligibility" (1979, 150), but sound, according to Chion (1991), "abounds in details; it is polyphonic but vague in its outlines and borders" (73). Notably, Chion says, modern sound design resembles the representation of visual space in pre-Renaissance painting where "the void between these bodies is not constructed" (73). The site of the wound is again displaced, but it now paralyzes the image: "being no longer functional or structuring, the image becomes interestingly idle" (73).

As discussed in chapter 8, rendering can serve to traverse the screen of fantasy that music of classical cinema supports. Rendering is the auditory correlate to—and the quiet revolution is the actual driving force of—the impoverished (and space-destroying) close-ups that constitute an important attribute of what David Bordwell (2006) has called "intensified continuity" (121–38) and what Lev Manovich (2001) calls the "painterly" quality of the contemporary image (295). Just as *King Kong* responds to the horror of silence by masking it with music and noise, so too the contemporary action film seems to respond to the threat of the catatonic image by covering it with frenetic editing and other visual wizardry designed both to energize and to distract. But once we note that Cavell's description of *King Kong* passes over the sound in the initial sequence in New York—a sequence where the silence is in fact allowed to resound in all its emptiness and words register only the pain of human interaction reduced to economic relations—we can understand the film's soundtrack less as an evasion of the wound than as a dramatization of the bitter breaking of silence, the conversion of trauma into myth. The film earns its screams and its evocation of Wagner.

And so it may be for the contemporary film. Digital filmmaking extends the principle of rendering from the soundtrack to the image. In this respect, the analytical emphasis on the digital image in Manovich's *Language of New Media* is misleading, as it reinvests in the visual basis of film. The action genre in particular makes the special effect into the norm and accompanies it with a sonic blast from the soundtrack. Now routinely built and framed in postproduction, the digital image floats, like the soundtrack, in the nether region between (imaginary) reproduction and (symbolic) representation. As Rick Altman noted already in 1992, "today, the customary electronic manipulation and construction of sound has begun to serve as a model for the image" (1992c, 44). But whereas rendered sound establishes a continuity that grounds the sequence, the rendered image loses depth, fragments rather than consolidates space, and disassociates in editing, which assembles a series of striking glances that relate as much through the soundtrack as to each other (Kerins 2011). With sound anchoring the continuity, the management of sync points for visceral impact more than for visual logic drives the montage.

Rendering, in other words, figures the loss of what Cavell calls "automatic world projections," a fading of the cherished indexical quality of film, and in this loss film registers the experience of a final terrible mortality as nature's withdrawal from us. It raises the question: does digital filmmaking still produce cinema? This has been a much-debated question and I will return to it in the next section. Digital film raises the specter of animation at the heart of the photorealistic image. Animation may not exactly make movies—or rather it might be worth upholding a distinction between animation and movies because animation retains a profound artistic dignity to the extent it denies itself and us a view of the world. Nature as such does not exist in animation, which is therefore a pure expression of subjective will. According to Cavell (1979), for instance,

> the difference between this [animated] world and the world we inhabit is not that the world of animation is governed by physical laws or satisfies metaphysical limits which are just different from those which condition us; its laws are often quite similar. The difference is that we are uncertain when or to what extent our laws and limits do and do not apply (which suggests that there are no real *laws* at all), (169–70, emphasis in original)

As Manovich (2001) argues, digital filmmaking follows animation in this respect.

> What happens to cinema's indexical identity if it is now possible to generate photorealistic scenes entirely using 3-D computer animation; modify individual frames or whole scenes with the help of a digital paint program; cut, bend, stretch, and stitch digitized film images into something with perfect photographic credibility, even though it was never actually filmed? (295)

A rendered world is a virtual world. It is a world that looks and sounds just the way it does because it has been made to order: nothing in it escapes the determinations of rendering. Compare this situation with nature, which, although captured, is not determined by its appearance as an automatic projection. The depiction of the rendered world is governed by resemblance rather than by cause; in semiotic terms it is iconic rather than indexical. Yet the world of digital filmmaking cannot acknowledge its denial of nature, its loss of "sacred contact" (Altman 1992c, 43), the fading of the index—at least not directly: the virtual world of digital filmmaking must still look indexical, must still look like automatic world projections. Nature's withdrawal therefore appears within it instead as an incorporation, as a destruction of distance—a destruction that makes the void between bodies unfathomable and the fixing of the coordinates of any narrative based on them uncertain. If we are not absent from nature, if we cannot escape responsibility for its representation, which is the only way we know it, the laws of nature assume form in the virtual world by force of subjective intention. This passage to the subjective interior is the reverse side of the fading of the index, the denial of nature. Following the path of sound, digital rendering has "radically desacralized cinema, substituting circuitry for direct contact, constructed iconicity for recorded indexicality" (Altman 1992c, 44). The wound of sound, which made silence apparent, articulate, and unbearable insofar as it figured social isolation, passes into the wound of rendering, which does the same to the unfathomable void between bodies that now asserts itself not in silence but in a conspiratorial hum of the world.

Animated Image, Stylized Sound: The Radical Effects of Digital Rendering

The Adventures of Tintin (2011) opens in a city marketplace buzzing with activity. An artist is working on a portrait and talking with the subject, who is not shown. An accordion, violin, and bass play in the background, presumably diegetically, and the sounds of the place fill the soundtrack in a more or less realistic manner. A close-up on the feet of a man bring with it prominent sound effects of his shoes on the pavement and the movement of his joints as he rises to his tiptoes. A pan up then reveals gloved hands cracking knuckles as the man chuckles. When the piano begins to play a tango rhythm, the man begins to move, and the sound effects of his footfalls remain apparent. These figures of audiovisual synchronization mark him for attention, and Snowy, the dog, confirms his importance by taking an interest. The man begins picking pockets, and each theft is emphasized by a distinct sound effect, as well as his footfalls through the market. Snowy follows, accompanied by his pawfalls. The scene returns to the artist, who now shows his finished caricature in a style that resembles Hergé, the artist who created the comic books on which the film is based. Tintin takes the picture and turns to show it to Snowy, only to realize that his dog is missing. Tintin pays and moves through the market looking for Snowy. Ambient crowd noise is now quite prominent until we hear distant barks, as a clarinet is also added to the music. Tintin is reunited with Snowy.

When Tintin spots a model ship in a mirror, the music cadences and pauses momentarily; it then changes to a repeated note in the piano, which is joined by a saxophone. Meanwhile, the sounds of a creaking ship, waves, and wind are also heard. Where the music previously had drifted ambiguously between diegetic and nondiegetic, it now becomes unambiguously nondiegetic, and evidently the sound effects have as well. At any rate, the effect of the sound and musical treatment here is to endow the model ship with a magical quality. When Tintin begins to describe the ship, the sound effects disappear even as the music maintains the aura of magic. Tintin talks with the merchant and the sound effects are muted, but when he buys the model boat the ambient noises return. Still, the music remains orchestral for much of the rest of the scene as Tintin encounters first the detective (whose approach is announced by a set of cacophonous sounds) and then Sakharine, both of whom try to buy the boat. The orchestral music ducks out only for the conversation with Sakharine, where the background music seems to come from a rather off-key carousel. The orchestral music returns with Sakharine's exit and continues into the next scene.

Sound designer Randy Thom (2013) opens a recent essay with the remark that directors of animated features "want their films to sound essentially like live-action films" (227). In fact, the sound design of the opening scene of *The Adventures of Tintin* largely conforms with the codes of live-action film. Indeed, it is hard to imagine that a live-action version would have approached the soundtrack for this scene in a substantially different way. A live-action version might have used somewhat less music (or initially localized it more clearly), and it might have de-emphasized the actions of the pickpocket. But since both of these choices serve to stylize the sound design and to underscore the humor and mystery of the scene rather than its menace and suspense, it is entirely conceivable that a live-action version would have adopted more or less this same strategy.

The animation of *The Adventures of Tintin* was accomplished through motion capture, which gives it a high degree of photorealism especially in the renderings of the facial expression. This is much the same computer-generated imagery (CGI) technology that was used to animate creatures such as Gollum from *The Lord of the Rings*. Gaudreault and Marion (2015) write about the technology: "Motion capture thereby makes possible a kind of mimetic dissociation: actors are dissociated from their photo-realist appearance while photo-realist illusion is maintained. Motion capture is thus a kind of *animated imitation of real filmed images*" (166, emphasis in original). Where a live-action film places its CGI creatures in photorealistic settings so that the creatures seem part of the live action, *Tintin* places its CGI figures in an animated setting. Or perhaps it would be better to say that the settings of live-action films are constructed to appear as photographs of something real (whether or not it is in fact real), whereas the settings of *Tintin* are constructed to appear as drawings or representations of something real. What practice and genre conventions have taught us to treat as dichotomies—photography and animation—are today better conceived as poles of a continuity, and the image of contemporary filmmaking makes frequent use of the space between. Indeed, *Tintin* floats in the space between to such an extent that initially there was some dispute about whether to classify it as animation or live action. But this is true of many special effects–driven films as well, where large portions of the film are created with CGI creatures and backgrounds. Even films as committed to traditional filmic values as *Amélie* (2001) or *Hugo* use a significant amount of digital processing to give the settings the look and feel that the filmmakers want. Manovich (2001) indeed argues that live-action film has become a special case of animation: "Digital cinema is a particular case of animation that uses live-action footage as one of its many elements" (302).

If photography and animation represent poles of a continuum rather than absolutes, then the convergence of sound design in live action and animation under the press of digital effects is consistent with this understanding. Moreover, as I suggested in chapter 6, the live-action soundtrack has long been similarly structured between realistic (diegetic) sound and music on the one hand and unrealistic (nondiegetic) music on the other, poles that in this respect resemble those of photography and animation. Robynn Stilwell's "fantastical gap" (2007) offers one way of charting a continuity between the dichotomous pair. Jeff Smith (2009) suggests thinking of the soundtrack in terms of degrees of stylization, and David Neumeyer (2015) similarly makes an explicit call for a continuum structured by poles of realistic sound and stylized music. Ben Winters (2010) sees nondiegetic music as a "fallacy" principally because the concept of the nondiegetic posits an absolute divide between the space of diegetic sound and the space of nondiegetic music that he finds untenable. (And I am willing to concede that the status of the sound and music associated with the ship in this scene from *The Adventures of Tintin* does not quite seem nondiegetic.) Despite their considerable differences, these accounts all call into question the dichotomous construction of diegetic and nondiegetic sound and music, and they all argue in their own way for charting more thoroughly the space between. In this sense, the classical soundtrack that allowed both realistic diegetic sound and unrealistic nondiegetic music was always already prepared for this convergence between live action and animation, once the boundary between the diegetic and the nondiegetic could be made sufficiently porous. And the soundtrack devices of classical animation, especially mickey-mousing, where music seems to merge into effect, transmute into the stylized soundtrack of the contemporary action sequence, where effects seem to merge into music. In both cases, at any rate, the soundtrack renders sound much as animation or CGI renders movement. The whole is gauged, however, not to reproduce an identity in action, as in the image of classical cinema, but rather, as Chion (1991) claimed about Dolby stereo, to make the audience feel the force of the action.

For Manovich (2001), the digital basis of contemporary film means that "cinema can no longer be clearly distinguished from animation" (295). And Gaudreault and Marion (2015) concur: the digital image carries with it "a *return of the repressed*" (139, emphasis in original). Tom Gunning (2007) argues that "the marginalization of animation" is "one of the great scandals of film theory," and he works to unify cinema under the kinesthetic, the impression of movement, which bears affinities with rendering inasmuch as the visceral impact of movement also displaces both reproduction and representation as the ground for assessing the "believability" or "reality" of the imagined world (38, 45). The price of unity, however, is the loss of distinction, and the wound of rendering is bound up with this loss. Gunning (2006) explores the consequences of this loss. "Animation," Gaudreault and Marion write,

> is thus *returning* to cinema, or rather the contrary: cinema is *returning* to animation. And it is animation, as a form of cinema in the broad sense, that is rising up as cinema's primary structuring principle in the digital age. In our view, animation thus represents the path of the future for understanding and apprehending this *medium in crisis in the digital age.* (175, emphasis in original)

The animated image has become the frontier of digital film; it "has *ontologized* the 'marvelous' quality of the special effect" (187, emphasis in original), much as rendered sound has ontologized the "musical" quality of the sound effect.

Music, though never marginalized on the soundtrack the way that animation has been in the image, has often been called upon to authorize the fantasy of the image, to habituate the audience to its fabricated, representational quality. And this classical function of suspending disbelief perhaps explains something of its ubiquity in both CGI live-action spectacles and animated films. Realistic sound effects perform a contrary function of extending an analogy and placing the characters within it. William Whittington (2013) argues that early work in computer animation "relied on sound to animate and anchor their designs by borrowing perceptual audio codes and practices" (65). Writing specifically of Pixar films, Daniel Goldmark (2014) remarks on the complex constructions of the films' soundtracks: "The multiple layers of effects and music serve to embellish the new worlds that Pixar seeks to fabricate and also evokes the historical, geographic, or purely imaginative spaces that the studio draws on as inspiration for those narrative spaces" (219). Music acclimates us to the fantasy of the CGI image, while carefully modulated sound effects ground its appeals to a sonic modality of photorealism.

for documenting real life and film as a medium for fashioning fictional worlds. Not surprisingly, on an overt level, *Hugo* takes the side of Méliès in this dialectic, celebrating the act of audacious storytelling while downplaying the other side, the recording of life and time, which it dismisses as a cheap novelty. The film repeatedly valorizes Georges's ability to conjure fantastic narratives out of the machine, just as it bemoans that his accomplishment of founding film fiction has been unjustly forgotten.

Or at least the film wants us to believe this story, which is almost worthy of one of Georges's tales. For the setting, the train station, and the mechanical, deterministic tracking of both clock and film belong more to the world of Lumière than to Méliès. *Hugo*, the film, knows that trains were a popular early subject of the Lumière brothers and many other filmmakers. The astonishment at the reality of the train's appearance was a principal attraction of the early shows, and the naïveté of the first spectators flinching at the image of the train hurling at them was already a common motif early in film reception. Phantom train rides featuring film in a theater designed to mimic the train's motions and sounds formed the basis of an early stand-alone film theater (Hale's Tours). Hugo, the character, also falls closer to this conception with his watchmaker's investment in efficient design—there are no extra parts—and his mechanistic conception of causality that would follow a reel of film through the machine without break.

Georges, on the contrary, may proclaim that he and Hugo are much the same; yet he admits to creating his first camera out of parts left over from constructing his automaton. He also admits to creating his magic by cheating the causality of the camera. Cutting the film, he alters the course of recorded events and thereby conjures the real appearance of something that never happened. If Georges at the beginning of the film is seemingly forgotten by history, this forgetting is recorded time exacting its revenge against one who would excise time to fashion fiction. In the cut, the basis of filmic fiction, we encounter the excess that is trimmed—precisely the fate of excess that Hugo, the character, fears and that Georges, the character, experiences.

The anxieties of *Hugo* and its principal characters are thus the displaced anxieties of digital filmmaking. Georges's initial encounter with Hugo, where Georges grabs Hugo and forces him into the reality of sound film—this is the first moment in the film featuring synchronized dialogue—points to the ambivalence of technological change, just as the film's iconographic insistence on a past modernity of mechanical technologies recalls a past when film as a medium was a product of the age of mechanical reproduction, its reality secured by the indexical relationship between the photograph and the subject. Today, film, especially a 3D film, no longer runs the old mechanical track. Digital film conforms fully to the logic of Méliès, driven not by what could be recorded but by how the rendering of the story could astonish.

Music, Sound Design, and Digital Audio Production

Inception (2010) is best known for its elaborate plotting, a kind of Russian doll structure of dreams within dreams such that it becomes indiscernible whether the level the film presents as reality is in fact reality or another level of the dream. The opening of the film is appropriately disorienting and unsettling: against black, a musical chord of indefinite timbre sounds. Listened to carefully, it sounds like the music has been faded up quickly so that we do not hear the transient, that is, the attack of the chord. The Warner Brothers Studio logo sequence then appears along with a low thump and vaguely pitched airy noise. A high piano, likely the instrument that produced the opening chord, enters and plays along with another low thump, and new sounds, perhaps synthesized, begin to emerge in the lower register. With the change to the Legendary Pictures logo sequence, the well-known "braaams" begin to form in the lower register along with some agitated strings, and the whole thing quickly crescendos. Low brass and a high whistling sound—perhaps processed string harmonics—are added as the Syncopy logo sequence appears. Everything continues to crescendo into black.

The sound of the "braaam" crescendo dissipates only with the cut to the beach, where very loud crashes of ocean waves are seemingly reinforced in the low-frequency range. As the protagonist (Cobb) begins to wake up, the wave sounds also diminish, displaced by a low bass sound and children's laughter. As he lifts his head to look at the kids, a distorted music begins, punctuated by sounds of the children and occasional waves, but now much quieter. Cobb closes his eyes and puts his head down, and another deep wave roar sounds. A soldier jabs Cobb's back with a rifle. When the soldier sees a gun, he begins to bark commands to soldiers near a beach house, and the sound turns ominous with the addition of a new airy sound that is more effect than music.

A deep thud shifts the scene, evidently inside the beach house. As two men speak Japanese, low strings brood, alternating regularly between a low bass sound, some tremolo strings, and yet another airy noise. Sound effects of the gun and a little toy top being placed on the table are heard. Cobb is carried in noisily by two soldiers, as the music and airy sound continue their ominous ostinato, which is a constant presence through an apparent forward temporal jump showing the older Japanese man now eating. The Japanese man asks if Cobb is there to kill him. High harmonics play in the strings along with some more midrange gurgling airy noise. When the Japanese man picks up the top, a realistic sound effect is heard, and an even more prominent sound effect, again realistic, is heard once he starts the top spinning. A sound advance of Cobb's voice brings the next scene, where we see an apparently younger version of the same man eating with Cobb. The music and other nondiegetic noises quickly drop out and are replaced by normal ambient sounds but also a very low-frequency drone that unsettles the new scene.

This opening is very characteristic of contemporary digital sound design, albeit more thorough than most in its implementation. Although the sequence contains clear examples of dialogue, music, and effects—the voice of the soldier barking orders, the speech of the older Japanese man; the piano that opens the film, the low strings; the sound of the waves, the sound of the top—it also contains extensive blurring of these categories, especially between music and effects. The "braaams" that conclude the credit sequence are perhaps the best example of a sound between music and effects, but the intensity of the waves initially seems reinforced by added low-frequency sound, and the low thud that accompanies the change to the interior of the beach house seems more narrative than musical punctuation. Then too, the children's laughs are also processed to give them a dreamy, uncertain, and subjectivized character that seems to focalize Cobb's perspective. Together, the sound and music fuse into a singular, if disorienting, sound design that we come to understand as the film's dream world.

If digital processes have brought the digital image closer to animation, something similar has happened with the soundtrack, where sound and music have increasingly converged. As Kevin Donnelly (2013) notes, this convergence has been at least partly driven "by the overwhelming adoption of digital technologies, with their new filtering and enhancing procedures, sounds and music have increasingly become conceptualized in electronic terms (envelopes, bandpass filters, frequency spikes, pitch shifting, etc.)" (358). Sergi Casanelles (2016) understands composing for the films today as increasingly determined by what he calls "hyperorchestration," which involves using recorded and virtual instruments, as well as signal processing, to affect the sound (58). One important aspect of this form of musical composition is that it breaks fundamentally with the notion of real musical sound. In the hyperorchestrated score, the "live" sound carries no special ontological weight. The only sound that matters is what comes out of the speakers in the auditorium mixed with the other sounds of the film. Casanelles calls this state "hyperreality," following Jean Baudrillard's (1994) definition: "The generation of models of a real without origin or reality" (1, quoted in Casanelles 2016, 58). But it actually accords directly with the conception of the diegetic as triangulated in the imaginary from a scene played out in front of the camera (and microphone) and shot (and recorded) for how it will appear on film. In terms of the opening of *Inception*, it matters little whether the musical sounds derive from real instruments, processed recordings of noises, virtual instruments, synthesizers, or some combination thereof. It also matters little if we can distinguish what belongs to the ambient sound from what belongs to the music. For Casanelles, this means that "the process of music composition is just a subset of sound design" (62) and that "music becomes a process of sound sculpting" (68).

Oddly, Casanelles's proposal that music is a species of sound design seems to follow from a realist ontology of film. Sound design takes priority over musical composition because sound design lies closer to the diegetic level of representation; sound design retains a stronger indexical relation to the image. William Whittington similarly sees sound design as linked to a mode of perceptual realism, what he, following Tomlinson Holman (2002, ix), also calls "hyperrealism." "Within visual design," Whittington (2013) writes,

> hyperrealism is a movement interested in our *perception* of the "real". . . . Within the sound design movement, the approach is also interested in perception because it fosters a heightened and often exaggerated use of sound that is attentive to emotional intents, expectations . . ., and intertextual connections such as historical homage. (64–65, emphasis in original)

If James Lastra (2008) is right that the "founding gesture" of sound design is a move away from mimetic reproduction (134–35), then sound design is always a step toward stylization. Where the digital image is structured by the poles of photography and animation, that is, between a mimetic or stylized representation, the soundtrack might be taken to be structured analogously by the poles of phonography and music. Sound design in this sense would be a move in this direction toward stylization, but that is also in the direction of music. That is, music is the stylized structuring pole of the soundtrack, not a subset of sound design. In this sense sound design is better understood as the musicalization of the soundtrack. Donnelly (2013) argues in this way:

> Film soundtracks now often evince a conceptual or aesthetic unity along the lines of musical principles, both in structure and suppositions about individual sounds. The increasing involvement within a larger sonic scheme of elements of the film soundtrack partners with the enhanced importance of offscreen sound (it is no longer necessary to painstakingly show *everything* on screen) in modern audiovisual aesthetics. The crucial point is that sound *implies* visuals. (357, emphasis in original)

The opening of *Inception* uses a lot of sound that is not tightly synchronized to the images. Some of these sounds, like the thump that marks the cut to the interior of the beach house, seem to mark the nondiegetic articulation of the narrative unit rather than belonging to diegetic sound or music. Others, like the low-frequency reinforcement of the waves, suggest an outsized power that seems calculated to prepare the distortions of the dream world. At the same time, although the music has gestural properties—the low basses, the tremolos, the alternating organization—it is not strongly articulated into clear motives or themes, so it seems like it might be unsettling ambience, especially the airy noises. Through its implication of a world beyond the image we see, the soundtrack establishes a degree of relative autonomy determined by a logic that relates to the image without being determined by it. As Donnelly (2013) puts it, film soundtracks can constitute an aesthetic unity, with music incorporating sound effects and the whole having something of a "musical" sense to it. Rather than simply being a cog in a mechanism, soundtracks are able, to a degree, to become autonomous without explicit moving images but through the implication of accompanying visuals. (358)

The ambient stereo field—what Chion calls the "superfield"—is similarly autonomous, and perhaps this autonomy is accomplished through a refusal of the indexical relation with the image much as nondiegetic music had. What this autonomy of the superfield recognizes is a sound that extends the world of the image into the theater but that no longer indexically implies the image. In this respect it connects to the displacements of rendering and the contested nature of the diegetic representation discussed at the end of chapter 8.

Theories of Stereophonic Sound

The methods or effects described in the previous section are grounded in the techniques of stereophonic sound, which has its own history. Stereo was introduced in a reasonably large number of theaters only in the 1950s. After some initial experiments, stereo mixing settled on a practice that placed dialogue in the center channel to conform better with the established conventions of monaural recording. Under this arrangement, side and surround channels still allowed for impressive effects of spatialization, including music, offscreen sounds and voices, the ability to create richly layered ambiences, and the use of moving sound, which could be created through panning or recording the movement with an array of microphones. (Such spatial effects were used carefully because the film also had to play in theaters equipped only for monaural sound.) The basic schema was to put foreground sound to the center channel and background and special effects elsewhere.

Dolby SVA, the four-channel matrix stereo that helped popularize stereo soundtracks in the 1970s, did not alter this situation much: the center channel still carried dialogue and the sides and surrounds emphasized music, effects, and ambience. Dolby SVA adapted those conventions to the limitations of its matrix, which was designed to also reproduce monaural sound from the same soundtrack and so greatly simplified mixing of release prints. The matrix technology of Dolby SVA did demand a different approach to mixing than the discrete multichannel stereo systems of 1950s, but mixing for matrixed stereo could in many respects be conceptualized as monaural sound with an ambient field.

The Dolby matrix was designed so that the channels were not completely separate. This had a particular effect on the lateral stereo field, which would not sound nearly as wide as stereo with discrete channels, even with speakers placed in the same positions. While Dolby SVA reproduced music well and opened depth into and out of the image orthogonally to the picture plane, lateral panning of sound was not as predictable. The result was a mixing style that functionalized the channels even more than the stereo systems of the 1950s, with the center channel for foreground and everything else for music and ambient background. Indeed, it is arguable that Dolby SVA even facilitated the codification of stereo mixing in part because the lack of discrete channels in the matrix made its stereo behave even more like mono in mixing than did other stereo systems.[1] Dolby SVA, Jay Beck (2016) says summarizing Chion, creates "a 'passive' offscreen presence" (205) that can be evocative and enveloping but works best when "the axis of cinematic action [is] along a line extending from the screen into the auditorium rather than along the lateral dimensions of the screen" (207).

Chion (1994) calls this effect of stereo the "superfield," where layers of sound produce a sense of space by laying ambient sound over the natural acoustic properties of the theater (149–50). All multichannel systems with surround channels can create a superfield, but the matrix of Dolby SVA required it to be especially stable and passive since the channel leakage from the matrixing meant that movement was unpredictable. The "passive" quality of the superfield, however, also emphasized its background function of creating a continuity that was "quasi-autonomous" from the images in the sense of not being narratively foregrounded and of not being directly anchored to the image (150). Kevin Donnelly (2013) explains that "such passive offscreen sound works to establish more close-ups and wide spaces, as well as freer movement among shots. Sound also helps prevent the audience from experiencing spatial disorientation, while contributing to a new group of aesthetics that rework the basic conceptions and practices of film" (359). Donnelly invokes the example of horror film and its characteristic use of offscreen sound, but the example is not especially effective inasmuch as such offscreen sound was a staple of horror long before the superfield.

Donnelly is correct that offscreen and ambient sound do take on a larger role in constructing cinematic space once the superfield is developed as a standard approach to multichannel sound. Summarizing Chion, Mark Kerins (2011) writes:

> The superfield is the sensation of a complete space, produced by a multichannel ambiance. This suggests a reversal of cinematic hierarchy: where historically it has been the responsibility of the image to explain the

---

[1] Eric Dienstfrey (2016) argues that the Dolby six-track stereo used for 70mm exhibition also did not require new mixing protocols but was rather an extension of existing multichannel mixing conventions.

soundtrack by visually confirming the sources of sounds, it is now the soundtrack that provides the context of the image. (86)

Thomas Elsaesser (2013) concurs, suggesting that, since the wide acceptance of Dolby SVA,

> sound has been experienced as three-dimensional (3D), "filling" the space the way that water fills a glass, but also emanating from inside our heads, seemingly empowering us, giving us agency, even as we listen passively. In the cinema, the traditional hierarchy of image to sound has been reversed in favor of sound now leading the image, or at least, giving objects a particular kind of solidity and materiality. (27)

As intimated earlier, Dolby SVA's achievement was to codify a style of mixing that retained many of the conventions of the older monaural sound of classic Hollywood while augmenting it with stereo effects of the superfield that allowed sound to take on the role of providing the context for the image.

Kerins considers Dolby SVA an intermediate stage between monaural sound and the digital surround sound that has been emerging since 1990. For Kerins, the important thing about monaural sound is that all sound comes through the same speaker (or speaker set) so that there is no aural distinction between onscreen and offscreen sound or foreground and background with respect to the sound source of the loudspeaker. Although Dolby SVA follows monaural sound in placing dialogue in the center channel, it also uses the other channels to create an ambient superfield around it. The left and right speakers were positioned behind the screen as well, and the superfield thus created an acoustical space that extended out from the screen and into the auditorium. Offscreen sound could now sound from around the auditorium, although the peculiarities of the Dolby matrix made the lateral positioning of sound less secure. It also allowed sound to place objects as points in space (2011, 66). In this scheme, onscreen and offscreen no longer simply define a relation of sound to a visible source, but offscreen in particular becomes a placement within the superfield, and similarly the foreground function is now not just marked by synchronization cues but also reinforced through the presence in the center speaker.

Finally, Kerins identifies a new arrangement that begins to take hold with the introduction of digital surround sound (DSS), which are systems that use digitally encoded sound on five or more full discrete channels and an additional channel for low-frequency effects. These systems first appeared in cinemas during the early 1990s. Besides improving the dynamic and frequency range over magnetic sound, DSS also offered a return of the discrete channels of earlier stereo sound. (In terms of the stereo field, it is actually quite similar to six-track sound that had been developed for 70mm.) DSS provides much better handling of lateral movement than does Dolby SVA, and the greater precision of movement allows for a more dynamic treatment of the stereo field. Kerins calls the stereo field of DSS the ultrafield. "Where the superfield is passive, continuous, and stable, the [ultrafield] is active, jumpy, and constantly shifting" (2011, 91). As with Dolby SVA, the principal advantage that DSS has over something like the earlier six-track 70mm was the number of theaters that installed DSS and the knowledge that most venues would be able to play the film in an auditorium equipped for DSS. During the 1990s, filmmakers increasingly explored the potential of the ultrafield, especially for rendering point-of-audition sound that could seem to track the aural trajectories of multiple individual objects from a specific audition point. In the scene on Omaha Beach in *Saving Private Ryan* (1999), for instance, multiple individual bullets whiz simultaneously through the ultrafield, as ricochets and various thuds indicate what sort of surface the bullet has hit (some in the image, some not).

Like the superfield, the ultrafield allows the soundtrack to do much of the work of establishing the setting, which in turn allows the image to roam much more freely. But DSS does not simply overwrite the theater sound with a stable extension of the image. Instead, the ultrafield moves with and extends (or distends) according to the action. Moreover, the ultrafield no longer uses the center channel as a reliable anchor point. In particular, it decenters dialogue so that it can become part of the ultrafield and move along within it. "The ultrafield encompasses not just these background sounds [of ambience and noises] but the entire aural world of the film, including sound effects, dialogue, and diegetic music" (Kerins 2011, 92). The idea, Kerins says, is to "[maintain] consistent spatial correlation between image and sound" to suggest "that the filmgoers are actually in the world of the film: they hear exactly what they would hear where they would hear it, based on their implied position in the diegesis indicated by the onscreen image" (134). The description here recasts the figure of synchronization in an interesting way, since it no longer involves just relating the coincidence of a sound to some onscreen image, but now it involves a precise experience of sound and body in action. The synchronization, moreover, is not simply a joining but also captures a moving orientation, a gesture.

> The idea is that the audience is literally placed in the dramatic space of the movie, shifting the conception of the cinema from something "to be watched from the outside"—with audience members taking in a scene in front of them—to something "to be personally experienced"—with audience members placed in the middle of the diegetic environment and action. (130)

Where Dolby SVA reduces our distance from the action on the screen, DSS eliminates the distance completely (132).

Kerins argues that the full exploitation of DSS yields a profoundly different filmic construction than do other multichannel treatments of sound and image, and he claims that many scenes in contemporary cinema use sound rather than image as the principal means of orientation. Action sequences have increasingly destabilized the terms of classical scene construction, and in these instances, Kerins's claim that DSS yields a somewhat different organizational principle seems plausible. A sequence such as the chase in Waterloo Station from *The Bourne Ultimatum* (2007) does seem to use sound both to orient and to disorient in a way that does not correspond with the terms of the classical continuity system but still serves the narrative. In particular, the vectors of synchronization are often oblique and uncertain, making the images on their own difficult to assess. From a visual standpoint, the construction of the scene seems either confused or to be operating on principles other than the continuity editing of classical narrative. Sound sometimes clarifies but often distends with the images and even plays outside them to create confusion. Much of this treatment serves to establish the virtuosity of Bourne, his ability to see, hear, and act in the situation with far greater skill than any camera can capture (Buhler and Newton 2013). Inasmuch as Kerins is explaining how contemporary action scenes especially seem constructed for the experience of "energy" and excitement rather than for showing coherent kinetic action through space, the idea of DSS style is persuasive. Yet, the idea that this has become the dominant style of films since the 1990s is implausible. Even in a film like *The Bourne Ultimatum*, the DSS style is contrasted with more staid treatment that follows the principles of the superfield. Most scenes, in fact, are still quite intelligible even in mono.

The argument that stereo technology has the capacity to upend the relation of sound and image is undoubtedly provocative. Certainly, stereo has affected the functions of sound through channelization where the foreground function becomes associated with the center channel and the background function with the sides and surrounds. The ultrafield does have the power to explain the construction of certain action scenes that become somewhat incoherent without the capabilities of DSS. In some cases, it does seem that the ultrafield sharpens these relationships so we can experience them clearly, but they still do not simply disappear when DSS is unavailable. The dubious quality of such arguments becomes clear when we recognize that such films are still most often screened at home, in two-channel stereo off the television or computer or using headphones (Whittington 2013, 71). And home surround systems are frequently set up suboptimally because the room arrangement takes precedence over speaker placement in most homes. DSS may well be pushing some filmmaking in new ways, and it may well represent an approach that gives greater emphasis to sound to establish the grounds of coherence. But to the extent that these films are still comprehensible in noncinematic screenings, we have to wonder whether Kerins's account is adequate.

To examine music in the environment of the surround field, we turn to *Gravity* (2013), which provides a good example because it pushes the use of surround to new extremes. Early on, astronaut Ryan Stone is working on the Hubble Space Station as another astronaut, Matt Kowalski, helps and chats on the radio with ground control. As Kowalski tells a story, an urgent radio voice cuts in to inform the astronauts that a debris field from a destroyed Russian satellite is en route. Ominous synthesized music enters with this information. The stereo staging of the music is initially relatively stable, but as the situation deteriorates, the music loses its usual anchoring to the image plane and begins to move about the stereo field. Initially this movement is slow, but after the robotic arm becomes detached from the shuttle with Stone on it, the speed markedly increases. Only when Stone manages to separate herself from the arm and begins to tumble through space do the movement and dynamics of the music relent to some extent. As the shot stabilizes on the still-rotating Stone, the music continues to move about the stereo field to suggest the tumbling movement of her body with respect to Earth and her own disorientation. Indeed, along with the regular throbbing synthesized sound, a string line, which enters when the camera fixes on Stone's face, now also moves prominently around the surround field. The use of a recognizable orchestral gesture here is striking precisely because its movement in the stereo field emphasizes the dynamic quality of the musical reference frame. Even as she loses her bearings relative to Earth, Stone acclimates to her body in motion as a stable reference point of immediate experience, which the stable matched perspective of the camera captures; but the dynamic frame of the music retains an awareness of the larger reference, her tumbling relative to Earth and her need to orient with respect to that.

Gravity is an extreme case, but its use of the surround field to immerse the audience in its diegesis and render the feeling of an experience is typical of cinematic uses of stereo sound since the 1950s. Miguel Mera (2016) distinguishes immersion from presence. "Immersion is achieved by replacing as many real-world sensations as possible with the sensations of a virtual environment" (92), whereas presence "is the perceptual outcome of that immersion. It is the psychological perception of 'being in' the virtual environment in which one is immersed" (93). The importance of this distinction is that it can help us account for stylization. In *Gravity*, music serves as a stylization of silence; it substitutes for the noises that we expect from actions but that do not sound in space. Music is therefore doubly immersive in this film, replacing the sounds of the theater but also the silence of space with the musical sounds. Because music creates a highly dynamic field, it also creates a strong sense of presence, of being in space, of experiencing space in much the way that Stone experiences space.

Mera suggests that *Gravity* offers a new approach to surround sound that he calls 3D sound (2016, 92). Mera is convinced by Kerins's argument that the ultrafield creates a dynamic ambient field that distinguishes its treatment from the superfield. Importantly, Mera notes a qualification that Kerins places on the ultrafield: it affects only diegetic sound. That is, the nondiegetic music retains the stability of the superfield even as the diegetic ambient field continually distends to orient with the image. Indeed, in a film like *The Bourne Ultimatum*, the stable staging of the music, especially the propulsive percussion track, serves as a measure of the torsion of the ultrafield, which continually orients on the image. In 3D sound, by contrast, the stable staging of the music gives way to the same dynamic treatment as the ultrafield. "The result is the divisions between music and sound design collapse when the spatial domain is enacted as the dominant feature in the construction of a soundtrack" (92) As Mera points out, "In Kerins' definition sound moves but non-diegetic music does not. The ultrafield, then, defines its boundaries in the 3-D sonic environment of the diegetic world, but does not resolve the use of non-diegetic music in spatial terms" (100). In some situations, this is a representational advantage. Music, Mera notes, "is not tied to environmental 'reality' in quite the same way as sound design so music is, in some ways, able to move *more* freely" (103, emphasis in original). Mera shows how freeing music from the stable stereo staging allows *Gravity*, perhaps the first film to incorporate nondiegetic music systematically into the ultrafield, to "[play] radically with point of view and point of audition so that the soundscape moves beyond a purely internal perspective and encourages the audience to *become* Ryan Stone. Music in rotation, for example, clearly embodies Stone's disorientation" (107, emphasis in original).

Mera's analysis of *Gravity* is excellent; in particular, he is careful to avoid relying on claims that would presuppose a specificity argument requiring, say, auditioning the film in a properly equipped theater. But *Gravity* is an unusual case, and even if the ultrafield is most often today deployed intermittently, reverting to a superfield in most instances, 3D sound seems likely to be used even less often.

Affective Intensities, the Withering of the Leitmotif, and the Withdrawal of Identity

One consequence of a sound design that blurs the boundary of music and sound is an effacement of thematic articulation of music. The opening of *Inception*—discussed earlier in this chapter—illustrates this well, and one consequence of the blurring of effects and music is that the music will often be less articulated into distinctive themes. For instance, the opening piano gesture from the credits of *Inception* gives a rudimentary thematic shape, and the braaam serves as something of a leitmotif throughout the film, but neither of them, nor any other music in the opening sequence of the film, establishes a firm musical identity in the way, say, the theme of *Raiders of the Lost Ark* (1981) marks the identity of Indiana Jones. *Raiders*, although classical in the way theme ultimately underscores identity, is something of a harbinger of this later practice in that it takes a surprisingly long time to reach the initial statement of its theme. The film begins mysteriously with its title sequence superimposed over the opening scene. A line of men are winding their way through a jungle, and thematically underarticulated music and jungle sounds mix to produce a rich ambient field where it is difficult to distinguish clearly between music and sound effects. Throughout the sequence, shots of Indiana Jones are made in a shadowy manner that suggests he might be a villain. This is especially true when one of the men draws a gun, but Indy deftly disarms him with his whip and steps out of the shadows; the music punctuates the moment with a melodramatic "bad guy entering" gesture. Indeed, not until Indy swings out into the river while being pursued does the music at last sound the main theme that will become associated with him; it is in that moment that the ambiguities of his character fall away into the identity marked by the theme.

As Janet Halfyard (2013) notes, a shift from these kinds of big themes positing a fixed thematic identity for the protagonist occurs around the year 2000 (171), and she links the changes in strategies for scoring films to the technological developments of the image. Although she writes specifically about superhero films, the tendency that she identifies applies broadly: most action films exhibit these shifts and in fact many dramatic films do as well. Before 2000, themes are generally prominent but are reserved to punctuate and valorize moments of action that validate the hero's intervention as consistent with the hero's identity; music thus compensates for a certain deficiency in the action. After 2000, however, themes almost disappear; Halfyard attributes the change to improved techniques in digital visual rendering: "the action has become so thoroughly convincing that it does not need music to bolster its effectiveness. Heroic themes might, in fact, detract from the slick hyperrealism" of the digital effects (182).

Halfyard writes of John Williams's treatment of the theme in *Superman: The Movie* (1978): "While the music's construction encodes ideas of the heroic, its close connection to moments of action articulates the idea that Superman's heroism lies not in what he is so much as in what he *does* and the decisions he makes" (2013, 173, emphasis in original). Halfyard perhaps places too much emphasis here on the deed and not enough on the identity that the theme announces and the deed merely confirms: Superman acts because he is always already who the theme calls him to be. The deed makes him worthy of his theme. Nevertheless, she is correct to note that the doing of deeds is part of the identity of the hero. In *Batman* (1989), by contrast, she detects a new emphasis, which she attributes to director Tim Burton's personal vision: the director, she says, "chooses to emphasize not what Batman does, but what he is" (175). The theme does not so much mark Batman as a man of action, much less call him to it, as it simply asserts that he is "an intrinsically powerful figure" (176). "The music," she writes, "constructs Batman as heroic icon more than heroic agent" (176–77). Still, the theme marks an identity, even if that identity is not realized in action.

Under the digital press of "hyperrealism," films made after 2000 abandon even the firm connection between theme and identity. The leitmotif withers, and music recedes to basic functions of providing "pace" and underscoring gesture and affect (2013, 182–83). If big themes still occasionally occur, they are displaced from action to being. They no longer represent the call to identity, to act in accordance with who the hero always already is, but instead serve to establish the hero as a site of potential or power. Halfyard understands the scoring for gesture and affect as a regression to "a potentially more traditional position of constructing character and emotion, rather than depicting the superhero as a man of action" (191). The primary criticisms of this approach to scoring, however, have not been that it reverts to an older style of scoring, but that it results in an anonymous, corporate style and has abandoned the thematic articulation providing the hero with musical identity (Lehman 2017a). The situation is similar to *Raiders of the Lost Ark* if Indy had never received the confirmation of his thematic identity as he swings into the river.

In *Batman Begins* (2005)—one of the more characteristic examples of this new style and a film that Halfyard analyzes—the rising minor third, which in fact sounds like a recurring call to the hero without ever expanding into anything more than that, is the dominant motive of the entire Dark Knight trilogy. But the fact that this motive does not bring forth a more elaborate thematic identity, that it is content to show affective faces of the motive, and that its signifying relation to Bruce and Batman is quite diffuse means that it relates more to affective quality than to identity: it establishes a quality of identity and suggests a potential for the character, but it does not offer an encompassing world that might define the hero (Buhler and Neumeyer 2016, 484–86; Buhler 2017, 17). Batman may be the hero that Gotham needs, but Halfyard (2013) concludes that *Batman Begins* deploys music to explore new qualities of its hero, not to mark his deeds (191).

Nicholas Reyland (2015) notes that films today are frequently structured around what he calls "affective intensities" (116), and he takes up Halfyard's observations about themes: "Melody, most strikingly, is entirely absent: the heroes and villains of modern blockbusters get few big themes. . . . Thematicism . . . is still present, but reduced to the barest of essentials" (118–19). For Reyland, contemporary film is about the rendering of feeling through "affective short hands" (123)—propulsive rhythms, musical topics abstracted to the smallest signifying particles, condensed bits of lyrical intensity, loops of pads and minimalist textures, and so forth. In general, "'secondary' compositional parameters, such as timbre, texture and rhythm, do the heavy dramatic lifting, with manipulations thereof providing musical nuance and variety" (119). Reyland connects this emphasis to the emergence of a new postclassical cinema organized around an impact aesthetic as defined by Geoff King

(2002) and intensified continuity as defined by David Bordwell (2006) (2015, 117). In general, contemporary scores favor "affective accentuation over other forms of narrative representation" (127). To the extent that this affective turn runs against narrative as the primary organizational principle of contemporary cinema, Reyland takes the side of those who see intensified continuity and impact aesthetic as marking a postclassical cinema rather than a continuation of classical narrative procedures.

Reyland identifies two dominant strategies of musical scoring for realizing affective intensities: "corporate classicism" and "the metaphysical style" (2015, 117). Corporate classicism focuses on pads, textures, and propulsive percussion, whereas the metaphysical style focuses on condensed bits of lyrical reflection. The classicism of corporate classicism relates to earlier scoring practice much as intensified continuity relates to classical continuity as a kind of distillation. One of the traits that Bordwell attributes to intensified continuity is the emphasis on the rarefied close-up that permits much quicker rates of cutting. As noted in chapter 4, Gilles Deleuze identifies the affection-image with the close-up that allows images to concatenate in unexpected assemblages, and Reyland similarly identifies affective intensities of film music with an attenuation of the theme. Without a strong obligation to respect thematic structure, music gains in its potential to score the subtleties of affective play rather than identity. In some respects, then, corporate classicism resembles what Copland called "neutral background music." Recall Aaron Copland's description of Max Steiner's practice as cited in chapter 3: "for certain types of neutral music, a kind of melodyless music is needed. Steiner does not supply mere chords but superimposes a certain amount of melodic motion, just enough to make the music sound normal and yet not enough to compel attention" (2010a, 91). The primary difference is that where Copland understood the music as "neutral," related in its way to the indistinct background that Deleuze associates with the any-space-whatever that defines the close-up, Reyland hears the music as engaging in affective intensities, precisely the qualities and potentials that Deleuze also locates in the face of the close-up.

Vice versa, the condensation and brevity of lyrical material in the metaphysical style mean that it too places emphasis on affect. If these themes of the metaphysical style deploy a more articulated material than that of corporate classicism, the tunes are often wispy or taut rather than broad, as we would expect of more traditional film themes. The metaphysical style is concerned less with marking identity with its theme than with deploying characteristic lyrical figures to reflect an affect or express a gesture. Once again the comparison to the close-up as analyzed by Deleuze is instructive. If for Deleuze the close-up divests the face of its individuality, the thematic material of the metaphysical style similarly receives affective quality in exchange for a distinct identity. Reyland himself suggests a comparison of corporate classicism and the metaphysical style with Deleuze's movement-image and time-image, respectively

(2015, 121). In support of this claim, he points to corporate classicism's dominance in action blockbusters and the metaphysical style's importance in prestigious, art-house productions.

But the lines are not so neat, and the metaphysical style is as likely to make an appearance in action film as corporate classicism—at least in its pared-down minimalist form—is in prestige productions. It may be better to think of these in terms of Deleuze's analysis of the poles of the affection-image between the pensive face and the feeling face, between what Delueze calls "facefication" and "faceicity" (1986, 88). Initially, it might seem difficult to orient these poles to Reyland's distinction: does the lyrical expression of the metaphysical style belong more to thought or feeling? But we can recall that for Deleuze facefication and faceicity order two distinct series: the reflective and the intensive (88–89). The wispy melodic figures of metaphysical style do not fluctuate in affective quality to create a series of affects but instead draw what they accompany into a singular expression. They belong to the reflective series. The aim of the metaphysical style is thus "to express a pure Quality, that is, 'something' common to several objects of different kinds" (90). Corporate classicism, by contrast, forms an intensive series, and aims "to express a pure Power—that is to say, [it] is defined by a series which carries us from one quality to another" (90). Affective intensity, then, can be understood as a series that transforms one quality into another. The hero is not moved to action as in the classical cinema; instead, any action is incidental to this expression of virtual power.

Man of Steel (2013), for instance, is dominated by the affective intensities of corporate classicism. Superman is never scored with music that features a strong thematic profile. In the sequence when he learns about his powers, the music broods while an interactive computer hologram of his dead father, Jor-El, tells the story of the planet Krypton, and this music is interspersed with occasional lyrical passages, such as the subtle vocalese that recalls the scene from the prologue where Superman's mother prepares him for departure, or the cello and violin duet when Jor-El talks about rejecting the genesis chamber and about the dream for Superman, respectively. Only when Superman begins to practice flying does the music at all start to coalesce, and even here the motives remain rudimentary, more a sequence of chords with percussion than a theme. The intensive series is particularly noticeable as he prepares to launch again after his crash, as the music moves from a gentle piano figure to a brass chorale.

Near the end of the film, Superman is dragged down into the gravity beam of the world engine, and the situation seems desperate, but gradually the music begins to build across various lines of action. A cut to the gravity beam shows Superman struggling against it, first outstretching his arm and then making a fist. The music continues for a cut to another line of action and then the scene returns to Superman, as he now stands securely, looks up, and then begins to test his powers. Music similar to the brass chorale that accompanied his successful flight plays, driving to an epic climax when the world engine explodes. Here again, the musical material lacks thematic definition to represent Superman's identity as a man of action or to represent a reflective series despite the intercutting from other lines of action. What emerges instead is an intensive series: the crescendo of the music, the addition of the brass as Superman stands upright, the swoosh as he begins to ascend, the addition of the choir, his yell of exertion, and finally the explosion itself accompanied by a dissonant chord that hangs in the background until the engine is destroyed in a second, more intense explosion. Although this is a crucial action in the film, the music here does not underscore Superman's identity as the one acting or really even the action of ascent. Instead, the soundtrack traces the changes of affective intensity as he literally rises to the challenge and overcomes it, one affective state passing to another, yielding ultimately the cadence of the double explosion. This is a qualitative leap—Superman disappears in the initial explosion, only to emerge a bit later lying on the beach, reaching for the sun as the music recalls again the vocalese from the prologue when his mother prepared him for departure.

Postclassical Cinema and the Fraying of Narrative

If music no longer serves to mark identity but has instead turned to underscoring gesture and affect, the soundtrack has also become less committed to clarifying the terms of narrative. Along with a blurring of sound effects and music into sound design, the soundtrack has participated in the postclassical loosening of causality, with sounds and music moving fluidly through narrative levels without thereby opening a fantastical gap.

Near the end of *Arrival* (2016), as the alien ships shift orientation from a vertical to a horizontal position that seems to portend final disaster, the personnel at a temporary army base are preparing to evacuate, with warning sirens blaring. Over the course of the film, Louise Banks, an expert in linguistics who was called in to help communicate with the aliens, has been experiencing a series of "memory images" from the future as she masters the aliens' visual language of logograms, and during the next few minutes she is flooded with a series of additional images from the future rapidly alternating with her wandering disoriented at the base. Her daughter asks why she is called Hannah. Louise staggers through a corridor in a tent. Louise explains that Hannah's name is a palindrome. This explanation prompts a recognition for Louise, though it remains opaque to us. In the next cut to the future, Louise opens a cardboard box. At the base, she types at a computer. In the future, she unpacks copies of her newly published book, *Universal Language*. At the base, she looks through an enormous database of logograms that the aliens had given her. In the future, she turns to the dedication page, "For Hannah." At the base, she continues to stare at the database on the screen while Ian tries to get her to leave. As Ian speaks, music enters with a buzzy vocalized tone that soon silences all other sounds and takes her back to the future where she realizes that her book is a guide to translating the aliens' logograms. At the base with this music continuing, she studies the logograms on the computer screen. In the future, she is lecturing on the logograms to a class, though we hear the music rather than her voice. At the base the music continues, and Louise speaks at last: "I can read it." As the scene shifts outside, the music continues, and Louise explains to the Colonel that the aliens' language is not a weapon, as they had supposed, but rather a gift: learning this language allows one to see the future. But the Colonel says the exercise is over, as the music sneaks out. In the future, Hannah tells Louise to wake up. Music enters again, at first sounding synthesized but then morphing into the Larghetto from Dvorak's Serenade in E Major, apparently diegetic music from a reception in the future. It is at this reception that Louise learns the key piece of information that allows her to defuse the situation. Throughout this sequence, music and sound serve to knot temporal strands of present and future together so that the needed information can flow together in the present and forestall a fateful decision.

A comparison with the climactic first contact scene from *Close Encounters of the Third Kind* (1977) is instructive. There, music plays its traditional role of universal language, becoming a conduit allowing communication between the aliens and humans. This makes music a crucial plot device in the film, and the scene of first contact necessarily grants music a decisive communicative role. In *Arrival*, by contrast, communication is managed not through music or speech but through image, through the decipherment of hieroglyphs. On one level this comparison suggests that *Arrival* believes in the dominance of the image. It is the ability to read an image, not to interpret a sound, that is decisive to "universal" communication; in the film the speech of the aliens, which often sounds like the "braaams" of *Inception*, is in fact never comprehended. Early in the film, sound is analyzed over and over to find meaning and significant patterns, Louise flatly declares that "I can tell you that it's impossible to translate from an audio file," and the alien speech resists revealing its secrets. Indeed, an important conceptual breakthrough is the recognition that the aliens' system of writing, the logogram, conveys meaning without representing sound. This exclusion of sound is important, the film implies, because sound imposes a temporal order on meaning. The need for thought to pass through the sound chain of arbitrary phonemes requires temporal expression and thereby radically limits its ability to think through and beyond time. As Louise learns to decipher the visual language and then becomes fluent in it, time increasingly frays, she dreams of the future, and the future talks back to her, allowing her access to needed information that only the future possesses.

On another level, however, this visual dominance is only ever apparent. If the visual language allows universal communication, it does so by destroying narrative order, revealing the causal chain to be akin to the stream of arbitrary phonemes that binds spoken language to a deterministic temporal order. By contrast, Ian tells us, "the logogram is free of time." If the traditional critique of writing argues that it is suspect because it necessarily breaks with the real presence that serves to authorize and anchor meaning by binding the words to a speaking body, the logogram represents autonomous thought as essentially timeless, and evidently free of physical constraint. The aliens form their logograms in the ephemeral substance of air, and these logograms dissolve and reform with the passing of thought. The idea is that thought free of time can see the future, and that thought bound to time is necessarily antagonistic because it must struggle against the constraints of the present pressing up against and passing into a largely unknowable future. Once thought is open to time and free to roam the future so that past, present, and future all intersect and become indiscernible, antagonism apparently disappears as well—at least for those who can handle the idea that the future is always already determined. (The film makes clear, for instance, that Ian cannot handle the foreknowledge of his daughter's death.)

Coming to understand the logograms—comprehending the language without sound—cracks open the flow of time, disrupting the linearity of the image sequence and narrative. Nearly every insight Louise has about the logograms comes via a flashforward to an image of her daughter triggered by the logograms, and beyond that the flashforwards are usually hailed through sound that accompanies the image of a logogram. Sometimes this sound seems reminiscent of the always unintelligible speech of the aliens; more commonly it is a sound advance from the flashforward. The effect, however, is to associate a sound not belonging to the diegetic present with comprehension of the logogram. These sounds, in other words, are anchored to particular temporal moments and serve to distinguish the temporal layers and secure their integrity even as they offer passage to the new temporal layer.

Music's role in the film is more diffuse. On the one hand, Max Richter's composition "On the Nature of Daylight" bookends the film. Although this piece did not originate as film music, it has appeared frequently in films, perhaps because its melancholy strains and highly condensed lyricism exhibit in nearly perfect form the traits of what Reyland identifies as the metaphysical style. The piece is immediately arresting and bears a marked affective quality, but it also lacks the kind of thematic articulation that would turn its lyrical reflection toward identity. If it is nevertheless the most overtly musical sounding cue of the film, its lyricism underscores both the fraying of narrative in the opening voiceover and the attempt to bind together the temporal fragments at the end. The lyricism of this music in that respect suggests an organization that escapes the temporality and causality of narrative. On the other hand, the other music of the film by Jóhann Jóhannsson relies more on the minimalist pads and ambient textures that Reyland attributes to corporate classicism.

Often, especially in the scenes with the aliens, this music merges with sound design so completely that it is difficult to say what is sound and what is music, or for that matter what is diegetic and what is nondiegetic, without thereby also opening up a pronounced fantastical gap. In fitting with the theme of the film, the fantastical gap—if we still want to call it that—opens more on to time than to narrative level, and so it extends only so far as making the aliens seem sublimely musical creatures, and their speech too has a musical quality that suggests an affinity between music and thought unbound from time.

This kind of fraying of narrative is a feature often associated with post-classical cinema. Elelftheria Thanouli (2006) notes that many films today have reconfigured the terms of classical style sufficiently that they constitute a distinct mode of narration.

> Whereas the classical film subordinated the realistic and the generic motivations to the tight cause-and-effect logic and the compositional parameters of the plot, the post-classical films invite an increased freedom among the various motivational factors that loosens the tight causal chain, without abolishing it, and allows other elements to come regularly into prominence, such as the heightened sense of realism in intense moments or the playful parodic references. (187)

Scholars such Justin Wyatt (1994), Geoff King (2002), and Carol Vernallis (2013a) have similarly argued that impact and sensation frequently trump narrative causality as the basis for organizing films' larger structures. If an audiovisual experience is spectacular enough, an audience may be willing to overlook even substantial plot holes and other narrative incoherencies. Or like a musical, a film comes to be organized around a series of set pieces that are graduated to build energy from one high point to another, as is commonly found in action film (King 2002). A deft handling of music and sound is often crucial in leading the action scene to its release, especially when it culminates in an "explosion point," contemporary cinema's answer to classical cinema's "screaming point" (Celeste 2007).

But spectacle is a feature of other kinds of scenes as well, and Vernallis argues that techniques from the music video frequently cut across and even disrupt the norms of contemporary scene construction. Vernallis (2017) offers the party sequence from *The Great Gatsby* (2013) as an especially rich example of what she calls the "audiovisual sublime," which aims at spectacle, opulence, and sublimity rather than coherence: "Luhrmann's sequence aims for barrage and bedazzlement. It buries its processes and techniques, especially those meant to establish audiovisual relations. . . . It can be hard to find patterns. Many features contribute simultaneously to a texture that can only be understood in retrospect, if ever" (182–83). The causal chain loosens to such an extent that other principles of construction take over. In classical sound films, musical numbers and dream sequences allowed for the kind of loose, associative editing that Vernallis identifies, and the party sequence from *The Great Gatsby* does have many attributes of a production number (and even a dream). But in the context of the film, the sequence serves to introduce Gatsby and establish an irrepressible quality to him. The whole point, in essence, is that the spectacle cannot yield to cogent analysis, for Gatsby makes the party go, but he is a cipher. We are asked to enjoy the spectacle but not to draw too much sense out of it, and these are in many respects the terms of Gatsby's acquaintance. The musical treatment is giddily incoherent throughout the film, careening from period popular music to orchestral underscore to anachronistic contemporary rap and everything in between with little mediation. The treatment of the music coupled with Nick's narration creates a highly stylized narrative effect that often crosses and confuses narrative levels in a way that we become uncertain whether what we are seeing and hearing is real or imagined, as though the spectacle of Gatsby has resisted the power of narration to make sense of him. As with *Arrival*, music and sound in *The Great Gatsby* contribute to a fraying of narrative that is one characteristic of postclassical cinema.

Conclusion

As noted earlier, critics and theorists as varied as David Bordwell, Geoff King, Lev Manovich, Carol Vernallis, Justin Wyatt, Elelftheria Thanouli, Tom Gunning, and André Gaudreault and Philippe Marion have remarked on the ways filmmakers have changed how they make and use images to tell stories since the advent of the new Hollywood, and these changes have only accelerated with the conversion to digital. Even Bordwell (2006), who has strongly resisted the idea that the new Hollywood produces films that are fundamentally different in structure from classical Hollywood, has codified these changes into a set of visual strategies he calls "intensified continuity." But, as noted throughout in this chapter, the soundtrack has also been intimately involved in these changes as well: a significant aspect of this change has been the development and refinement of audiovisual figures designed to take advantage of the new digital representational technologies and, as the previous analyses revealed, these problems have been thematized and worked through in a number of contemporary films. Even though Bordwell ignores the significant changes in sound technology and techniques for exploiting it that have occurred in the new Hollywood, the visual dominance of cinema is generally no longer taken for granted. This is a product of the collapse or at least weakening of the theory of cinema itself in the face of the changed situation. A theory of cinema no longer certain of cinema's boundaries, of its reason to exist, grows uncertain about the plausibility of its ontological claims. Its convergence with other media calls into question the privileged status of its image, a status that rarely held in the practice of sound film.

In any event, the importance or at least presence of the soundtrack is today frequently acknowledged, even by those who do not make it their object of study. The contemporary action film may still be denigrated as "big and loud," but auditoria are designed specifically to accommodate the audiences who seek out this spectacle of sound, and the health of the industry is largely determined by studios' ability to reliably provide it. Filmmakers have learned to tap the potential of digital sound production and multichannel sound not just for rendering the feeling of bone-rattling explosions or for accurately tracking the individual sonic trajectories of a hail of bullets, but also for capturing the subtle play of quiet ambiences and small noises that make spaces feel intimate.

If the digital turn has greatly affected the soundtrack, the theory of the soundtrack in the age of the digital media remains uncertain (although, to be sure, no more uncertain than the theory of the image). The digital basis of the "new" media has increasingly seemed to demand a "convergence" (Jenkins 2006) that erodes all distinctions in mediums. Film, television, and video are increasingly difficult to tell apart; video games frequently adopt cinematic codes, and films adopt the looping structures of games in turn. As Holly Willis (2005) explains:

> The tools used in digital film and sound work have created an undeniable sense of creative convergence: because the tools for creating music, designing video games and doing graphic design overlap with those for making films, they have affected and influenced each other, and the impact is seen in many films created at the turn of the new century. (45)

Even amusement parks increasingly integrate cinematic elements into the rides—and music is one of the primary elements used to facilitate these adaptations. Digitalization has also served to unify both image and soundtrack under a general principle of "rendering" that seeks to make experience of the cinema match the feeling of being in the diegetic world. This is the nature of audiovisual world-building, which seeks to create fictional settings whose digital "assets"—images, backgrounds, sounds, music, and so forth—can be exploited across a variety of products and platforms (Jenkins 2006, 116).

The investment in these assets as tangible intellectual property belies a fundamental instability in their deployment and a willingness to ignore resistances to convergence in the underlying legacy media (Elsaesser 2013, 19). In the era of digital media, nothing is what it seems; everything is manipulated and sculpted. Digital actors increasingly populate screen images: not just in animated form or as digital creatures such as Gollum or as composite images transposed into another setting such as in *Forrest Gump* (1994), but as new images performing new actions, as the youthful Carrie Fisher portraying Princess Leia and the dead Peter Cushing reprising his role as Tarkin in *Rogue One* (2016). Much as Fisher and Cushing were digitally animated to reprise earlier roles, whole vocal performances can be constructed from the legacy of digital assets left by dead actors, such as when Paul Newman's voice was synthesized for use in *Cars 3* (2017) almost a decade after the actor's death.[2] Music and sound effects are losing their autonomy to constitute poles of an overriding sound design. This fluidity destabilizes traditional analytical categories and radically changes artistic practices and workflows. Rendering reaches an apotheosis, determining the terms of both image and soundtrack and indeed the relation between them that still serves to bind image, sounds, and music into audiovisual figures.

Film in the age of digital media continues to pose problems for critics and theorists, perhaps for some of the same reasons it did in its earliest days. If few today doubt that film is an aesthetic object or believe that the fact of mechanical reproduction discounts aesthetic value, the cultural shift, positive in so many ways, has been largely accomplished by refusing to distinguish art from entertainment. This is another aspect of the convergence of digital media: the elimination of any valuation not based in the market or the idiosyncrasies of personal taste as more or less irrelevant. "Convergence," Thomas Elsaesser (2013) reminds us, "happens under the sign of capitalist concentration, merger, and cartelization" (22). At the same time, digitalization has required rethinking at a fundamental level what film is. The virtual quality of digital media is one reason ontological questions, especially those concerning the identity of film, seem so pressing again even if the question of art itself is difficult to pose without imposing a necessarily problematic cultural hierarchy. The urge to erect such hierarchies persists, as with Raymond Bellour's attempt to posit the cinema screen as the only authentic site of film spectatorship. (I discussed Bellour's attempt in the introduction to this chapter.)

Recalling the struggle of theorists such as Sergei Eisenstein, Vsevolod Pudovkin, Béla Balázs, Rudolf Arnheim, and Harry Potamkin with the sound film—and recalling in particular their attempts to specify the terms under which the sound film could come into its own and assume the status of art—is perhaps helpful today when we face similar ontological uncertainty with digital media. Of course, the fact of the soundtrack does not pose an ontological crisis for film today as it did during the transition to sound. Theories of the contemporary soundtrack instead reflect the ontological crisis posed by digitalization; Michel Chion's account of rendering arguably anticipated a general response to this crisis. Whether this response will continue to be effective as digitalization facilitates the proliferation of screens and audio playback situations is an open question. One of the few things of which we *can* be certain is that we will continue to need theories to explain the presence, attributes, constructive principles, and work of the soundtrack in the age of digital media.

---

[2] Cushing's voice, however, was not used in *Rogue One*. Instead, Guy Henry voiced the part in imitation of Cushing. Henry also provided the motion capture.

BIBLIOGRAPHY

Anon. 1928. "Too Much Vocal Attention." *Variety,* September 19, 7.

Abbate, Carolyn. 1991. *Unsung Voices: Opera and Musical Narrative in the Nineteenth Century.* Princeton, NJ: Princeton University Press, 1991.

Abbate, Carolyn. 2004. "Music—Drastic or Gnostic." *Critical Inquiry* 30 (3): 505–36.

Abbate, Carolyn. 2016. "Sound Object Lessons." *Journal of the American Musicological Society* 69 (3): 793–829.

Abel, Richard, ed. 1988. *French Film Theory and Criticism, vol. II: 1929–1939.* Princeton, NJ: Princeton University Press.

Abel, Richard, and Rick Altman, eds. 2001. *The Sounds of Early Cinema.* Bloomington: Indiana University Press.

Adorno, Theodor W. (1960) 1996. *Mahler: A Musical Physiognomy.* Translated by Edmund Jephcott. Chicago: University of Chicago Press.

Afra, Kia. 2015. "'Vertical Montage' and Synesthesia." *Music, Sound, and the Moving Image* 9 (1): 33–61.

Agamben, Georgio. 2009. *What Is an Apparatus and Other Essays.* Translated by David Kishik and Stefan Pedatella. Stanford, CA: Stanford University Press.

Agawu, V. Kofi. 1991. *Playing with Signs: A Semiotic Interpretation of Classic Music.* Princeton, NJ: Princeton University Press.

Almén, Byron. 2008. *A Theory of Musical Narrative.* Bloomington: Indiana University Press.

Althusser, Louis. (1970) 1995. "Ideology and Ideological State Apparatuses (Notes towards an Investigation)." In *Mapping Ideology,* edited by Slavoj Žižek, 100–140. New York: Verso.

Altman, Rick. 1980a. "Introduction: Cinema/Sound." *Yale French Studies* 60: 3–15.

Altman, Rick. 1980b. "Moving Lips: Cinema as Ventriloquism." *Yale French Studies* 60: 67–79.

Altman, Rick. 1984. "Toward a Theory of the History of Representational Technologies." *Iris* 2 (2): 111–25.

Altman, Rick. 1985. "The Technology of the Voice: Part I." *Iris* 3 (1): 3–20.

Altman, Rick. 1986. "The Technology of the Voice: Part II." *Iris* 4 (1): 107–19.

Altman, Rick. 1992a. "General Introduction: Cinema as Event." In *Sound Theory/Sound Practice,* edited by Rick Altman, 1–14. New York: Routledge.

Altman, Rick. 1992b. "The Material Heterogeneity of Recorded Sound." In *Sound Theory/Sound Practice,* edited by Rick Altman, 15–31. New York: Routledge.

Altman, Rick. 1992c. "Four and a Half Film Fallacies." In *Sound Theory/Sound Practice,* edited by Rick Altman, 35–45. New York: Routledge.

Altman, Rick. 1992d. "Sound Space." In *Sound Theory/Sound Practice,* edited by Rick Altman, 46–64. New York: Routledge.

Altman, Rick. 1999. "Film Sound—All of It." *Iris* 27: 31–48.

Altman, Rick. 2004. *Silent Film Sound.* New York: Columbia University Press.

Altman, Rick, with McGraw Jones and Sonia Tatroe. 2000. "Inventing the Cinema Soundtrack: Inventing the Hollywood Multiplane Sound System." In *Music and Cinema,* edited by James Buhler, Caryl Flinn, and David Neumeyer, 339–59. Hanover, NH: Wesleyan University Press.

Andrew, Dudley. 1976. *The Major Film Theories: An Introduction.* New York: Oxford University Press.

Andrew, Dudley. 1984. *Concepts in Film Theory.* New York: Oxford University Press.

Andrew, Dudley. 1985. "The Neglected Tradition of Phenomenology in Film Theory." In *Movies and Methods,* vol. II, edited by Bill Nichols, 625–32. Berkeley: University of California Press.

Appadurai, Arjun. 1999. "Disjuncture and Difference in the Global Cultural Economy." In *Cultural Studies Reader,* 2nd ed., edited by Simon During, 220–30. London: Routledge.

Arnheim, Rudolf. (1931) 1933. *Film.* Translated by L. M. Sieveking and Ian F. D. Morrow. London: Faber and Faber.

Arnheim, Rudolf. 1957. *Film as Art.* Berkeley: University of California Press.

Arnheim, Rudolf. 1997. *Film Essays and Criticism.* Translated by Brenda Benthien. Madison: University of Wisconsin Press.

Attali, Jacques. (1977) 1985. *Noise: The Political Economy of Music.* Translated by Brian Massumi. Minneapolis: University of Minnesota Press.

Aumont, Jacques, Alain Bergala, Michel Marie, and Marc Vernet. (1983) 1992. *Aesthetics of Film.* Translated by Richard Neupert. Austin: University of Texas Press.

Bakhtin, Mikhail. 1981. *The Dialogical Imagination.* Austin: University of Texas Press.

Bal, Mieke. 2009. *Narratology: Introduction to the Theory of Narrative.* 3rd ed. Toronto: University of Toronto Press.

Balázs, Béla. (1945) 1970. *Theory of the Film: Character and Growth of a New Art.* Translated by Edith Bone. New York: Dover.

Balázs, Béla. (1924) 2010a. *Visible Man.* In Balázs, *Early Film Theory: Visible Man and the Spirit of Film.* Edited by Erica Carter. Translated by Rodney Livingstone. Oxford: Berghahn Books.

Balázs, Béla. (1930) 2010b. *The Spirit of Film.* In Balázs, *Early Film Theory: Visible Man and the Spirit of Film.* Edited by Erica Carter. Translated by Rodney Livingstone. Oxford: Berghahn Books.

Banfield, Ann. 1992. *Unspeakable Sentences: Narration and Representation in the Language of Fiction.* London: Routledge.

Bartoli, Jean-Pierre. 2000. "Propositions pour une definition de l'exotisme musical et pour l'application in musique de la notion d'isotopie sémantique." *Musurgia* 7 (2): 61–71.

Baudrillard, Jean. 1994. *Simulation and Simulacra.* Translated by S. Glaser. Ann Arbor: University of Michigan Press.

Baudry, Jean-Louis. (1970) 1974–75. "Ideological Effects of the Basic Cinematographic Apparatus." *Film Quarterly* 28 (2): 39–47.

Baudry, Jean-Louis. (1975) 1976. "The Apparatus." *Camera Obscura* 1 (1): 104–26.

Baudry, Jean-Louis. 1986. "The Apparatus: Metapsychological Approaches to the Impression of Reality in the Cinema." In *Narrative, Apparatus, Ideology,* edited by Philip Rosen, 299–318. New York: Columbia University Press.

Bazelon, Irwin. 1975. *Knowing the Score: Notes on Film Music.* New York: Arco.

Bazin, André. (1958–62) 2005. *What Is Cinema?* 2 vols. Translated by Hugh Grey. Berkeley: University of California Press.

Beck, Jay. 2016. *Designing Sound: Audiovisual Aesthetics in 1970s American Cinema.* New Brunswick, NJ: Rutgers University Press.

Beck, Jay, and Tony Grajeda, eds. 2008. *Lowering the Boom: Critical Studies in Film Sound.* Urbana: University of Illinois Press.

Belton, John. 1992. "1950s Magnetic Sound: The Frozen Revolution." In *Sound Theory/Sound Practice,* edited by Rick Altman, 154–67. New York: Routledge.

Bhabha, Homi K. 1983. "The Other Question . . .." *Screen* 24 (6): 18–36.

Biancorosso, Giorgio. 2001. "Beginning Credits and Beyond: Music and the Cinematic Imagination." *Echo* 3 (1). http://www.echo.ucla.edu/Volume3-Issue1/biancorosso/biancorosso1.html.

Biancorosso, Giorgio. 2009. "The Harpist in the Closet: Film Music as Epistemological Joke." *Music and the Moving Image* 2 (3): 11–33.

Bogue, Ronald. 2003. *Deleuze on Cinema.* New York: Routledge.

Bonitzer, Pascal. (1971–72) 1990. "Off-Screen Space." Translated by Lindley Hanlon. In *Cahiers du Cinéma: 1969–1972,* edited by Nick Browne, 291–305. Cambridge, MA: Harvard University Press.

Bonitzer, Pascal. (1975) 1986. "The Silences of the Voice (*A propos* of *Mai 68* by Gudie Lawaetz)." In *Narrative, Technology, Ideology,* edited by Philip Rosen, 319–34. New York: Columbia University Press.

Bordwell, David. 1980. "The Musical Analogy." *Yale French Studies* 60: 141–56.

Bordwell, David. 1985. *Narration in the Fiction Film.* Madison: University of Wisconsin Press.

Bordwell, David. 1989. *Making Meaning: Inference and Rhetoric in the Interpretation of Cinema.* Cambridge, MA: Harvard University Press.

Bordwell, David. 1996. "Contemporary Film Studies and the Vicissitudes of Grand Theory." In *Post-Theory: Reconstructing Film Studies,* edited by David Bordwell and Noël Carroll, 3–36. Madison: University of Wisconsin Press.

Bordwell, David. 2005a. *Figures Traced in Light: On Cinematic Staging.* Berkeley: University of California Press.

Bordwell, David. 2005b. "Slavoj Žižek: Say Anything." *David Bordwell's Website on Cinema.* http://www.davidbordwell.net/essays/zizek.php.

Bordwell, David. 2006. *The Way Hollywood Tells It.* Berkeley: University of California Press.

Bordwell, David, and Noël Carroll, eds. 1996. *Post-Theory: Reconstructing Film Studies.* Madison: University of Wisconsin Press.

Born, Georgina, and David Hesmondhalgh, eds. 2000. *Western Music and Its Others: Difference, Representation, and Appropriation in Music.* Berkeley: University of California Press.

Branigan, Edward. 1992. *Narrative Comprehension and Film.* New York: Routledge.

Brett, Philip, Elizabeth Wood, and Gary Thomas, eds. 2006. *Queering the Pitch: The New Gay and Lesbian Musicology.* 2nd ed. New York: Routledge.

Bribitzer-Stull, Matthew. 2015. *Understanding the Leitmotif: From Wagner to Hollywood Film Music.* Cambridge: Cambridge University Press.

Brown, Royal S. 1994. *Overtones and Undertones: Reading Film Music.* Berkeley: University of California Press.

Browne, Nick, ed. 1990. *Cahiers du Cinéma: 1969–1972: The Politics of Representation.* Cambridge, MA: Harvard University Press.

Brownrigg, Mark. 2007. "Hearing Place: Film Music, Geography and Ethnicity." *International Journal of Media and Cultural Politics* 3 (3): 307–23.

Bryukhovetska, Olga. 2010. "'Dispositif' Theory: Returning to the Movie Theater." *Art It Magazine*, August 10. http://www.art-it.asia/u/admin_ed_columns_e/ apskOCMPV5ZwoJrGnvxf/.

Buhler, James. 2001. "Analytical and Interpretive Approaches to Film Music (II): Analysing Interactions of Music and Film." In *Film Music: Critical Approaches,* edited by Kevin Donnelly, 39–61. Edinburgh: Edinburgh University Press.

Buhler, James. 2008. "'Everybody Sing': Family and Social Harmony in the Hollywood Musical." In *A Family Affair,* edited by Murray Pomerance, 29–44. London: Wallflower Press.

Buhler, James. 2009. "Music and the Adult Ideal in A Nightmare on Elm Street." In *Music in the Horror Film,* edited by Neil Lerner, 168–86. New York: Routledge.

Buhler, James. 2010. "Wagnerian Motives: Narrative Integration and the Development of Silent Film Accompaniment, 1908–1913." In *Wagner and Cinema,* edited by Jeongwon Joe and Sander L. Gilman, 27–45. Bloomington: Indiana University Press.

Buhler, James. 2013. "The Agitated Allegro as Music for Silent Film: Origins, Nature, Uses and Construction." In *Studies in Honor of Eugene Narmour,* edited by Lawrence Bernstein and Lex Rozin, 25–55. New York: Pendragon.

Buhler, James. 2014a. "Ontological, Formal, and Critical Theories of Film Music and Sound." In *The Oxford Handbook of Film Music Studies,* edited by David Neumeyer, 188–225. Oxford and New York: Oxford University Press.

Buhler, James. 2014b. "Gender, Sexuality, and the Soundtrack." In *The Oxford Handbook of Film Music Studies,* edited by David Neumeyer, 366–82. Oxford and New York: Oxford University Press.

Buhler, James. 2014c. "Psychoanalysis, Apparatus Theory, and Subjectivity." In *The Oxford Handbook of Film Music Studies,* edited by David Neumeyer, 383–417. Oxford and New York: Oxford University Press.

Buhler, James. 2017. "Branding the Franchise: Music, Opening Credits, and the (Corporate) Myth of Origin." In *Epic Music in Film,* edited by Stephen Meyer, 3–26. New York: Routledge.

Buhler, James, Caryl Flinn, and David Neumeyer, eds. 2000. *Music and Cinema.* Hanover, NH: Wesleyan University Press.

Buhler, James, and David Neumeyer. 1994. "Review of Caryl Flinn, *Strains of Utopia* and Kathryn Kalinak, *Settling the Score.*" *Journal of the American Musicological Society* 47 (2): 364–85.

Buhler, James, and David Neumeyer. 2005. "Music—Sound—Narrative: Analyzing *Casablanca.*" In *Interdisciplinary Studies in Musicology* 5, edited by Maciej Jablonski and Michael Klein, 279–93. Poznan, Poland: Rhytmos.

Buhler, James, and David Neumeyer. 2016. *Hearing the Movies: Music and Sound in Film History.* 2nd ed. New York: Oxford University Press.

Buhler, James, David Neumeyer, and Rob Deemer. 2010. *Hearing the Movies: Music and Sound in Film History.* New York: Oxford University Press.

Buhler, James, and Alex Newton. 2013. "Outside the Law of Action: Music and Sound in the Bourne Trilogy." In *The Oxford Handbook of Sound and Image in Digital Media,* edited by Carol Vernallis, John Richardson, and Amy Herzog, 325–49. New York: Oxford University Press.

Burch, Noël. 1981. *Theory of Film Practice.* Princeton, NJ: Princeton University Press.

Burnand, David, and Benedict Sarnaker. 1999. "The Articulation of National Identity through Film Music." *National Identities* 1 (1): 7–13.

Burt, George. 1994. *The Art of Film Music: Special Emphasis on Hugo Friedhofer, Alex North, David Raksin, Leonard Rosenman.* Boston: Northeastern University Press.

Butler, Judith. 1990. *Gender Trouble: Feminism and the Subversion of Identity.* New York: Routledge.

Carroll, Noël. 1978. "Lang, Pabst and Sound." *Cine-Tracts* 2 (1): 15–23.

Carroll, Noël. 1986. "Notes on Movie Music." *Studies in the Literary Imagination* 19 (1): 73–81.

Carroll, Noël. 1988. *Mystifying the Movies: Fads and Fallacies in Contemporary Film Theory.* New York: Columbia University Press.

Carroll, Noël. 1996a. *Theorizing the Moving Image.* Cambridge: Cambridge University Press.

Carroll, Noël. 1996b. "Prospects for Film Theory: A Personal Assessment." In *Post-Theory: Reconstructing Film Studies,* edited by David Bordwell and Noël Carroll, 37–68. Madison: University of Wisconsin Press.

Casanelles, Sergi. 2016. "Mixing as a Hyperorchestration Tool." In *The Palgrave Handbook of Sound and Music in Screen Media: Integrated Soundtracks,* edited by Liz Greene and Danijela Kulezic-Wilson, 57–72. London: Palgrave Macmillan.

Casetti, Francesco. 1999. *Theories of Cinema, 1945–1995.* Austin: University of Texas Press.

Cavalcanti, Alberto. 1939. "Sound in Films." *Films* 1 (1): 25–39.

Cavell, Stanley. 1979. *The World Viewed: Reflections on the Ontology of Film.* Enlarged ed. Cambridge, MA: Harvard University Press.

Celeste, Reni. 2007. "The Frozen Screen: Levinas and the Action Film." *Film-Philosophy* 11 (2): 15–36.

Chatman, Seymour. 1980. *Story and Discourse: Narrative and Structure in Fiction and Film.* Ithaca, NY: Cornell University Press.

Cheng, Anne Anlin. 2000. *The Melancholy of Race: Psychoanalysis, Assimilation, and Hidden Grief.* New York: Oxford University Press.

Chion, Michel. (1982) 1999. *The Voice in the Cinema.* Translated by Claudia Gorbman. New York: Columbia University Press.

Chion, Michel. (1990) 1994. *Audio-Vision: Sound on Screen.* Translated by Claudia Gorbman. New York: Columbia University Press.

Chion, Michel. 1991. "Quiet Revolution . . . or Rigid Stagnation." Translated by Ben Brewster. *October* 58: 69–80.

Chion, Michel. (2003) 2009. *Film, a Sound Art.* Translated by Claudia Gorbman. New York: Columbia University Press.

Clair, René. (1930) 1988. "Film Authors Don't Need You." In *French Film Theory and Criticism, vol. II: 1929–1939,* edited by Richard Abel, 57–60. Princeton, NJ: Princeton University Press.

Cohen, Annabel J. 2013. "Congruence-Association Model of Music and Multimedia: Origin and Evolution." In *The Psychology of Music in Multimedia,* edited by Siu-Lan Tan, Annabel Cohen, Scott D. Lipscomb, and Roger Kendall, 17–47. New York: Oxford University Press.

Cohen, Annabel J. 2014. "Film Music from the Perspective of Cognitive Science." In *The Oxford Handbook of Film Music Studies*, edited by David Neumeyer, 96–130. New York: Oxford University Press.

Comolli, Jean-Louis. (1971) 1986. "Technique and Ideology: Camera, Perspective, Depth of View [Parts 3 and 4]." In *Narrative, Technology, Ideology*, edited by Philip Rosen, 421–43. Originally published as Part III: "Pour la première fois." *Cahiers du cinéma*, no. 231 (August–September 1971): 42–50; Part IV: "La profondeur du champ 'primitive.'" *Cahiers du cinéma*, no. 233 (November 1971): 39–45.

Comolli, Jean-Louis. (1971) 1990. "Technique and Ideology [Parts 1 and 2]: Camera. Perspective, Depth of Field." Translated by Diana Matias. In *Cahiers du Cinéma: 1969–1972: The Politics of Representation*, edited by Nick Browne, 213–47. Cambridge, MA: Harvard University Press.

Comolli, Jean-Louis. 1971–72. "Technique et Idéologie (5): Caméra, perspective, perfondeur de champ." *Cahiers du Cinéma* 234–35 (December–February): 94–100.

Comolli, Jean-Louis. 1972. "Technique et idéologie, 6: Quelle parole?" *Cahiers du cinéma* 241 (September–October): 20–24.

Comolli, Jean-Louis. 1980. "Machines of the Visible." In *The Cinematic Apparatus*, edited by Teresa de Lauretis and Stephen Heath, 121–42. Milwaukee: MacMillan Press.

Comolli, Jean-Louis, and Jean Narboni. 1971a. "Cinema/Ideology/Criticism." *Screen* 12 (1): 27–36.

Comolli, Jean-Louis, and Jean Narboni. 1971b. "Cinema/Ideology/Criticism (2)." *Screen* 12 (2): 145–55.

Comolli, Jean-Louis, and Jean Narboni. 1972. "Cinema/Ideology/Criticism 2 Continued." *Screen* 13 (1): 120–31.

Cook, Nicholas. 1998. *Analysing Musical Multimedia*. New York: Oxford University Press.

Cooke, Deryck. 1959. *The Language of Music*. London and New York: Oxford University Press.

Cooke, Mervyn, ed. 2010. *The Hollywood Film Music Reader*. New York: Oxford University Press.

Copjec, Joan. 1989. "The Orthopsychic Subject: Film Theory and the Reception of Lacan." *October* 49: 53–71.

Copjec, Joan. 1994. *Read My Desire: Lacan against the Historicists*. Cambridge, MA: MIT Press.

Copland, Aaron. 2010a. "*Our New Music* (1941)." In *The Hollywood Film Music Reader*, edited by Mervyn Cooke, 83–91. New York: Oxford University Press.

Copland, Aaron. 2010b. "Aaron Copland in the Film Studio (1949)." In *The Hollywood Film Music Reader*, edited by Mervyn Cooke, 317–26. New York: Oxford University Press.

Dancy, Jonathan. 1985. *Introduction to Contemporary Epistemology*. London: Wiley-Blackwell.

Davis, Glyn. 2008. "Hearing Queerly: Television's Dissident Sonics." In *Queer TV: Theories, Histories, Politics*, edited by Glyn Davis and Gary Needham, 172–87. Hoboken, NJ: Routledge.

Davy, Charles, ed. 1937. *Footnotes to the Film*. New York: Oxford University Press.

Dayan, Daniel. 1974. "The Tutor-Code of Classical Cinema." *Film Quarterly* 28 (1): 22–31.

Deaville, James. 2006. "The Topos of 'Evil Medieval' in American Horror Film Music." In *Music, Meaning and Media*, edited by Erkki Pekkilä, David Neumeyer, and Richard Littlefield, 26–37. Imatra: International Semiotics Institute.

Deleuze, Gilles. (1983) 1986. *Cinema 1: The Movement-Image.* Minneapolis: University of Minnesota Press.

Deleuze, Gilles. (1985) 1989. *Cinema 2: The Time-Image.* Minneapolis: University of Minnesota Press.

Dienstfrey, Eric. 2016. "The Myth of the Speakers: A Critical Reexamination of Dolby History." *Film History* 28 (1): 167–93.

Doane, Mary Ann. 1980a. "The Voice in the Cinema: The Articulation of Body and Space." *Yale French Studies* 60: 33–50.

Doane, Mary Ann. 1980b. "Ideology and the Practice of Sound Editing and Mixing." In *The Cinematic Apparatus,* edited by Teresa de Lauretis and Stephen Heath, 47–56. Milwaukee: MacMillan Press.

Doane, Mary Ann. 1987. *The Desire to Desire: The Woman's Film of the 1940s.* Bloomington: Indiana University Press.

Doane, Mary Ann. 2002. *The Emergence of Cinematic Time: Modernity, Contingency, the Archive.* Cambridge, MA: Harvard University Press.

Dolar, Mladen. 2006. *A Voice and Nothing More.* Cambridge, MA: MIT Press.

Donnelly, Kevin J. 2013. "Extending Film Aesthetics: Audio beyond Visuals." In *The Oxford Handbook of New Audiovisual Aesthetics,* edited by John Richardson, Claudia Gorbman, and Carol Vernallis, 357–71. New York: Oxford University Press.

Donnelly, Kevin J. 2014. *Occult Aesthetics: Synchronization in Sound Film.* New York: Oxford University Press.

Doolittle, Hilda [H. D.]. 1927. "The Cinema and the Classics: I. Beauty." *Close Up* 1 (1): 22–33.

Doty, Alexander. 1993. *Making Things Perfectly Queer: Interpreting Mass Culture.* Minneapolis: University of Minnesota Press.

Doty, Alexander. 1998. "Queer Theory." In *Oxford Guide to Film Studies,* edited by John Hill and Pamela Church Gibson, 148–52. New York: Oxford University Press.

Doughty, Ruth. 2009. "African American Film Sound: Scoring Blackness." In *Sound and Music in Film and Visual Media: An Overview,* edited by Graeme Harper, Ruth Doughty, and Jochen Eisentraut, 325–39. New York: Continuum.

During, Simon, ed. 1999. *Cultural Studies Reader.* 2nd ed. London: Routledge.

Dyer, Richard. 1993. *The Matter of Images: Essays on Representation.* New York: Routledge.

Eagleton, Terry. 1990. *The Ideology of the Aesthetic.* Cambridge, MA: Basil Blackwood.

Eco, Umberto. 1979. *A Theory of Semiotics.* Bloomington: Indiana University Press.

Edison, Thomas. 1888. [Caveat] Handwritten Caveat 110, filed 17 October 1888 (PT031AAA; TAEM 113:236).

Eisenstein, Sergei. (1942) 1975. *The Film Sense.* Revised ed. Translated by Jay Leyda. New York: Harcourt Brace.

Eisenstein, Sergei. 1949. *Film Form: Essays in Film Theory.* Translated by Jay Leyda. New York: Harcourt Brace.

Eisenstein, Sergei. 1988. *Selected Works, vol. 1: Writings, 1922–1934.* Edited and translated by Richard Taylor. London: BFI Publishing.

Eisenstein, Sergei. 1991. *Selected Works, vol. 2: Towards a Theory of Montage.* Edited by Michael Glenny and Richard Taylor, translated by Michael Glenny. London: BFI Publishing.

Eisenstein, Sergei, Vsevolod Pudovkin, and Grigori Alexandrov. (1928) 1988. "Statement on Sound." In Eisenstein, *Selected Works, vol. 1: Writings, 1922–1934.* Edited and translated by Richard Taylor. London: BFI Publishing.

Eisler, Hanns [and Theodor W. Adorno]. 1947. *Composing for the Films.* New York: Oxford University Press.

Elsaesser, Thomas. 2013. "Digital Cinema: Convergence or Contradiction?" In *The Oxford Handbook of Sound and Image in Digital Media*, edited by Carol Vernallis, John Richardson, and Amy Herzog, 13–44. New York: Oxford University Press.

Erdmann, Hans, and Giuseppe Becce, with Ludwig Brav. 1927. *Allgemeines Handbuch der Film-Musik.* 2 vols. Berlin-Lichterfelde: Schlesinger.

Farmer, Brett. 2005. "The Fabulous Sublimity of Gay Diva Worship." *Camera Obscura* 20 (2): 165–95.

Faulkner, Robert R. 1971. *Hollywood Studio Musicians: Their Work and Careers in the Recording Industry.* Chicago: Aldine-Atherton.

Faulkner, Robert R. 1983. *Music on Demand: Composers and Careers in the Hollywood Film Industry.* New Brunswick, NJ: Transaction Publishers.

Feuer, Jane. 1993. *The Hollywood Musical.* 2nd ed. Bloomington: Indiana University Press.

Flinn, Caryl. 1992. *Strains of Utopia: Gender, Nostalgia, and Hollywood Film Music.* Princeton, NJ: Princeton University Press.

Gabbard, Krin. 1996. *Jammin' at the Margins: Jazz and the American Cinema.* Chicago: University of Chicago Press.

Gaines, Jane, and Neil Lerner. 2001. "The Orchestration of Affect: The Motif of Barbarism in Breil's *The Birth of a Notion* Score." In *The Sounds of Early Cinema*, edited by Richard Abel and Rick Altman, 252–68. Bloomington: Indiana University Press.

Gaudreault, André, and Philippe Marion. 2015. *The End of Cinema? A Medium in Crisis in the Digital Age.* New York: Columbia University Press.

Genette, Gérard. 1980. *Narrative Discourse: An Essay in Method.* Ithaca, NY: Cornell University Press.

Genette, Gérard. 1988. *Narrative Discourse Revisited.* Ithaca, NY: Cornell University Press.

Girard, René. (1972) 1977. *Violence and the Sacred.* Translated by Patrick Gregory. Baltimore: Johns Hopkins University Press.

Goldmark, Daniel. 2014. "Drawing a New Narrative for Cartoon Music." In *The Oxford Handbook of Film Music Studies*, edited by David Neumeyer, 229–44. Oxford and New York: Oxford University Press.

Goldmark, Daniel, Lawrence Kramer, and Richard Leppert, eds. 2007. *Beyond the Soundtrack: Representing Music in Cinema.* Berkeley: University of California Press.

Gorbman, Claudia. 1987. *Unheard Melodies: Narrative Film Music.* Bloomington: Indiana University Press.

Gorbman, Claudia. 1991. "Hanns Eisler in Hollywood." *Screen* 32 (3): 272–85.

Gorbman, Claudia. 2000. "Scoring the Indian: Music in the Liberal Western." In *Western Music and Its Others*, edited by Georgina Born and David Hesmondhalgh, 234–53. Berkeley: University of California Press.

Gorbman, Claudia. 2001. "Drums along the L. A. River: Scoring the Indian." In *Westerns: Films through History*, edited by Janet Walker, 177–95. New York: Routledge University Press.

Gorbman, Claudia. 2004. "Aesthetics and Rhetoric." *American Music* 22 (1): 14–26.

Green, Fitzhugh. 1929. *Film Finds Its Tongue.* New York: G. P. Putnam's Sons.

Greenberg, Harvey R., and Krin Gabbard. 1990. "Reel Significations: An Anatomy of Psychoanalytic Film Criticism." *Psychoanalytic Review* 77 (1): 89–110.

Greene, Liz, and Danijela Kulezic-Wilson, eds. 2016. *The Palgrave Handbook of Sound Design and Music in Screen Media: Integrated Soundtracks*. London: Palgrave Macmillan.

Gross, Larry. 1995. "Big and Loud." *Sight and Sound* 5 (8): 6–10.

Gross, Robert F. 1995. "Consuming Hart: Sublimity and Gay Poetics in *Suddenly Last Summer*." *Theatre Journal* 47 (2): 229–51.

Gunning, Tom. 2001. "Doing for the Eye What the Phonograph Does for the Ear." In *The Sounds of Early Cinema*, edited by Richard Abel and Rick Altman, 13–31. Bloomington: Indiana University Press.

Gunning, Tom. 2006. "Gollum and Golem: Special Effects and the Technology of Artificial Bodies." In *From Hobbits to Hollywood: Essays on Peter Jackson's* Lord of the Rings, edited by Ernest Mathijs and Murray Pomerance, 319–49. Amsterdam and New York: Rodopi.

Gunning, Tom. 2007. "Moving Away from the Index: Cinema and the Impression of Reality." *Differences* 18 (1): 29–52.

Halfyard, Janet, ed. 2012. *The Music of Fantasy Cinema*. London: Equinox Publishing.

Halfyard, Janet. 2013. "Cue the Big Theme? The Sound of the Superhero." In *The Oxford Handbook of New Audiovisual Aesthetics*, edited by John Richardson, Claudia Gorbman, and Carol Vernallis, 171–93. New York: Oxford University Press.

Hall, Stuart. (1976) 1999. "Encoding, Decoding." In *The Cultural Studies Reader*, 2nd ed., edited by Simon During, 507–17. London: Routledge.

Hall, Stuart. 1985. "Signification, Representation, Ideology: Althusser and the Post-Structuralist Debate." *Critical Studies in Mass Communication* 2: 91–114.

Hanson, Ellis. 1999. "Introduction." In *Outtakes: Essays in Queer Theory and Film*, edited by Ellis Hansen, 1–20. Durham, NC: Duke University Press.

Harpham, Geoffrey Galt. 2003. "Doing the Impossible: Slavoj Žižek and the End of Knowledge." *Critical Inquiry* 29 (3): 453–85.

Hatten, Robert S. 1994. *Musical Meaning in Beethoven: Markedness, Correlation, and Interpretation*. Bloomington: Indiana University Press.

Hatten, Robert S. 2004. *Interpreting Musical Gesture, Topics and Tropes: Mozart, Beethoven, Schubert*. Bloomington: Indiana University Press.

Hayward, Philip. 1997. "Danger Retro-Affectivity! The Cultural Career of the Theremin." *Convergence* 3 (4): 28–53.

Hayward, Philip, ed. 2004. *Off the Planet: Music, Sound and Science Fiction Cinema*. Eastleigh: John Libbey Publishing.

Hayward, Philip, ed. 2006. *Terror Tracks: Music, Sound, and Horror Cinema*. London: Equinox Publishing.

Heath, Stephen. 1977–78. "Notes on Suture." *Screen* 18 (4): 48–76.

Heath, Stephen. 1981. *Questions of Cinema*. Bloomington: Indiana University Press.

Heldt, Guido. 2013. *Music and Levels of Narration in Film: Steps across the Border*. Bristol: Intellect.

Hill, John, and Pamela Church Gibson, eds. 1998. *Oxford Guide to Film Studies*. New York: Oxford University Press.

Hitchcock, Alfred. 1937. "Direction." In *Footnotes to the Film*, edited by Charles Davy, 3–15. New York: Oxford University Press.

Holman, Tomlinson. 2002. *Sound for Film and Television*. 2nd ed. Los Angeles: Focal Press.

Hopkins, Edwin. 1928. "Re-Vocalized Films." *Transactions of the Society of Motion Picture Engineers* 12–35: 845–52.

Hubbert, Julie, ed. 2011. *Celluloid Symphonies: Texts and Contexts in Film Music History*. Berkeley: University of California Press.

Jacobs, Lea. 2015. *Film Rhythm after Sound: Technology, Music, and Performance*. Berkeley: University of California Press.

Jacobs, Lewis. 1977. "Introduction." In Harry Alan Potamkin, *The Compound Cinema: The Film Writings of Harry Alan Potamkin*, xxv–xliii. Edited by Lewis Jacobs. New York: Teachers College Press.

Jagose, Annamarie. 1996. *Queer Theory: An Introduction*. New York: New York University Press.

Jameson, Fredric. 1981. *The Political Unconscious: Narrative as a Socially Symbolic Act*. Ithaca, NY: Cornell University Press.

Jaubert, Maurice. (1936) 1988. "The Cinema: Music." In *French Film Theory and Criticism, vol. II: 1929–1939*, edited by Richard Abel, 206–11. Princeton, NJ: Princeton University Press.

Jaubert, Maurice. 1937. "Music on the Screen." In *Footnotes to the Film*, edited by Charles Davy, 101–15. New York: Oxford University Press.

Jenkins, Henry. 2006. *Convergence Culture: Where Old and New Media Collide*. New York: New York University Press.

Joe, Jeongwon, and Sander L. Gilman, eds. 2010. *Wagner and Cinema*. Bloomington: Indiana University Press.

Johnson, Albert. 1960. "[Review of] *Suddenly, Last Summer*." *Film Quarterly* 13 (3): 40–42.

Johnson, Russell. 2017. "'Better Gestures,' A Disability History Perspective on the Transition from (Silent) Movies to Talkies in the United States." *Journal of Social History* 51 (1): 1–26.

Johnston, Claire. 1976. "Towards a Feminist Film Practice: Some Theses." *Edinburgh Magazine* 1: 50–59.

Kalinak, Kathryn. 1992. *Settling the Score: Music and the Classical Hollywood Film*. Madison: University of Wisconsin Press.

Kalinak, Kathryn. 2001. "How the West Was Sung." In *Westerns: Films through History*, edited by Janet Walker, 151–76. New York: Routledge.

Kalinak, Kathryn. 2007. *How the West Was Sung: Music in the Westerns of John Ford*. Berkeley: University of California Press.

Kaplan, E. Ann. 1983. *Women and Film: Both Sides of the Camera*. New York: Methuen.

Kaplan, E. Ann. (1983) 2000. "Is the Gaze Male?" In *Feminism and Film*, edited by E. Ann Kaplan, 119–38. New York: Oxford University Press.

Karlin, Fred, and Rayburn Wright. 1990. *On the Track: A Guide to Contemporary Film Scoring*. New York: Schirmer.

Kassabian, Anahid. 2001. *Hearing Film: Tracking Identifications in Hollywood Film Music*. New York: Routledge, 2001.

Kassabian, Anahid. 2008. "Rethinking Point of Audition in The Cell." In *Lowering the Boom: Critical Studies in Film Sound*, edited by Jay Beck and Tony Grajeda, 299–305. Urbana: University of Illinois Press.

Kerins, Mark. 2011. *Beyond Dolby (Stereo): Cinema in the Digital Age*. Bloomington: Indiana University Press.

King, Geoff. 2002. *New Hollywood Cinema: An Introduction*. New York: Columbia University Press.

Kivy, Peter. 1990. *Music Alone: Philosophical Reflections on the Purely Musical Experience*. Ithaca, NY: Cornell University Press.

Knapp, Lucretia. 1993. "The Queer Voice in 'Marnie.'" *Cinema Journal* 32 (4): 6–23.

Knapp, Raymond. 2006a. *The American Musical and the Formation of National Identity*. Princeton, NJ: Princeton University Press.

Knapp, Raymond. 2006b. *The American Musical and the Performance of Personal Identity*. Princeton, NJ: Princeton University Press.

Kozloff, Sarah. 1988. *Invisible Storytellers: Voice-Over Narration in American Fiction Film*. Berkeley: University of California Press.

Kozloff, Sarah. 2000. *Overhearing Film Dialogue*. Berkeley: University of California Press.

Kracauer, Siegfried. (1960) 1997. *Theory of Film: The Redemption of Physical Reality*. Princeton, NJ: Princeton University Press.

Kraft, James P. 1996. *Stage to Studio: Musicians and the Sound Revolution, 1890–1950*. Baltimore: Johns Hopkins University Press.

Kramer, Lawrence. 2014. "Classical Music, Virtual Bodies, Narrative Film." In *The Oxford Handbook of Film Music Studies*, edited by David Neumeyer, 351–65. Oxford and New York: Oxford University Press.

Lacan, Jacques. (1949) 1968. "The Mirror-Phase as Formative of the Function of the I." *New Left Review* 51: 71–77.

Lacan, Jacques. (1975) 1998. *On Feminine Sexuality: The Limits of Love and Knowledge. Encore: the Seminar of Jacques Lacan, Book XX*. Translated by Bruce Fink. New York: W. W. Norton.

Laing, Heather. 2007. *The Gendered Score: Music in 1940s Melodrama and the Woman's Film*. Aldershot: Ashgate.

Lastra, James. 1992. "Reading, Writing, and Representing Sound." In *Sound Theory/Sound Practice*, edited by Rick Altman, 65–86. New York: Routledge.

Lastra, James. 2000. *Sound Technology and the American Cinema: Perception, Representation, Modernity*. New York: Columbia University Press.

Lastra, James. 2008. "Film and the Wagnerian Aspiration: Thoughts on Sound Design and the History of the Senses." In *Lowering the Boom: Critical Studies in Film Sound*, edited by Jay Beck and Tony Grajeda, 123–38. Urbana: University of Illinois Press.

Lauretis, Teresa de, and Stephen Heath, eds. 1980. *The Cinematic Apparatus*. Milwaukee: MacMillan Press.

Lawrence, Amy. 1991. *Echo and Narcissus: Women's Voices in Classical Hollywood Cinema*. Berkeley: University of California Press.

Lebel, Jean-Patrick. 1971. *Cinéma et idéologie*. Paris: Editions Sociales.

LeBlanc, Michael. 2006. "Melancholic Arrangements: Music, Queer Melodrama, and the Seeds of Transformation in *The Hours*." *Camera Obscura* 21 (1): 105–45.

Lehman, Frank. 2017a. "Manufacturing the Epic Score: Hans Zimmer and the Sounds of Significance." In *Music in Epic Film: Listening to Spectacle*, edited by Stephen Meyer, 27–55. New York: Routledge.

Lehman, Frank. 2017b. "Methods and Challenges of Analyzing Screen Media." In *The Routledge Companion to Screen Music and Sound*, edited by Miguel Mera, Ron Sadoff, and Ben Winters, 497–516. New York: Routledge.

Lehrdahl, Fred, and Ray Jackendoff. 1983. *A Generative Theory of Tonal Music*. Cambridge, MA: MIT Press.

Lerner, Neil. 2001. "Copland's Music of Wide Open Spaces: Surveying the Pastoral Trope in Hollywood." *Musical Quarterly* 85 (3): 477–515.

Lerner, Neil, ed. 2009. *Music in the Horror Film: Listening to Fear*. New York: Routledge.

Levin, Tom. 1984. "The Acoustic Dimension: Notes on Cinema Sound." *Screen* 25 (3): 55–68.

Leydon, Rebecca. 2004. "*Forbidden Planet* Effects and Affects in the Electro Avant-garde." In *Off the Planet: Music, Sound and Science Fiction Cinema*, edited by Philip Hayward, 61–76. Eastleigh: John Libbey Publishing.

Lidov, David. 2005. *Is Language a Music? Writings on Musical Form and Signification*. Bloomington: Indiana University Press.

Lindsay, Vachel. 1916. *The Art of the Moving Picture*. New York: MacMillan.

Locke, Ralph. 2009. *Musical Exoticism: Images and Reflections*. Cambridge: Cambridge University Press.

London, Kurt. 1936. *Film Music: A Summary of the Characteristic Features of Its History, Aesthetics, Technique, and Possible Developments*. London: Faber and Faber.

Lott, Eric. 1995. *Love and Theft: Blackface Minstrelsy and the American Working Class*. New York: Oxford University Press.

Lowe, Donald M. 1982. *History of Bourgeois Perception*. Chicago: University of Chicago Press.

Manovich, Lev. 2001. *The Language of New Media*. Cambridge, MA: MIT Press.

Manvell, Roger, and John Huntley. 1957. *The Technique of Film Music*. London: Focus Press.

Marshall, S. K., and A. Cohen. 1988. "Effects of Musical Soundtracks on Attitudes to Geometric Figures." *Music Perception* 6: 95–112.

Martin, Wallace. 1986. *Recent Theories of Narrative*. Ithaca, NY: Cornell University Press.

Mast, Gerald. 1983. *Film/Cinema/Movie: A Theory of Experience.* Chicago: University of Chicago Press.

McClary, Susan. 2007. "Minima Romantica." In *Beyond the Soundtrack: Representing Music in Cinema*, edited by Daniel Goldmark, Lawrence Kramer, and Richard Leppert, 48–65. Berkeley: University of California Press.

McGowan, Todd. 2003. "Looking for the Gaze: Lacanian Film Theory and Its Vicissitudes." *Cinema Journal* 42 (3): 27–47.

McGowan, Todd. 2007. *The Real Gaze: Film Theory after Lacan*. Albany, NY: SUNY Press.

Mera, Miguel. 2016. "Towards 3-D Sound: Spatial Presence and the Space Vacuum." In *The Palgrave Handbook of Sound Design and Music in Screen Media: Integrated Soundtracks*, edited by Liz Greene and Danijela Kulezic-Wilson, 91–111. London: Palgrave Macmillan.

Mera, Miguel, Ron Sadoff, and Ben Winters, eds. 2017. *The Routledge Companion to Screen Music and Sound*. New York: Routledge.

Metz, Christian. (1968) 1974a. *Film Language: A Semiotics of the Cinema*. Translated by Michael Taylor. Chicago: University of Chicago Press.

Metz, Christian. 1974b. *Language and Cinema*. Translated by Donna Jean Umiker-Sebeok. The Hague: Mouton.

Metz, Christian. (1977) 1982. *The Imaginary Signifier: Psychoanalysis and the Cinema*. Translated by Celia Britton, Annwyl Williams, Ben Brewster, and Alfred Guzzetti. Bloomington: Indiana University Press.

Metz, Christian. 1980. "Aural Objects." *Yale French Studies* 60: 24–32.

Meyer, Stephen, ed. 2016. *Music in Epic Film: Listening to Spectacle.* New York: Routledge.

Miller, D. A. 1990. "Anal Rope." *Representations* 32: 114–33.

Miller, D. A. 1997. "Visual Pleasure in 1959." *October* 81: 34–58.

Mirka, Danuta, ed. 2014. *The Oxford Handbook of Topic Theory.* New York: Oxford University Press.

Mitchell, Juliet. 1982. "Introduction—I." In *Feminine Sexuality: Jacques Lacan and the école freudienne,* edited by Juliet Mitchell and Jacqueline Rose, 1–26. New York: W. W. Norton.

Mitry, Jean. (1963) 1997. *The Aesthetics and Psychology of the Cinema.* Translated by Christopher King. Bloomington: Indiana University Press.

Mitry, Jean. 2000. *Semiotics and the Analysis of Film.* Translated by Christopher King. Bloomington: Indiana University Press.

Monelle, Raymond. 2006. *The Musical Topic: Hunt, Military and Pastoral.* Bloomington: Indiana University Press.

Morris, Mitchell. 2004. "Cabaret, America's Weimar, and Mythologies of the Gay Subject." *American Music* 22 (1): 145–57.

Mulvey, Laura. 1975. "Visual Pleasure and Narrative Cinema." *Screen* 16 (3): 6–18.

Munsterberg, Hugo. 1916. *The Photoplay: A Psychological Study.* New York: D. Appleton and Co.

Nattiez, Jean-Jacques. 1990a. *Music and Discourse: Toward a Semiology of Music.* Translated by Carolyn Abbate. Princeton, NJ: Princeton University Press.

Nattiez, Jean-Jacques. 1990b. "Can One Speak of Narrativity in Music?" *Journal of the Royal Musical Association* 115: 240–57.

Neale, Stephen. 1985. *Cinema and Technology: Image, Sound, Colour.* Bloomington: Indiana University Press.

Neumeyer, David. 2009. "Diegetic/Nondiegetic: A Theoretical Model." *Music and the Moving Image* 2 (1): 26–39.

Neumeyer, David, ed. 2014. *The Oxford Handbook of Film Music Studies.* Oxford and New York: Oxford University Press.

Neumeyer, David. 2015. *Meaning and Interpretation of Music in Cinema.* Bloomington: Indiana University Press.

Neumeyer, David, and James Buhler. 2008. "*Composing for the Films,* Modern Soundtrack Theory, and the Difficult Case of *A Scandal in Paris.*" *Eisler-Studien* 3: 123–41.

Newton, Alex. 2015. "Semiotics of Music, Semiotics of Sound, and Film: Toward a Theory of Acousticons." PhD diss., University of Texas at Austin.

Nichols, Bill. 1992. "Form Wars: The Political Unconscious of Formalist Theory." In *Classical Hollywood Narrative: The Paradigm Wars,* edited by Jane Gaines, 49–77. Durham, NC: Duke University Press.

Ohi, Kevin. 1999. "Devouring Creation: Cannibalism, Sodomy, and the Scene of Analysis in *Suddenly, Last Summer.*" *Cinema Journal* 38 (3): 27–49.

Oudart, Jean-Pierre. (1969) 1977–78. "Cinema and Suture." *Screen* 18 (4): 35–47.

Parakilas, James. 1998. "How Spain Got Its Soul." In *The Exotic in Western Music,* edited by Jonathan Bellman, 137–93. Boston: Northeastern University Press.

Percheron, Daniel. 1980. "Sound in Cinema and Its Relationship to Image and Diegesis." *Yale French Studies* 60: 16–23.

Pisani, Michael. 2005. *Imagining Native America in Music.* New Haven, CT: Yale University Press.

Pleynet, Marcelin, and Jean Thibaudeau. (1969) 1978. "Economic—Ideological—Formal." In *May '68 and Film Culture,* edited by Sylvia Harvey, 149–64. London: British Film Institute.

Potamkin, Harry Alan. 1929a. "Music and the Movies." *Musical Quarterly* 15 (2): 281–96.

Potamkin, Harry Alan. 1929b. "The Compound Cinema." *Close Up* 4 (1): 32–37.

Potamkin, Harry Alan. 1929c. "The English Cinema." *Close Up* 4 (3): 17–28.

Potamkin, Harry Alan. 1929d. "The Compound Cinema: Further Notes." *Close Up* 4 (4): 10–17.

Potamkin, Harry Alan. 1929e. "Phases of Cinema Unity." *Close Up* 4 (5): 27–38.

Potamkin, Harry Alan. 1929f. "The French Cinema." *Close Up* 5 (1): 11–24.

Potamkin, Harry Alan. 1929g. "The Aframerican Cinema." *Close Up* 5 (2): 107–17.

Potamkin, Harry Alan. 1929h. "Phases of Cinema Unity III." *Close Up* 5 (3): 171–84.

Potamkin, Harry Alan. 1929i. "Kino and Lichtspiel." *Close Up* 5 (5): 387–98.

Potamkin, Harry Alan. 1929j. "Movie: New York Notes." *Close Up* 5 (6): 493–505.

Potamkin, Harry Alan. 1930a. "In the Land Where Images Mutter." *Close Up* 6 (1): 11–19.

Potamkin, Harry Alan. 1930b. "Movie: New York Notes." *Close Up* 6 (2): 98–113.

Potamkin, Harry Alan. 1930c. "Movie: New York Notes." *Close Up* 6 (3): 214–23.

Potamkin, Harry Alan. 1930d. "The Personality of the Player: A Phase of Unity." *Close Up* 6 (4): 290–97.

Potamkin, Harry Alan. 1930e. "Phases of Cinema Unity II." *Close Up* 6 (6): 463–74.

Potamkin, Harry Alan. 1930f. "Playing with Sound." *Close Up* 7 (2): 112–15.

Potamkin, Harry Alan. 1930g. "Movie: New York Notes." *Close Up* 7 (2): 115–19.

Potamkin, Harry Alan. 1930h. "Movie: New York Notes." *Close Up* 7 (4): 235–52.

Potamkin, Harry Alan. 1930i. "Film Novitiates, etc." *Close Up* 7 (5): 314–24.

Potamkin, Harry Alan. 1930j. "Reelife." *Close Up* 7 (6): 386–92.

Potamkin, Harry Alan. 1931a. "The New Kino." *Close Up* 8 (1): 64–70.

Potamkin, Harry Alan. 1931b. "Novel into Film." *Close Up* 8 (4): 267–79.

Potamkin, Harry Alan. 1932. "Dog Days in the Movie." *Close Up* 9 (4): 268–72.

Potamkin, Harry Alan. 1933. "The Year of the Eclipse." *Close Up* 10 (1): 30–39.

Potamkin, Harry Alan. 1977. *The Compound Cinema: The Film Writings of Harry Alan Potamkin.* Edited by Lewis Jacobs. New York: Teachers College Press, 1977.

Prendergast, Roy M. 1977. *Film Music: A Neglected Art.* New York: New York University Press.

Prince, Stephen. 1996. "Psychoanalytic Film Theory and the Problem of the Missing Spectator." In *Post-Theory: Reconstructing Film Studies,* edited by David Bordwell and Noël Carroll, 71–86. Madison: University of Wisconsin Press.

Propp, Vladimir. 1968. *Morphology of the Folktale.* 2nd ed. Austin: University of Texas Press.

Pudovkin, V. I. 1949a. *Film Technique.* In Pudovkin, *Film Technique and Film Acting: The Cinema Writings of V. I. Pudovkin.* Translated by Ivor Montagu. New York: Bonanza Books.

Pudovkin, V. I. 1949b. *Film Acting.* In Pudovkin, *Film Technique and Film Acting: The Cinema Writings of V. I. Pudovkin.* Translated by Ivor Montagu. New York: Bonanza Books.

Pudovkin, V. I. 1949c. *Film Technique and Film Acting: The Cinema Writings of V. I. Pudovkin.* Translated by Ivor Montagu. New York: Bonanza Books.

Rapée, Ernö. 1925. *Encyclopedia of Music for Pictures.* New York: Belwin.

Ratner, Leonard. 1980. *Classic Music.* New York: Schirmer Books.

Reisz, Karel. 1953. *The Technique of Film Editing.* London and New York: Focal Press.

Reyland, Nicholas. 2012. "The Beginnings of a Beautiful Friendship? Music Narratology and Screen Music Studies." *Music, Sound, and the Moving Image* 6 (1): 55–71.

Reyland, Nicholas. 2015. "Corporate Classicism and the Metaphysical Style: Affects, Effects, and Contexts of Two Recent Trends of Film Scoring." *Music, Sound, and the Moving Image* 9 (2): 115–30.

Rich, Adrienne. 1980. "Compulsory Heterosexuality and the Lesbian Experience." *Signs* 5 (4): 631–60.

Richardson, John, Claudia Gorbman, and Carol Vernallis, eds. 2013. *The Oxford Handbook of New Audiovisual Aesthetics*. New York: Oxford University Press.

Ricoeur, Paul. 1970. *Freud and Philosophy: An Essay on Interpretation*. New Haven, CT: Yale University Press.

Ringer, Alexander L. 1953. "The 'Chasse' as a Musical Topic of the 18th Century." *Journal of the American Musicological Society* 6 (2): 148–59.

Rodman, Ronald. 2010. *Tuning In: American Narrative Television Music*. New York: Oxford University Press.

Rodowick, David. 1997. *Gilles Deleuze's Time Machine*. Durham, NC: Duke University Press.

Rodowick, D. N., ed. 2010. *Afterimages of Gilles Deleuze's Film Philosophy*. Minneapolis: University of Minnesota Press.

Rogin, Michael. 1996. *Blackface, White Noise: Jewish Immigrants in the Hollywood Melting Pot*. Berkeley: University of California Press.

Rosen, Philip, ed. 1986. *Narrative, Technology, Ideology*. New York: Columbia University Press.

Rothman, William. 1975. "Controversy and Correspondence: Against 'The System of the Suture.'" *Film Quarterly* 29 (1): 45–50.

Sabaneev, Leonid. 1935. *Music for the Films: A Handbook for Composers and Conductors*. Translated by S. W. Pring. London: Pitman and Sons.

Said, Edward. 1993. *Culture and Imperialism*. New York: Alfred A. Knopf.

Schmidt, Lisa. 2010. "A Popular Avant-Garde: The Paradoxical Tradition of Electronic and Atonal Sounds in Sci-Fi Music Scoring." In *Light Years from Home: Music in Science Fiction Film*, edited by Mathew Bartkowiak, 23–41. Jefferson, NC: McFarland.

Schubert, Linda. 1998. "Plainchant in Motion Pictures: The Dies Irae in Film Scores." *Florilegium* 15: 207–29.

Sedgwick, Eve. 1990. *The Epistemology of the Closet*. Berkeley: University of California Press.

Seldes, Gilbert. 1928. "Movies Commit Suicide." *Harpers Magazine*, June, 706–12.

Seldes, Gilbert. 1929a. "Talkies' Progress." *Harpers Magazine*, September, 454–61.

Seldes, Gilbert. 1929b. "The Mobile Camera." *New Republic*, October 30, 298–99.

Seldes, Gilbert. 1929c. *An Hour with the Movies and the Talkies*. Philadelphia: J. B. Lippincott Company.

Shapiro, Ann Dhu. 1984. "Action Music in American Pantomime and Melodrama, 1730–1913." *American Music* 2 (4): 49–72.

Shaviro, Steven. 2012. "Post-Continuity: Full Text of My Talk." *Pinocchio Theory* (blog), March 26. http://www.shaviro.com/Blog/?p=1034.

Sheppard, Anthony. 2001. "An Exotic Enemy: Anti-Japanese Musical Propaganda in World War II Hollywood." *Journal of the American Musicological Society* 54 (2): 303–57.

Siegel, Janice. 2005. "Tennessee Williams' *Suddenly Last Summer* and Euripides' *Bacchae*." *International Journal of the Classical Tradition* 11 (4): 538–70.

Silverman, Kaja. 1983. *The Subject of Semiotics*. New York: Oxford University Press.

Silverman, Kaja. 1988. *The Acoustic Mirror: The Female Voice in Psychoanalysis and Cinema.* Bloomington: Indiana University Press.

Sjogren, Britta. 2006. *Into the Vortex: Female Voice and Paradox in Film.* Urbana: University of Illinois Press.

Slowik, Michael. 2014. *After the Silents: Hollywood Film Music in the Early Sound Era, 1926– 1934.* New York: Columbia University Press.

Smelik, Anneke. 1998. "Gay and Lesbian Criticism." In *Oxford Guide to Film Studies,* edited by John Hill and Pamela Church Gibson, 135–47. New York: Oxford University Press.

Smith, Jeff. 1996. "Unheard Melodies? A Critique of Psychoanalytic Theories of Film Music." In *Post-Theory: Reconstructing Film Studies,* edited by David Bordwell and Noël Carroll, 230–47. Madison: University of Wisconsin Press.

Smith, Jeff. 1998. *Sounds of Commerce: Marketing Popular Film Music.* New York: Columbia University Press.

Smith, Jeff. 2009. "Bridging the Gap: Reconsidering the Border between Diegetic and Nondiegetic Music." *Music and the Moving Image* 2 (1): 1–25.

Spadoni, Robert. 2007. *Uncanny Bodies: The Coming of Sound Film and the Origins of the Horror Genre.* Berkeley: University of California Press.

Spottiswoode, Raymond. 1935. *The Grammar of Film: An Analysis of Film Technique.* London: Faber and Faber.

Stam, Robert, Robert Burgoyne, and Sandy Flitterman-Lewis. 1992. *New Vocabularies in Film Semiotics: Structuralism, Poststructuralism, and Beyond.* New York: Routledge.

Stam, Robert, and Louise Spence. 1983. "Colonialism, Racism and Representation: An Introduction." *Screen* 24 (2): 2–20.

Steiner, Max. 1937. "Scoring the Film." In *We Make the Movies,* edited by Nancy Naumberg, 216–38. New York: Norton.

Stern, Seymour. 1965. "Griffith: I—*The Birth of a Nation,* Part I." *Film Culture* 36: 1–210.

Stilwell, Robynn. 2007. "The Fantastical Gap between Diegetic and Nondiegetic." In *Beyond the Soundtrack: Representing Music in Cinema,* edited by Daniel Goldmark, Lawrence Kramer, and Richard Leppert, 184–202. Berkeley: University of California Press.

Tagg, Philip. (1979) 2000. *Kojak: Fifty Seconds of Television Music: Toward the Analysis of Affect in Popular Music.* New York: Mass Media Music Scholars' Press.

Tagg, Philip. 1982. "Nature as a Musical Mood Category." Philip Tagg Website: http://www. tagg.org/articles/xpdfs/nature.pdf.

Tagg, Philip. 1987. "Open Letter about 'Black Music', 'Afro-American Music' and 'European Music." http://www.tagg.org/articles/xpdfs/opeletus.pdf.

Tagg, Philip. 1989. "Open Letter: 'Black Music', 'Afro-American Music' and 'European Music.'" *Popular Music* 8 (3): 285–98.

Tagg, Philip, and Bob Clarida. 2003. *Ten Little Title Tunes: Toward a Musicology of the Mass Media.* New York: Mass Media Music Scholars' Press.

Tan, Siu-Lan, Annabel Cohen, Scott D. Lipscomb, and Roger Kendall, eds. 2013. *The Psychology of Music in Multimedia.* New York: Oxford University Press.

Taruskin, Richard. 2007. "Nationalism." *Grove Music Online, Oxford Music Online.* http:// www.oxfordmusiconline.com.

Taylor, Henry M. 2007. "The Success Story of a Misnomer." *Offscreen* 11 (8–9). http://www. offscreen.com/Sound_Issue/taylor_diegesis.pdf.

Thanouli, Eleftheria. 2006. "Post-Classical Narration." *New Review of Film & Television Studies* 4 (3): 183–96.

Thom, Randy. 2013. "Notes on Sound Design in Contemporary Animated Film." In *The Oxford Handbook of New Audiovisual Aesthetics*, edited by John Richardson, Claudia Gorbman, and Carol Vernallis, 227–32. New York: Oxford University Press.

Thompson, Kristin. 1980. "Early Sound Counterpoint." *Yale French Studies* 60: 115–40.

Thompson, Kristin. 1988. *Breaking the Glass Armor: Neoformalist Film Analysis*. Princeton, NJ: Princeton University Press.

Thompson, Kristin. 1999. *Storytelling in the New Hollywood: Understanding Classical Narrative Technique*. Cambridge, MA: Harvard University Press.

Tiomkin, Dimitri. 1951. "Composing for Films." *Films in Review* 2 (9): 17–22.

Vernallis, Carol. 2013a. *Unruly Media: YouTube, Music Video, and the New Digital Cinema*. New York: Oxford University Press.

Vernallis, Carol. 2013b. "Accelerated Aesthetics: A New Lexicon of Time, Space, and Rhythm." In *The Oxford Handbook of Sound and Image in Digital Media*, edited by Carol Vernallis, John Richardson, and Amy Herzog, 707–31. New York: Oxford University Press.

Vernallis, Carol. 2017. "Partying in The Great Gatsby: Baz Luhrmann's Audiovisual Sublime." In *Indefinite Visions: Cinema and the Attractions of Uncertainty*, edited by Martine Beugnet, Allan Cameron, and Arild Fetveit, 180–205. Edinburgh: Edinburgh University Press.

Vernallis, Carol, John Richardson, and Amy Herzog, eds. 2013. *The Oxford Handbook of Sound and Image in Digital Media*. New York: Oxford University Press.

Verstraten, Peter. 2009. *Film Narratology*. Toronto: University of Toronto Press.

Walker, Janet, ed. 2001. *Westerns: Films through History*. New York: Routledge University Press.

Waugh, Thomas. 1996. "Cockteaser." In *Pop Out: Queer Warhol*, edited by Jennifer Doyle, Jonathan Flatley, and José Estaban Muñoz, 51–77. Durham, NC: Duke University Press.

Weis, Elisabeth, and John Belton, eds. 1985. *Film Sound: Theory and Practice*. New York: Columbia University Press.

Whitesell, Lloyd. 2006. "Trans Glam: Gender Magic in the Film Musical." In *Queering the Popular Pitch*, edited by Sheila Whiteley and Jennifer Rycenga, 263–77. New York: Routledge.

Whittington, William. 2013. "Lost in Sensation: Reevaluating Cinematic Sound in the Digital Age." In *The Oxford Handbook of Sound and Image in Digital Media*, edited by Carol Vernallis, John Richardson, and Amy Herzog, 61–73. New York: Oxford University Press.

Wierzbicki, James. 2002. "Weird Vibrations: How the Theremin Gave Musical Voice to Hollywood's Extraterrestrial 'Others.'" *Journal of Popular Film and Television* 30 (3): 125–35.

Wierzbicki, James, Nathan Platte, and Colin Roust, eds. 2012. *The Routledge Film Music Sourcebook*. New York: Routledge.

Williams, Alan. 1980. "Is Sound Recording Like a Language?" *Yale French Studies* 60: 51–66.

Willis, Holly. 2005. *New Digital Cinema: Reinventing the Moving Image*. London and New York: Wallflower Press.

Wimsatt, W. K., and M. C. Beardsley. 1946. "The Intentional Fallacy." *Swanee Review* 54 (3): 468–88.

Winters, Ben. 2010. "The Non-Diegetic Fallacy: Film, Music, and Narrative Space." *Music and Letters* 91 (2): 224–44.

Winters, Ben. 2012a. "Music and Narrative: An Introduction." *Music, Sound and the Moving Image* 6 (1): 3–7.

Winters, Ben. 2012b. "Musical Wallpaper? Towards an Appreciation of Non-Narrating Music in Film." *Music, Sound, and the Moving Image* 6 (1): 39–54.

Wollen, Peter. 1972. *Signs and Meaning in the Cinema*. London: Secker and Warburg.

Wood, Nancy. 1984. "Towards a Semiotics of the Transition to Sound: Spatial and Temporal Codes." *Screen* 25 (3): 16–24.

Wyatt, Justin. 1994. *High Concept: Movies and Marketing in Hollywood*. Austin: University of Texas Press.

Yacavone, Daniel. 2012. "Spaces, Gaps, and Levels: From the Diegetic to the Aesthetic in Film Theory." *Music, Sound, and the Moving Image* 6 (1): 21–37.

Žižek, Slavoj. 1991a. *Looking Awry: An Introduction to Jacques Lacan through Popular Culture*. Cambridge, MA: MIT Press.

Žižek, Slavoj. 1991b. "Grimaces of the Real, or When the Phallus Appears." *October* 58: 44–68.

Žižek, Slavoj. 1996. "'I Hear You with My Eyes'; or, the Invisible Master." In *Gaze and Voice as Love Objects*, edited by Renata Salecl and Slavoj Žižek, 90–126. Durham, NC: Duke University Press.

Žižek, Slavoj. 2001. *The Fright of Real Tears: Krzystof Kieślowski between Theory and Post-Theory*. London: BFI.

Žižek, Slavoj. 2006. "Against the Popular Temptation." *Critical Inquiry* 32 (3): 551–74.

Žižek, Slavoj. 2010. *Living in the End Times*. London: Verso.

INDEX